1995

Songs about Work

Essays in Occupational Culture for Richard A. Reuss

Songs about Work

Essays in Occupational Culture
for Richard A. Reuss

Edited by Archie Green

Special Publications of the Folklore Institute No. 3
Indiana University
BLOOMINGTON
1993

Distributed by Indiana University Press,
Bloomington and Indianapolis

Printed in the United States of America

Library of Congress Cataloging-in-Publication Data

Songs about work : essays in occupational culture for
Richard A. Reuss / edited by Archie Green.
       p.   cm. — (Special publications of the Folklore
Institute : No.3)
   Includes bibliographical references.
   ISBN 1-879407-05-1 : $39.95
   ISBN 1-879407-04-3 : $17.50
   1. Work songs—History and criticism. 2. Folk songs—
History and criticism. 3. Folk music—History and criticism.
4. Reuss, Richard A.   I. Reuss, Richard A.   II. Green, Archie.
III. Series.
ML55.R46   1993
782.42'1593'09—dc20   93-34120
                                                          CIP

Contents

Part I
Remembrances

Judith McCulloh
A Tribute to Dick Reuss

Dick Reuss remains strong in our minds and memories, as much for his personal integrity as for the strength of his scholarship. To say that Richard August Reuss was born May 24, 1940, in New York City, got a B.A. in history from Ohio Wesleyan in 1962 and an M.A. and Ph.D. in folklore from Indiana University in 1965 and 1971, respectively, married Joanne Lynch in 1971, received a Master of Social Work degree from Michigan in 1981, and died August 17, 1986, in Ann Arbor gives the barest outline of a short life, little of its texture.

Dick's detailed research on American folksong and left-wing politics remains unsurpassed. His dissertation has become something of an underground classic. In that work he brought together a singer's enthusiasm and a historian's clear explication of one of the most volatile, complex periods in recent times.

The Women's Section of the American Folklore Society noted his early support for their efforts and his recognition of the important contributions women have made to the Society and the discipline. In 1987, in appreciation of Dick's concern for the field's development, the Folklore and History Section of the Society established a prize in his name for the best student paper dealing with the history of folklife studies. Dick's extensive historical and biographical research on Woody Guthrie led not only to several publications, but also to involvement with the Committee to Combat Huntington's Disease (CCHD), as a member of the CCHD national board and founder of the Michigan chapter.

Dick's passion for thoroughness extended to activities perhaps less well known. He traced family histories for himself and for his wife, Jo, where no records had seemed to exist. His hobby of collecting baseball cards—he collected and researched gum, candy, and cigarette cards as well—was written up in a 1971 front-page feature in the *Wall Street Journal*.

Dick touched many of us with his generosity of time, knowledge, and friendship. He had a way of making our concerns his—whether personal or professional—of taking up our questions and thoughts, exploring them, pushing them to their limits, at once curious and gentle and enthusiastic. He became truly involved with people and ideas. That, I think, is the model we'll miss most and will remember.

University of Illinois
Urbana

David King Dunaway

Staking the Territory: Dick Reuss and the U.S. Protest-Political Song Tradition

Richard Reuss met me in the spring of 1976, at the old Archive of American Folk Song in the depths of the Library of Congress. He had come to Washington that day for a dinner in honor of folklorist Archie Green and the recently passed American Folklife Preservation Act at the invitation of an old friend, Joe Hickerson, director of the Archive. I was there beginning research on *How Can I Keep From Singing: Pete Seeger,* a book Reuss later confessed that he had once hoped to write. His interview with Pete Seeger on April 9, 1968 served as a model for my own (1976–1979) and remains one of the most thoughtful attempts to confront Seeger with his past.

I knew of Richard Reuss through a droll article on the folklore of folklorists, "That Can't Be Alan Dundes: Alan Dundes Is Taller Than That." (Since Dundes, a resourceful man who conducted his letter-reading and telephone calls while meeting students, was my graduate director at Berkeley, I found the piece particularly apt.)

I also knew Reuss as the preeminent scholar of the American folksong revival, a fact hammered into me as I read, with initial despair, his brilliant doctoral dissertation at Indiana, "American Folklore and Left-wing Politics: 1927–1957." In this work, perversely still unpublished, and in his accompanying articles in the *Journal of the Folklore Institute* and *Western Folklore,* Richard Reuss set down the basic underpinnings for later research on the folk music revival of the 1930s and 1960s. In doing so, he restored credibility to folklore studies of those periods; in effect, he reclaimed the subject for folklorists after distorted and bitterly anti-Communist treatment by hostile outsiders, such as sociologist R. Serge Denisoff.

Denisoff's *Great Day Coming* suggested that the interest of New Deal radicals in American folk music resulted from distant ideological shifts of the world Communist movement. Though Denisoff thanked Reuss for providing "esoteric documents," *Great Day Coming* merely fine-tuned earlier anti-Communist diatribes such as *Rhythm, Riots, and Revolution* by an Oklahoma fundamentalist preacher, David Noebel. In these studies, chauvinist patriots and "folksingers" were portrayed as locked in a Zoroastrian conflict between good and evil. To many in the folksong revival community, such studies seemed modern holdovers from days of the Tenney Committee of California, the House Committee on Un-American Activities (HUAC), or the Senate Internal Securities Committee—all of which chorused a litany of extreme-right attacks on liberals by the John Birch Society.

To Dick Reuss, this legacy was a travesty, though reasonably characteristic of the treatment which social protest materials received from the academic establishment of folklore in the forties, fifties, and sixties. Ever since Thelma Jones's bitter denunciation of the People's Songs Movement in the late 1940s, a politically conservative tone dominated discussion of political-protest song. When the first book-length study appeared, John Greenway's *American Folksongs of Protest* (1953), reviewers of his collection of folk-protest songs discounted this material from the canon of American folklore.

This was the temper of the times. In June 1950, *Red Channels* (published by a group of ex-FBI agents bent on commercializing anti-Communism) skewered Pete Seeger and other proponents of folk-protest music. Harvey Matusow, the HUAC witness who first denounced the singing group The Weavers, has recounted in detail how editors of *Counterattack* (a monthly anti-Communist broadside) conjured up false testimony against the group, with the aid of the redoubtable Roy Cohn, Senator Joe McCarthy's former aide. In 1951, according to documents released under the Freedom of Information Act, the Senate Internal Security Committee (under Senator Pat McCarran) made Pete Seeger and The Weavers the first musicians in U.S. history to be formally investigated by their government for sedition.

This red-baiting atmosphere, out of which Noebel's and Denisoff's work came, was the background to studies of the American folksong revival of the 1960s, before Reuss's dissertation. Dick Reuss participated in the folk-cultural revival movement starting in the late 1950s as a subscriber and, eventually, as a volunteer at both *Sing Out!* and *Broadside* magazines in the early and mid-sixties. In the 1970s, as I interviewed one figure after another from this movement, many said that this was the second time they'd been interviewed on these matters—mentioning a tall, shy kid with ruffled hair and a great deal of inside information, the Kilroy of the revival, Dick Reuss. (The first time I looked through Reuss's detailed files from his days at *Sing Out!* and *Broadside,* at his house in Ann Arbor, I suspected that he'd begun planning his doctoral thesis, already an acolyte at age thirteen.)

Despite the above-mentioned resistance to considering folk-protest materials as folklore, some welcomed such studies. Ben Botkin, Charles Seeger, Herbert Halpert, and Alan Lomax (among others) accorded folk-protest materials respectability and attention, as noted in John A. William's "Radicalism and Professionalism in Folklore Studies," an essay answered by Reuss's graduate professor at Indiana, Richard Dorson. To Dorson's credit, though he held with those who disclaimed folk-protest songs as a traditional genre, he supported Reuss's work, directing him into the history of folklore which resulted in Reuss's role in creating *The Folklore Historian.*

My extensive professional correspondence with Reuss began, ironically enough, at the time his dissertation was rejected by the press of Wayne State University, where he was teaching. On May 11, 1976 he wrote me that one (of four) outside readers "accused me of being too gullible and sympathetic to the old left radicals. . . . You run into this sort of thing from all sides when writing about controversial periods and people." (Here was advice I might well have heeded, as I reflect back on damning reviews—for the reasons Reuss expressed—on my Seeger biography in the *Nation* and *National Review.*) After another rejection, Reuss dropped efforts to see his dissertation into print, a decision which may have cost him his academic folklore appointment and eventually led him out of the field of folklore into counselling.

Intellectual counselling is what Reuss provided to myself and to many others in the second half of the 1970s, as my studies proceeded. Rarely would two months pass without some missive: a clip file, suggestions of obscure individuals to interview, outtakes from the massive bibliography (and his projected biography) of Woody Guthrie, which a subsequent biographer, Joe Klein, mined without mentioning Reuss's work.

In his comments Reuss always cut to the intellectual core; on September 10, 1977, he challenged my (and Seeger's) assumption that folk music was a logical medium for protest songs: "Every urban protest movement from the mid-1800s on based its songs on hymns, national patriotic songs, and popular tunes. The Wobblies were by far the best singing organizers we've had in the U.S., and they had no interest in folksong per se. . . . The logical path [for radical composers such as Charles Seeger and Elie Siegmeister of the N.Y. Composers Collective] was to write protest songs to Rudy Vallee or Bing Crosby songs, Benny Goodman music and Broadway show tunes."

By the end of the 1970s, Reuss had moved away from folklore as a vocation, though he continued to work on a few chosen projects. In 1979, a group of radical folklorists established a short lived section of the American Folklore Society on "Folklore and Social Struggle," which Dick Reuss soon joined. He had previously established links with colleagues who were to become active in the "Public Programs" and "Occupational Folklife" sections of the American Folklore Society. These two units particularized many of Dick's deepest concerns.

At the 1980 AFS meeting, Reuss read a paper "The American Folklore Society and Left-Wing Folklore Activities in the 1940s" (unpublished) to support the fledgling "Social Struggle" section. That year, while beginning his course work for a Masters in social work, he also assisted Barbara Kopple and myself on a film concerning the Ku Klux Klan–police riots at a Peekskill, New York concert in 1949. (In 1962, for an undergraduate history class at Ohio Wesleyan, Reuss had visited the Peekskill area to conduct historical interviews.)

The last major folklore publication Dick Reuss worked on was a discography of industrial song for the Institute of Labor and Industrial Relations at the University of Michigan. Once again Reuss brought to this task a gargantuan appetite for detail; in the letter that accompanied a draft for me to critique, he was seeking further information on a Seeger album he had purchased twenty years before.

He was also at that time beginning to be concerned with the effects of *glasnost* on left-wing folk musicians, and particularly on Pete Seeger. This was in the era of the first worker rebellions in Poland organized by Solidarity. A Seeger appearance at an Ann Arbor coffeehouse led Reuss to wonder if Seeger would hold to his uncritical three-decade long allegiance to the Soviet Union. (Seeger eventually did sing at a Solidarity benefit in New York City in 1982, publicly aligning himself with anti-Soviet critics for perhaps the first time.)

In a letter dated April 13, 1981—representative of the changes the decade would bring—Reuss wanted Seeger "to continually test and retest his own values and beliefs in the light of the changing world scene before asking audiences again to identify with them (or beguiling listeners though song)." The present-day collapse of the Eastern bloc nations (once naively called "Eastern Democracies" by the American left) arrived at the same period some former leftists proclaimed a new-found allegiance to neo-conservatism; this marks a turning-point which students of the folklore revival have yet to explore fully.

The question of what to make of now acknowledged Communist Party membership among the folklore-protest song crowd disturbed Reuss as he began revising his dissertation in 1985. For twenty years, defenders of freedom of speech had insisted that a person's membership in political campaigns should not abridge his right to perform for audiences—that the two were sides of the same First Amendment coin. Yet Reuss found "the old rationalizations less plausible," as he wrote on February 4, 1985, weighing the importance of individual memberships in the Communist Party. As important to him as post-factum admissions of memberships were details of F.B.I. harassment of folksong groups in the forties and fifties, which I obtained under the Freedom of Information Act. Such infiltration was not a matter of paranoia—the People's Songs and People's Artists groups actually did have paid informers and phony typewriter repairmen installing phone taps and stealing trash by the bag; elected officials—such as the governor of Ohio— were illegally providing restricted F.B.I. files on the Weavers in an unconstitutional (and ultimately unsuccessful) effort to put that singing quartet out of business.

In the last letter I received from Dick Reuss before his death in 1986, he asked about such matters, though typically, he did not mention his illness, only his curiosity as to the names of informers in the folk music community of the 1950s. He closed his letter with his plans for revising his dissertation amid regrets that he was "such a tortured writer."

Thus ended a decade of friendship born in the Archive of Folk Song. Other, younger scholars will take up the folksong revivals of the 1930s and 1960s, but they will not be former participants with first-hand knowledge, materials, or interviews which date from the period itself. Yet if those studying the revivalists now lack a scholar with a comprehensive perspective comparable to, say, Leon Edel's on the Bloomsbury group, they will bring to this study a frame of reference free of the great moral questions of the 1950s: who was or was not a member of the Communist Party and what difference this might have made in their musical careers. The point is not to forget the past or the ghosts fitfully sleeping there, but to draw the inspiration and lessons which still lie buried in that oft-suppressed era; to test and retest beliefs of the past (in Reuss's phrase) in the light of painstaking research and to offer up its lessons for the future. In such a task we will miss Dick Reuss's simultaneous circumspection and courage.

University of New Mexico
Albuquerque

Robbie Lieberman
Memories of Dick Reuss

In 1989 the University of Illinois Press published my book, *My Song is My Weapon: People's Songs, American Communism, and the Politics of Culture, 1939–1950*. It was dedicated in part "to the memory of Dick Reuss, whose thoughtfulness and enthusiasm is missed by all." I welcome the opportunity to explain that dedication.

I was a graduate student in American Culture at the University of Michigan in the late 1970s, searching for a dissertation topic. I had a great interest in the history of American radicalism and had spent much of my graduate career studying late nineteenth- and twentieth-century movements: populist, socialist, labor, and communist. I was particularly eager to learn more about the cultural aspects of those movements. I had taken courses and read books that addressed literary radicalism, but could find almost nothing about the songs and the singing of the American left. I thought at first that I would do a history of the American Communist movement's use of folksongs (from a very different perspective than the one that informed R. Serge Denisoff's *Great Day Coming: Folk Music and the American Left*). In the course of beginning my research, however, I discovered Dick's dissertation: "American Folklore and Left-Wing Politics: 1927–1957."

At first dismayed by this discovery, thinking the topic had been covered already, I soon became pleased with having Dick's narrative as a source. He had done a detailed history of the left's interest in and use of folk culture, especially folk music, which forced me to define my own topic more sharply. His dissertation also encouraged me to develop my perspective on some of the theoretical issues involved, such as the relationship between art and politics, and the meaning of singing in people's lives and in social movements. Dick's dissertation was in many ways my introduction to the history, the people, and the issues I would have to confront in working on my own dissertation, and it helped me realize what a rich subject I had chosen to address. His work also illustrated that one could write successfully about such a subject from a balanced point of view; he was critical and sympathetic at the same time.

Then I found out that Dick lived in Ann Arbor, a lucky coincidence for me. I called him to tell him what I was doing and he immediately invited me to come to his house and talk with him. My memories of Dick stem from those nice evenings of tea and talk at his house in Ann Arbor. He became a mentor who had a great interest in my work and in helping me get the details right. He also just enjoyed talking about the subject of folksongs and the American left. We had a great time exchanging stories and trivia. Dick seemed delighted to have found someone who shared one of his passions, and it was clear he found these evening pleasurable as well.

The quality of Dick's that stands out most in my mind is his generosity. Anyone who has worked in the academic world knows that people are often stingy, and sometimes paranoid, about sharing sources and information. My first experience with this made me wary: I was working on a graduate paper and found out that someone was working on a book on the same subject. When I wrote this "colleague" to ask him to recommend sources, he replied with a nasty letter saying in essence that he had got there first and I should stay off his turf. Thus I was all the more overwhelmed and gratified by Dick's response to my questions about sources. He was willing to share everything he had, in a generous spirit that went beyond the boundaries that most academics would set. He had reel-to-reel tapes of recordings from the 1940s and 1950s that were obviously very precious. He had put much of his collection of sources together when he worked at *Sing Out!* some years before. Yet he allowed me to take these tapes with me when I moved from Ann Arbor to Columbia, Missouri, to send back at my own convenience. My impression was that this sort of generosity and trust was typical of Dick. I will always remember him as a gentle, caring soul.

Southern Illinois University
Carbondale

Joyce L. Kornbluh

A Conversation with Jo Reuss

Dick Reuss's attraction to folklore began with his passion for history, interest in human nature, and curiosity about the relationship of culture to civilization.* He felt, however, that formal history concentrated more on economic and political issues than on cultural matters. Although he chose to focus on folklore at Indiana University, he never lost his passion for history. He knew that an understanding of the present was informed by an understanding of the past.

The notion of people's inherent creativity motivated Dick. He believed that ordinary people developed folktales, folksongs, and rituals to celebrate community. Folkloric traditions become the inevitable glue, the matrix for human culture. His scholarly concern was not only to understand human experience broadly, but to look at the less obvious aspects of folklore's role: What are the functions of folklore for individuals, families, and communities? How does folklore reflect and touch the psychological aspects of human behavior? How can folklore be used in holding people together, for example, in labor organizing?

Dick identified with people popularly described as "underdogs" rather than with people in power. Although he treasured classical music, he loved especially folk music and folk literature, which he considered people's culture, the product of our whole civilization rather than the product of a few. He felt strongly that folk music could serve as a vehicle for organizing because workers identify with folklore; they understand intuitively that their experience generates lore.

For Dick society's most important ideological goal was equal rights. These rights underpinned societal groups. Dick saw that wide gaps between classes did not serve society. He viewed great disparity in economic resources as unhealthy. Although he held a strong interest in the political process, he did not identify himself as a political person. Dick believed strongly in democ-

* This is a summary of an interview with Jo Reuss, Dick's wife, in Ann Arbor, Michigan.

racy, and indeed, the capitalist system, but knew that the latter would not work unless it concerned people without ready access to economic power. Dick asserted the need to make the democratic polity and the capitalistic economy work to benefit all people.

Although he lived in Ann Arbor, a college town, Dick's identification with workers held firm. He chose to research the life of Woody Guthrie because he saw him as a people's champion—one who used folksong to win rights for the oppressed. Woody symbolized those persons willing to take a stand, to dedicate their lives to articulating people's rights. Further, Dick identified with Guthrie's creativity in that his songs worked well and communicated effective messages. As a musician (Dick played the guitar), he respected Guthrie's craftsmanship.

After graduate school, Dick taught at Wayne State University in Detroit. When Wayne cut back its folklore program, Dick taught briefly at UCLA and Indiana. As college jobs declined, Dick became a social worker employed in a publicly-supported community mental health clinic in Detroit. After the clinic's staff workers organized a union local (AFSCME), Dick was elected the first shop steward. This assignment by his peers greatly pleased him. Dick always celebrated collectivity, whether in Guthrie's songs or in his AFSCME local.

Dick had many mentors, among them, Archie Green with his abiding interest in workers' culture. Dick Dorson, with his passion for collecting folklore and his interest in American history, inspired Dick. Ellen Stekert, who had recruited Dick to the Wayne State faculty became a third guide. (That's where Dick and Jo met while the latter worked on a study project in the folklore program.) Dick drew ideas from many folklorists; his interest in urban folklore flowered during his association with Professor Stekert. At Wayne State, he focused on the problem of how folklore generated in rural society could be transferred and modified in urban settings.

During his years in social work, Dick's scholarship turned to the emotional and psychological applications of folklore. He paid attention to the uses of ritual and ceremony within family life. He studied the deliberate application of such ritual in community events, rallies, and parades. He continued his interest in community members' participation in their own culture. The commitment to people's intuitive wisdom animated all of Dick's work. Folklore served as a vehicle for collective intuition.

Dick identified with groups lacking equal rights. He developed an interest in women's contributions to folklore and wrote an early article for *Feminist*

Folklore Studies. On his last job, Dick became interested in clerical workers and their office folklore, an area previously overlooked. Had Dick lived, he would have continued to study folklore within female-intensive office-work settings.

Dick was ahead of his time in many interests. Facing the problem of diminishing positions for college folklorists, he turned to a second career, social work. Still, he continued to see himself as a scholar and teacher. Not one to bend to the summer breeze, he maintained a strong sense of himself as a researcher able to withstand trends and fads. He continued to study and write on folkloric subjects to the very end of his life. From adolescence until his last days in a Detroit community agency, Dick Reuss lived every day as a folklorist.

Labor Studies Center
University of Michigan
Ann Arbor

Archie Green

Goodnight Irene, Goodbye Dick

Dick Reuss and I shared a long interest in labor and radical song—a concern intertwined with close friendship. In 1960, I had put blue-collar work behind in San Francisco to take up a librarian's calling at the University of Illinois. Dick, upon completing undergraduate studies at Ohio Wesleyan in 1962, had enrolled in Indiana University's folklore program. The few hours of travel from Urbana to Bloomington made frequent trips possible. I met Dick at his student quarters shortly after he arrived at I.U.

Reuss entered graduate school enthusiastic about the "folksong revival." For tools, he brought a good phonograph record collection and the start of a huge gathering of ephemeral "revival" publications. Above all, he came to Bloomington with a yen to explore the role of Communists in their turn to American folklore. Beyond his affection for popularized folksong, Dick responded as a scholar to the fascinating contradiction between claims of Communists that they served the folk and their actual role in homogenizing and commercializing folk music.

Reuss knew that his chosen path seemed hazardous within Cold War as well as radical circles. In the 1960s, some of his teachers of conservative bent felt his subject to be dangerous. A few brave souls encouraged him. Meanwhile, listening to euphemisms such as "progressive" or "left-wing," Dick puzzled over the Aesopian speech employed in "the movement." He did not choose his life work from within a Red family's ambience. Rather, he embraced the world of Pete Seeger, Woody Guthrie, and Paul Robeson from the distance of a comfortable suburban home in Long Island.

Secure in his commitment to liberal democracy, and free from totalitarian impulse, Reuss plunged into a thicket of protest music, strident polemic, and People's Songs appeal. Armed with a strong faith in "value-free" empiricism, it never entered his mind that he should subscribe to Marxism in order to understand Communist party policy. Conscious that a few comrades viewed him with suspicion as a bourgeois outsider, while other radicals castigated him for naiveté in treating Stalinism, Dick persisted in his journey.

I recall my earliest visits with Dick; charged with enthusiasm and curiosity, he made our every exchange an adventure. Despite age difference, we approached labor-song study as peers. We used the term "labor song" as a bridge between my sense of toil and his of cause. We ranged from sea shanties and railroad-construction calls to ideological pieces such as "Which Side Are You On?" Conscious of separate perspectives, we constantly shared detailed information, taking pleasure in each other's discoveries.

Dick knew far more than did I about the "folksong revival," but I could help him with first-hand portraits drawn from job experience. Among areas of preference, I was more partial to Joe Hill than to Woody Guthrie. Dick suggested that my interest in the Wobbly bard stemmed from libertarian values, while his belief in the Oklahoma troubadour flowed from Guthrie's affective power. Despite such contrasts, we shared questions about Guthrie. (My case study, "Woody's Oil Songs," published within this volume, pursues a query raised by Reuss more than two decades ago.)

It is with deep trepidation that any friend erects a monument, literal or symbolic, for a colleague who has not completed his life work. A few years after finishing his thesis at Indiana University in 1971, Reuss submitted it to the Wayne State University Press. Unwisely, the editors rejected it. Unimpressed by their decision, I urged Dick to update it and resubmit it to another press. He found the task difficult, in part because of the vagaries of academic employment. Also, changes in position by People's Songs partisans forced Dick to look anew at radical attitudes and practices in the "revival."

Reuss did not live long enough to see the fall of Ceausescu or the rise of Havel, the Soviets' turn to Salvation Fronts and Black Berets in the Baltics, or the failed coup in Moscow. Yet, Dick did have the opportunity to ponder the challenge of Walesa, Fang Lizhi, and Sakharov. In short, as he turned back in the early 1980s to his thesis, Reuss had to ask a new set of questions about protest and freedom. I am confident that the very act of revising early formulations would have resulted in a fine ethnography grounded in liberal thought. I use the term "liberal" in its best and most traditional sense.

Within Part One of this volume, four of Dick's friends (McCulloh, Dunaway, Lieberman, Green) offer opening remembrances, while Joyce Kornbluh reports a conversation with Jo (Mrs. Richard) Reuss. Joyce had worked with Yvonne Lockwood and Dick in Ann Arbor on his 1983 labor discography. Our informal pieces overlap in that colleagues join in describing a peer.

In Part Two, we leave memory behind in favor of fourteen specialized essays on worksong, labor song, and songs about work. Five have appeared in a special issue of the *Journal of Folklore Research*. A few articles are reprinted from other publications with credit and thanks. The authors have edited these latter items to various degrees for reprinting in this volume. I have not tried to force our chapter studies into a unitary mold, either of philosophic position or rhetorical style. Readers will note a variety of subjects, perspectives, and values. If a thread of unity need be defined, it is work's many faces.

I offer readers a caveat. Our collected essays do not comment upon all of Dick Reuss's many interests in either the "folksong revival," or in the music of political and civil rights groups. I leave to others the task of preparing essay anthologies about "freedom" and "contestational" song. All contributors to this volume are well aware of interconnections between worksong, songs about work, and music of social significance. Further, we know that the rubric "labor song" holds its share of special ambiguities; nevertheless, we trust that our narrow compass on work will have the virtue of showing the complexity needed to decode themes within popular culture and folklore studies.

A brief chronology illustrates Dick's path from teenage interest in popu-larized folksong to an unsurpassed dissertation, "American Folklore and Left-Wing Politics: 1927–1957" (1971).

A) In 1954, Dick purchased a 78–RPM disc—"Goodnight Irene" by The Weavers with Gordon Jenkins's Orchestra. Liking the sound, Dick became a fan before he could identify folksong.

B) As an undergraduate, Dick helped organize a folksong club at Ohio Wesleyan.

C) In 1959, at Camp Quinipet (a Methodist Youth Center at Shelter Island, New York), Dick participated in a ukelele group, The Folkmeisters. The group sang "Michael, Row the Boat Ashore" and "Tom Dooley," among other then current favorites.

D) While at Ohio Wesleyan, Dick projected a book on the history of the "folksong revival." Pete Seeger suggested that he train himself in academic folklore. Following this advice, Dick applied and was accepted at Indiana University.

E) In 1965, Dick spent a summer in Manhattan as a volunteer reorganizing the People's Songs library at *Sing Out!* magazine. During the 1960s, he interviewed nearly every living participant in protest-song composition and performance.

F) Completing his I.U. dissertation in 1971, Dick taught folklore in several universities. Although the thesis remains unpublished, his views are available in several key articles, a bibliography, and a discography:

1) *A Woody Guthrie Bibliography, 1912–1967.* New York: Guthrie Children's Trust Fund, 1968.

2) "Woody Guthrie and His Folk Tradition." *Journal of American Folklore* 83 (1970):273–308.

3) "The Roots of American Left-Wing Interest in Folksong." *Labor History* 12 (1971):259–79.

4) "American Folksongs and Left-Wing Politics: 1935–56." *Journal of the Folklore Institute* 12 (1975):89–111.

5) "Folk Music and Social Conscience: The Musical Odyssey of Charles Seeger." *Western Folklore* 38 (1979):221–38.

6) *Songs of American Labor, Industrialization and the Urban Work Experience; A Discography.* Ann Arbor, Institute of Labor and Industrial Relations, University of Michigan, 1983.

Reuss studied labor song for twenty-five years before he joined a union. In a letter to me (May 4, 1984), he described a problem at the Detroit social agency where he then worked. His colleagues, facing an office "hassle," responded by signing "green cards enabling us to hold an election to bring in AFSCME as our collective bargaining unit." As a new unionist, Dick noted ironically that he would have to "trot out all the old Almanac albums like *Talkin' Union* for our folks."

Complementing this formal turn to union organization, Dick reported happily that he continued to assist "our younger laborlore colleagues." Typical of his enthusiastic spirit, he wrote that Deborah George, after reading his labor discography, had stumbled upon two twelve-inch 78-RPM discs issued by the ILGWU Chorus in 1934. Previously, Dick and I had noted that no known copies of these rare recordings had been located in union archives or private collections. We revelled in Deborah's lucky find—one more chip in work culture's mosaic, a building block in our continuous effort to represent and re-present the expressive treasures of working people.

I dwell upon the role of Reuss in uncovering the ILGWU discs as a metaphor for years of patient research. Dick never met Deborah George; I talked to her only by telephone. Standing alone, the recovery of a single artifact holds little significance. Yet, Dick Reuss for all of his adult life searched for ephemera—correspondence, publications, sound recordings. Such material, of course, shored up careful analysis of labor and radical tradition.

I close with thanks to all who helped memorialize Dick Reuss in this collection. In addition to contributors, Tim Lloyd and Pat Mullen of the American Folklore Society helped us move from idea to action. Robert McCarl of the Society's Occupational Folklife Section encouraged our efforts. John McDowell, Inta Carpenter, and Maria Hetherton at the Folklore Institute, Indiana University, made possible the monograph's appearance in the Folklore Institute's Special Publications series. Tom Adler, of Lexington, Kentucky, contributed numerous hours to earlier phases of the project, converting rough-draft copy to final manuscripts on computer disk.

The many who have helped write and prepare this volume desire that readers will continue to find richness of detail and balance of perspective in Dick's published writings. His journey carried him far from The Weavers and "Goodnight Irene." He will be remembered as long as working people remain curious about their songlore, as long as radicals of any persuasion interpret their past. My colleagues and I trust that our book will become a marker on the road that Richard A. Reuss helped explore.

San Francisco

Part II
Essays

Lori Elaine Taylor

Joe Hill Incorporated:
We Own Our Past

In November of 1990, on the 75th anniversary of the death of
Joe Hill, the Joe Hill Organizing Committee invited interested
scholars, publishers, artists, and others in a wide range of
related fields to gather at the University of Utah for a conference: "'Don't Mourn: Organize!' Joe Hill, the IWW, and
Western Labor Militancy." I offered the following personal
narrative in the section on "The IWW in Music, Poetry, and
Cartoons" at the AFL-CIO Labor Center in Salt Lake City.

In this presentation's original form, ideas expressed
themselves through audio examples, short excerpts from songs
and finally a longer collage. Listeners were asked to make what
they would of a variety of songs influenced by Joe Hill and of
an assortment of related facts. In a written presentation of the
same ideas, many of the conclusions implied in the juxtaposi-
tion of sound must now be made explicit in print. The
experience of reading will not allow the pleasant rediscovery of
familiar sounds in new historical contexts, but perhaps it will
facilitate subtle realizations of a different sort.

This essay is dedicated to Earl Robinson, who believes
"death is just a change of address." He "changed his address" on
July 20, 1991. I leave my references to him in the present tense.

On the bag that I carry around, I have a few buttons that the Joe Hill
Organizing Committee has been selling. One says "Joe Hill," his signature;
another says "Don't Mourn—Organize!" I have had people stop me and tell
me why these words are familiar to them, recounting personal experiences
that relate to Joe Hill. I began this paper in my quest to find out why, to find
out how people use the words "Joe Hill" and "Don't Mourn—Organize!" to
give meaning and structure to certain experiences. For the people who
stopped me, these button slogans, these products of popular and mass culture,
marked me like membership badges as someone who shared common knowl-

edge and experience. As the quest has progressed, I realize that the intriguing question is much larger. I find myself wondering not just who uses the words, but who has the right to use the words or the right to use the past.

Recently in the *Industrial Worker*, the newspaper of the Industrial Workers of the World (IWW or Wobblies), and in the *Bay Branch Bulletin* of the union, Jess Grant (later the General Secretary-Treasurer of the IWW) attempted to reclaim Wobbly history from the "graverobbing antics of those who would mythologize Joe Hill without ever acknowledging the radical context in which he wrote his songs." He referred specifically in these two articles to the Western Workers Labor Heritage Festival in San Francisco, January 1990, telling his Fellow Workers about the "dangerous sentimentalism" of non-Wobblies who sang, to the piano accompaniment of composer Earl Robinson, the song "Joe Hill." He clearly resented what he saw as the appropriation of early IWW history by mere "'progressive' trade unionists." He attempted to assert his union's control over the context of "Joe Hill" and "Don't Mourn— Organize!" His indignant report implied not just who has a right to the past but when (1990b:n.p.; 1990a:n.p.).

The IWW does not hold exclusive claim to the influence of Joe Hill. The words and ideas associated with Joe Hill have depth of meaning far beyond slogans and far beyond the current membership of the Industrial Workers of the World. To emphasize radical politics is just one way to use his name. Artists cannot determine the meaning of art; speakers cannot control the life of their words once they are given to an audience. And the IWW cannot determine the meaning of its martyrs any more than Earl Robinson can determine who knows the tune he wrote for the song "Joe Hill" or where they sing it.

Joe Hill, named and unnamed, came to be recontextualized by poets, songwriters, singers, and audiences who used him to comment upon their personal, political, or artistic lives. I would like to follow with examples, far from comprehensive, of how Joe Hill's name, words, and influence travelled between ears and mouths and pages.

Creating the influence of Joe Hill

Why is Joe Hill such a celebrated figure, probably the *most* celebrated figure, in the labor movement? Why not Wesley Everest or Frank Little, both of whom died horrible deaths while on Wobbly business? Why not Big Bill Haywood or Elizabeth Gurley Flynn, two great organizers of the early IWW? And why not a non-Wobbly? Exceptional circumstances started the legend of Joe Hill. He became a hero because of the popularity of his case at the time. He was in jail long enough for sympathy and solidarity to build up to the tragic moment of his execution and to guarantee a massive outcry at his death.

But we remember him because he wrote songs. Exceptional circumstances also guaranteed the long life of the legend. The life of Joe Hill—the artist fighting the system—inspired other artists who commemorate him in a way they can easily pass on to us. "A song," Joe Hill wrote, "is learned by heart and repeated over and over; and I maintain that if a person can put a few cold, common sense facts into a song, and dress them up in a cloak of humor to take the dryness off of them, he will succeed in reaching a great number of workers" (Foner 1965:16).

In the early-twentieth century Joe Hill appeared in literature as both a "good guy" and a "bad guy." He appeared in many characterizations, Wobbly and Communist, by writers from James Stevens to John Dos Passos; in novels, in poetry, and particularly in song. Joe Hill was a hero to follow and celebrate, a role model to imitate. Through the role and idea of Joe Hill, the IWW has had immeasurable influence on the role of music in society. Joe Hill has led many people to investigate the radical politics of the IWW because music attracts people to ideas (see, e.g., Stevens 1948, Dos Passos 1932).

Many first met Joe Hill through songs and stories about him. It starts with a story, in song or narrative. Then perhaps the listener digs for more: learns his songs, reads books about him, learns the facts of his life. When this listener begins to shape the tradition by telling stories and writing songs about Joe Hill, or by organizing an arts night at a union hall, this listener becomes a tradition bearer. In this way, one makes the songs and stories of Joe Hill one's own. A listener comes to own the past.

The stories about Joe Hill strayed from verifiable fact even during his own lifetime. Growing out of these stories, many glorifying eulogies were written soon after his death. One poem of the period, Ralph Chaplin's "Joe Hill," appeared regularly in The Little Red Songbook. Though he never met Joe Hill alive, he met him dead—he witnessed Joe Hill's cremation:

> Singer of many songs, laughter and tears;
> Singer of Labor's wrongs, joys, hopes and fears;
> Though you were one of us, what could we do?
> Joe, there was none of us needed like you.
> (Chaplin 1964:6)

Chaplin's poem began, and what life it has continues, within the context of the IWW. To show that origins do not necessarily determine destination, I present two other poems, written less than twenty years after Joe Hill's death. These poems, "Joe Hill Listens to the Praying" by Kenneth Patchen and "I

153, 188

Dreamed I Saw Joe Hill Again" by Alfred Hayes, develop the persona of Joe Hill as hero. Both were first published in *New Masses,* then collected in an anthology of Communist writing, *Proletarian Literature in the United States—* the Patchen poem in its entirety and several verses of the Hayes poem in an article on "The Wobbly in American Literature." Kenneth Patchen's free verse remains an interesting footnote while Alfred Hayes's traditional rhyme and verse have become some of the best known words in labor and the left internationally as the song "Joe Hill," "The Ballad of Joe Hill," or "I Dreamed I Saw Joe Hill Last Night."[1]

Hayes's poem would be consigned to footnotes if not for Earl Robinson. During the summer of 1936, at Camp Unity in upstate New York, Hayes gave a copy of his poem to fellow staff member Earl Robinson. There was to be a Joe Hill campfire that evening, and they needed a song to sing. The young composer took a guitar into a tent and came out forty minutes later with the song we know. It did not get much applause, but a few people asked for the words. By the end of that summer unionists heard the song at the New Orleans Labor Council, on a San Francisco picket line, and with the Lincoln Brigade in Spain. That first evening, Alfred Hayes's words escaped. He owned the moment of creation and the original text, but he no longer had control over the use and influence of his words (much to his chagrin). Alfred Hayes avoided association with the song throughout his life. Earl Robinson, by contrast, has gladly spread the song, and along with it the fame of Joe Hill and of Earl Robinson, by recording and performing "Joe Hill" for more than fifty years. The song, however, began to lead a life apart from either of its creators the very evening of its debut.[2]

When Earl Robinson met Paul Robeson in 1939, he found that Robeson had learned "Joe Hill" in the Workers' Theatre in England. Paul Robeson played a very important role in popularizing both the hero and the song, singing it as one of his standards for several decades, recording it several times. It was a year after Robinson and Robeson met, four years after Robinson first wrote the music, that Michael Loring made the first recording of the song, with Earl Robinson playing piano. Then, in 1941, Robinson released his own version.[3]

The song "Joe Hill" has become an international standard. It has been collected in the field as an English folksong;[4] it has been translated into twelve languages (as close as Earl Robinson can tell); and the variety of people who not just know it but who hold it dear goes far beyond any knowledge I could hope to acquire (see apppendix for recordings of "Joe Hill").

At another important moment in perpetuating the name of Joe Hill, also in 1941, Elizabeth Gurley Flynn, who met Joe Hill just once for one hour, brought a few of Joe Hill's papers to the Almanac Singers. When Mike Gold had written in the *Daily Worker* nearly a decade earlier (1933) that what the movement needed was "a Communist Joe Hill," the meaning of "Joe Hill" was clear enough that the writer could assume his readers' familiarity with the songwriter. The Almanac Singers dedicated their album *Talking Union* to the memory of Joe Hill. Text in the album described The Almanacs as "young minstrels who work and sing their way around the country, in the tradition of Joe Hill." In particular, the movement got "a Communist Joe Hill" with a twist in Woody Guthrie, who wrote a song about Joe Hill which he titled "Joseph Hillstrom," but which appears in the Guthrie songbook, edited by Pete Seeger, as "Joe Hillstrom."[5]

Most individuals who had been involved in the Almanac Singers before World War II joined People's Songs (a political song clearing house) after the war. These activists knew the story of Joe Hill and wrote songs, attaching themselves to the story, and turning it into a kind of family saga. Their association held together through the war, and in tracing their tenacity, they found Joe Hill. Editors at People's Songs wrote, "If we were to try to choose some singing figure who best symbolized the work of People's Songs so far . . . that person would be Joe Hill. For Joe Hill . . . was sort of a one-man People's Songs outfit all by himself back in the days of the IWW, and he has left us a great singing and fighting tradition" (1947:5). Other periodicals have also dedicated issues to Joe Hill with similar claims to continuity of tradition, including *Sing Out!* (1954) and, nearly thirty years later, *Talkin' Union* (1983).

Through Pete Seeger, Woody Guthrie, Cisco Houston, and others, the story and songs of Joe Hill reached the folk revival and all of its young practitioners during the 1950s and 1960s. The young political songwriters traced their history back to People's Songs and the Almanac Singers, who owed, in turn, their legacy to Joe Hill; they added to the growing family saga. Bob Dylan carried The Little Red Songbook around with him. In emulating Woody Guthrie, he emulated, by extension, Joe Hill. From Woody Guthrie, Phil Ochs borrowed a tune (from the West Virginia ballad of the hanged steel-driver "John Hardy"), which Guthrie had borrowed for his song about "Tom Joad" from a Carter Family recording. With it Ochs wrote a song called "Joe Hill," published in *Broadside* magazine in 1966 and recorded, with guitar backup from Ramblin' Jack Elliott, in 1968. Billy Bragg recently recorded Phil Ochs's "Joe Hill" also.[6]

Young songwriters knew Joe Hill as a character and wrote about him. They also wrote about heroes closer in time: Phil Ochs wrote "Bound for Glory" about Woody Guthrie; Bob Dylan wrote a poem, "Last Thoughts on Woody Guthrie," suggesting that hope can be found either in the Church of

Your Choice or at Brooklyn State Hospital (where Guthrie was ill at the time); and Dylan's first record included "Song to Woody," in which he wrote "Hey, Woody Guthrie, I wrote you a song, about a funny old world. It's a coming along." I thought the last line an indecipherable Dylan quirk until I read the words of Guthrie's "Joe Hillstrom" in which the Joe Hill character says, "Hey Gurley Flynn I wrote you a song, It's to the dove of peace; it's coming along," which is a paraphrase and combination of letters Joe Hill wrote to Elizabeth Gurley Flynn. Other young songwriters continued the saga, writing about Cisco Houston, Pete Seeger, even Bob Dylan. And they continued to sing Joe Hill's songs for popular audiences. A major event in spreading the popular character of Joe Hill to a massive audience was Joan Baez singing the song "Joe Hill," "an organizing song" as she called it, at Woodstock and the song's later inclusion on the soundtrack record. The tune was not, however, so well known that Baez's quite competent Nashville session musicians could use prior knowledge of the song to breathe life into the studio version released on Vanguard in 1969. The audience for "Joe Hill" remained limited.[7]

Another group of musicians, singer-songwriters influenced by the folk revival and folk rock, spread the name of Joe Hill. Si Kahn, for example, whose music publishing company is Joe Hill Music, wrote a song he called "Joe Hill" for a 1976 play (*200 RPM*, that is, 200 revolutions per minute) about American history, later renaming the song "Paper Heart" (recalling the paper target pinned on Joe Hill's chest at his execution). The song leaves out the name Joe Hill completely, saying only "I guess you know his name," because, of course, the character and the details of his death are already well-known. Rather than drawing a new audience to the idea, this song acts as a confirmation of in-group knowledge.[8]

Abstracting the influence of Joe Hill

The abstraction and influence of the idea of Joe Hill is well underway in song (see fig. 1). People sing the singer's songs, like "Casey Jones" and "There Is Power in a Union"; songs about the singer, like "Joe Hill" (Robinson/Hayes), "Joe Hill" (Ochs), "Joe Hillstrom" (Guthrie), and "Joe Hill" (Kahn); and there is even a song about the singer's ashes—Mark Levy's "Joe Hill's Ashes." People sing songs based on a song about the singer, like Bob Dylan's "I Dreamed I Saw St. Augustine," in which he sings how great it is *not* to be a hero or a martyr. He even fantasizes about killing the martyr himself. The song "Joe Hill," on which Dylan's song is based, has in fact become a "zipper song"—often a picket line song in which you can just zip in details of the present protest. Joe Glazer zipped together a fast-forgotten song about a politician called "The

Ballad of Joe Smith" ("I dreamed I saw Joe Smith last night . . . "), published in *Sing Out!* in 1957. A verse of "Joe Hill" about Earl Robinson has surfaced recently at labor gatherings. People sing songs about singing songs about the singer, as in Si Kahn's "They All Sang Bread and Roses," the chorus of which claims the power of music to create solidarity: "We all sang 'Bread and Roses,' 'Joe Hill,' and 'Union Maid.'/ And we all joined hands together saying, We are not afraid./ 'Solidarity Forever' will go rolling through the hall./ 'We Shall Over-

Fig. 1 *Don't Mourn–Organize! Songs of Labor Songwriter Joe Hill* (Smithsonian/ Folkways SF 40026)

come' together, one and all." All but one of the five songs he mentions appear in the most recent edition of The Little Red Songbook—which has had a special printing as the "Joe Hill Commemoration Song Book" with a drawing of Joe Hill on the cover.[9]

Singers, songwriters, and storytellers create lines of influence and ownership by commemorating their past then passing it on, as they have created it, to their present audience—who become the next generation in the family saga. Through mass media (renting a video, buying a CD, playing a 78-RPM record, reading reprints of a magazine), we can go back, in a way, to any previous stage in the continuing story of Joe Hill. New Dylans, Seegers, and Guthries, new Lou Reeds, R.E.M.s, and Billy Braggs discover their roots in popular culture. They learn stories about their heroes, gathering details until the stories are their own. And they pass them along.

Sometimes a storyteller is conscious of a connection with earlier singing heroes, sometimes not. Bruce Springsteen was definitely aware of Bob Dylan's influence on his music and his image, but not until a decade into his career did he discover Dylan's hero, Woody Guthrie, and stretch his own repertoire of stories to include Guthrie. Perhaps he also knows of Guthrie's hero, Joe Hill?

Billy Bragg, described by a *Village Voice* reporter as a cross between Joe Hill and Benny Hill, in his liner notes for the recent release of a Phil Ochs recording wrote, "Everybody wants to be somebody else. Phil Ochs wanted to be Elvis Presley. I wanted to be the Clash. Both of us at one time or another wanted to be Bob Dylan, who had originally wanted to be Woody Guthrie." Thus Joe Hill begat Woody Guthrie, who with Elvis begat Phil Ochs, who with the Clash begat Billy Bragg—there are endless ways to trace the musical and political genealogy because it is not simply linear. The storyteller creates his own past by choosing to emphasize or invent certain influences, by wanting to be someone else.[10]

Bragg is a good example of a contemporary performer in whose past a variety of Joe Hill influences are tangled. Bragg wrote a song called "There Is Power in a Union," a title he borrowed from a Utah Phillips recording of Joe Hill's song. He learned one verse of the Robinson/Hayes song "Joe Hill" from a drunken friend in the streets of London (but no more because his friend kept falling down) and the rest from a Paul Robeson recording. Then he borrowed Earl Robinson's tune—just called him up on the phone to ask permission— and wrote "I Dreamed I Saw Phil Ochs Last Night," another characterization within the zipper song. And Billy Bragg, along with other inheritors of the tradition, following the suggestion of Abbie Hoffman, swallowed a tiny fragment of Joe Hill's ashes which were recently returned to the IWW. A bite of ash and a swig of beer. Can one get closer to Joe Hill than that? There are so many layered and parallel influences at work here that the story could be told almost any way you like.[11]

The idea of Joe Hill becomes just one model for the singing hero image. All of the singing heroes are familiar to us because we know the image through so many who have taken on the role. The heroes are familiar because they model themselves on one another, and in retelling the stories deliberately emphasize similarities, creating an emotional truth, an abstraction from the factual lives, from the radical or not so radical context in which the actor took on the image.

Using Joe Hill to organize

In Jess Grant's article, "Joe Hill Is Dead. Long Live the I.W.W.," he wonders why trade unionists "don't read the *Industrial Worker* to stay in touch with current affairs" (1990b:n.p.). But not all of the people who carry around versions of the Joe Hill legend relate the story to an IWW or even a union context.

Joe Hill and Joseph Hillstrom are versions, even in death, of Joel Hägglund. Joseph Hillstrom the murder suspect had come a long way on the road from "Julle" Hägglund of Gävle, Sweden, and even from the wandering Wobbly, Joe Hill, working and singing. Joe Hill is a figure abstracted from the life of a man. Joe Hill is a hero, a character of legend. His name, even his history and his legend are without owners, though not without heirs.

The process by which a person becomes a hero emphasizes the teller of the tale, who gradually modifies the story according to changing circumstance. Context, the ever-changing contemporary context, reveals more about the meaning of the tale than its time-bound origins or its static texts. That the story of Joe Hill is told around a campfire to a group of ten-year-olds or on a picket line to striking coal miners reveals more about the meaning of the hero than a Salt Lake City jail or a letter to Big Bill Haywood. Every person who hears the legend owns a version, and every teller owns the moment.

In the case of any hero, it is not necessary that the person be what the legend claims. We act on that which we believe to be true. Followers may know that what they read is not verifiable fact, but they can still perceive the value of emotional truths. People do not want facts; they want a hero who embodies the ideal—an abstraction whose real life has been sifted through the receivers' expectations. In its retellings, a story tends to emphasize heroic aspects of a person's life. By the evolution of unlikely but poetic truths in retelling stories, an individual human being loses the chains of personality to become immortal as a hero, as a reflection of the group of tradition bearers, telling stories and writing songs. All societies gradually fit their heroes into particular patterns based on their own values.

Part of the process of coming together and making sense of our present, of organizing, is looking back to compare and to learn—using the past to comment on the present. Many different communities use the story of Joe Hill to comment upon their present.

The labor arts community gathers at regional and national festivals, where participants learn about their common past and present. When Earl Robinson sat at the piano in San Francisco at one of these festivals, the Western Workers Labor Heritage Festival, and played piano and sang "Joe Hill" for "the millionth time," as a Wobbly reporter wrote, or when Earl Robinson sang in September 1990 in Salt Lake City at the Joe Hill Organizing Committee's Labor Day concert (see fig. 2), did events go beyond the senti-mentalism Jess Grant feared? Earl Robinson was not only celebrating the songs and life of Joe Hill, teaching the whole story to young workers and others, but he was reinforcing in our minds the fact that the historical character Earl Robinson is *Alive and Well,* as his most recent record proclaims, and he is still part of this saga. He owns Joe Hill as part of his own story; Earl Robinson was telling his own story by association. And when people leave these gatherings, they tell the story of Earl Robinson, hero, in whatever way seems appropriate to their situation.[12]

Joe Hill is a teaching metaphor, an idea to confirm in-group knowledge, and bait to draw new like-minded listeners to similar ideas. I do not think Earl Robinson sings "Joe Hill" out of sentimentalism all of the time. Alfred Hayes's poem may have been sentimentalism—maybe. But the fifty-five years Robinson

Fig. 2 The event was planned and presented by the Joe Hill
Organizing Committee. Sugarhouse Park is the former site of the
Utah State Prison, where Joe Hill was executed.

has been singing this is a long time for a man to sing his song for nostalgia's sake alone. The song is responsible (and, by extension, so is Earl Robinson) for the popular acceptance and immediate recognition of Joe Hill's name. My participation in a conference on labor radicalism, perhaps even my chosen career, depends on an abstracted Joe Hill. It has less to do with the song "Joe Hill" in my childhood *Fireside Book of Folk Songs* than with the fact that I dragged my guitar in with that book and sang the song for my class in graduate school when everyone else droned on about turn-of-the-century reform movements. I could probably find a lot of us—maybe most of us—who would not gather but for this song.

Joe Hill's words, texts of the legend, also create common ground: "Don't Mourn—Organize!" (Foner 1965:84).The day before his death, Joe Hill wrote to Big Bill Haywood, "Don't waste any time mourning—organize!" The evolution of this statement into one of the best known lines in labor history may be traced through at least some of its transformations. Haywood told mourners at Joe Hill's funeral that Joe had said, "Don't mourn. Organize!"— turning a phrase in a letter to a death cry. Editorial cartoons showed Hill, blindfolded and tied to the executioner's chair, yelling this out. In its most recent manifestations you can read Big Bill Haywood's abstraction of Joe Hill's words as a record title, a button slogan, or the title of a conference.

Joe Hill wrote to his fellow workers in the San Francisco local of the IWW to "Forget me and march right on to emancipation" (Foner 1965:86). He seemed to be of a mind to reduce the hype about himself the day before he died, to focus attention on labor's larger battle rather than on himself, but it is precisely in remembering that we organize. By mourning, not in the sense of sorrow but in the positive sense of continually reminding ourselves, we give structure to events. We give ourselves reasons to gather in groups and find power in our solidarity. Joe Hill's execution gives us a holiday, a memorial day. For example, the commemoration of the 75th anniversary of his death brought scholars together at a conference to discuss formally not just Joe Hill but the radical context of the IWW—just as the Wobbly reporter had hoped. And in hallway conversations participants covered endless other related topics, but they were drawn by the several ideas of radical politics, labor, non-conformism, art as a tool, or just songwriting. By singing the song, by continually talking about Joe Hill, by looking to the labor movement and working people, we create common ground.

We may know Memorial Day as a civic holiday, perhaps a memorial to those who died at war, but members of my family generally decorate the graves of grandparents, aunts, fathers who died less patriotic deaths. And then we come together to do what families do: eat, talk, burp, sing, and gossip. Memorial Day is an excuse. Joe Hill is also an excuse, and a good one, for us to make time and space to discuss issues and events that affect our work and lives, to use the past to comment on our present either plainly or subtly. "Don't Mourn—Organize!" and "Joe Hill" are very familiar to us as a phrase, a legend about a hero, as songs, books, records, and as button slogans. They facilitate the gathering of like-minded individuals, giving us a forum, a holy day to use as we will. So by continually bringing up Joe Hill's death as our past, though not exactly by mourning, we organize.

Who owns Joe Hill?

Joe Hill's personal effects, some envelopes of his ashes, even his songs until recently, all belonged to the Industrial Workers of the World. Seventy-five years seems an appropriate anniversary of his death to discuss who "owns" Joe Hill because his lasting legacy, his songs, are all now in the public domain. Copyright expires seventy-five years after the death of the author. That means you can sing and record Joe Hill's songs without any permissions from the IWW. But you could always change his songs significantly and copyright your own arrangement—Hazel Dickens did this with "The Rebel Girl." She changed a few of the sexist lines and broadened the union references beyond the IWW; she made the song a contemporary bluegrass song. I find Joe Hill's version offensive when performed in a contemporary context, but not all singers or audience members feel that way. At the opening of the 75th anniversary candlelight vigil at the site of Joe Hill's execution, a singer sang the original version of "The Rebel Girl." She feels an ethical obligation, she told me, to preserve songs as the songwriters intended them. But original intention is fleeting—even the songwriter's intent, instrumentation, or inflections may change in subsequent performances. A performer is a mediator between present audience and chosen past.

Who owns the past? I do. I own Joe Hill. You do, too. We may not be his legal heirs, but we control what he means to us. Anyone owns Joe Hill now, ethically and legally. We use ideas and words associated with him to our own ends, shouting "Don't mourn—organize!" at a peace rally or a strike, or singing "I dreamed I saw . . . " and zipping in the name we think appropriate.

When we hear the past in the teller's words, we hear the teller as much as the tale. Joe Hill is continually recontextualized, without particular regard for "the radical context in which he wrote his songs" or even for the songs as he wrote them. We are not obligated to serve the past at the expense of the present. It is in the new contexts, created by the teller and the listener, that we find meaning in Joe Hill and his words. And in that common ground between teller and listener, between attendees at a conference, between family members on a holiday, we use the past to give shape to our present.

Folkways and Folklife Archives
Smithsonian Institution
Washington, D.C.

Notes

1. Kenneth Patchen, "Joe Hill Listens to the Praying," *New Masses* (20 November 1934), 8–9; Alfred Hayes, "I Dreamed I Saw Joe Hill Again," (18 September 1934), 21. Granville Hicks, et al., eds., *Proletarian Literature in the United States* (New York: International Publishers, 1935), Patchen, 179–80; Hayes in Alan Calmer, 340–45. "Joe Hill Listens to the Praying," recorded in its entirety by Joe Glazer for *Don't Mourn—Organize! Songs of Labor Songwriter Joe Hill*, Smithsonian/Folkways Recordings SF 40026. Recorded 29 January 1990; released 24 June 1990.

2. The obituary headline in Earl Robinson's hometown paper referred to him as "'Joe Hill' composer Robinson." *Seattle Post Intelligencer* (22 July 1991), B1.

3. Michael Loring,"Joe Hill," TAC Records GM–430. Earl Robinson, "Joe Hill," Timely Records, 1941; later General Records G–30, 503–A.

4. *English Folk Music Anthology*, Folkways FE 38553.

5. Almanac Singers. *Talking Union*, Keynote 106, 1941; Folkways FH 5285, 1955. "Joseph Hillstrom," Woody Guthrie, typescript 5 March 1946, Moses and Frances Asch Collection, Office of Folklife Programs, Smithsonian Institution. "Joe Hillstrom," Woody Guthrie. In Pete Seeger, ed., *The Nearly Complete Collection of Woody Guthrie Folk Songs* (New York: Ludlow Music, 1963).

6. Woody Guthrie, "Tom Joad," *Dust Bowl Ballads*, Folkways FH 5212. Phil Ochs, "Joe Hill," *Broadside* 76 (1966):5; "Joe Hill," *Tape from California*, A & M SP–4138. Billy Bragg, "Joe Hill," *Don't Mourn—Organize!*

7. Phil Ochs, "Bound for Glory," *All the News That's Fit to Sing*, Elektra EKL 269, 1964. Bob Dylan, "Last Thoughts on Woody Guthrie," *Bob Dylan: The Bootleg Series, Volume 1*, Columbia 47382. Recorded 12 April 1963, live at Town Hall, New York City. Bob Dylan, "Song to Woody," *Bob Dylan*, Columbia CL 1779, 1962. Letters, primarily Joe Hill to Elizabeth Gurley Flynn, 18 November 1915. In Foner (1965:83). Joan Baez, "Joe Hill," *Woodstock*, Cotillion SD 3–500, 1970. Joan Baez, "I Dreamed I Saw Joe Hill," Vanguard VSD–79310, 1969.

8. *Don't Mourn—Organize!*

9. Mark Levy, "Joe Hill's Ashes," *Sheroes/Heroes*, New Clear Records 0008, 1990 [P.O. Box 559, Felton, CA 95018]; and *Don't Mourn—Organize!* Bob Dylan, "I Dreamed I Saw St. Augustine," *John Wesley Harding*, Columbia CL 2804, 1968. Joe Glazer, "The Ballad of Joe Smith," *Sing Out!* 6 (1957): 26. Earl Robinson verse of "Joe Hill," David Sawyer. 1991. Si Kahn, "They All Sang Bread and Roses," *I Have Seen Freedom*, Flying Fish 70578, 1991. *I.W.W. Songs* (The Little Red Songbook). 35th ed. (Chicago: Industrial Workers of the World, 1984). Special printing, 1990, for the 75th anniversary of Joe Hill's execution for the Joe Hill Organizing Committee, Salt Lake City, Utah.

10. Billy Bragg. Notes for Phil Ochs, *There and Now: Live in Vancouver, 1968*, Rhino, 1991.

11. Billy Bragg, "There Is Power in a Union," *Talking with the Taxman about Poetry*, Elektra 60502–1; *Help Save the Youth of America*, Elektra 60787–2. Utah Phillips, "There Is Power in a Union," *We Have Fed You All a Thousand Years*, Philo 1076, 1984. Paul

Robeson, "Joe Hill," *Paul Robeson Live at Carnegie Hall,* Vanguard VDS 72110, 1958. Billy Bragg, "I Dreamed I Saw Phil Ochs Last Night," *The Internationale*, Utility 11, 1990. See also Gary L. Baran, "I Dreamed I Saw Phil Ochs Last Night," *Sing Out!* 36 (August-October 1991): 59.

    12. Earl Robinson. *Alive and Well,* Aspen SPN 30101, 1986.

References Cited

Chaplin, Ralph. 1964. "Joe Hill." *I.W.W. Songs*. 31st ed. Chicago: Industrial Workers of the World.

Dos Passos, John. 1932. *1919*. New York: Harcourt, Brace.

Foner, Philip S., ed. 1965. *The Letters of Joe Hill*. New York: Oak Publications.

Grant, Jess. 1990a. "Western Workers Labor Heritage Festival." *Bay Branch Bulletin* January: n.p.

————. 1990b. "Joe Hill is Dead! Long Live the IWW." *The Industrial Worker* March: n.p.

————. "Joe Hill." 1947. *People's Songs Bulletin* 2:5.

Stevens, James. 1948. *Big Jim Turner*. New York: Doubleday.

Appendix

I wrote my version of "Joe Hill" in the form of a collage of excerpts from the following recordings, which accompanied the original version of the preceding essay. I challenge any reader looking for the creative aural experience to rewrite the song, as well as the man and the tale. Songs are "Joe Hill" (tune: Earl Robinson, words: Alfred Hayes and others), except where noted.

Michael Loring,TAC Records GM–430, 1940.

Earl Robinson, Timely Records 503, 1941; *Don't Mourn—Organize!,* Smithsonian/ Folkways SF 40026, 1990.

Paul Robeson, *Paul Robeson at Carnegie Hall,* Vanguard VRS 9051, 1958.

Paul Robeson, *Freedom Songs,* Topic Records TOP 62; *Don't Mourn—Organize!,* Smithsonian/Folkways SF 40026, 1990.

Joan Baez,*Woodstock,* Cotillion SD 3–500, 1970.

Pete Seeger, with Si Kahn and Jane Sapp, *Carry It On,* Flying Fish FF 104.

George Strattan, *English Folk Music Anthology,* Folkways FE 38553, 1981.

ILGWU Members Choral Group, Festival of American Folklife, Working Americans Program, Smithsonian Institution, 1976.

Joe Glazer,*Songs of Joe Hill,* Folkways FA 2039, 1954.

Joe Glazer,*Songs of the Wobblies,* Collector Records 1927, 1977.

Bob Dylan, "I Dreamed I Saw St. Augustine," *John Wesley Harding,* Columbia CL 2804, 1968.

Billy Bragg, "I Dreamed I Saw Phil Ochs Last Night," *The Internationale*, Utility 11, 1990.

Utah Phillips,*We Have Fed You All a Thousand Years,* Philo 1076, 1984.

Earl Robinson, Western Workers Labor Heritage Festival, San Francisco, California, 13 January 1990.

Earl Robinson, Joe Hill Organizing Committee Concert, Salt Lake City, Utah, 1 September 1990.

Earl Robinson, *Alive and Well,* Aspen APN 30101, 1986.

John Minton

"The Waterman Train Wreck": Tracking a Folksong in Deep East Texas

During a century of folklore scholarship, the generic obituary has become something of an academic commonplace. Among the more notorious instances of that motif, we may cite Francis Barton Gummere's characterization of Anglo-American balladry as a "closed account," a fiat instantaneously annulled by ballad hunters in the tradition of John Avery Lomax, the patriarch of Texas folksong collectors. Balladry was a closed account neither then nor, somewhat more surprisingly, now, and ballad season is still open.[1]

So was deer season on the second day of December, 1989, as I tramped through the dead undergrowth in a stand of pines in southwestern Shelby County. I was looking for any trace of a tragic railroad mishap that had occurred over seventy-five years before on a narrow-gauge logging spur serving the sawmill community of Waterman. The previous September, I had been directed to the site by eighty-two-year-old Judge V. V. (Verbon Vester) Pate, who lived up the road in Arcadia community and who as a boy was taken by his father to the scene of the accident. Judge Pate remembered that the right of way for the tracks was still visible when he had revisited the area five or ten years earlier, along with the massive scars raised in the earth when the freshly cut timber cascaded from the derailing log cars, crushing workers riding back to town after a day in the woods. At that time I had driven down the isolated red dirt road to the spot he indicated, but my camera was malfunctioning, the underbrush was impassable, and the "No Trespassing" signs were hardly encouraging. When I returned in December, the signs were still there, but most of the brush was gone and my camera was working, so I ducked under the barbed wire and headed into the woods.

About a hundred yards into the trees, I found what had to be the dry creek bed paralleling the tracks that Judge Pate had described, but no remaining feature suggested the horrific impact he recalled, and, after about a half hour of traversing the creek, snapping photos of tree trunks and any discernable impression in the earth, I suddenly remembered that it was deer season. Obviously, all signs of the wreck had vanished, I assured myself, and expeditiously made my way through the pines back to the road and the car.

The casual visitor to Shelby County might not believe that the pines were ever taller or more numerous, but the virgin longleaf forest that covered this country before the arrival of the lumber industry around the turn of this century would dwarf the stands of loblolly that have since reclaimed the cut-over land and the communities organized to harvest the timber, company towns whose success ensured their own extinction. The park-like floor of the old-growth forest, recalled in photographs and memoirs describing an unobstructed expanse beneath trees four or five feet in diameter rising a hundred feet, now nourishes underbrush and hardwoods that have sprung up with the young pines on the clear-cut tracts.[2] That new growth conceals most of what was Waterman, once the largest payroll in Shelby County, today a few homes and outbuildings scattered along a red dirt road, a community existing primarily in the memories of the elderly. Reforestation has also ostensibly obliterated the physical evidence of a catastrophe evidently recorded in no contemporaneous official document save an image captured by a part-time photographer. The account of the Waterman wreck reposes instead in the folklore of Shelby County, circulating in the oral histories of witnesses and their descendants and in the ballad they made and sang. Judge Pate provided this account as we sat behind his house late one afternoon in September on a rise overlooking the bottoms where the wreck occurred:

> Way back yonder, . . . the Waterman people, Mr. Waterman, come in here and established a big sawmill at Waterman, Texas. And that was below here a few miles, below where I'm a-living now. And he laid railroads all over this country in here for the purpose of delivering his logs in these big forests over here to the Waterman mill on a train. An' in the period of nineteen and twelve . . . one day they was coming in from off of the, out of the woods and they was coming down what we call the "Shoat Hill." And I live here, well, there's less than half a mile to where the wreck occurred. And Mr. Eli Sanford lived down there right close to where it happened and he told me that he heard the whistle as it began to scream, because the train was running away. The brakes had failed and the train was coming down Shoat Hill, and it was might'ly moving along, it was real fast. Well, after a while, it got so fast, well, that couldn't get no faster, well, it left the track. When it left the track, the logs bursted all over the place and they began to spin in there, some of 'em went as high as fifty, seventy-five feet in the air, and these men that was killed on that wreck was a-riding on those cars, a-coming out of this—what they call "flatheaders"—back in the big woods. And I've been told by a fellah that knew that Mr. Wise, who was killed, Mr. Ernest

Wise was one of these, one of the men that was killed here in that wreck, lived where I'm a-living now. I been here ever since nineteen and fourteen, so I been around here a while, I'm nearly seventy-three, eighty-three-years-old. But anyhow that train come down there, well, those men was on there when the train, the boxcars began to pile up on one another, I mean logcars, loaded with these big logs, 'gan to pile up there's, everything they had was bursted loose and those logs was free agents. They's going through the air. And these men was there, and I talked to Mr. Gilmer Tyson about it who, one of those around helped pick 'em up, and they used washtubs and such to put 'em in, part of 'em. It was real sad. And Mr. Mansfield—Mr. Adams, Mr. Mansfield, and Mr. Haynes, and Mr. Wise all lost their lives in that wreck. It 'as a sad thing. Well, then the next day after it happened, my father hooked up to the wagon and carried us young uns, kids over there to see the Waterman wreck. Well, we drove over there, and we never did know what day it was. The date has slipped everybody's mind but it 'as 1912. And we drove over there and I remember this much, that the flies was so bad in there that you couldn't hardly stand it. And they showed me where they laid these people out there on the, where the wreck happened. And next day after the wreck happened, then they began to pick up all the casualties in this wreck. O' course there's several of 'em hurt, . . . I heard that one man got his back broke. And a lot of 'em got hurt real bad, their arms broke, leg broke, this thing, that thing. And the next day they told everybody to come, they wanted us 'at could come over there at where the wreck occurred. So my daddy carried us over there, well, everybody had to have on a white shirt. And as this picture I've got of the Waterman wreck here with logs everywhere, everybody's, their picture's made, everybody had on a white shirt.

Judge Pate was studying a clipping of Mattie Dellinger's column "Box 744," published in the old Shelby County *Champion* a decade ago. This particular installment was devoted to the Waterman tragedy and featured a locally renowned photograph of the wreck's aftermath by Loving Sabel, at that time a local jack-of-all-trades, photography and the ministry among them (fig. 1). Some residents can still identify relatives or acquaintances in the scene, but Judge Pate was cautious. "Well, it's hard to recognize people after seventy-five years. . . . Your mind begins to lose traces of things that made an impression on me," he confessed before continuing his story.

So, Mr. Eli Sanford told me that he was a-plowing so we have a reason to believe that—you plow in the spring and the summer—so we have reason to believe it was in the spring or summer because he was plowing over there and he heard this whistle a-blowing as it 'as a-coming down the hill and it 'as running away and Mr. Sanford said it was a curious, most blood-curdling sound that you ever heard in your life and said just a few minutes he heard the thump and the bump and the logs and things a-falling. And when we got there the next day this train was laying over on its side. And they come up with another train there, and we called it the "steam loader." And the—maybe you might call it something else

Fig. 1 The Waterman Train Wreck, photographed by Loving Sabel. The crane-like device behind the Shay locomotive is a steam skidder. Otto MacDonald is in the front row, far right.   *Courtesy Buren McNease.*

this day and time, probably a "lift" or something or 'nother—and they 'as in there trying to get the cars back on there, back on the track. And the way this train was pickin' these, this loader sat on a flat boxcar, and they had it tied down, buckled down. And as he would pick up a car, a flat car, a log car, you might say, he would place that on there and then they'd shove it back behind 'em. And they kept a-working until they worked out there at the end and they finally put the train back on. I used to know the number of the train, seem like it 'as Old Forty-Four or something 'nother like that, I'm not sure 'bout that. But that 'as about the worst tragedy that's happened in this country right here, that four young men lost their lives. We know that many, and they could've been some more, because those logs was driven into the ground twenty, twenty-five feet deep. They had such a force as they come down. And there's one sad thing. And I'm living here and I've been in this place ever since 1914, and that happened when I's about five, six, and it's just as fresh in my mind today as it was yesterday. And we've had our ups and downs in this community but I believe that 'as 'bout as a worse thing as we ever had here.[3]

Judge Pate's vivid account is practically a composite of the memories of elderly Shelby Countians who recall the wreck. Typical too was his response when I mentioned "an old song people used to sing about it": "There was a song written about Asbery Adams [the Mr. Adams numbered among the dead], also one about the Waterman wreck," he acknowledged. "Now, brother, now I wanna tell you something. Such as that'll make your hair stand up. It'll make tears come in your eyes." But though he recalled once singing the song (or songs), and though the emotional force of those performances was palpable in that recollection, he could no longer summon text or tune, and he seems to have compounded one ballad as two. Sensing my interest, he struggled to describe their contents. "I don't know whether it states in the Waterman, in the Asbery Adams song, now if I could think of the tune I might sing a little of it but I can't think of the tune. And I know that it was written about him 'cause we all sing it and it also sang about the Waterman wreck." When I quoted the opening of a text recovered on an earlier fieldtrip—"Was it that one that starts, 'September, Friday morning, this lonesome train did come'?"—he still hesitated, excusing his lapse with unassailable logic: "I don't know just exactly how it's worded," he admitted. "I've forgotten that. It's been so long, you think about seventy-five years since you've sing something. You gonna forget it. 'Specially if you get old and you live long enough, you gonna get old."

But seventy-five years after the event, "The Waterman Train Wreck" does survive, in a couplet of verse and the strain of a tune an octogenarian remembers his mother singing around their home in Waterman nearly as many years ago; in a pair of handwritten "ballets" set down by eye witnesses who participated in the song's making; and in a homemade audio cassette tape, contemporary analogue of the ballet, recorded by Waterman native Marcille Hancock Hughes for Homer Bryce, a friend and neighbor who also recalled the traditions surrounding the disaster. Marcille's text follows with an outline of its tune (musical example 1), harmonized on the tape by her daughter, Regina Hughes Wright, and Laurie Butler, who accompanies on guitar.

> (guitar break)

> September, Friday morning, this lonesome train did come,
> Out into the pine woods, it was our daily run.
> But on our trip returning, a tragedy occurred,
> The train derailed with four men killed, distress is what we heard.

> Chorus:
> We heard the cries in Waterman, it broke our hearts to hear,
> The wailing wives and sweethearts, they faced their deepest fear.

> The agony it lingered till Sunday night so late,
> From the old hotel Mr. Adams passed on through the golden gate.

Musical Ex. 1 "The Waterman Train Wreck," performed by Marcille Hancock Hughes, Regina Wright, and Laurie Butler. Homemade audio-cassette, Center, Texas, c. 1987.

> The flat cars had been loaded with timber we had fell,
> The engine came uncoupled, this caused them to derail.
>
> We heard the cries in Waterman, it broke our hearts to hear,
> The wailing wives and sweethearts, they faced their deepest fear.
>
> (guitar break)
>
> Chorus:
> That fateful autumn morning, the year nineteen-eleven,
> Four men who rode that steaming train took their final run to heaven.[4]

"The Waterman Train Wreck" is self-evidently within the tradition of Anglo-American balladry, just as Waterman is of a kind with documented Anglo-American ballad communities. Although I went looking neither for a Waterman nor an Anglo-American ballad, I was not surprised to learn that this community once existed where it did, nor to discover that ballad singing and ballad-making were once customary features of daily life. I was somewhat more surprised that seventy-five years after the Waterman wreck, seventy-five years after the Waterman Company "cut out and pulled out" of the Attoyac bottoms, seventy-five years after most of Waterman's residents had scattered far beyond that tract, the ballad that those persons made about the tragedy that galvanized their community still enjoys something of a living tradition, still lives because, not in spite of, the forces of modernity that obliterated its original milieu.

Shelby County, lying along the Sabine River (now Toledo Bend Reservoir) on the boundary of Texas and Louisiana, was settled by Anglo-Irish migrants from the Deep South beginning around 1820, while the area was still part of the Mexican municipality of Tenehaw. Previously, this section had belonged to the "Neutral Ground," a vaguely defined strip along the Sabine so designated by Spain and the United States to forestall a border dispute following the Louisiana Purchase; predictably, the district attracted fugitives from both jurisdictions. This laissez-faire attitude persisted after Texas Independence and the formal organization of the county the following year in 1837. Between 1839 and 1844 Shelby County was the principal site of the Regulator-Moderator War, a struggle for political legitimacy that escalated into pitched battles before Sam Houston, then president of the Republic, sent in the militia. The subsequent lives of Shelby Countians were sometimes violent and typically trying though somewhat less dramatic, characterized mainly by hard work and want. Before the arrival of the railroads around 1900, and, with them, the lumber industry, small farms provided subsistence for most locals, whose descendants explain their families' endurance with a maxim used by rural Southerners who have been on the land for generations: "They (or 'We') were just too poor to move away." Neighborly cooperation was a necessity and families were large and close. Today, the people of Shelby County remain independent and self-reliant, the older residents truly astounding in their ability to specify some degree of kinship to almost any fellow resident.[5]

With the advent of large-scale commercial lumbering, however, the company town became temporary home or workplace for a significant portion of the county's established population, and for numerous newcomers. Waterman, one of several, was founded by William M. Waterman, reputedly a German emigrant who in 1905 established the lumber company bearing his name on the east bank of the Attoyac River. Not coincidentally, the Santa Fe had just extended its lines through the surrounding piney woods, providing the prerequisite transportation for extensive logging, and a much-needed link with the outside world. Marcille's mother recalled that the entire population of Grigsby, just south of the future site of Waterman, turned out to welcome the first train into town. Like many East Texas lines, the spur was soon rechristened by the locals. "My daddy always told us that the train was called 'The Boll Weevil,'" remembers Marcille, "because it ran through all the cotton in the river bottoms."[6]

The 1910 Census gives the population of Waterman, incorporated the previous year, as 476, with 1,803 persons combined in the town and its surrounding precinct, a steady increase from 986 in 1890 and 1,289 in 1900. There were 26,423 inhabitants in the county overall, around 3,000 more than registered by the 1980 Census. The largest town then (1,684) as now (5,827) was Center (*U.S. Census* 1910: 792; 1980 Census figures from Pass 1981: 332). Some residents estimate that the mill employed between 2,500 and 2,800 workers, probably an exaggeration. Nonetheless, Waterman at its height was a sizable place. Besides the depot and the mill with its company housing, the community included a commissary, a school, churches, a few businesses and finer residences, and a hotel. "We worked during the week, do most anything you could to get some money together and ride that little train down to Waterman," recalled Ashley N. Beasley, who grew up in the surrounding countryside. "It was kind of a show goin', it was like goin' to a city in Waterman. It was big, lots of people there, lots of tradin' goin' on in that store, big store" (fig. 2). In addition to locals, the operation depended on a succession of itinerant laborers who migrated with the mills. Wives and families may have effected some semblance of gentility and stability, but in a notoriously rough industry in a historically rough area, Waterman was by reputation a singularly rough place.[7]

That violent reputation combined with the community's remote location and the pronounced hostility of management toward outside interference to isolate Waterman's residents socially, economically, and politically as well as geographically, the common predicament of the lumber worker in the company town. When the Waterman establishment abruptly pulled out around 1913, the community collapsed (fig. 3). The reasons for the sudden action are unclear, though Marcille Hughes remembers the story that Mr. Waterman returned to Germany at the start of the First World War, an account suggesting the veiled truth intrinsic to oral history; William Waterman was apparently German, and his Shelby County mill did close around the start of the War, but more plausible is the concurrent explanation that the operation moved on when the timber was "cut out," the usual cause of closings. Marcille had also heard that when the lumber around the Attoyac

Fig. 2 Waterman, c. 1910. The Waterman mill is visible in the upper left. The note in the lower margin indicates that as of 1981 the old community water well still supplied six thousand broilers [chickens], two families, and forty cows.

Courtesy Homer Bryce/Marcille Hancok Hughes.

Fig. 3 Waterman, December 1989.   *Photographed by the author.*

was exhausted, the owner moved north ·to neighboring Panola County, founding "Waterman Front" near Deadwood, an account corroborated by Mr. Beasley.[8] Locals who stayed went back to farming. Others departed with the outsiders who had followed the mill into the Attoyac bottoms. Many of the county's current native residents lived and worked in Houston and its industrial environs for varying periods before returning home. Although logging continues in the new growth—the southeast portion of the county now comprises part of the Sabine National Forest—broilers are the big business today; Shelby County has been crucial to the development of a billion dollar poultry industry in East Texas.

The Waterman Lumber Company epitomized East Texas sawmills of the period. The mill itself was situated on the Santa Fe spur, the hub of a network of narrow-gauge tram tracks leading into the woods. Like most East Texas outfits, the operation depended on the "Shay," a gear-driven locomotive identified with its inventor (first name "Ephraim"), utilized in conjunction with a "steam skidder" or "loader," a crane equipped with booms, power drums, and steel cables and mounted on a railroad car (fig. 4; see also fig. 1). The locomotive daily hauled the skidder and a train of empty logcars to the work site, simultaneously ferrying the "flatheads" (tree cutters) to the job. As the workers felled the trees, the "skidder man" fed out the cables, which were attached to the timber. The operator then reeled the lines back in, dragging the logs (and anything in their path) to the side of the track, where they were loaded on the cars. After a day in the woods, the flatheads commuted aboard the laden logcars back to the mill, where the lumber was processed then shipped out on the mainline (fig. 5). "I had a friend, got a job back in the thirties, he just lasted half a day," Waterman native Buren McNease recalled of a similar operation. "He'd ride a horse, an' he'd drag them grabs [the skidder's tow lines] to them [the flatheads]. An' they'd come draggin' with 'em, draggin' down great big trees. He said that 'as the hardest work he'd ever done in his life an' he quit at dinner, he just lasted half a day.'"[9]

The labor was grueling, the pay low but about average. Buren McNease recalls his stepfather working at the Waterman mill for eighty-five cents a day, probably for the standard ten-hour shift. The company adhered to the accepted practice of paying workers in tokens redeemable only at the company commissary (Mr. McNease remembered that the Waterman Company "merchandise checks" were red and yellow: "That's the only kind I ever seen," he laughed. "I taken a few of 'em myself"), and of off-setting the company doctor's salary by docking workers one day's pay a month as "health insurance." Even that purely pragmatic precaution was conspicuously inadequate. During the first decades of this century, the Bureau of Labor Statistics reck-

Fig. 4 A Shay locomotive reputedly used by the
Waterman Company. (Note the off-center boiler,
a distinguishing feature of the Shay.)

Courtesy Mattie Dellinger.

Fig. 5 The Waterman Company's mainline log train with its engineer, Samuel Tilton
Smith.   *Courtesy Bessie Smith Alford.*

oned the lumber worker seven times as likely to be hurt on the job as workers in other manufacturing trades, and logging in the woods was by far the most dangerous aspect of lumbering, ranking first for all U.S. industries in both disabling injuries and fatalities. Despite its efficiency from the company's standpoint, the steam skidder was both wasteful and hazardous, destroying young trees and other growth, preventing reforestation and encouraging erosion. Viewing a photograph of a locomotive reportedly used by the Waterman Company, Buren McNease's son Bill, himself a railroad man for thirty years, commented ruefully, "Yeah, them little Shay engines ruined many a forest around here."[10] The logs hurtling to trackside could crush unwary workers, who also risked becoming entangled in the cables, which frequently snapped, whipping through the woods and killing or critically injuring—even decapitating—loggers. Given the disproportionate risk posed by railroading, the two occupations were a foreboding combination, more so since the narrow-gauge trains favored in logging were particularly prone to derailment.[11]

If serious injury and death were shockingly routine in mill towns, statistics only further understate the problem. Especially before the passage of the first Texas workers' compensation law in 1913, accident figures for the East Texas lumber industry are suspiciously low. Owners, who ran their towns as virtual fiefdoms, were understandably reluctant to publicize such conditions, and in this as in other matters, workers, accustomed to violence on and off the job, and to handling such matters themselves, had little recourse to official channels; the impact of organized labor on East Texas lumbering was negligible to nonexistent (Maxwell and Baker 1983: 123–35). These factors may explain the lack of documentary evidence concerning the Waterman wreck. Of the few written works on the community, fewer still record the tragedy, and even the precise date is uncertain. Judge Pate argued persuasively for the spring of 1912; the ballad sets the date as September 1911. The only complete run of the newspaper most likely to have carried the story, the *Champion*, perished when its offices burned in the late seventies. The minutes of the Shelby County Commissioners' Court and the County Death Records (which have survived) make no mention of the crash or the victims, whose names are likewise absent from the WPA inventory of the County Probate Records.[12] But Loving Sabel's photograph is highly convincing, the local accounts insistent and consistent with the lumbering practices of the day and their attendant risks. Excepting that compelling image, then, my knowledge of the wreck derives almost solely from those traditions, with which I first became acquainted through Marcille Hughes.

I met Marcille through our mutual friend Terry McDevitt, a classmate from Stephen F. Austin State University across the Attoyac in Nacogdoches and then a colleague at the Institute of Texan Cultures in San Antonio. Terry had worked as a journalist in Shelby County for several years, so when she, Rick Burns, and I set out in June of 1989 to broaden the Institute's coverage of Deep East Texas, her contacts were an obvious resource. Marcille got the project off to a propitious start.

Marcille Hancock Hughes was born at Waterman April 9, 1925, on land settled by her family the previous century. An avid researcher of county history herself, Marcille's grasp of local affairs was readily apparent when Rick and I first visited her in June of 1989 at the Pine Colony Inn, a bed and breakfast she and her husband, Pershing, also a Waterman native, run in Center. We were all in a hurry that rainy day, but in our brief conversation she fortuitously alluded to the wreck and the ballad, topics which had always interested her. They interested me as well, and I welcomed her invitation to return when we all had more time.

Later that month, Terry, Rick, and I sat and talked with Marcille in the front room of the Inn. As the rain again beat down outside, she related the facts of the wreck as she knew them, even locating and reading her ballet of the song. Though she was born a decade after the mill closed, people still sang "The Waterman Train Wreck" during her childhood, and the stories still circulated. Her account differed slightly from Judge Pate's, paralleling instead her version of the ballad in attributing the derailment to the uncoupling of the cars:

> After they cut the timber this day and loaded the flat cars, and the train was coming into the mill, somehow the engine became uncoupled from the train, and they tried, the engineer tried to beat the train, and there wasn't—the load of logs—there wasn't nothing he could do really, they could've jumped off, I guess, but he tried to stay ahead of the logs but as they were coming down the hill, the logs overtook the train and it caused a wreck. A lot of men were riding the logs, and they did jump off, but there were a lot of men killed, and it was such a sad thing that they wrote a song.

She related another anecdote from Swinton Tyson, brother of the Gilmer Tyson who figures in Judge Pate's narrative.

> It was Mr. [Swinton] Tyson, that I talked to, helped lay out the bodies. He and a black woman was the ones, and he told me this, it doesn't make too much sense, but he was a young man, and he was helping her, and she told him, he said he would—it was so bad that he would have to take time to vomit—and she told him finally to, just to wash his hands good and to cut her a plug of tobacco and put it in her mouth, and that she would lay the men out. So she did, and

> that's, he said he just put the tobacco in her mouth and she'd, I guess the
> tobacco calmed her nerves enough to. They were crushed!

So after nearly two decades the wreck was still a topic of conversation. "This tragedy was the only thing they talked about for a long, long time. And we have pictures of the wreck, and these big logs rolled over these men and killed 'em and crushed 'em," Marcille commented, referring to Loving Sabel's photo and remembering in particular the sympathy accorded the Adamses, who were especially grieved at the death of their son, Asbery.

> And I don't know, don't remember off-hand the names of the men that was
> killed. But Mr. Adams was—his family lived there in Waterman—and I can
> remember they talked about his mother, how bad it hurt his mother. Now, I
> don't know if he was a young man, if he was married or not, but I remember
> that people felt so sorry for his mother.

Besides the migratory songs general to the Anglo-American South, Marcille's neighbors numbered among their repertoire the local composition commemorating young Adams, the one victim named in that ballad, though Marcille, like most, has no idea who actually made the song. East Texas is also a bastion of the "shape-note" method of sacred singing, and of the religious fundamentalism associated with it, and with her neighbors, Marcille attended the "singing schools" that convened in the county every summer (Judge Pate was himself a "singing teacher" for many years). Significantly, although she recited the ballad's text and praised its tune, we could not persuade her to sing, since she insisted that she needed someone to harmonize in the shape-note style. However, she remembered the tape that she, her daughter, and a family friend had recorded for Homer Bryce, a neighbor at Waterman. As far as she knew, the cassette was still at his place, so maybe we could retrieve it the next day when we were to visit out that way.

Leaving the Inn, we drove south to Todd Springs Community to meet Judge Pate's younger brother, Shade, another native of the Waterman area recommended by Marcille. Born in 1916 at Arcadia, Shade Pate was also too young actually to recall the wreck, or even the Waterman mill, but he had heard the stories—and the ballad. "I can't remember much about the Waterman Front," he admitted, adding with a chuckle, "but I can remember 'em telling some things that happened down there; it used to be pretty rough around there." Still, the tragedy was common knowledge. "Well, that train wreck happened about, aw, I reckon three mile, two or three mile below where I 'as raised," he confirmed. "I can't remember the Waterman train wreck when-ever it happened. But I know where it happened, I been to the spot and heard 'em talk about it and the people that got killed and what have you on it, but

I can't remember the wreck." As bass fiddle player in a local string band, Mr. Pate had actually pursued music as an occupation for a time in the thirties, progressing from local house dances to radio broadcasts, recording sessions, and touring, but his response was tentative when queried on the "old song about the Waterman wreck." "Yeah, uh-huh," he assented. "One of 'em killed was Bery Adams. He 'as a brother to Mr. Clayton Holts's wife. But I forgot, I used to know some of the words to it but I forgot it. 'Course it mentioned Bery Adams, his name in there." In any case, he assured us, this piece wasn't featured by his ensemble.

The next day, we drove with Marcille to Waterman. June was wet even for East Texas. Rain still fell in sheets, the dark pines dripped constantly, and the overflowing road had turned to red mud. We stopped first at the family farm to meet Marcille's parents, Mr. and Mrs. Elmer Hancock, who entertained us with stories of wild times in the county before the railroad and the mill arrived. Marcille had told us they were both fine singers, but they weren't in a singing mood that day and, by Marcille's account, "The Waterman Train Wreck" was never a part of their repertoire anyway (she'd heard the song from neighbors), so after a short visit we drove down the road to Homer Bryce's.

Born in a log dog trot at Waterman in 1909, Mr. Bryce is today one of the most successful businessman in East Texas, a regent of Stephen F. Austin State (the SFA Lumberjacks play in the stadium named in his honor). Like Marcille, he pursues an interest in local history, and the walls of his new home at Waterman display scenes of Shelby County's past, including Loving Sabel's photo and a rare view of the town itself (see fig. 2). Although he couldn't remember off-hand where he'd put Marcille's tape he promised to locate it for our next trip. Leaving his place, we dropped Marcille at her family's, then hydroplaned through the rain-lashed pines and red mud back to the blacktop.

When Rick and I returned to Center in late August, East Texas badly needed rain. Our first visit was with Mattie Dellinger, an ex-newspaperwoman who was now hosting a call-in show, "Mattie's Party Line," on radio KDET (as in Deep East Texas). Mattie had written about the Waterman tragedy, and just about every other conceivable aspect of local history, in her old "Box 744" column for the *Champion,* and during our first two trips we'd gone on the air with her, hoping thus to elicit lore and establish contacts, with considerable success, incidentally, though my requests for "The Waterman Wreck" had gone unanswered. Mattie had repeated my inquiries in the interim, but still no luck. She had, however, found a photo of a Shay Engine, reputedly one of the Waterman locomotives, and she promised to ask her listeners about the wreck again on that afternoon's broadcast. Before leaving the station, I phoned the Pine Colony Inn, but there was no answer, so Rick and I started back to Nacogdoches for the night. It was past three, and I switched on the car radio to Mattie's show. Marshall Alvis was singing "The Waterman Train Wreck."

The next morning we met Mr. Alvis in front of his house trailer just west of Center, within sight—and sound—of the Cedar Gap Mill. As a log truck roared by (quite audible on the tape), he sang the ballad's opening couplet to the first strain of the tune (musical example 2):

> It was on a Friday morning, the train with its lonesome sound,
> Went out into the wildwood to make its final run.

Like Shade Pate, Mr. Alvis, born in Shelby County in 1909, had pursued music professionally for a time. Moving to California in 1926, he played guitar and sang with various groups, even appearing on records and in motion pictures before returning to Center around the time of his mother's death in 1959 or 1960. He recalled this snatch of "The Waterman Train Wreck" from his mother, Callie Starling Alvis (born c. 1880), who "just sang around home." "There's about eight or ten verses in it," he explained. "You know, they used to write songs long and now they just make 'em 'bout two minutes, that's all they have." He didn't know who made the song—"Don't have any idea," he replied when asked—nor could he clarify the facts of the case. "I don't even know what year," he admitted. He couldn't even recall specifically hearing anyone besides his mother sing the ballad, but, he assured us, "it was real popular around Center." "Then another thing she told me," he elaborated. "There was a guy on the train, he was a-going on it. And he begged his wife to cook him some peas and cornbread. And she wouldn't do it. And he got killed on the train wreck." (When he had told the story the previous day on Mattie's program, she immediately responded, "And I bet she was sure sorry!" "She sure was!" he emphatically concurred.)

When I reached Marcille the next morning, she'd still been unable to retrieve the tape, but she hadn't forgotten either. In the meantime, she suggested we contact Buren McNease, a distant relative who, she thought, had the print of Loving Sabel's photo that Homer Bryce had copied and perhaps other information as well. We found Mr. McNease at the home of his son Bill in Garrison, just across the Attoyac in Nacogdoches County, a couple of miles from where he was born on the first of May, 1905.

Mr. McNease's own memory of the event is understandably vague. "Well, just six years old," he explained, "I can still 'member the disturbance, you know, I didn't know just what was goin' on." However, he had heard the

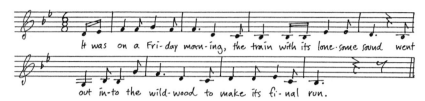

It was on a Fri-day morn-ing, the train with its lone-some sound went out in-to the wild-wood to make its fi-nal run.

Musical Example No. 2 "The Waterman Train Wreck," performed by Marshall Alvis, Center, Texas, August 25, 1989.

stories—and the ballad—most notably from his uncle, Otto MacDonald, and aunt, None ("No-nee") MacDonald Scoggins. By his estimation his uncle was seventeen or eighteen at the time of the wreck, a contemporary and close friend of Asbery Adams, with whom he had worked in the woods on the day of the tragedy:

> But this Asbery Adams, now, was this uncle of mine's friend and they worked together, see, they goed out, you drag up, they called it "draggin' up" . . . back into the mill. Sometime on Saturday or Friday, . . . you could get your payday but then you'd have to wait for the next day, so they caught the train. They's sawin' logs, called it "stock" in them days, and he said they caught the train, and he's, Mr. Asbery Adams caught this one, well, he's in the office a little longer and he caught the car next to it, I mean, but he wasn't on the car that wrecked, he's on the same train but what I mean one of 'em caught one car and one of 'em the other'n', but they'd been friends for years.

Like Eli Sanford, Mr. McNease's Aunt None, also nearby at the time of the accident, recalled the lonesome sound of the train's whistle, the poignant image that opens the ballad.

> She was, oh, I guess she's fourteen or fifteen years old and she, they knew there's something when they heard this whistle blowin', see, when they're comin' in to Waterman, see, there's seven different rails went out in the woods from that mill, seven different directions. But anyhow, when they heared this she said it was one of the lonesomest whistles she thought she'd ever heard, but they knew there's something wrong. The people gathered up around the depot or close to the mill. Now, well, there's a store at that time there and they used it as kind of a depot too and so she said that they knew there's something but in a few minutes they knew what it was. They had Mr. Asbery Adams on the train and the other wounded, there's another 'as wounded, he died too later but there's two of 'em killed outright.

Mr. McNease did indeed have a print of the photo by Loving Sabel, to whom he was himself kin. As we sat surveying the picture—he identified his Uncle Otto in its foreground—he gave still a third account of the accident.

> Now the train didn't wreck, it 'as the four cars. You see, what happened, if I understood it right, see they didn't try to level up them roads haulin' logs in

them days. You'd go over the hill then down a valley. Well, as they went, them boys could've got off that train, they would've done it, but see when it pulled the top of this hill, it broke loose an' it goes back down, . . . well, it went up there and it stopped. And they could've got off but they thought it 'as gonna come back and stop and it went over that other hill, back where it broke loose. Well, the engineer seen what 'as happenin' so they said he went to hookin' 'em up, to try to get out of the way of it, because he's 'fraid it's gonna hit him. An' it like to caught him 'fore it wrecked, but there's four cars, four cars of logs, they's all left the track an' course it'd done got up right close to him, I think, when it did wreck. If he hadn't o', it'd wrecked the engine and all.

To my delight Mr. McNease not only possessed the celebrated photograph, he also had photocopies of two ballets, both set down from memory around 1960, one by his aunt, the other by Preacher Sabel's son, Tommie (figs. 6, 7). While these latter-day ballets were primarily resuscitative rather than creative acts, intended to salvage something of the distant past, the handwritten medium evidently sustained the piece from its inception. "Yeah, she [None Scoggins] wrote that herself an' the Sabel boy wrote this," he explained as I examined the ballets. "But he didn't copy from no—they didn't have no ballet or nothin' like, well, they had a ballet but I don't know what become of it. Might near everybody had one around Waterman at that time, but I don't know what become of them. I don't know whether anybody livin's got any of 'em or not."

Like most ballets, intended only as personal communications or memory aids, never the equivalents of actual performance, these texts were obviously produced by individuals somewhat unaccustomed to communicating through writing. Tommie Sabel's version, composed in a cramped hand on a single sheet of ruled paper, foregoes stanza or even line divisions.

tommie
Rote By tommie Sabel 19-60

it was on one friday morning the train
was some lonesom tune it went out into
the log woods it was on it daley rome
and on it way returning this sad accident
ocurred the train did wreck and did kill to men
later to more did die it was own one sunday
night at Eleavon tharty o clock we heared the
cryes of mercy that cause me to start
I stept into the Watermon Hotel and gaze
up on the Bed and it concurning this reck
Mr asbery adam was dead. it was in
sept 1911 the day the reck occured the train
did Reck and did kill to men and later to more

did die the sun was sloly sinking the
Bird had gone to rest all thro the day
is lonely we all shall meet again there
Be no Wreck up younder cause By the
Watermon Wreck the Engion near says
to the farmer we must shead down the train
the train has lost it manel guide to
Wreck this train its Bound

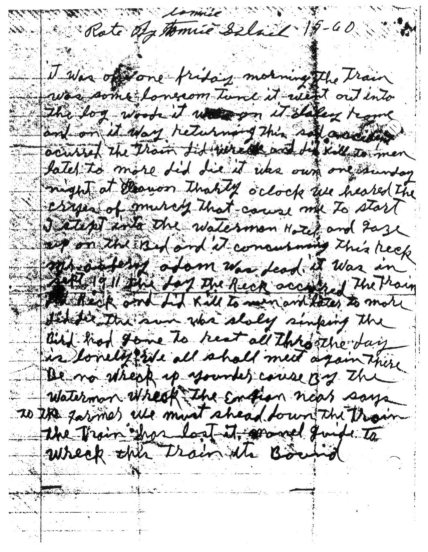

Fig. 6 Tommie Sabel's ballet.   *Courtesy Buren McNease.*

None Scoggins's script, covering two pages, is more fluid, generally arranged by line and stanza, but her ballet too suggests a stilted graphic representation of a fluent oral manifestation.

1   The Watermon Wreck
Aunt None wrote:[13]

it was on one Friday Morning
This Train of Lonesome Tone
Went out in The Logs Wood
Witch was our Dailey Run
&. on it way Returning This
Accident Accured This Train
Did Wreck & Killed 4. men
Distress was Soonley heard

2

we heard The Cryes in Watermon
it was Thire Wives &. Sweet to
&. Also one Dear old mother
Would Break The Heart of you

3

it was on one Sunday night
At Elevon Thirty O Clock I. heard
The Growns of Mercey. That
Caused me to start
I Stepped in to The Watermon
Hotel &. Gazed upon The Bed
&. Thire I Saw Conserning
This Wreck. Mr. Asbery Adams
Was Dead.

4

The Engion Nearmon Said to the
Firmon We Must Shut Down
This Train for if We Dont
We Loose Controll & Cause
This Train to Wreck.

5

it was on Sept 1911 The Day
This Train Did Wreck.
&. The Sun was Sloley Sinking
&. The Birds had gone to Rest
All Thro The Day was so
Loneley far it had Brought
to us. Distress

for The Steaming Train was
Cooling Down That Caused
The Watermon Wreck.

1 The watermon wreck.
aunt Mone wrote:

it was on ome Friday marning
This Train of Lonsome Tone
Went out in The Togswood
Witch was aur Dailey Run
S. on it way Returning This
accident Occured This Train
Did Wreck S Killed 4. men
Distress was Soon ley heard

(2)
we heard The Cryes in Watermon
it was Thire Wives S. Sunt to
S. Also ome Dear ald mother
Wauld Break The Heart of jau

(3)
it was on ome Sunday night
at Elevon Thirty a clok I heard
The Grawns of Mercey. That
Caused me To start.
I Stepped in to The Watermon
Hotell S. Gazed upon The Bed.
S. Thire I Saw Conserning
This Wreck. Mr. Asfery Adoms
was Dead.

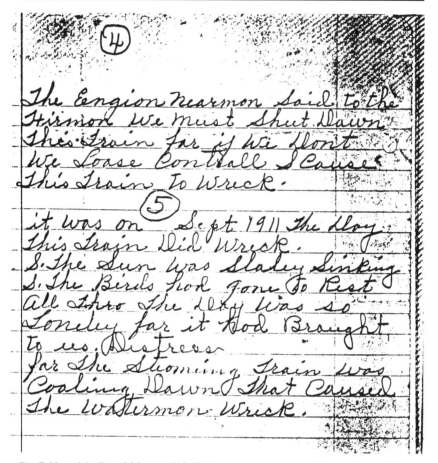

Fig. 7 None MacDonald Scoggin's ballet.   *Courtesy Buren McNease.*

Despite the lapse of several decades between the song's origin and the production of these texts, despite Mr. McNease's tentative memories, the recreative acts of Tommie Sabel and None Scoggins and the recollections of Mrs. Scoggins's nephew provide the most complete view of the making and early history of the Waterman ballad.

Just as Loving Sabel preserved the physical evidence of the crash, his son Tommie seemingly played a considerable role in popularizing the ballad that recorded its emotional impact. Like many county residents, the Sabels lived the balance of their lives within its boundaries, farming or pursuing odd jobs, though Tommie also acquired a reputation as a local entertainer, identified, moreover, with the ballad. "He 'as a g'itar picker and he used to sing it ["The

Waterman Train Wreck"] hisself," Buren McNease remembered, adding with a laugh, "He tried to learn me how to pick a g'itar but I never could learn." His association with this logging ballad notwithstanding, Preacher Sabel's son apparently avoided the mills; asked if Tommie had ever actually worked lumber, Mr. McNease replied, "No, not that I ever knew of. They was four of 'em [Loving Sabel's children], one girl and three boys, an' nary a one of 'em never did marry, either one of 'em never did marry, but he [Tommie] could play might anything and he played for the church a whole lot an' finally he worked at White Rock Graveyard." "But Tommie never did do nothin' but farm that I ever knew of, either one of 'em," he asserted, explaining, "They'd never been nowhere, what I'm a-gettin' at, to travel nowhere or, probably never been out of the county a dozen times. 'Course they daddy's a preacher an' sometime they'd go with him when he went, you know. O' course, them days you couldn't go very far in a buggy or horseback."

Whatever role Tommie played in remaking and popularizing "The Waterman Train Wreck," the ballad's actual maker, according to Mr. McNease's Aunt None, was a traveling salesman lodged at the hotel where they brought the victims. "He's some kind of a drummer, I don't know whether he's a clothes man, shoe man, or what he was, but he goes and writes this song, he composed the song, but I don't know his name," Mr. McNease volunteered. "I never did get it, never did know. Course Aunt None knew who it was an' she might've told me, but I forgot what his name was." As the ballad's point of view so strongly intimates, the drummer reputedly made the ballad in the immediate aftermath of the accident at his lodgings in the hotel-cum-hospital, "fixing" it to "a pretty tune" and committing it to writing.

> This drummer I was tellin' you about, he composed it, I don't know what his name was, but he was happened to be, he happened to be at the hotel when they come in with him [Asbery Adams]. I don't know whether he was spendin' the night or the day or what, but anyhow he 'as, I guess he 'as registered in the hotel, it had, I think it 'as several rooms in it, pretty good sized hotel and there 'as around three thousand people there [in Waterman] at that time, that worked the mills and in the woods and first one place and then another, and I can't, now, I never did hear his name an' if I did I forgot it, but he 'as the one that composed the song. [JM: So he just made it up right after?] Oh, yeah, he made it up hisself, but now if that's all of it, I don't know, but seem like there's more to it than what they got there [in the ballets], and it had a pretty tune to it, what I mean, the way he had it fixed, and now, whatever come of the original to whether somebody wrote it down from him or he wrote it down, I don't know just what happened. But might near everybody around Waterman when I was a kid, they knew that song there.

Nor were such performances limited to the wreck's immediate vicinity. Like many Shelby Countians, Mr. McNease was obliged to take what work he could find when the mills weren't running. "An' one time I went out to West Texas to pick cotton and they was singin' this song out there around Roscoe and Sweetwater out there," he marveled. "They still singin' this song, people that could sing it," adding "It had a pretty tune to it but I can't think of it no more." (He did, however, remember that he once could play the melody on a French harp.)

Attributed to an outsider, the ballad nevertheless won the approval of the community, readily incorporated within, and assimilated to, its performance repertoire, perhaps even diffusing beyond Shelby County, though the people "singin' this song out there around Roscoe and Sweetwater" (two towns near Abilene, over 300 miles west of the Attoyac) were apparently, like Buren McNease, displaced East Texans. Mr. McNease's uncle and aunt, both fine singers, were themselves quite explicably drawn to the ballad about a tragedy that affected them so very personally, a disruption in community life of such magnitude that it registered, if only faintly, on their young nephew. "That mornin' it 'as happened, I knowed there's a 'sturbance but I didn't know exactly what 'as happenin'," he reiterated. "What I mean, it just faint in my mind, although this aunt was six, seven years older than me, she was, always talked about, she'd always worried about that, you know, them men gettin' killed. She 'as kind of a Christian lady and been that way all her life and died that a-way." He well remembered his aunt's singing, particularly her performances of "The Waterman Train Wreck" with her brother, Asbery Adams's friend, Otto MacDonald, and another sister, his description again implicating Southern hymnody.

> Well, she's sung lots of religious songs. Yeah, she, I don't know whether she ever composed many but she used to sing lots of religious songs, and she sung a lot of just love ballads too. She 'as a pretty good singer. O' course, now, this uncle that I, he had one o' the prettiest voices that I ever, and if it'd been now, he could've went somewhere, you know what I mean, had some trainin'. But he had an awful pretty voice an' he might sing near anything. An' o' course they sung together an' then there's a sister in between there that sung with 'em a whole lot. But they sung some pretty songs.

"But this here one here," he emphasized, indicating the ballet in his Aunt None's hand and echoing V. V. Pate's assessment of the ballad's effect, "they could make the hair rise on your head singin'."

I drove over to East Texas alone at the end of September to return Mr. McNease's photograph. (On the day of our first meeting in August, I'd duplicated his own copies of the ballets at the video cassette rental outlet in Garrison, a typical East Texas storefront facing the increasingly disused tracks that inevitably parallel Main Street.) When I reached Center, Marcille apologized once more for having been unable to lay hands on the tape, but I'd brought her duplicates of the texts and photo, and with these as prompts, she filled in a few more gaps.

Marcille reckoned herself and Buren McNease kin both to one another and to Loving Sabel, whose personal effects, including the ballets and the photo of the crash, were transmitted to her by Mr. McNease before finally passing to another relative. Though Marcille hadn't time to make copies, she'd based the version she recorded for Homer Bryce on the texts from None Scoggins and Tommie Sabel, supplementing these with a few details recalled from childhood and slightly "modernizing" the tune as she remembered (but still would not sing) it. "Back when I got this," she explained, recounting the events a decade ago when the ballets first came into her possession, "I tried to sing it, and it was kind of jumbled up as you can see, so we begun to kind of change the words to make it rhyme better. We did change the words to fit them in a little better," adding "The tune may be a little changed—you'll have to hear it, it's on the same order the way they sung back then and we may have given a little bit of change to it, you know, every singer makes his style, and it's got a little of our style in it, but it's basically the same."

Marcille also shared with me a series of vignettes on Waterman that she'd just written—or rather word-processed on the personal computer at the Inn— for the local paper, among them her account of the wreck with the ballad's text.[14] As I left, it occurred to her that I might contact Shade Pate's older brother, Verb, in Arcadia. She remembered hearing him speak of the wreck; maybe he could help me. As always, her advice was well-taken.

At the end of November, I made a final foray into Deep East Texas on the trail of the Waterman Wreck. I stopped first in Tyler to see Mr. Ashley N. Beasley, whom I'd contacted through the Shelby County Historical Society. Born in Louisiana in 1902, Mr. Beasley was raised in the Waterman area, where his grandfather worked skidding logs with a yoke of oxen before the introduction of steam loaders, and where his father was later employed as a house carpenter, building company homes and lumber warehouses for the Waterman mill. Certainly he recalled the talk of the tragedy, but his memories were vague and at variance with others—he gave the date as 1914 and numbered the dead at fourteen—understandably, since his knowledge was limited to hearsay.[15] "I did not actually see the wreck itself," he acknowledged.

I knew about it, but transportation was a problem in those days. It wasn't a matter of jumpin' in a car, and runnin' down yonder, seein' something. It was walkin'. You walked down there, and, if you hear about it, you may be two or three days hearin' about it, 'cause you didn't have a telephone like you do now. We had no telephones. Somebody come along and tell you about it, then you go down there, provided you can get through with your work, go look at it. But it was a bad thing and very much talked about at that time.

The next day, December 1, I drove down to Shelby County, stopping first in Nacogdoches at Stephen F. Austin State to check the Forest History Collection; there was nothing on Waterman, the Waterman Lumber Company, or the Waterman wreck. I crossed the Attoyac and spent an overcast afternoon driving the backroads of what was Waterman, photographing red dirt and dark pines. But the real find of the trip awaited me in Center the following morning: Marcille had the tape.

She and I sat and listened to the cassette—three renditions of "The Waterman Train Wreck" in a row, all of them stunning—on the side porch of the Inn. Marcille was disappointed; the performances weren't as good as she'd remembered. I was pleased beyond all hope. The performances were not only magnificent; they confirmed my premonitions, based on a reasonable acquaintance with Southern balladry, as to their probable character. The harmonies suggest bluegrass more than shape-note singing, perhaps what Marcille meant when she said they'd modernized their performance. The chromaticism in the bridge seems similarly anachronistic, though the general correspondence of the tune's first strain to Marshall Alvis's performance suggests that this component at least is derived from the original tradition. In fact, the chorus itself—apparently elaborated from the second stanza of None Scoggins's ballet—impresses me as a concession to more recent musical expectations, where the obligatory refrain is conventionally signaled, as here, by a second melodic strain with a concomitant shift to the major IV chord. Although the tune implicates a triple tempo more typical of older a cappella ballad singing, the insistent duple rhythm and commonplace chord progression of the guitar likewise suggest updating, though by no means in a negative sense. Indeed, such features parallel the evolution of Anglo-American balladry as a whole, and particularly its adaptation to instrumental traditions and choral performance, developments documented, beginning in the 1920s, by "hillbilly" records—78-RPM discs produced by Northern corporations for commercial distribution in the South. Even disregarding its ties to purely oral entities, Marcille's recording is traditional as well in its adherence to the conventions of that particular stream of Southern balladry that evolved through the interaction of local folksong, semi-professional entertainment, popular print, and electronic media, her tape constituting a quite consciously poised, cleverly arranged media production; the three "takes" are practically identical, with simple instrumental breaks in the introduction and then before the climactic final chorus, followed by a carefully orchestrated coda in which, as the tempo slows to a standstill, the voices fade in a wordless reprise of the refrain ("Oooo-ooo-ooo-ooo-ooo . . . ").

Departing Center once more, I headed north to Timpson to see Bessie Smith Alford, another contact from the Shelby County Historical Society whose late father, Samuel Tilton Smith, was the engineer on the Waterman Log Train, the mainline locomotive that transported the milled lumber out of the Attoyac bottoms. Bessie was actually born at Blocker, to the north in Harrison County, where her father had moved after the Waterman mill closed. She had heard him, and others from the county, speak of the wreck, but she recalled few specifics. She did remember his story of a black man who lost an arm in a railway accident near the mill, but it was unclear whether this was the same catastrophe which occasioned the ballad or a separate incident.[16] Bessie also had a photograph of her father with his engine, however, which she graciously loaned me. Before I said good-bye, we sat in her front room and listened to Marcille's tape, her first exposure to the song. She seemed quite pleased. As I left she apologized for having so little for me. If only her father were alive; he could have told me everything I wanted to know.

It was mid-afternoon when I left Timpson, heading back south toward Waterman. I had another appointment in Center, this one unrelated to my trip's main purpose, but first there was time for one more stop. Under overcast skies and shadowy pines, I drove once more down the red dirt road past Judge Pate's to see if I could find the scene of the Waterman wreck as he remembered it.

In my pursuit of the Waterman train wreck, I have hardly exhausted the field. Any trip produces new leads, and I've tallied my share. After the closing of the Waterman Mill, most of the residents of that company town scattered far beyond the borders of Shelby County, though many have remained in touch with the folks who stayed and who have supplied me with the names and whereabouts of some who left, a few with whom I've corresponded, with or without reply. A sister of Asbery Adams reportedly is, or until recently was, still alive, though I have yet to locate her. I have thus far spared myself the arduous and dubiously useful task of perusing the various contemporaneous Texas dailies for the years 1911 and 1912 on the off-chance that one of these carried the story (the outright suppression of such reporting by the lumber bosses and the general disinterest to this day of outsiders in insular Shelby County argue against such an eventuality). Maybe the facts of the incident repose with one of these sources, or perhaps in an undiscovered family Bible, or on a tombstone in one of the innumerable private cemeteries in Shelby County, many of which have themselves been reclaimed by the pines.

But for a folklorist, the real interest lies in the manner in which the "facts," whatever these might be, have clearly gravitated toward a traditional model, the folk ballad, revealing once more that, while Southern folksong has not exactly thrived in the face of increased competition from other media, it has survived precisely because of such alternative means of expression. Certainly the proximity of the ballad model to the Waterman train wreck, and to that tragedy's subsequent depiction in "The Waterman Train Wreck," is indisputable. We know little of the ballad's reputed maker, the drummer lodged at the hotel where they brought the victims, the narrator at the scene whose presence is especially sensed behind the third stanza of None Scoggins's ballet and the corresponding portion of Tommie Sabel's text ("I Stepped in to The Watermon Hotel &. Gazed upon The Bed"). However, traveling salesmen, habitual tradition bearers transmitting materials between the isolated stops along their routes, were identified with the circulation of folklore in East Texas as elsewhere; since their itineraries coincided with the expanding rail lines, it is accordingly quite credible that such an individual played some role in creating "The Waterman Wreck."[17] In any case, the persons who made and remade this piece were clearly conversant in the poetics of Southern songs of tragedy and disaster generally, and more particularly in one of that genre's prodigious subdivisions, the train wreck ballad, a product of the successive, recursive interaction of folk singers, written texts, and commercial phonograph records.

Such electronically mediated materials were, of course, initially disparaged by folksong purists, who dismissed them as corrupting and corroding to "true" folk balladry, and deferred instead to the older strata of Anglo-American oral tradition circumscribed by Francis James Child in his canon of *English and Scottish Popular Ballads* (1956 [1882–98])—the "closed literary account" to which Gummere appealed as absolute standard. Such injunctions aside, this integral facet of the Anglo-American ballad tradition has since been rescued from academic ignominy by Anglo-American ballad scholars in the tradition of D. K. Wilgus, the foremost authority on hillbilly records whose "broadside analogy" cogently characterizes the unmistakable functional parallels between, and the historical crossings and re-crossings of, the commercial discs that adapted the oral traditions of the American South to the age of electronic media and the broadsides and chapbooks that previously accommodated British folksong to the rise of literacy. The writers and printers of these song sheets ("broadsides") and cheap folios ("chapbooks" or "songsters") quickly learned that pieces from folk tradition or new compositions after that pattern were favorably received among their target audience, the semi-literate rural and urban working classes of Britain and, subsequently, their North American progeny, and many venerable and venerated Anglo-American folksongs owe their continued vitality or even their origins to the broadside presses of the seventeenth, eighteenth, and nineteenth centuries.

Beginning in the 1920s, "hillbilly broadsides"—commercial recordings by white Southerners informally tutored in the region's traditions, or calculated imitations by formally trained musicians—served an identical function in preserving and transmitting older folksongs and in contributing new compositions to the Southern folk for whom these commodities were primarily intended, abetting the publishers of popular sheet music, the nineteenth- and twentieth-century heirs of the broadside presses, in circulating materials within, and recirculating materials from, the folk milieu. Eventually, these multiple cycles of mutual influence—tempered, moreover, by contact with African-American folksong—rendered the creations and recreations of oral tradition, popular print, and hillbilly broadside interchangeable in style and substance, producing a uniquely American offspring of the English and Scottish popular ballad.[18]

The oikotypal subcategory within this tradition was the "blues ballad," one avatar of the "ballad idea" which, in the definitive formulation of D. K. Wilgus and Eleanor Long, "boldly departs from the linear narration, gapped or circumstantial, of its congeners: to sing a story not by directly relating that story but by celebrating it; not by following a chronological sequence, but by creating a sequence of concepts and feelings about it" (1985: 439). Topically, these pieces reflect the unique experiences of Southern working class men and women in the late-nineteenth and early-twentieth centuries, paralleling geographically as well "the post-Civil War expansion of American industry in river traffic, railroading, coal mining, and mass labor no longer confined to the plantations." Emanating from "river towns, construction camps, 'frolic houses,' hobo jungles—situations for the cross-fertilization of Black and White traditions in relatively uninhibited fashion," this subgenre "is clearly a product of the rural South in the throes of industrialization" (Wilgus and Long 1985: 458). And one obvious and especially significant effect of this transformation of Southern life and livelihood was the incorporation of Southern folksong within modern media like the phonograph, media that preserved, circulated, and motivated compositions whose contents were accordingly consonant with their technological format.

Like their predecessors in print, composers for the hillbilly market immediately discovered the appeal of the sensational topical tragedy, always a
commonplace subject as well for the oral folksongs that nurtured, and were
nourished by, both printed and recorded broadsides—one such cycle of
mutual influence that accordingly provided a well-tested precedent and
conventional mold for the depiction of contemporaneous calamities in any
or all of these separate yet inseparable media. As one might expect, many of
these pieces concerned specifically the occupational hazards of the historical
epoch described by Wilgus and Long, documenting the inherent risks of
industrial life.[19] In the late- nineteenth and early-twentieth centuries, railroad
disasters were among the most common and compelling of such tragedies,
and the recurring verbalization, through word of mouth, on printed page, and
in sound recording, of their significance for the Southern sensibility produced
the subgenre of the train wreck ballad. One of the most famous compositions
of the type, "The Wreck of Old 97" (Laws G2), was also one of the most
famous hillbilly records. Inspired by an actual event, the ballad began as a folk
creation based loosely on a popular nineteenth century song sheet, a recasting
immediately adopted by, and adapted to, the phonograph trade, reinvesting
or reinvigorating the song in both oral tradition and print.[20]

Marcille Hughes compared "The Waterman Wreck" to another renowned
example of the train wreck genre, "Casey Jones" (Laws G1), which her mother
sang: "Mama rocked us kids to sleep with this song. I'll never forget, 'Turn on
the water, shovel in the coal, stick your head out the window and watch the
drivers roll.'" The piece is omnipresent in American oral tradition, but
popular print and commercial recordings were both essential to that remarkable currency. Although Ashley Beasley had never heard the Waterman
ballad, he correctly surmised, given the popularity of "Casey Jones," that such
a song existed. Asked if he'd heard any songs about the wreck, he replied, "I
never did hear that. I'm sure there were. We had a song at that time that
everybody sang, young and old. It was 'The Wreck of Casey Jones,' now, I do
have that song." And, while he realized that "that song had no connection
with the Waterman wreck," he reasoned, "I'm sure that somewhere out there
floating around must be a song about the Waterman wreck."[21]

The Waterman ballad's affinity to Southern broadside tradition generally
was likewise remarked. Buren McNease was reminded of "Floyd Collins,"
(Laws G22), a fixture in Southern tradition that originated as a phonograph
disc, just one composition by a preeminent songmaker in that medium, the
Reverend Andrew "Blind Andy" Jenkins. "But might near everybody around
Waterman when I was a kid, they knew that song ["The Waterman Wreck"]

there," he assured me. "Just like that 'Floyd Collins in the Cave,' you know that, I gonna tell you, they singin' that song out there, that's the first radio we ever heard over." Shade Pate, who himself performed on radio and record with a hillbilly string band, likened "The Waterman Train Wreck" to "The Santa Barbara Earthquake" (Laws dG45), a composition by another prolific composer of hillbilly broadsides, Carson Robison. Unable to recall any of the Waterman piece, Shade quoted the opening lines of the Robison song instead: "Way out in California, among the hills so tall,/A town named Santa Barbara they thought would never fall."[22]

Marshall Alvis's earliest exposure to music was through a mother who "just sang around home," though he himself advanced to professional status among Hollywood's media moguls. Older songs from the domestic tradition persisted, of course, for example, the ubiquitous "Barbara Allen" (Child 84), itself the subject of innumerable broadsides, records, and broadcasts, but these pieces seemed a bit dated to a younger generation attuned to the topical expressions and alternative media of a particularly Southern, specifically twentieth-century ethos. "Oh, yeah, o' course that," acknowledged Buren McNease when I mentioned "Barbara Allen." "I guess that 'as 'fore my time, it 'as already here when I got big enough to hear that 'bout 'Barbary Allen.'" Marcille also remembered her mother performing that venerable item, though it hardly excited in her the same interest as "The Waterman Wreck" or even "Casey Jones," songs that directly addressed her own generation's experiences and expectations through the artistic conventions of a familiar though fast-changing present; quite tellingly, she prefaced her tale of the Waterman tragedy with an account of that topical aesthetic: "In the nineteen-hundreds, about the turn of the century, the trains, it was their heyday, so to speak, and there were lots of stories about train wrecks, and it was interesting to me and I was always fascinated by stories of train wrecks, but we had the train went right through our place, right down the 'Toyac River to Waterman."

So "The Waterman Train Wreck" numbers among those American ballads that grew from, contributed to, and prevailed through the interaction of oral tradition, popular print, and commercial recording, abetted in this instance by numerous other media, for example, the handwritten ballet and its contemporary equivalent, the homemade cassette, whose analogous relation to one another, and homologous interrelation with popular graphic and phonograph disc (handwritten script : individually produced audio tape :: mechanical type : commercially manufactured sound disc) reveal both the theoretical facility and practical utility of Wilgus's felicitous analogy for describing the increasingly complex interaction of an increasing number and variety of media in Southern folksong. Recall that the ballets providing one link to "The Waterman Wreck" were transmitted not as manuscripts but as photocopies, a medium customarily associated with the lore of corporate offices in urban centers (cf. Dundes and Pagter 1975, 1987). This admittedly limited account of a single song nonetheless describes an intertwining host of media presently assimilated within the interpersonal networks of rural Deep East Texas—verbal communication, handwritten ballet and type-written correspondence, audio tape, photograph and photocopy, radio, telephone, newsprint, personal computer (the fax and videotape, while not represented here, are present as well).

And even after my prolonged quest for the unmediated essence of an oral tradition, even after repeatedly insinuating myself into the personal presence of so many invariably helpful and incomparably hospitable Shelby Countians, there is this: of all my data, Marcille's recent recreation of "The Waterman Train Wreck" most closely approximates, in origin, form, function, meaning, and context, an actual folksong performance, even though this particular performance was electronically implanted within a plastic cassette filled with magnetic tape; patched together from memories of an oral tradition, aided by photocopies of commonplace manuscripts and both a native sense of folk expression and a contemporary acquaintance with media conventions; recorded and replayed on portable high-tech tape decks; yet rearranged and recorded at home cooperatively with kith and kin for a lifelong friend and neighbor; inspired, that is, by the interpersonal concerns and considerations criterial to the folk ballad; performed moreover without the goading of an intrusive university-trained folklorist; created essentially as an artistic expression of community, albeit a community mainly of memories and the media that preserve them.

So despite these fading memories of Waterman's past or the jading influences of modern experience, influences apparent even in the secluded piney woods, despite the intercession of electronic media definitive of contemporary sensibilities or the inspired intervention of an exceptional individual, folk balladry is still alive, if only barely, in Deep East Texas. Marcille's revival of the ballad is no mere resurrection of a fossilized skeleton but rather an imaginative implementation of that form in the kind of interpersonal act governing such conventional expressions in customary communication. And the fluid and resilient ballad form is manifest in this and the rest of our selective sample. The texts are cast in the traditional ballad verse, an approximation of iambic pentameter malleable either as couplets of seven stress lines or in four line stanzas, rhymed ABCB and alternating four and three accents.

Set to a rounded tune, the narrative proceeds in the "leaping and lingering" fashion peculiar to the ballad,[23] a series of episodic flashes that successively reveal the story, as the viewpoint shifts abruptly from the log woods to Waterman to the hotel then back to the wreckage. More particularly, this technique embodies the "blues ballad idea" as explicated by Wilgus and Long (1985), a loose stanzaic sequence stressing affects and responses as much as actions and their consequences, emotional reflexes as much as temporal relations.

Thematically as well, the tale is filtered through the ballad sensibility. Consider the manner in which aural/oral imagery pervades the piece, beginning with the train whistle recalled as well in the narrative Verb Pate heard from Eli Sanford, or the story None Scoggins told her nephew, Buren McNease. Intriguingly, their descriptions of the emotive impact of that recollected image—"the train of lonesome tune (tone, sound)," "a curious most bloodcurdling sound that you ever heard in your life," "the lonesomest whistle she thought she'd ever heard"—parallel their similarly cognate accounts of the ballad that opens on that signal of distress: "Such as that'll make your hair stand on end," mused V. V. Pate, sentiments echoed by Buren McNease: "This here one here, they could make the hair rise on your head singin'." Add to the image of that discordant tone the distress heard from Waterman, the cries and wailing of the wives and sweethearts and especially of Asbery Adams's dear old mother, the groans for mercy from Adams himself as he lays dying in the Waterman Hotel, the engineer's frantic instructions to the fireman, the sudden silence of the forest birds at sunset opposed to the hiss of steam from the cooling train that caused the wreck. These figures cumulatively evoke a world in which life was regulated not by the precise dates of a calender but by the whistles of sawmills and locomotives marking a perpetual cycle of labor, a milieu likewise summoned in the proverbial report that "Along both branches of the 'Wobblety-Bobblety' [another East Texas logging line] sawmills were so close together that it was said that one was never out of the sound of a mill whistle" (Maxwell and Baker 1983: 42). This was a world where, despite the proliferation of alternative media (albeit many themselves, like the hillbilly disc, oral/aural in essence), most news was still heard, not read, a world, that is, of oral traditions like balladry.

The depiction in ballad and tale of the grieving women—the "Wives &. Sweet[hearts] to[o] &. Also one Dear old mother [who] Would Break The Heart of you," the woman whose doomed husband "begged [her] to cook him some peas and cornbread, and she wouldn't do it"—no doubt reflects empirical fact, though this selective account (such grief was obviously general if of varying degrees) simultaneously accords with the conventions of the train wreck ballad, where the waiting wife, sweetheart, or mother is a constant in the tragedy's revelation. Marshall Alvis's anecdote of the wife whose grief was cruelly compounded by remorse ("And I bet she was sure sorry!" "She sure was!") aptly suggests the logic of a detail which has long puzzled folklorists, the stanza concluding one subtype of "The Wreck of Old 97."

> Now ladies, you must take warning,
> From this time now and on;
> Never speak harsh words to your true love and husband,
> He may leave you and never return.

Folklorists have often remarked that this stanza, borrowed from a ballad predating "The Old 97," "is completely out of place in the railroad song."[24] To an outsider the feature indeed seems "rather inappropriate" since "no indication is given in the ballad that harsh words were spoken to anyone" (Laws 1964:30), the assumption being, apparently, that the folk, as thralls of tradition, are dutifully reproducing an incoherent and inconsistent narrative as they heard it. In spite of its ostensible sensibility, the argument belies the fact that this conclusion was obviously comprehensible, obviously seemed quite appropriate to the Southerners who made, remade, and sang the ballad, persons who inhabited a world where most occupations were intrinsically hazardous, where working men routinely died young, where grief-stricken women often found small comfort in a culture where inherent individual guilt was a fundamental religious doctrine. That moral was quite clearly viewed as a fitting conclusion for train wreck ballads, as evidenced by "The Old 97" or by Callie Alvis's tale of the remorseful Waterman widow.

The ballad's chronology, suspect from the "historical" standpoint, also suggests folksong convention, and East Texas' fervent fundamentalism, the latter implicated especially through the song's association with Preacher Sabel's son Tommie, who "played for the church a whole lot"; with None Scoggins, the "Christian lady" who "sung lots of religious songs" and who "always worried about them men gettin' killed"; and with shape-note singing, as recalled by Marcille and recreated on her recording. I attribute greater reliability to V. V. Pate's claim that the wreck occurred in 1912 than to the ballad's alternative account in part because "nineteen-eleven" rhymes with "heaven," a ballad commonplace for the fate of persons killed in that year.[25] Marcille's closing couplet also evokes the central trope of the popular "Life's Railway to Heaven" (Cohen 1981:611–18), a moralistic touch typical of the Southern broadside, found as well in the other texts. The tragedy, of course, takes place on Friday, the day cursed by the crucifixion of Christ and ever after a harbinger of bad luck, most pertinent here, in ballads such as "The Mermaid" (Child 289), in which a ship's crew who foolishly set sail on Friday are doomed from the outset. Within our own example, Asbery Adams, the only named victim, serves as a sacrificial symbol not only of the dead and injured in this particular mishap but of all the young men who suffered and died in a high-risk industry to earn a living for their families. And Adams is mortally stricken on a Friday, lingers briefly on earth and then on Sunday, the third day, ascends into heaven.

Perhaps the prominence of Asbery Adams in this ballad motivated Judge Pate's recollection of a separate song devoted exclusively to him. None of my other informants remembered such a piece, though its existence is certainly plausible. However, when asked about other compositions on local disasters, Marshall Alvis replied, "Well, 'nother un on the Garrison flood down there." Questioned further, he hesitated. "No, I don't remember none of that. 'Course it was recorded, it was real popular for a while. I don't know who wrote it but. . . ."[26]

Ballads are not evergreen nor will they ever grow as they once did. But while they may be an endangered species, they are neither extinct. There may be a few more loose in the piney woods of Deep East Texas.

Indiana University–Purdue University
Fort Wayne

Notes

Support for this project was provided by the University of Texas Institute of Texan Cultures at San Antonio, whose assistance I gratefully acknowledge. I wish also to thank Terry McDevitt, whose rapport with the people of Shelby County provided the indispensable link to "The Waterman Train Wreck"; Rick Burns, who also participated in fieldwork for this study; and Roger deV. Renwick, who read and commented perceptively on the manuscript. Finally, heartfelt thanks to the many Shelby Countians, far outnumbering those listed in n. 3, who contributed their time and knowledge; the extent of my debt notwithstanding, I must express special gratitude to Marcille and Pershing Hughes, Mattie Dellinger, and Howell and Pam Howard.

1. Gummere pronounced his post-mortem in *The Popular Ballad* (1959 [1907]:16, 337). Lomax recounts his collecting experiences in *Adventures of a Ballad Hunter* (1947).

2. The definitive history of lumbering in East Texas before the Second World War is Robert S. Maxwell and Robert D. Baker's *Sawdust Empire* (1983), which also contains an excellent account of the land and the people (see esp. 3–16).

3. Unless otherwise noted, all direct quotations are taken, with occasional minor emendations, from the following taped interviews (Prefixes refer to the archives of the Institute of Texan Cultures and also identify the interviewers: JM=John Minton; TMcD=Terry McDevitt; RB=Rick Burns. Except for Buren McNease and Ashley N. Beasley, all subjects were interviewed in Shelby County.): JM/TMcD/RB89–1–1:1 Marcille Hancock Hughes, Center, June 29, 1989; JM/TMcD/RB89–2–1:1 Shade Pate, Todd Springs Community, June 29, 1989; JM/TMcD/RB89–4–1:1 Mr. and Mrs. Elmer Hancock, Waterman Community, June 30, 1989; JM/TMcD/RB89–5–1:1 Homer Bryce, Waterman Community, June 30, 1989; JM/RB89–3–1:1 Marshall Alvis, Center, August

25, 1989; JM/RB–5–1:1 Buren McNease, Garrison, Nacogdoches County, August 26, 1989; JM89–1–1:1 Marcille Hancock Hughes, Center, September 21, 1989; JM89–2–1:1 V. V. Pate, Arcadia Community, September 21, 1989; JM89–3–1:1 Ashley N. Beasley, Tyler, Smith County, November 30, 1989.

4. The organization of Marcille's ballet differs slightly in its divisions, giving lines 1–4, 9–10, and 13–14 as stanzas and lines 5–8 as the chorus, with a few minor contrasts in wording.

5. In addition to the interviews listed in n. 3 above and the other materials cited herein, information on Shelby County may be found under the appropriate entries in Webb (1952).

6. On railroads in East Texas lumbering, see Maxwell and Baker's chapter "Whistle in the Piney Woods" (1983:34–50) and Reed (1941:292–94). Marcille recalled the railroad through Waterman as a branch of the Gulf, Colorado and Santa Fe, a Texas company employed by the Santa Fe as an umbrella for its interests in the state. Technically, however, Waterman was apparently on another Santa Fe route, the Texas and Gulf, a shortline running south from Marshall and Carthage as far as Grigsby, then connecting the Gulf, Beaumont and Great Northern, which reached Center in 1903 (Maxwell and Baker 1983:39).

Maxwell and Baker also enumerate the nicknames of several other East Texas logging roads, based on the carriers' acronyms as well as purported attributes. For example, the Houston, East and West Texas Railroad, the HE&WT, was known both as "Hell Either Way Taken" and the "Rabbit," the latter "because of its short, bobbing narrow-gauge cars, its up- and downhill roadbed, its 'out-of-breath' engines, its tendency to jump the track, and, above all, its proclivity for 'stopping behind every stump'." Other lines so distinguished were the Texas and New Orleans (T&NO)— "Time No Object" or "Turnips and New Onions"; the Waco, Beaumont, Trinity and Sabine (WBT&S)—"Wobblety-Bobblety, Turnover, and Stop"; the Texas South-Eastern (TS-E)—"Tattered, Shattered, and Expired"; and the Nacogdoches and Southeastern (N&SE)—"Never Say Early." One narrow-guage shortline, consisting of five miles of track and a single Shay locomotive, was "The Great Sweetgum Yubadam and Hoo Hoo Route" (Maxwell and Baker 1983:38–46).

7. According to one Shelby County historian, "Though Waterman had businesses, schools, churches and other trappings of a normal community, it became a wild and woolly town with a penchant for violence. It is said that even the women carried guns and learned to swing knives" (McCoy 1982:66). Many of my own informants gave hair-raising accounts of routine violence in the community.

8. The term "front" applied generally to such temporary mill towns located as close as possible to the timber source (Maxwell and Baker 1983: 65; McCoy 1982:64), and Waterman's Shelby County operation was also apparently known as the "Waterman Front" (see the quote from Shade Pate below). However, there currently is a "Front Community" near Deadwood in eastern Panola County, possibly substantiating this account of the move. Stating that "The Waterman Mill was abruptly closed in 1912 or 1913," McCoy, who places the relocation a bit farther north, at Waskom in Harrison County, quotes an informant who "recalled that there was 'a labor dispute or something'" (1982:66), but given the tenuous position of organized labor in East Texas lumbering, this seems less likely than the more common depletion of timber.

9. The typicality of the Waterman operation as recollected by my informants is corroborated in Maxwell and Baker (1983:51–69) and McCoy (1982:64).

10. Conversation at Garrison, Nacogdoches County, September 23, 1989. This photo (see fig. 4), printed without attribution on a vintage postcard, was provided by Mattie Dellinger, who also relayed this account of its provenience (below), but the

uncertain ethnicity of the man with the engine led some to challenge that identification. Viewing the photo, Bill's father, Buren McNease, confirmed that the locomotive was a Shay of the type employed by the Waterman mill but then remarked, "I don't know if he's a black man. If it 'as Waterman, it wasn't a black man," relating how the company's attempts to import black workers were thwarted by the violent opposition of white residents. According to Mr. McNease, blacks did not begin settling around Waterman until the 1940s. However, other data strongly suggest that at least some blacks lived in or around Waterman and were involved in the mill's operation, e.g. the stories from Marcille Hancock Hughes and Bessie Smith Alford below and the photograph of Mrs. Alford's father and his work mate with the Waterman train (fig. 5). It is also possible that the individual in the contested photograph is a white male whose face is merely covered in soot or shadows.

11. For the experiences of East Texas lumber workers in company towns, see Maxwell and Baker (1983:116–54). Statistics on the relative risks of lumbering appear on p. 123. On the hazards of railroading during this period, see Cohen (1981:169–80). Although my informants all recalled the wreck as the greatest tragedy to befall their community, most remembered the endemic accidents at the Waterman operation and other area mills. For instance, Buren McNease had heard his grandfather tell of a man who was knocked into a saw "and got cut half in two"; on another occasion, he recalled an uncle who was among several millhands scalded to death in a boiler explosion (conversation at Garrison, September 23, 1989).

12. Peaches Conway, Shelby County Clerk, to John Minton, December 8, 1989. WPA *Index*. In her column featuring Loving Sabel's photo, Mattie Dellinger (1978) gives the date of the wreck as 1912, although her account was provided by Gilmer Tyson, one of V. V. Pate's sources. Patricia McCoy also specifies Spring 1912, but her information comes in turn from Judge Pate (McCoy 1982:66). Mattie credited the copy of the Sabel photo reproduced with her article to Mrs. W. L. Miller of Austin. Mrs. Miller, a Shelby County native, stated that she in-herited the picture from her father, who, she believed, had worked in the Waterman mill (Mrs. W. L. Miller to John Minton, December 12, 1989). Her photo is identical to Figure 1 except that "Wreck on the Waterman" is superimposed across the bottom in mechanical type, suggesting the extent to which the image circulated, perhaps even commercially.

13. This notation was added in a different hand, presumably by Mr. McNease.

14. Marcille supplied me with undated clippings of the articles, published by the *Light-Champion* in October and November 1989.

15. Mr. Beasley was, in fact, aware of this discrepancy, having just read Marcille's stories in the Center paper (n. 14 above).

16. A lady in Center had told Marcille that there were actually two Waterman train wrecks, certainly a possibility given the safety record of the East Texas lumber industry.

17. The customary association of itinerant drummers and oral tradition is reflected in one familiar American folklore genre, the traveling salesman joke. In East Texas, the Houston, East and West Texas Railway (HE&WT) apparently received its nickname— "Hell Either Way Taken" (n. 6 above)—from the drummers who depended on the company's service, individuals who "usually traveled up and down a given railroad line, calling on the milltowns along the route, [and who] also brought news and gossip from neighboring mills" (Maxwell and Baker 1983:38,149). We may only speculate on the role of our own drummer in the largely undocumented diffusion of the Waterman ballad. One might also wonder if this attribution was influenced or even inspired by the stereotype of the traveling salesman as a source of folklore.

18. The standard descriptions of the Anglo-American adjuncts of Child's *English and Scottish Popular Ballads* (1956 [1882–98]) are G. Malcolm Laws, *Native American*

Balladry (1964) and *American Balladry From British Broadsides* (1957). D. K. Wilgus expounded his broadside analogy in his definitive history of *Anglo-American Folksong Scholarship Since 1898* (1959:198, 232–35, 283–84, 430), refining it in subsequent analyses (cf. 1968, 1965, and 1964).

19. For two exemplary applications of Wilgus's broadside analogy to commercially recorded occupational song, see Archie Green, *Only a Miner* (1972) and Norm Cohen, *Long Steel Rail* (1981). I also explore Wilgus's analogy and develop a complementary approach to the relation between oral tradition and sound recording in my doctoral dissertation, "Phonograph Blues" (1990).

20. For an authoritative consideration of the American train wreck ballad, and particularly of the respective contributions of oral tradition, popular print, and commercial recordings, see Norm Cohen's outstanding study *Long Steel Rail*, especially Chapter 5, "The Fatal Run" (1981:169–274); his painstaking account of "The Wreck of Old 97" appears on pp. 197–226. In this regard, "The Waterman Train Wreck" has interesting implications for the classification of American balladry, particularly the system developed by Laws, which has met with criticism from D. K. Wilgus, among others (see Laws 1964:12, n. 10), since this arrangement's constituent categories clearly are not mutually exclusive, topically exhaustive, logically of a kind, internally consistent, and so forth. Indeed, given subject matter alone—the primary criterion in the Laws scheme—we would be hard-pressed to classify "The Waterman Train Wreck" with either "Ballads of Lumberjacks" (C1–28) or "Ballads of Tragedies and Disasters" (G1–33). Provincially, thematically, and stylistically, however, the piece obviously belongs among the Southern train wreck ballads classified under the G subdivision, not with the songs of the Northern woods represented by C, though its relation to many other items in the "Tragedies" category is equally tenuous. The Shelby County background of another famous Southern railroad song/hillbilly recording seems pertinent here: the alliterative names of four Shelby County stops along the celebrated HE&WT (nn. 6 and 17 above)—Tenaha, Timpson, Bobo, and Blair—were adopted locally as a dice call, used when rolling for ten points (a pun on "Tenaha"). This conductor's cant/crap shooter's rant in turn served as title and refrain of a popular composition by Woodward Maurice "Tex" Ritter, a native of neighboring Panola County (Reider and Davis 1977; Maxwell and Baker 1983:38). Ritter's record is still regularly broadcast over area stations like KDET, and a billboard by a lumberyard south of Timpson portrays a locomotive with the refrain billowing from its smoke-stack.

21. On "Casey Jones," see Cohen (1981:132–57). Mr. Beasley did indeed "have that song," in a tattered songbook from which he sang. Regrettably, I neglected to note the title of the songster.

22. For brief accounts of Jenkins and Robison respectively, see Cohen (1981:159–61 and 268 and passim). It is also noteworthy, given this line of analysis, that the East Texas Serenaders, one of the most successful hillbilly recording units of the 1920s, were from Center.

23. This oft-repeated characterization of the ballad style was also coined by Gummere (1959 [1907]:90–91, 117).

24. Friedman (1956:318). The specific instance of this stanza above is from Vernon Dalhart's immensely successful recording—the only indisputable hillbilly million seller—as given in Cohen (1981:213, 222). The fact that the verse was borrowed from "The Parted Lover," a parody of Henry C. Work's popular composition "The Ship That Never Returned" (1865) which contributed to "The Wreck of Old 97" (Cohen 1981:201; Friedman 1956:318), no doubt reinforced the sense of its incongruity in the last item.

25. A convenient example is "The Cross Mountain Explosion (Coal Creek Disaster)" (Laws G9), as quoted in Laws (1964):

> The ninth day of December,
> Nineteen hundred and eleven,
> Many were killed in the Coal Creek mine
> And I hope they are in heaven.

Unfortunately for this reconstruction, the trope does not appear in the Sabel and Scoggins ballets, though both specify the date as 1911, and Tommie Sabel's text alludes to heaven as well, though not by name (instead, we find "up younder"). Possibly the detail was forgotten, but this seems a bit unlikely, if hardly inconceivable, for such an obvious commonplace rhyme. Marcille herself may have inserted the figure, in which case the convention is, of course, the effect, not the cause of this detail, and cannot then account for the discrepancy in the dates. On the other hand, Marcille very likely recalled the couplet from versions she heard in her youth (she asserted that she had rearranged the song the "way [she] remembered it"). The conflicting dates remain puzzling, however, especially since Tommie Sabel, None Scoggins, and Judge Pate were all eye witnesses to the wreck's aftermath.

There is, of course, an inverted ballad commonplace for the fate of persons who died in 1912, appearing in some of the songs concerning the most famous disaster to occur in that year, the sinking of the Titanic, as in a North Carolina variant of "The Titanic I" (Laws D24), which attributes the calamity to God's displeasure at the refusal of the rich to ride with the poor:

> You read about that mighty ship,
> In nineteen hundred and twelve,
> That moved upon the mighty seas
> And landed those people in hell.
> (Belden and Hudson 1952:668)

This sentiment was, however, quite obviously inappropriate for the Waterman ballad.

26. Buren McNease remembered the Garrison flood, or at least a Garrison flood, but knew nothing of the ballad, stating "They had a flood there in '33, I don't know if you'd call it a Garrison flood or a Stockman flood, it as closer to Stockman. . . . It 'as on the 'Toyac. That's the highest they claim it got since nineteen hunerd, back in nineteen hunerd it got that high. But I never did hear of no 'Garrison Flood'."

References Cited

Belden, Henry M. and Arthur Palmer Hudson, eds. 1952. *The Frank C. Brown Collection of North Carolina Folklore, Volume Two: Folk Ballads from North Carolina*. Durham: Duke University Press.

Child, Francis James. 1956 [1882–1898]. *The English and Scottish Popular Ballads*. 5 vols. New York: The Folklore Press.

Cohen, Norm. 1981. *Long Steel Rail: The Railroad in American Folksong*. Urbana: University of Illinois Press.

Dellinger, Mattie. 1978. "Box 744." The Shelby County *Champion*, March 16, 1978, A8.

Dundes, Alan and Carl R. Pagter. 1975. *Work Hard and You Shall Be Rewarded: Urban Folklore from the Paperwork Empire*. American Folklore Society, Memoir Series, vol. 62. Bloomington: Indiana University Press.

————. 1987. *When You're up to Your Ass in Alligators . . . : More Urban Folklore from the Paperwork Empire.* Detroit: Wayne State University Press.

Friedman, Albert B. 1956. *The Viking Book of Folk Ballads of the English-Speaking World.* New York: The Viking Press.

Green, Archie. 1972. *Only a Miner: Studies in Recorded Coal-Mining Songs.* Urbana: University of Illinois Press.

Gummere, Francis B. 1959 [1907]. *The Popular Ballad.* New York: Dover Publications.

Laws, G. Malcolm. 1957. *American Balladry from British Broadsides: A Guide for Students and Collectors of Traditional Song.* American Folklore Society, Bibliographical and Special Series, vol. 8. Philadelphia.

————. 1964. *Native American Balladry: A Descriptive Study and a Bibliographical Syllabus.* Rev. ed. American Folklore Society, Bibliographical and Special Series, vol. 1. Philadelphia.

Lomax, John Avery. 1947. *Adventures of a Ballad Hunter.* New York: The Macmillan Company.

Maxwell, Robert S. and Robert D. Baker. 1983. *Sawdust Empire: The Texas Lumber Industry, 1830–1940.* College Station: Texas A&M University Press.

McCoy, Patricia R. 1982. *Shelby County Sampler.* Lufkin, Texas: Lufkin Printing Company.

Minton, John. 1990. "'Phonograph Blues': Folksong and Media in the Southern United States Before the Second World War." Ph.D. dissertation, University of Texas.

Pass, Fred, ed. 1981. *The Texas Almanac and State Industrial Guide 1982–1983.* Dallas: A. H. Belo Corporation.

Reider, David and Stuart Davis. 1977. "Tenaha, Timpson, Bobo, and Blair." *Loblolly* 5/2:51–52.

Reed, S. G. 1941. *A History of Texas Railroads: And of Transportation Conditions under Mexico and Spain and the Republic and the State.* Houston: St. Clair Publishing Company.

U.S. Census. 1910. Washington, D.C.: U.S. Bureau of the Census.

Webb, Walter Prescott, ed. 1952. *The Handbook of Texas.* 2 vols. Austin: The Texas State Historical Association.

Wilgus, D. K . 1959. *American Folksong Scholarship Since 1898.* New Brunswick, New Jersey: Rutgers University Press.

————. 1964. "Folksong and Folksong Scholarship: Changing Approaches and Attitudes. IV. The Rationalistic Approach." In *A Good Tale and a Bonnie Tune,* edited by Mody C. Boatright, Wilson M. Hudson, and Allen Maxwell, 227–37. Publications of the Texas Folklore Society No. 32, Dallas: Southern Methodist University Press.

————. 1965. "An Introduction to the Study of Hillbilly Music." *Journal of American Folklore* 78:195–203.

————. 1968. "The Hillbilly Movement." In *Our Living Traditions: An Introduction to American Folklore,* edited by Tristram Potter Coffin, 263–71. New York: Basic Books.

————, and Eleanor R. Long. 1985. "The *Blues Ballad* and the Genesis of Style in Traditional Narrative Song." In *Narrative Folksong, New Directions: Essays in Appreciation of W. Edson Richmond,* edited by Carol L. Edwards and Kathleen E. B. Manley, 435–82. Boulder: Westview Press.

WPA Index to Probate Cases: Shelby County. Box 4G202, Archives and Manuscripts, Eugene C. Barker Texas History Center, University of Texas, Austin.

Doug DeNatale and Glenn Hinson

The Southern Textile Song Tradition Reconsidered

The development of the textile industry in the southeastern United States exacted more than its share of human costs. From a region of small, inter-dependent farms where people had long struggled "to raise their bread and meat," the southern Piedmont region became a land of tenant farms, cash crops, and cotton mills. Country people turned to "public work" in the mills hoping to earn a decent living, pay off debts, and perhaps return to farming. Instead, they encountered new hardships. In villages owned and closely supervised by the mill companies, they worked twelve-hour days in hot, dusty, and noisy mills, for wages as low as ten cents an hour near the turn of this century. Children as young as eight worked full-time to help support their families. More prosperous townspeople despised mill workers as "lint heads" and "factory tacks."

The story is well-known, but the achievements of Southern mill workers are less often acknowledged. If Southern mill workers managed to raise their families despite such conditions, it was in large measure a tribute to the strength and support of fellow workers, sustained by elements of traditional culture that they adapted to mill village life. Workers counted on the continu-ity of rural norms—for domestic aid in times of sickness, for borrowed goods to cover short pay.

Music was an important element of rural culture, and music occupied its own place in the social relations of the mill village. Song had power in addressing the conditions of mill life. Thanks to the efforts of a few dedicated collectors, a generous sample of the textile songs composed by Southern workers is available to us.[1] At the very least, these songs are invaluable historical documents, for they express a perspective distinct from the institu-tional sources of Southern labor history. They are eloquent statements from people too often considered inarticulate. Yet the nature of textile songs as historical evidence for the mind of the mill worker is problematic. Unless we have a firm sense of their social context, the messages they convey may seem ambiguous and even contradictory.

Our comments here provide something of the larger context in which textile songs were born and shared. The basis for this discussion is a selection of interviews from the Piedmont Social History Project, a long-term oral history project conducted by the Southern Oral History Program of the University of North Carolina. The major findings of this study have been published in *Like a Family: The Making of a Southern Cotton Mill World* (1987). This study involved over three hundred interviews with textile workers throughout the Carolina Piedmont. As participants in the project, together with fellow folklorists Della Coulter and Allen Tullos, we paid particular attention to the place of music in mill workers' lives. Our exploration of textile songs involved interviews with mill workers who composed songs about the mills, or their closest living relatives; mill workers who did not sing or play music; and mill workers who played and wrote music but did not compose songs about the mills. In the process, we gathered a few previously uncollected songs. More important, we gained a fuller appreciation for the strengths, and serious limitations, of song in addressing the inequities of mill life.

John Greenway's *American Folksongs of Protest* first treated the body of Southern textile songs as a coherent tradition. According to Greenway, only miners "have produced more songs of social and economic protest than the textile workers." In a chapter devoted to textile songs, and in a subsequent discussion of Ella May Wiggins—the tragic martyr and song maker of the 1929 Gastonia strike—Greenway took the majority of his examples from the southeast. In all, he attributed twenty-two songs to Southern textile workers, "richer in sincerity, quality, genuine folk content, and protest, than those emanating from any other industry" (1953:16,121–45,248–52; See App. A).

Greenway's emphasis on Southern textile songs as a vehicle for direct protest established the framework for subsequent interpretation. Over two-thirds of the songs in Greenway's collection emerged from particular strikes—in keeping with his belief that "the best songs, as always, are born of conflict." Attacking the tendency of scholars to reject protest songs from the folksong canon on the basis of their controversial, individualistic, or ephemeral nature, Greenway rightly argued for their consideration as individual expressions of a common sentiment. Though folksongs of protest might be "spontaneous outbursts of resentment" aimed at particular wrongs, they emerged from a groundswell of shared feeling. As Greenway depicted the dynamics of social protest among Southern mill workers, unionization drives brought "social enlightenment that might not appear for years without outside stimulation," and the ensuing, often violent, conflicts between mill owner and strikers "inevitably produced songs of protest" (129,7,3,127).

The example of Gastonia, with violent conflict directly proportional to the wealth of songs produced, supported Greenway's analysis of the forces giving rise to strike songs. Such songs were indeed an active collaboration between local songsters, traditional models, and new ideologies. As Archie Green suggests, the charge that strike songs were "imposed on cretinous workers by wiley organizers" is a partisan reduction of a more complex reality (1965a:55).

It is true that outside labor organizers had a crucial influence on the production of such songs. From available evidence, it appears that all of the workers who composed songs voicing direct protest against the mill companies participated in labor drives organized by the United Textile Workers or the National Textile Workers Union, or attended the labor education centers of the Highlander Folk School and the School for Southern Women Workers (see e.g., Adams 1975:72–80; Frederickson 1981:156–59; Horton 1939; Larkin 1929: 383–83; Tippett 1931:250–51). Claims of outside influence were most vehement in regard to the Gastonia strike.

Nonetheless, the impetus to use local song models came from workers themselves. Serge Denisoff notes, "The Loray strike appears to have been the first significant contact the urban-centered Communists had with folk material as a propaganda form" (1971:19-20). It is apparent from the accounts of the organizers of the Gastonia strike that the use of song was initiated by local female strikers, most notably Ella May Wiggins, and encouraged as an effective tool by the outside organizers (see, e.g., Beal 1937:159; Weisbord 1977:233, 260). As Greenway suggests, songsters such as Ella May Wiggins (or Ella May, as she identified herself) gave mill workers an effective voice for their discontent precisely because they expressed their newly acquired knowledge through locally familiar models for song:

> Come all of you good people, and listen while I tell;
> The story of Chief Aderholt, the man you all knew well.
> It was on one Friday evening, the seventh day of June,
> He went down to the union ground and met his fatal doom.
>   (Ella May, "Chief Aderholt.")

> It is for our little children,
> That seem to us so dear,
> But for us nor them, dear workers,
> The bosses do not care.
>   (Ella May, "The Mill Mother's Lament.")

> The bosses will starve you,
> They'll tell you more lies,
> Than there's crossties on the railroads,
> Or stars in the skies.
>   (Odell Corley, "Up in Old Loray.")[2]

By all accounts, such songs were enthusiastically accepted and used by fellow strikers, for they successfully restated traditional values under the polarized conditions of a strike.

One recent account of the Gastonia strike makes the counterclaim that Ella May was "in fact, anti-Communist; she was a patriotic, loyal and devout American" (Williams and Williams 1983:82). The irony becomes sharper when it is known that the source of this characterization was one of Ella May's children, embittered at being elevated as a symbol of labor while an infant, then abandoned to an orphanage. On the fiftieth anniversary of Ella May's murder, a car scrawled with anti-union sentiments was driven by her children.[3] The statement from a Gastonia resident unwittingly alludes to the difficult position of the Gastonia songsters, taking sustenance from an outside ideology, but casting it in their own vision of proper relations. A recent thesis by Lynn Haessly effectively traces the cultural context for Ella May's fragmented legacy (1987).

Greenway's argument for protest song was a much needed corrective, but his characterization of the Southern textile song tradition was nevertheless limited, if only by the sad yet justified reputation of Southern textiles for being among the least unionized of occupations. It subsumes too many songs under the category Archie Green has called "labor lore," to denote items associated with trade-union movements. Instead, Southern textile songs need to be considered under Green's more general heading of "industrial lore" (1972:9). The collected body of textile songs contains many composed by workers about the everyday life of mill work, with no connection to the labor movement.[4] These songs present a far more ambiguous range of content and style. Consider, for example, the curious mixture of grievance and humorous commentary in Lester Smallwood's "Cotton Mill Girl:"

> Combed my hair and it would not curl,
> Caught my fellow with another girl.
>
> And it's hard times in this old mill,
> Hard times everywhere.
>
> Stooped down one day to get a drink of water,
> Around come the boss and he docked me a quarter.
>
> When I marry, I'll marry a weaver,
> She won't work and I won't neither.

> The belt got hot and the pulley flew off,
> And knocked Joe Peterson's derby off.
>
> Chew my tobacco and spit my juice,
> I love my honey till it ain't no use.

Contrast this with the ironic cynicism of Wilmer Watts's "Cotton Mill Blues":

> Uptown people call us trash,
> Say we never have no cash,
> That is why the people fret,
> Call us the ignorant factory set.

Unlike the strike songs, none of these pieces carries a call to action or suggests a means for changing conditions. From this large sample, it is clear that Greenway's emphasis on the quality of direct protest in Southern textile songs does not accurately comprehend the tradition as a whole. A consideration of the meaning of textile songs must both embrace and properly relate the entire range of expression in mill workers' songs.

While we know most of the strike songs through period accounts and the collections of labor centers, many of the non-strike pieces remain because of commercial recordings recovered through the discographic research of Archie Green and others. Like Greenway, Green at first considered Southern textile songs primarily the result of labor drives until he and other researchers had traced the artists who recorded these songs (1961:5).

Among the recorded textile songs, a few must be considered completely irrelevant to the lives of Southern workers, for they were neither composed by mill workers nor accepted by them. Bob Miller's "Little Cotton Mill Girl" is one example. Miller was a Tin Pan Alley songwriter who specialized in composing tear-jerkers for the "hillbilly" market. His song is full of a maudlin sentimentality foreign to any of the songs composed by workers themselves:

> My heart is sad and lonely,
> I have no friends in the world,
> Nobody seems to love me,
> I'm only a cotton mill girl.

One of the strike songs quoted by Greenway, "The Marion Massacre," must also be rejected, together with its accompanying "North Carolina Textile Strike." These were composed and recorded by Frank Welling and John McGhee of West Virginia, a vaudeville entertainer and a lay preacher hoping to cash in on the notoriety of the strike with these event songs. Welling and McGhee's homiletic call for reconciliation sets them apart from the sentiments of the strikers:

> Why is it over money, these men from friends must part,
> Leaving home and loved ones with a bleeding, broken heart?
> But some day they'll meet them on that bright shore so fair,
> And live in peace forever, there'll be no sorrow there.

A second group of later recordings stands in more ambiguous relationship to mill workers themselves. Performers affiliated with organized labor
such as Pete Seeger, Hedy West, Joe Glazer, and later, Si Kahn, brought strike
songs to greater public attention and, in turn, composed new songs inspired
by the synthetic model of overt protest couched in traditional forms that
arose in Southern strikes. These performers and occasional composers have
served as an important conduit to a wider audience and should rightly be
considered as mediating figures between mill workers' own forms of community expression and the ideology of organized protest. As such, they stand in
curious relationship to mediating figures from the mill worker side, such as
Ella May, but fall outside the emphasis of this discussion.

A third group of commercial recordings from the 1930s and 1940s were,
in fact, sung or composed by mill workers. Lester Smallwood, who first
recorded his version of "Hard Times in the Mill," worked at the New Holland
Mills in Gainesville, Georgia. The Lee Brothers Trio (whose members worked
in the same mill) recorded another version two years later entitled "Cotton
Mill Blues." Dorsey Dixon, who recorded three original mill songs in the
1930s, spent most of his working days at the Little Hanna Pickett mill in East
Rockingham, North Carolina. David McCarn, who recorded his "Cotton Mill
Colic" shortly after the Gastonia strike, worked near that troubled place in a
Belmont, North Carolina, mill. Wilmer Watts, an independent mechanic in a
number of mills around Belmont, recorded his acerbic "Cotton Mill Blues"
about the same time. Daddy John Love, who composed and recorded his own
"Cotton Mill Blues" in 1936, worked in a mill in Concord, North Carolina.
Jimmie Tarlton, who recorded Dorsey Dixon's "Weaver's Life" in 1932,
worked in a number of mills during his rambles and met the Dixon brothers
while working at the Little Hanna Pickett mill. Lester Pete Bivins, who
recorded David McCarn's "Poor Man, Rich Man," was a life-long mill worker
from Shelby, North Carolina. Although these artists never participated in any
labor drives, and although their songs contrast strongly with the strike-
generated songs, their music was an equally valid expression of mill worker
sentiment.[5]

If these recorded songs are set apart from the strike songs by their failure
to suggest alternatives to the unequal relations of labor, they are joined to
each other through a common approach to the problems of mill life. Though
they may present grievances, these are generally couched in a joking manner.

The quality of humor may not be readily apparent to the outsider, who might overlook the conscious irony in lines such as: "Country folks they ought to be killed / For leaving their farms and going to the mill" and take the expressed sentiment more or less literally. These lines from the Lee Brother Trio's version of "Hard Times" can be compared to a couplet from Daddy John Love's "Cotton Mill Blues," in which the irony may be lost without knowledge of the tenant farmer's enforced dependency on the country merchant.

> I'm going to the country, going to quit the old cotton mill,
> I'm going to the country where they got no grocer bill.

Similarly, when David McCarn sang "I'm gonna starve, everybody will, / 'Cause you can't make a living at a cotton mill," his exclamation was not a straightforward complaint, but a complicated result of anger transposed through deflecting humor. It was precisely McCarn's skillful blending of the two sentiments that made his "Cotton Mill Colic" one of the most powerful of the mill songs:

> They run a few days, and then they stand,
> Just to keep down the working man.
> We can't make it, we never will,
> As long as we stay at a lousy mill.
> The poor are getting poorer, the rich are getting rich,
> If I don't starve, I'm a son of a gun.

The song title itself proclaimed McCarn's strategy, for among rural people in North Carolina "to colic" was to make a fuss without taking action. As McCarn himself explained to Archie Green and Ed Kahn: "Around the town a lot of people say they have the colic when they are griping about something, and they will say let's attack about, let's colic about it and go do something else." McCarn made it clear that his main intention was to portray serious matters in a humorous light. "Things were just about that bad. . . . Of course I exaggerated some. It's mostly to be a humorous song, of course, it couldn't be anything else."[6]

According to the testimony of the artists, their families, and friends, an emphasis on humor was paramount in the performance of these songs. Ollie Melton, who lived in the same house with Dorsey Dixon when he composed "Weave Room Blues," remembers that fellow workers in the village took up the song before it was recorded: "They would sing them as a joke, you know. It was funny to them. And [Dorsey] finally recorded that. . . . I know it was funny, and we used to all sing it. And it was true, where they told about how much the meat and stuff cost, and how much they made. It was a fact."[7] Laura Chumbler, whose brother Archer belonged to the Lee Brothers Trio, remembered the version of "Hard Times" sung at the New Holland Mills in the same light: "It was a funny song, you know. It would sound real, you know."[8] And Bill Bolick, who grew up in a mill village and later sang with his brother as the Blue Sky Boys, recalls performing McCarn's "Cotton Mill Colic" only as a novelty piece: "I didn't sing "Cotton Mill Colic" with the idea of protesting. I thought it was more of a comedy song."[9]

It is not difficult to account for this use of irony in the portrayal of working conditions, but it was also directed toward the mill workers themselves. The manner in which the poverty of the workers could be caricatured in these songs can strike the outsider as particularly odd. When David McCarn sang, he presented a familiar stereotype that the mill worker might well find offensive:

> . . . I've got a wife and fourteen kids,
> We all have to sleep on two bedsteads.
> Patches on my britches, holes in my hat,
> Ain't had a shave since my wife got fat . . .

McCarn explained to Archie Green and Ed Kahn that the depiction was intended as exaggeration for comic effect. Dorsey Dixon aimed for similar comedy in his "Spinning Room Blues":

> I'm a factory worker and I work in the mill,
> I have to keep at it cause I live on the hill,
> Ain't got no clothes, ain't got no shoes,
> I ain't got nothing but the spinning room blues.

If the comic sense is not apparent to the outsider from the text, it was conveyed more strongly in the Dixon Brothers' tone during performance.

The most common and apparent stereotype presented in these songs was particularly problematic for mill workers. Daddy John Love sang:

> Well I drink my booze and I shoot my dice,
> I [swear?] if the mill don't get better,
> I'm going to have to divorce my wife.

This image of the dissolute mill worker was not directly challenged in these songs, but defused through humor. According to David McCarn:

> Now some people run the mill man down,
> But the cotton mill people make the world go round.
> They take a little drink, they have a little fun,
> Whenever they can manage to rake up the mon.

And Dorsey Dixon achieved a masterful touch of mock pathos in the well-known stanza from "Weave Room Blues":

> The harness eyes are breaking with the double coming through,
> The Devil's in your alley and he's coming after you.
> How our hearts are breaking, let us take a little booze,
> For we're going crazy with them weave room blues.

In so doing, Dixon steered carefully between fundamentalist sacrilege and self-mockery. The drinking theme also arises in one of the verses that was omitted from the recorded version of "Spinning Room Blues" because of the three-minute recording time limit:

> A doffer comes along piecing up ends,
> Acting just like he's about out of wind,
> Then he starts moving like he's had a drink of booze
> But he's never had nothing but the spinning room blues.
>   (Green 1966a:14)

The acerbic humor of Wilmer Watts's "Cotton Mill Blues" maps an extended period of mill village life. The convoluted history of this piece, which Watts adapted from a turn-of-the-century poem by Greensboro mill worker George Dumas Stutts, is traced fully in a study by Archie Green (1993). The original poem, written at a period when the perception of mill workers as a new class in Piedmont society was becoming a contentious issue, is a proclamation of personal worth, redolent with the self-conscious flourishes of a literate sensibility:

> Now, while I have a leisure time,
> I'll try to write a factory rhyme.
> I live in Greensboro, a lively town,
> And work in a factory, by name the Crown.

In the original of the stanza from Watts's song cited above, the landscape of Piedmont social relations seen from the perspective of mill workers is burdened with the racial politics of its time:

> The darkies call us "white factory trash."
> And say we never have a bit of cash;
> But I'll have all colors ne'er forget
> We are the "monied factory set."

Stutts published his poem in a commonplace book of verse in 1900. His son, J. S. Stutts, republished the book in 1919. This second printing apparently brought the song to the attention of Watts, who reworked the song as a humorous piece within the self-ironic conventions of his own time (Green 1993; Stutts 1900 and 1919).

This tendency toward self-irony could only be fully appreciated by mill workers themselves. Fisher Hendley's 1938 recording of "Weave Room Blues" points to the underlying issues. A college-educated singer who began as a nightclub performer interpreting "Southern tunes" on his banjo, Hendley had a popular radio program on station WBT in Charlotte. Hendley was careful not to offend because a great portion of his audience lived among the area's mill villages. In the pirated version of Dixon's song that Hendley claimed as his own, he bowdlerized the relevant stanza to become the vapid, "How our hearts are aching, let's take a little snooze." According to a member of his band, Hendley's recording of the song was a conscious attempt to appeal to his mill worker audience.[10]

Yet Hendley's version abounds with the marks of his outsider status. For example, in the succeeding stanza, beginning "Slam outs, break outs, mat ups by the score," Hendley replaces the last two lines with a repetition of the "snooze" lines. This is clearly because he could not make out the technical term in the stanza's original third line—a problem that has plagued every single transcription made of the song. The line *should* read: "The battery's running empty, strings are hanging to your shoes"—"battery" in this case referring to the ferris-wheel-like apparatus introduced on the Northrop loom that carried a supply of full shuttles. Hendley also attempted a mill song of his own, "The Weaver's Blues," which reveals his distance from the mill experience:

> Tobacco juice and language rare,
> In mild confusion mingled there,
> Up and down and all about,
> Cursing and cutting matups out.
> A shuttle flew out with a clicking spat,
> And the weaver reached for his coat and hat,
> It's no wonder he lost his grit,
> He did just what you'd do, he quit,
> I've got The Weaver's Blues.

In contrast to Hendley's propitiatory treatment of "Weave Room Blues," Cecil Kinzer of Fries, Virginia pushed his own version in the other direction:

> The ends are coming down, and the double's coming through.
> The Devil's in the alley, and he's coming after you.
> I'm a-fighting for my life, but I think I'm gonna lose.
> Done gone crazy with the cotton mill blues.
>
> Come on now, boss, with a little more pay.
> You know we're down to three or four days.
> Our pockets are empty and we've got no booze.
> All gone crazy with the cotton mill blues.

In this regard it was no coincidence that Kinzer, a member of the Grayson County Ramblers, was a long-term employee in the Fries textile mill.[11]

The pressures that the record companies placed on rural artists to don the hillbilly mantle might account for some of the self-deprecating humor in the recorded songs. The mill worker is explicitly paired with this image in David McCarn's "Serves 'Em Fine":

> Now all you mountaineers just listen to me,
> Take off your hats and a-holler "whoopee!"
> For I'm going back home in the land of the sky,
> Where they all drink moonshine and never do die.

McCarn, it should be noted, was *not* from the mountains, as is often assumed, but was born and raised in the mill village of McAdenville, North Carolina.[12]

Yet it is insufficient to attribute the contrast between these songs and those composed in the labor movement to the effects of the recording industry. Certainly expressions of direct protest were anathema to commercial recordings. But a number of non-strike songs were also collected from oral tradition during the same period, and these share some of the same qualities of deflected anger and ironic humor. In the Southern version of the "Lowell Factory Girl" collected by John Lomax, for instance, the descriptive list of working conditions drawn from the original New England broadside is framed by two new stanzas that invoke the worker's own physical condition in a muted humorous mode:

> No more shall I work in the factory
> To greasy up my clothes,
> No more shall I work in the factory
> With splinters in my toes . . .
>
> No more shall I wear the old black dress
> Greasy all around;
> No more shall I wear the old black bonnet
> With holes all in the crown.

The several orally collected versions of "Hard Times in the Mill" share the same humor found in the recorded versions, and it was no doubt the sardonic quality of this whole family of songs that made it applicable to mill work:

> The section hand thinks he's a man,
> And he ain't got sense to pay off his hands.
>
> They steal his ring, they steal his knife,
> They steal everything but his big fat wife.[13]

The "Winnsboro Cotton Mill Blues," sung to William Wolff in 1939 at the School for Southern Women Workers, is one of the finest examples of anger redirected through humor:

> Old man Sargent, sitting at the desk,
> The damned old fool won't give us no rest.
> He'd take the nickels off a dead man's eyes
> To buy a Coca-Cola and an Eskimo Pie . . .
>
> When I die, don't bury me at all,
> Just hang me up on the spool room wall;
> Place a knotter in my hand,
> So I can spool in the Promised Land.
>
> When I die, don't bury me deep,
> Bury me down on Six Hundred Street;
> Place a bobbin in each hand
> So I can doff in the Promised Land.

These songs are closer in temperament to the recorded textile songs than to the strike songs.

In order to understand the role of humor in these songs, and to relate the commercial recordings to the strike songs, we must acknowledge the troubled and heterogeneous nature of mill village society. A portion of the mill population belonged to the ranks of middle management as overseers and foremen. As a result, the everyday social relations of the mill village were complex, burdened by competing pressures of familial ties and management demands. The foreman responsible for increasing production in the mill might have a dozen ties by blood and marriage to the reluctant workers in his charge. The worker trying to quietly organize a resistance might have a dozen wavering kin to question his or her activities.

We must also recognize that music was part of a large range of expression employed by Southern mill workers in their everyday lives. An informal code of behavior, developed over time, governed these common cultural practices. Within this code of indirection, covert expressions of personal antagonism were protected by fellow workers, while open protest was considered the pre-lude to a possibly violent conflict in which the mill worker had the weaker hand. Because of the nature of social relations in the mill village, different forms of expression were unequally appropriate for communicating hostility.[14]

For the most part, the structural inequalities of power had to be accepted as a given by mill workers where no outside intervention made sense. The mill companies' ownership of the villages was a weapon used with telling effect in the event of open protest. When the Dixon brothers' fellow workers at the Little Hanna Pickett mill threatened to strike, for instance, the mill owner moved quickly against the leader to quell his activities:

> That was the night after he told us all to fight, and it was getting cold weather, children didn't have no shoes, we didn't have no coal, didn't have nothing to eat. And he got up there that next night, it was short and sweet. He said, "Go back to work. That's what I'm going to do." But they moved his stuff out. He was in our village over there, and they moved his furniture out to a [wooden tent platform that belonged to the Holiness Church]. . . . I passed it one time, and I saw him sitting up there on his furniture.[15]

The tactic was common elsewhere, as a conscious dramatization of the unwritten contract that mill workers were forced to accept when they came to the mills.[16]

The mills had less immediate control over the daily expressive activities of the workers, but mill owners certainly could exert pressure when those forms of expression found their way into the commercial media. A dramatic example occurred during the Danville, Virginia, strike of 1930–31, which coincided with the release of David McCarn's "Cotton Mill Colic." Seeing the commercial possibilities of the song during the strike, Luther B. Clarke, a Danville record store owner who had previously arranged recording sessions for several mill worker musicians, promoted the record through his store and arranged to have it played on a local radio station. Strikers then took up the song as an appropriate expression of their grievances. Tom Tippett described a union meeting where "a small boy, not yet in his teens, sang a solo accompanying himself with a guitar swung from his shoulder. It was called 'Cotton Mill Colic' and accurately portrayed in a comic vein the economics of the textile industry, as well as the tragedy of cotton mill folk. . . . " (Tippett 1931:250). In response, H. R. Fitzgerald, the president of Dan River Mills, pressured the local media to suppress the song on the grounds that "it was degrading to cotton mill work." According to one Danville musician, "Harry Fitzgerald . . . asked Mr. Clark to quit selling the records or something. I don't know exactly what happened, but they quit playing it anyway, didn't broadcast it no more."[17] Parenthetically, it should be noted that Jim and Jesse McReynold's song, "Cotton Mill Man," though not a mill worker composition, later received similar treatment. According to Neil Rosenberg, the song "appeared to be developing as a hit in 1963, but it lost valuable exposure when radio stations in several Southern mill towns refused to air it because of its protest-type lyrics" (1985:313).

Within the mill village itself, the ties of kinship and the presence of middle management personnel placed further constraints on the direct expression of protest through song. Mill village string bands often included members of middle management. The members of the Lee Brothers Trio, for example, regularly played with a larger group called Jim King's Brown Mules, which included two foremen. The presence of such supervisory personnel would certainly discourage the voicing of protest through song. Nonetheless, the Brown Mules could, and often did, sing their version of "Hard Times" at gatherings within the mill village.

The conscious establishment of a humorous context for mill songs made their performance possible in everyday life and allowed the performers, within limits, to avoid retribution. This was particularly important for individual performers. As an expressive genre with formal boundaries, songs were easily attributed to their creators in the close world of the mill village. But the overt harmlessness of songs considered comic by fellow workers furnished some protection against management reprisals. According to Archie Green, Dorsey Dixon's "Weave Room Blues" drew a mixed response from his overseers, but no retribution: "One disliked it and one was proud that a poet like Dorsey worked in the plant." In the case of David McCarn, the reaction of the company was stronger, but at least deferred: "McCarn was never actually fired for composing or recording 'Colic,' but after his job ended 'The guys told him that he was barred from the Victory Mill in South Gastonia.'"[18]

Because this group of textile songs was necessarily framed as overtly benign, its ability to actually transform the conditions of mill life was inherently limited. The underlying discontent resonated in the reactions of the mill audience ("it would sound real, you know"), and this fellow feeling helped nourish the seeds of open rebellion. But under the mores of everyday mill life, a direct attack was most feasible when it involved a personal wrong. It was easier to enumerate the wrongs felt at the hands of an overseer than to specify the particular inequities of a company's policy. For this reason, the most pointed comments were reserved for individuals:

> Old man Jones taking up cards,
> Won't give you half that you take off.

> If you lack one yard being two cuts to roll,
> He won't give you one but to save your soul.
>   ("Cotton Mill Blues," Lee Brothers Trio)

> Old Pat Goble thinks he's a hon,
> He puts me in mind of a doodle in the sun.
>   ("Hard Times in the Mill," Lessie Crocker)

> Old man Sargent, sitting at the desk,
> The damned old fool won't give us no rest.
>   ("Winnsboro Cotton Mill Blues")

Similarly, the larger injuries of labor relations were placed on a personal horizon:

> They'll hunt around and find a little educated man.
> He'll stand around with a watch in his hand:
> See if you been doing all that you can do.
> Now I'm a-going crazy with the cotton mill blues.
>   ("Cotton Mill Blues," Cecil Kinzer)

> Saying wait a minute fellow, now tell me where you're going,
> Don't you hear the doggone spinning room a-roaring?
> Can't fool me cause I'm on the scout,
> Get back on the job you ain't a-gonna slip out.
>   ("Spinning Room Blues," Dorsey Dixon)

In either case, the deflating laughter of mill-worker kin helped keep overseers' reactions within the realm of personal antagonisms.

Decie Smith of Siler City, North Carolina, exemplifies the constraints upon songwriters and the degree to which they were able to affect social relations in the mill village. A life-long employee of the Hadley-Peoples Manufacturing Company, she began writing poetry and songs at the age of nine and became known in the village for her compositions. In 1957, her mill was sold to a new company, which instituted management practices common in the larger factories. The company erected a fence around the mill and prevented workers from leaving during breaks. In response, the workers invited labor organizers to help them form a union. After a short strike, the company signed a one-year union contract, but it also brought in efficiency experts, or "time-study men" to streamline the production process and "to show the union who was boss." A year later, the company refused to renew the contract, and the workers began a new strike. After six months, during which the company evicted striking workers and brought in outside labor, the workers finally capitulated.

Decie Smith did not join the strike, fearing the possible results. Her mother and sisters had been employees of the Loray Mill in Gastonia during that bloody strike and had told her of the violence they had witnessed. Her fears were not unjustified, as demonstrated by the mill president's actions when the union organizers tried to intercept arriving strikebreakers at the bus station: "Mr. Thomas took a tire tool, and he whopped up that fellow up beside of the head. . . . He said, 'If any of the rest of you customers want any of it, come and get it.'"[19]

Mrs. Smith's sentiments were largely with fellow workers, though she chose to comply with the new policies. She found the efficiency expert especially obnoxious. She chose to deal with this threat to her autonomy on a personal basis: "I said, 'If I was Popeye I'd throw him clear out of Siler City.'" Summoned to the head office to hear a report on her production, Mrs. Smith staged her own protest:

> They was all sitting there, two of the union men, Mr. Thomas [the mill president], and Charlie [the time-study man], and Mr. Meyers, the superintendent. Charlie said, "Back in June...." I'd hit the table, I'd say, "Gee dee June, this is September!" And Mr. Thomas said, "Decie, let Charlie read his report." I said, "Gee dee Charlie." ... He never did get to read his report—how much I'd made back in June.... So when I got up to come on out and go back upstairs to my work, ... them union men shook hands with me, they said, "I sure am glad you said that." ... Boy, I laid it on old Charlie. But you know, after that, every time that he'd see me, he'd cut his eye around and give me a smile.[20]

Upon the efficiency expert's departure, Decie Smith used her poetic talents to summarize her feelings in song:

> It is so easy to stand and watch,
> And say what can be done,
> Through eyes that are inexperienced,
> Our jobs may look like fun.
>
> When you put it down on paper,
> To you it seems quite plain,
> But try doing some of the jobs yourself,
> You'll find it's not the same.
>
> For each of us God has a book,
> We fill a page each day.
> Be it good or bad, it won't be erased,
> As we go along life's way.
>
> He will not tear any pages out
> Of any wrong we do.
> So do unto others as you would have
> Them do the same to you.
>
> And when your life is over,
> And God adds up your score,
> Don't let him say, "Dear Charlie,
> You should have paid Decie more."
>
> I hope when you've reached the Pearly Gates
> St. Peter he won't say,
> "For what you done at Hadley-Peoples
> You'll have to go the other way.

Mrs. Smith's response stayed within the acceptable boundaries of mill village conduct and it did have material results. Mrs. Smith effectively challenged the efficiency expert's assessment and the reduction of her piece rate. Through this mode of humor, she could even address the actions of the mill president himself:

> I made a poem about him. . . . And I was scared to show it to him, you know. I said, "When he goes through the mill, and his coat don't fit, you better watch out, he's gonna have a fit." . . . And my daughter was working in the summertime up there reeling, and they all got a kick out of it, you know, and she said, "Mr. Thomas," said, "Mama made up a poem about you," but said, "she's scared to show it to you, scared you'll fire her." He come walking down my alley, I thought, "Oh oh, what's the matter?" . . . He said, "How about that poem you wrote about it," said, "bring it over here," said, "I might even agree with you." And so I took it over there, you know, . . . and he said his mother said, "Mason, that's just like you." You know, I told all about what he done—he locked all the doors and throwed away the keys, wouldn't let them go out no more, and all such as that. But he really got a kick out of that poem, and I really laid it on him. But it was all true.[21]

Such expression, finally, could not challenge the basic structure of labor relations. On the occasion of her fiftieth anniversary at Hadley-People's in 1970, Mrs. Smith composed a long song that she sang at a dinner in her honor. The composition typified the underlying dilemma. The opening promised to tell all:

> They say you will feel better,
> If you lay it on the line,
> So when I finish up tonight,
> I should be feeling fine. . . .
>
> I'm writing a book about Hadley-Peoples,
> It should be on the best seller list,
> For I want you to know when I get through
> There's not a thing I've missed.

And it continued by addressing the inequities of labor relations in general terms:

> Some overseers were honest
> And their names are in my book,
> But some have been as crooked
> As a barrel of fish hooks. . . .
>
> If you tell them something's wrong,
> Their authority they like to show,
> Well I'll tell you one thing—I've forgot more
> Than some of them will ever know.

When she listed particular faults, Mrs. Smith carefully placed these in the context of community humor: "The ones I was calling didn't like what I was talking about, but the others just stamped their feet, you know, and hollered." She tempered her summary by injecting stanzas that deflected the thread of criticism, and she ended with a panegyric to the mill's owner:

> Charlie has a high-price car,
> Nivens has his plane,
> Decie is still walking,
> But she gets there just the same.

> Martha is in personnel and time keeper too,
> And my it is a shame,
> Every time a check is wrong,
> She always gets the blame.

> A lot of people would get to the top,
> If they could sit down and slide up I'd say,
> But the ones that don't want to work,
> They always want the highest pay. . . .

> There's been a lot of easy jobs made,
> The price they pay is swell,
> But seniority didn't get them,
> I still have to work like _____ .

> H-E-L-L-E-L-U-J-A-H
> My Fifty's here today,
> And I'm hoping it'll be easier,
> As I go the rest of the way.

> I don't have no pension plan,
> Don't get no sick-leave pay,
> But Junior will give me a job and a half,
> If I'd run it every day.

> But I'm glad I made it,
> I'm as happy as can be,
> I won't ever be wealthy,
> But that don't bother me.

> Mr. Dee, he is our Super,
> Most of the time he has a smile,
> But don't let that fool you,
> He is watching all the while.

> A new hand said since I'd worked fifty years,
> St. Peter should let me through.
> Well it hasn't been quite that bad,
> Although there's been rough crews.

Now people like to be remembered,
For ever since the world began,
Eve took the prettiest apple,
And gave it to her man.

So I thank you Mr. Baker,
For all the nice things that you do,
Now God may not have you a mill up above,
But at Hadley-Peoples you'll always be loved.

When asked why she had felt the need to soften her satire in this fashion, Mrs. Smith laughed and gave a familiar answer: "I reckon I was scared of my job. I was scared they'd fire me."[22]

The indirect humor grounded in immediate conflict that characterized the non-strike songs may have been one reason for their limited distribution among mill workers. Fewer than ten of the hundreds of mill workers interviewed during the Piedmont Social History project could recall encountering these songs, and their recognition was limited to "Weave Room Blues" and "Cotton Mill Colic." These two songs appear to have most effectively expressed the general sentiment, for a common response among other workers after hearing one or the other was: "If he was a cotton mill man, I can understand him writing something like that!"[23]

This sparse response does not invalidate the notion of a general textile song tradition, but suggests that the majority of such songs did not go beyond their home communities. We did come across several references, but not the words, to other songs identified with particular communities. In Danville, J. Richard Bigger recalled a song "somebody composed [called] 'The Doffer's Dream' I believe—he went to heaven you know, and, I don't know what all, I've forgot how it went, it was a long way on back." In Glencoe, Ethel Faucette remembered a song by a fellow worker that reviewed the various jobs in the mill: "He rhymed it up and he made a song, a great long song. Because he started where it went in the breakers at the lap room and went on up. But I can't remember who it was, been so long ago." Anne Montgomery had heard a song about the workers in Saxapahaw, North Carolina, and Eula Durham of Bynum, North Carolina, remembered hearing songs "about our crazy bunch, you know, and things like that."[24] According to Charles Wolfe, the widow of Lindale, Georgia, textile worker and noted fiddler Joe Lee recalled that her husband "wrote some sort of songs about working in cotton mills" (Wolfe 1977:5). From such evidence, it might be best to view the textile song tradition as a submerged body of common sentiment that could be realized in many individual offshoots.

Finally, the major musical contribution of mill workers was not the body of textile songs. Mill workers' direct influence in shaping an entire region's music was far more important. As Kinney Rorrer (1982) has discussed, the mill village served as a cradle for the development of new instrumental techniques and as a meeting place for disparate musical styles. In some cases, instructors provided by mill welfare programs introduced new stylistic influences such as classical banjo and new instruments like the mandolin. Such places became hotbeds for the rapid development of new string band styles, and mill villages, in turn, became attractive venues for medicine and tent shows. A number of rambling mill workers like Charlie Poole or Jimmie Tarlton spread these new styles to other mill villages. Mill workers approached ensemble music-making with a seriousness that was impossible in rural society. Homer "Pappy" Sherrill recalls:

> They'd have a fiddler's convention. And they'd have it down in a mill village and man, you'd have—you get a little more classy type of bands, because they were closer together to practice. You know what I mean? See, they lived closer together, and they could practice and they were better bands. If you had an old country band, they played once a month, and sat on the porch and played all night long. And have a catfish fry or something like that. Maybe a little corn liquor around once in a while somewhere. But they didn't practice as well much as they did in the mill village, where they was closer together.
>
> See? So that made the difference where that you had more players, and they're a little more shiny, polished up in the mill village, you know, cause they were closer together where they could practice."[25]

In this fashion, the new conditions of mill life had a dramatic impact on the shape and social context of Southern music in general.

Mill musicians themselves perceived music more often as a means for self-advancement than as a vehicle for mass protest. The development of the fiddlers' convention as a paying contest and the increased popularity of small travelling shows first suggested the possibility of an alternative source of cash to mill musicians. It is no coincidence that Henry Whitter and Fiddlin' John Carson, the very first Southeastern musicians to make commercial recordings, were textile workers. Other mill workers such as G. B. Grayson, Ernest Stoneman, Kelly Harrell, Charlie Poole, J. E. and Wade Mainer, and many others soon followed their example. The number of mill workers who became significant recording artists in the 1920s and 1930s is impressive (see App. B), and indicates the extent to which mill workers attempted to cash in on their musical abilities. The story told of Charlie Poole's departure from the Spray mill captures the sense of optimism many must have felt:

> They came early in the morning, before the looms started, to draw their last paychecks. Bringing their instruments into the mill with them, they sat down at the end of one of the rows of looms. As their fellow mill workers gathered around, they played Don't Let Your Deal Go Down. When they finished, Poole spoke up and said, 'Goodbye, boys, we're gone.'" (Rorrer 1982:30)

It is equally significant how few of these musicians chose to compose songs about the mills they were trying to leave.

Unfortunately, for some like Charlie Poole, Kelly Harrell, or Dorsey Dixon, the attempt to escape mill work through music ultimately proved unsuccessful. Yet a good number were able to sustain careers as professional musicians for extended periods with the growth of local radio programs. Musicians such as the Mainers, Lester Flatt, Earl Scruggs, and Whitey and Hogan began their life-long professional careers on the radio. The comparative advantages of radio work over mill work were obvious, as Roy "Whitey" Grant recalled: "At the Firestone Cotton Mill in Gastonia [formerly the Loray Mill] we had fifteen dollars a week for forty hours at the mill. When Mr. Crutchfield [of WBT] called us up and offered us twenty-five dollars a week, we could hardly speak to each other. We was rich!'" (Coulter 1985:10). In turn, the broadcasts of such musicians nurtured the dreams of many a textile musician at home.

The hope of commercial success also left its mark on textile songs. Many composers, like Dorsey Dixon, recorded their mill songs because the approval of workers in their home villages promised a potential audience among other mill workers. But many, again like Dixon, did not consider these songs the most important part of their repertoire. David McCarn wrote the two follow-up songs to "Cotton Mill Colic" specifically for his later recording sessions, because he assumed the first song to be the reason Ralph Peer called him back: "I knew it sold pretty good or he wouldn't have done it."[26]

The fact that several textile song composers called their pieces "blues" further indicated their professional aspirations. This was less a reference to the conditions of mill work than an advertisement that these songs imitated Jimmie Rodger's phenomenally popular blue yodels. Tommy Scott, whose family worked in the mills, had this connection firmly in mind when he composed his own "Cotton Mill Blues":

> Jimmie Rodgers had come along about this same time, and I'm thinking two ways now, I'm thinking about hard labor in the mill, and I'm also thinking about the show business, and I'm watching and listening to Jimmie Rodgers, and he had blues after blues after blues, and yodels. The yodelling thing looked like it was the thing coming in, which it did and it was the thing for quite some time.[27]

The textile song tradition as a whole, then, must be seen as a range of expressive forms that arose from changing social contexts. Mill worker composers were free to express direct protest only when a strike suspended the conditions of everyday life and radically altered the structure of industrial relations. Nonetheless, strike songs were organically connected to the non-strike pieces. Many of the strike songs display small touches of the familiar sardonic humor, particularly in Odell Corley's Gastonia songs, or in the hymn of the Merrimac Mill strikers in Huntsville, Alabama:

> Hallelujah, here we rest;
> Hallelujah, Mr. Dean;
> Uncle Sammy, give us a handout
> 'Cause we're tired of these beans.

Where the humor of strike songs was largely submerged in direct protest, the quality of protest in the non-strike songs was deflected by their humorous cast.

Ultimately, the hallmark of mill village culture in general became the strategy of deflection. More evanescent forms of expression such as jokes and pranks put this mode of indirection to best use in affecting the conditions of everyday mill life. Mill workers used pranks played on fellow workers, for example, to restrict output and actively oppose management interests.[28] Songs were less suited to such purposes, although Decie Smith remembers a striking example from the Siler City mill in which a fellow worker's overbearing behavior was challenged through song. A creeler in the mill relied too heavily on the fellow workers' custom of covering for each other during breaks. When she attempted to brush their antagonism aside with a joke, the ploy was subverted:

> She'd come back—and they had a song: "Have I stayed away too long?" And she'd come back a-singing. . . . She'd see they'd done creeled it, you know. . . . She'd come back a-singing:
>> Have I stayed away too long?
>> Have I stayed away too long?
> And Carl would say:
>> While you was off with your head a-reeling,
>> We was down here doing your creeling,
>> Yes, you've stayed away too long.[29]

Decie Smith's example illustrates that textile songs must be seen as but one part of a large expressive tradition that helped mill workers maintain continuity, address the conditions of their common life, and deflect the high human costs extracted from their labor.

University of South Carolina Center for Folklife and Oral History
University of North Carolina

Notes

1. In particular, John Edwards, Archie Green, John Greenway, Zilphia Horton, Margaret Larkin, Mike Seeger, and William Wolff should be mentioned.

2. See Wiley for a discussion of the models for the Gastonia songs.

3. Doug DeNatale and Cliff Kuhn witnessed this scene.

4. See Appendix A for a current checklist of Southern textile songs.

5. For further information on these artists, see articles listed in bibliography, and biographical summary of textile worker artists in Appendix B.

6. Interview with David McCarn, Stanley, North Carolina, August 19, 1961, by Archie Green and Ed Kahn (Southern Folklife Collection, Southern Historical Collection, University of North Carolina).

7. Interview with Ollie Melton, East Rockingham, North Carolina, December 19, 1979, by Doug DeNatale and Della Coulter.

8. Interview with Laura Chumbler, Gainesville, Georgia, August 19, 1981, by Glenn Hinson.

9. Interview with Bill Bolick, August 28, 1981, by Glenn Hinson.

10. Interview with Joseph D. Miller, Monroe, Georgia, August 18, 1981, by Glenn Hinson.

11. Interview with Lucille Kinzer, Fries, Virginia, August 15, 1981, by Glenn Hinson and Della Coulter. Archie Green collected Cecil Kinser's version of "Weave Room Blues," August 24, 1961; Hedy West published it in 1969.

12. See Green 1965b:223, for a discussion of some of the broad cultural currents that might have been at work here.

13. Collected from Lessie Crocker, Columbia, South Carolina.

14. These observations are drawn largely from the series of interviews conducted by the Southern Oral History Program and incorporated in a number of forthcoming studies. For a discussion of the quality of indirection in mill life and mill worker protest, see DeNatale (1985), especially chapters five, seven, and eight.

15. Interview with Ollie Melton, East Rockingham, North Carolina, December 19, 1979, by Doug DeNatale and Della Coulter.

16. For another example, see Tippett 1931, 202–203, for a description of the unionization attempt in Greensboro, North Carolina in 1930.

17. Interview with J. Richard Bigger, Danville, Virginia, August 13, 1981, Glenn Hinson and Della Coulter. For a discussion of Clarke's efforts on behalf of Danville musicians, see Rorrer 1982:39–40.

18. Green, notes, "Babies in the Mill"; interview with David McCarn, Stanley, North Carolina, August 18, 1963, by Archie Green and Ed Kahn (Southern Folklife Collection, Southern Historical Collection, University of North Carolina).

19. Interview with Decie Smith, Siler City, North Carolina, January 21, 1986, by Doug DeNatale.

20. Interview with Decie Smith (above).

21. Interview with Decie Smith (above). Unfortunately, Mrs. Smith was unable to recall any more of the poem, and we have not yet received a copy that she believes to be in her son's possession.

22. Interview with Decie Smith, January 21, 1986 and February 4, 1986.

23. Interview with Bill Ellis, June 23, 1981, by Doug DeNatale.

24. Interviews with J. Richard Bigger, August, 13, 1981, by Glenn Hinson; Anne Montgomery, July 23, 1983, and Eula Durham, March 1, 1979, by Doug DeNatale.

25. Interview with Homer "Pappy" Sherrill, October 26, 1985, by Glenn Hinson.

26. Interview with David McCarn, August 19, 1961, by Archie Green and Ed Kahn

(Southern Folklife Collection, Southern Historical Collection, University of North Carolina).

27. Interview with Tommy Scott, July 17, 1980, by Glenn Hinson.

28. For an extended discussion of the varieties of active opposition achieved by mill workers through overtly humorous expressive forms, see DeNatale 1990.

29. Interview with Decie Smith, February 4, 1986.

References Cited

Adams, Frank. 1975. *Unearthing Seeds of Fire: The Idea of Highlander.* Winston-Salem, North Carolina: John F. Blair.

Ahrens, Pat J. 1970. *A History of the Musical Careers of Dewitt "Snuffy" Jenkins, Banjoist, and Homer "Pappy" Sherrill, Fiddler.* Columbia, South Carolina: Author.

Beal, Fred. 1937. *Proletarian Journey.* New York: Hillman-Curl.

Blackard, Malcolm V. 1969. "Wilmer Watts and the Lonely Eagles." *JEMF Quarterly* 16:126–40.

Conte, Pat. "Beyond Black Smoke: The Dixon Brothers, Original Recordings," County 6000, notes.

Coulter, Della. 1985. "The Piedmont Tradition." In *Charlotte Country Music Story,* 7–11. Raleigh: North Carolina Office of Folklife Programs.

DeNatale, Doug. 1985. "Bynum: The Coming of Mill Village Life to a North Carolina County." Ph.D. diss., University of Pennsylvania.

———. 1986. "Dorsey Dixon." In *Dictionary of North Carolina Biography.* Vol. 2. Edited by William Powell, 74–75. Chapel Hill: University of North Carolina Press.

———. 1990. "The Dissembling Line: Industrial Pranks in a North Carolina Textile Mill." In *Arts in Earnest: North Carolina Folklife.* Edited by Daniel W. Patterson and Charles G. Zug III, 254–76. Durham: Duke University Press.

Denisoff, R. Serge. 1971. *Great Day Coming: Folk Music and the American Left.* Urbana: University of Illinois Press.

———. 1983. *Sing a Song of Social Significance.* Bowling Green, Ohio: Bowling Green State University Popular Press.

Fowke, Edith and Joe Glazer. 1960. *Songs of Work and Freedom.* Chicago: Roosevelt University, Labor Education Division.

Frederickson, Mary E. 1981. "A Place to Speak Our Minds: The Southern School For Women Workers." Ph.D. diss., University of North Carolina, Chapel Hill.

Glazer, Joe. 1988. *Textile Voices: Songs from the Mills.* New York: Rieve-Pollock Foundation.

Green, Archie. 1961. "Born on Picket Lines, Textile Workers' Songs Are Woven into History." *Textile Labor* 22/4:3–5.

———. 1964a. "Dorsey Dixon: A Place in the Sun for a Real Textile Troubador." *Textile Labor* 25/11:4–5.

———. 1964b. "Babies in the Mill: Nancy Dixon: Dorsey Dixon: Howard Dixon." Testament Records T–3301, notes.

———. 1965a. "American Labor Lore: Its Meanings and Uses." *Industrial Relations* 4: 51–68.

———. 1965b. "Hillbilly Music: Source and Symbol." *Journal of American Folklore* 78:204–28.

———. 1966a. "Tipple, Loom & Rail." Folkways FH 5273, notes.

———. 1966b. "Dorsey Dixon: Minstrel of the Mills." *Sing Out* 6 (July):10–12.

———. 1972. *Only a Miner: Studies in Recorded Coal-Mining Songs.* Urbana: University of Illinois Press.

——. 1993. "A Southern Cotton Mill Rhyme." In *Wobblies, Pile Butts, & Other Heroes: Laborlore Explorations*. Urbana: University of Illinois Press.

Greenway, John. 1953. *American Folksongs of Protest*. Philadelphia: University of Pennsylvania Press.

Haessly, Lynn. 1987. "'Mill Mother's Lament': Ella May, Working Women's Militancy, and the 1929 Gaston County Strikes." M.A. thesis, University of North Carolina, Chapel Hill.

Hall, Jacquelyn Dowd, James Leloudis, Robert Korstad, Mary Murphy, Lu Ann Jones, and Christopher B. Daly. 1987. *Like a Family: The Making of a Southern Cotton Mill World*. Chapel Hill: University of North Carolina Press.

Hendley, Fisher. n.d. *Fisher Hendley and His Rhythm Aristocrats*. (Promotional Songbook.) Charlotte, North Carolina: Author.

Hinson, Glenn. 1981. "Cotton Mill Songs in the Southeastern Piedmont: The Search for a Regional Tradition." Paper presented at Annual Meeting of the American Folklore Society, San Antonio, Texas.

Horton, Zilphia. 1939. *Labor Songs*. Atlanta: T.W.U.A. Southeastern Regional Office.

——. 1964. *Registers, Number 6: Zilphia Horton Folk Music Collection*. Nashville: Tennessee State Library and Archives.

Larkin, Margaret. 1929. "Ella May's Songs." *The Nation* 129(October 9):382–83.

——. 1929. "The Story of Ella May." *New Masses* 5:3–4.

Lomax, Alan, Woody Guthrie, and Pete Seeger. 1967. *Hard Hitting Songs for Hard-Hit People*. New York: Oak Publications.

Lomax, John A. 1915. "Some Types of American Folk Song." *Journal of American Folklore* 28:1–17.

Nelson, Donald Lee. 1973. "'Walk Right in Belmont:' The Wilmer Watts Story." *JEMF Quarterly* 9:91–96.

Paris, Mike. 1973. "The Dixons of South Carolina." *Old Time Music* 10:13–16.

——. 1969. "J. E. Mainer—The Crazy Mountaineer." *Opry* 2:22.

Rhodes, Don. 1979. "Lester Flatt: Talking With a Bluegrass Giant." *Pickin'* 6/1:24–30.

Rorrer, Kinney. 1968. *Charlie Poole and the North Carolina Ramblers*. Eden, North Carolina: Author.

——. 1971. "The Bunch of Nuts from Hickory." *Old Time Music* 2:19.

——. 1982. *Rambling Blues: The Life and Songs of Charlie Poole*. London: Old Time Music.

Rosenberg, Neil V. 1985. *Bluegrass: A History*. Urbana: University of Illinois Press.

Russell, Tony. 1971. "Kelly Harrell and the Virginia Ramblers." *Old Time Music* 2:10.

Stutts, G. D. 1900. *Picked Up Here and There*. Raleigh: Edwards & Broughton.

Stutts, J. C. 1919. *"Picked Up Here and There" and "Gleanings from the Gullies."* Haw River, Alamance County, North Carolina: Author.

Tamburro, Frances. 1974–1975. "A Tale of a Song: 'The Lowell Factory Girl,'" *Southern Exposure* 2:42–51.

Tippett, Tom. 1931. *When Southern Labor Stirs*. New York: Jonathan Cape & Harrison Smith.

Tribe, Ivan M. 1981. "John McGhee and Frank Welling: West Virginia's Most-Recorded Old-Time Artists," *JEMF Quarterly* 17:57–63.

Tullos, Allen. 1989. *Habits of Industry*. Chapel Hill: University of North Carolina Press.

Weisbord, Vera Buch. 1977. *A Radical Life*. Bloomington: Indiana University Press.

West, Hedy. 1969. *Hedy West Songbook*. Erlangen, Germany: Rolf Gekeler.

Whisnant, David E. "'Our Type of Song': A Second Look at the Blue Sky Boys," *Presenting the Blue Sky Boys*. *JEMF Quarterly* 104 (reissue of Capitol ST 2483), notes.

Wiley, Stephen A. 1982. "Songs of the Gastonia Textile Strike of 1929: Models of and for Southern Working-Class Women's Militancy," *North Carolina Folklore Journal* 30/2:87–98.

Williams, Robert L. and Elizabeth Wise Williams. 1983. *The Thirteenth Juror*. Kings Mountain, North Carolina: Herald House Publishers.

Wolfe, Charles. 1977. "Lester Smallwood and His Cotton Mill Song," *Old Time Music* 25:22–23.

APPENDIX A

A Checklist of Southern Textile Songs

Composer, where known, is given in parentheses; earliest known source is given in brackets. Written sources are cited only where they are the earliest known. Variants are listed indented below earliest known appearance of song. Textile songs cited by Greenway are marked (G).

All Around the Jailhouse (Ella May Wiggins) [Reported by Margaret Larkin.] (G)

Babies in the Mill (Dorsey Dixon) ["Babies in the Mill: Nancy Dixon : Dorsey Dixon : Howard Dixon." Testament Records T–3301.]

    Babies in the Mill [Hedy West, "Love, Hell, and Biscuits for Two Centuries." Bear Family 15003.]

Ballad of the Blue Bell Jail (Blanch Kinett, Greensboro, North Carolina, 1939) [Zilphia Horton Folk Music Collection, Tennessee State Library.] (G)

The Big Fat Boss and the Workers (Ella May Wiggins) [Reported by Margaret Larkin.] (G)

Chief Aderholt (Ella May Wiggins) [Reported by Margaret Larkin.] (G)

Come On You Scabs If You Want to Hear (Odell Corley) [Reported by Margaret Larkin.] (G)

Cotton Mill Blues (Wilmer Watts, adapted from a poem by George Dumas Stutts) [Paramount 3254, Recorded 10/29/29.]

    Cotton Mill Blues [Roy Harper, "I Like Mountain Music," Old Homestead Records OHS–80081.]

Cotton Mill Blues (Daddy John Love) [Bluebird B–6491, recorded 6/20/36.]

Cotton Mill Blues (Tommy Scott) [Glenn Hinson interview, composed 1938.]

Cotton Mill Colic (Dave McCarn) [Victor 40274, recorded 5/19/30.]

    Cotton Mill Colic [Blue Sky Boys, "Presenting the Blue Sky Boys," *JEMF Quarterly* 104 (reissue of Capitol ST 2483).]

    Cotton Mill Colic [Joe Sharp, Scottsboro, Tennessee, recorded by Alan Lomax, 1939. Archive of Folk Culture, 1629 B2, Library of Congress.]

Cotton Mill Girl (Earl McCoy and Jessie Brock) [Columbia 15499, recorded 1/31/30.]

Cotton Mill Man (Jim and Jesse McReynolds) [Epic 5–9676, 1964.]

Fiftieth Anniversary Poem (Decie Smith) [Doug DeNatale interview, composed 1970.]

For The Time Study Man (Decie Smith) [Doug DeNatale interview, composed 1957.]

Flying Squadron (Unknown) [Zilphia Horton Folk Song Collection, Tennessee State Library.]

Give Me That Textile Workers Union (Unknown) [Zilphia Horton Folk Song Collection, Tennessee State Library.]

Hard Times (Unknown)

    Cotton Mill Blues [Lee Brothers Trio, Brunswick 501, recorded 11/14/30.]

    Cotton Mill Girl [Lester Smallwood, Victor V–40181, recorded 10/18/28.]

    Cotton Mill Girls ["Hedy West." Vanguard VRS 9124.]

    Hard Times at Little New River [Mrs. Coker, Townley, Alabama] (G)

    Hard Times in the Mill [Lessie Crocker, Columbia, South Carolina, collected by William Wolff, 1939.] (G)

Hard Times in the Mill [Workers in the Columbia Duck Mill, Columbia, South Carolina, collected by Margaret Knight and Norris Tibbetts, TWUA, 1940s.]

Hard Times in this Old Mill [Dorsey Dixon, "Babies in the Mill: Nancy Dixon : Dorsey Dixon : Howard Dixon." Testament Records T–3301. Adaptation of song learned from sister, Nancy Dixon.]

Spinning Room Song [Nancy Dixon, "Babies in the Mill: Nancy Dixon : Dorsey Dixon : Howard Dixon." Testament Records T–3301, learned in Darlington, South Carolina, ca. 1898.]

Here We Rest (Unknown) [Workers in Merrimac Mill Village, Huntsville, Alabama, 1934.] (G)

ILD Song (Ella May Wiggins) (G)

Let Me Sleep In Your Tent Tonight Beal (Odell Corley) (G)

Let Them Wear Their Watches Fine (Unknown) [Collected from unknown singer, West Virginia, by Will Geer. This song is related to Wilmer Watts's "Cotton Mill Blues." See Green (1993), "A Southern Cotton Mill Rhyme."] (G)

Little Mill Worker (Unknown) [Zilphia Horton Folk Song Collection, Tennessee State Library.]

Lowell Factory Girl (Unknown)

 Factory Girl [Nancy Dixon, "Babies in the Mill: Nancy Dixon : Dorsey Dixon: Howard Dixon." Testament Records T–3301, learned in Darlington, South Carolina, ca. 1899.]

 The Factory Girl [Dorsey Dixon, "Babies in the Mill: Nancy Dixon : Dorsey Dixon : Howard Dixon." Testament Records T–3301. Adaptation of song learned from sister, Nancy Dixon.]

 Untitled [Unknown singer, Fort Worth, Texas, collected by John Lomax, 1913, from "wandering singer" who had learned the song in Florida.]

 No More Shall I Work in the Factory [Peoples' Songs Library. Greenway attributes to North Carolina, but probably reworked from John Lomax version. See Tamburro (1974–75:49).] (G)

 Pity Me All Day [Hedy West, "Getting Folk Out of the Country." Bear Family 12008.]

Marion Massacre (Welling and McGhee) [Paramount 3194, recorded 10/22/29.] (G)

The Marion Strike (Unknown) [Peoples' Songs Library.] (G)

The Mill Mother's Lament (Ella May Wiggins) [Margaret Larkin, "Ella May's Songs."] (G)

North Carolina Textile Strike (Welling and McGhee) [Paramount 3194, recorded 10/22/29.]

Old Days At Hadley-Peoples (Decie Smith) [Doug DeNatale interview, composed 1968.]

On A Summer Eve (Daisy McDonald) [Margaret Larkin Collection, Peoples' Songs Library. See Greenway 1953:138.] (G)

Poor Man, Rich Man (Dave McCarn) [Victor 23506, recorded 11/19/30.]

 Cotton Mill Blues [Lester Pete Bivins, Decca 5559, recorded 6/9/38.]

Reade Shirt Factory Blues (Cleda Helton and James Pyl) [Zilphia Horton Folk Song Collection, Tennessee State Library.] (G)

Roane County Strike at Harriman, Tenn. (Hershel Phillips) [Archive of Folk Culture, Library of Congress AFS 31761; also Mike Seeger, "Tipple, Loom & Rail," Folkways FH 5273.]

Serves 'Em Fine (Dave McCarn) [Victor 23577, recorded 5/19/31.]

Snoopy Is the Stretchout Man (Unknown) [Zilphia Horton Folk Song Collection, Tennessee State Library.]

Soliloquy to the Shirt Mill Workers on Strike (Unknown) [Zilphia Horton Folk Song Collection, Tennessee State Library.]

Some More About My First Years (Decie Smith) [Doug DeNatale interview, composed 1974.]

Song of the Danville Strikers and Their Children (Unknown) [Zilphia Horton Folk Song Collection, Tennessee State Library.]

The Speakers Didn't Mind (Daisy McDonald) [People's Songs Library, see Greenway, 1953:136.] (G)

Spinning Room Blues (Dorsey Dixon) [Montgomery Ward 7042, recorded 6/23/36.] See also "Tipple, Loom & Rail."

Stretch Out Blues (Unknown) [Zilphia Horton Folk Song Collection, Tennessee State Library.]

Ten Little Textile Workers (Unknown) [Zilphia Horton Folk Song Collection, Tennessee State Library.]

The Twenty Third Shirt Factory Psalm (Unknown) [Zilphia Horton Folk Song Collection, Tennessee State Library.]

Tribute To Mr. Gregson (Decie Smith) (Doug DeNatale interview, composed 1973.]

Two Little Strikers (Ella May Wiggins) [Wiley—source?]

Up in Old Loray (Odell Corley) [Peoples' Songs Library, see Greenway 1953:135.] (G)

We Are Building a Strong Union (Unknown) [Fowke and Glazer 1960:72.]

The Weaver's Blues (Fisher Hendley) [?]

Weaver's Life (Dorsey Dixon) [Bluebird B–7802, recorded 2/18/37.] (G)
> *The Weaver's Blues* [Recorded by Jimmie Tarlton, Victor 23700, 2/28/32.]

Weave Room Blues (Dorsey Dixon) [Bluebird B–6441, recorded 2/12/36.] (G)
> *Weave Room Blues* [Recorded by Fisher Hendley, Vocalion 04780, 11/3/38.]
> *Cotton Mill Blues* [Cecil Kinzer, collected by Archie Green, 1961.]

Winnsboro Cotton Mill Blues (Unknown) [Zilphia Horton Folk Song Collection, Tennessee State Library.] (G)

Appendix B

Early Southeastern Textile Recording Artists

This list is by no means exhaustive and represents only those artists identified as mill workers in secondary sources. Further documentary research would no doubt reveal that many other recording artists came from a mill-worker background.

ATLANTA AREA:

Fiddlin' John Carson: b. ca. 1868, Fannin Co., Georgia, alternated between mill work and painting.

Archer Chumbler: b. 1902, Clermont, Georgia, mandolin player with the Lee Brothers Trio, worked in the New Holland Mill, Gainesville, Georgia, also played in Jim King's Brown Mules, a group that included two mill foremen.

Howard Coker: fiddler with the Lee Brothers Trio, worked in the New Holland Mill, Gainesville, Georgia, also played in Jim King's Brown Mules, a group that included two mill foremen.

Ed Freeman: mandolin player for Scottdale String Band, recorded for OKeh and Paramount, band named after Scottdale mill village, near Atlanta.

Marvin Head: mandolin player for Scottdale String Band, recorded for OKeh and Paramount, band named after Scottdale mill village, near Atlanta.

Bill Helms: b. 1902, Thomaston, Georgia, leader of Upson Co. (Georgia) Band, recorded with Home Town Boys, loom fixer in Thomaston, Georgia, mill all his life.

Elias Meadows: member of Georgia Yellow Hammers, boss weaver at Echota Cotton Mill.

Bonnie and Eunice Pritchard: guitar players for Scottdale String Band, recorded for OKeh and Paramount, band named after Scottdale mill village, near Atlanta.

Lester Smallwood: b. 1900, Banks Co., Georgia, began work in Pacolet Mill, Gainesville, Georgia, at age fourteen.

Henry Thomas: tenor banjo player with the Lee Brothers Trio, worked in the New Holland Mill, Gainesville, Georgia, also played in Jim King's Brown Mules, a group that included two mill foremen.

SPRAY/DANVILLE/ROANOKE AREA:

Lonnie Austin: member of North Carolina Ramblers, worked in Spray.

J. Richard Bigger: fiddler with the Four Virginians, worked in Danville Knitting Mill, Danville, Virginia.

Glen Ease: fiddler with the Grayson County Boys, worked in the Washington Mill, Fries, Virginia.

Kelly Harrell: b. 1889, Drapers Valley, Virginia, worked in Fries, Virginia, leader of Virginia String Band.

R. D. Hundley: worked in Fieldale mill, member of Virginia String Band.

Leonard Jennings: banjo player with the Four Virginians, worked in various Danville, Virginia, area mills.

Cecil Kinzer: b. 1912, Pine Mountain, Virginia, guitarist with the Grayson County Boys, worked in the Washington Mill, Fries, Virginia.

Charley Laprade: b. 1888, Franklin Co., Virginia, family moved to Spray in 1900, later moved to Danville, leader of Blue Ridge Highballers.

Gil Nowlin: member of North Carolina Ramblers, worked in Spray.

Fletcher "Red" Patterson: b. ca. 1900, Leaksville, North Carolina, went between farm and mill work in Leaksville, moved to Fieldale in mid-1920s and played with fellow mill workers Kelly Harrell, Lee and Dick Nolen, leader of Piedmont Log Rollers.

Charlie Poole: b. 1892, Randolph Co., North Carolina, family worked in various mills throughout north central Carolina Piedmont, living in Spray by 1918, leader of North Carolina Ramblers.

Fred Richards: guitarist with the Four Virginians, worked in various Danville area mills.

Posey Rorer: b. 1891, Franklin Co., Virginia, worked in Spray, North Carolina, played with North Carolina Ramblers, Virginia String Band, The Carolina Buddies, and The Dixie Ramblers.

Jesse and Pyrhus Shelor: b. 1894 and 1888, Meadows of Dan, Virginia, fiddlers with Dad Blackard's Moonshiners (alternately identified as the Shelor Family), both worked as children in various mills in Danville/Spray area.

Odell Smith: member of North Carolina Ramblers, worked in Spray.

Walter "Kid" Smith: b. 1895, Carroll Co., Virginia., worked in Spray.

Alfred Steagall: worked in Fieldale, Virginia, mill, member of Virginia String Band.

Ernest V. "Pop" Stoneman: b. 1893, Monurat, Virginia., worked in mill with Henry Whitter.

Henry Whitter: b. 1892, Fries, Virginia., worked in Fries, learned "Wreck of the Southern Old 97" from a fellow millworker.

Norman Woodlief: member of North Carolina Ramblers, worked in Spray, member of The North Carolina Buddies and The Virginia Dandies.

CHARLOTTE AREA:

Lester Pete Bivins: b. near Shelby, North Carolina, life-long mill worker.

Claude Casey: b. 1912, Enoree, South Carolina, worked at Schoolfield Cotton Mills, Danville, Virginia, member of Briarhoppers.

Dorsey Dixon: b. 1897, Darlington, South Carolina, family moved to East Rockingham, North Carolina, member of Dixon Brothers, associate of Jimmie Tarlton, life-long mill worker.

Howard Dixon: b. 1903, Darlington, South Carolina, family moved to East Rockingham, North Carolina, member of Dixon Brothers, associate of Jimmie Tarlton, life-long mill worker.

Lester Flatt: b. 1914, Overton Co., Tennessee, worked in Sparta, Tennessee, silk mill and in Covington, Virginia, mill before joining Charlie Monroe's Kentucky Pardners and then Bill Monroe's Blue Grass Boys.

Gwen Foster: worked in Gastonia, Belmont, Dallas, North Carolina, mills, member of Carolina Tar Heels, Carolina Twins, recorded with David McCarn.

Charles Freshour: b. 1900, Newport, Tennessee, worked in Belmont, North Carolina, mill, guitarist with Wilmer Watts and the Lonely Eagles.

Roy "Whitey" Grant: b. 1916, Shelby, North Carolina, met his longtime partner Arval Hogan while the two were working at the Firestone Cotton Mill, Gastonia, North Carolina, in the late 1930s, originally identified as the Spindle City Boys, in honor of Gastonia's heavy concentration of cotton mills, recorded as Whitey and Hogan, and as part of the Briarhoppers.

Jay Hall: b. 1910, Waynesville, North Carolina, worked in various cotton mills prior to becoming a professional musician, recorded with the Hall Brothers, and later with Roy Hall and his Blue Ridge Entertainers.

Roy Hall: b. 1907, Waynesville, North Carolina, worked in various cotton mills prior to becoming a professional musician, recorded with the Hall Brothers, and later led the Blue Ridge Entertainers.

Arval Hogan: b. 1911, Robbinsville, North Carolina, met his longtime partner Roy "Whitey" Grant while the two were working at the Firestone Cotton Mill, Gastonia, North Carolina, in the late 1930s, originally identified as the Spindle City Boys, in honor of Gastonia's heavy concentration of cotton mills, recorded as Whitey and Hogan, and as part of the Briarhoppers.

Roy Lear: b. Pineville, North Carolina, worked in Cone Mills in mid-fifties to supplement music work, member of Tennessee Ramblers, Carolina Crackerjacks.

Howard Long: Gastonia, North Carolina, mill worker, recorded with David McCarn

Daddy John Love: worked in Concord, North Carolina, mill, member of Mainer's Mountaineers, Hilliard Brothers, Dixie Reelers.

J. E. Mainer: b. 1898, High Cove, Weaverville, North Carolina, worked in mills in Knoxville, Tennessee, Glendale, South Carolina, and Concord, North Carolina, leader of Mainer's Mountaineers.

Wade Mainer: b. 1907, Weaverville, North Carolina, worked in Glendale, South Carolina, and Concord, North Carolina, mills, member of Mainer's Mountaineers, leader of Wade Mainer and his Little Smilin' Rangers and Wade Mainer and the Sons of the Mountaineers.

David McCarn: b. 1905, McAdenville, North Carolina, worked in Belmont and Gastonia, North Carolina, recorded with Howard Long and Gwen Foster.

Julius Plato "Nish" McClured: b. 1897, Cleveland County, North Carolina, worked in Newton, North Carolina, mill, member of Hickory Nuts.

Claude "Zeke" Morris: b. 1916, Old Fort, North Carolina, after playing with the Mainers and the Smiling Rangers, left music to work at a Gastonia, North Carolina, cotton mill, low pay and long hours led him to return to music, leading to the formation of the Morris Brothers.

Palmer Rhyne: worked in Gastonia, North Carolina, mill, guitarist with Wilmer Watts and the Lonely Eagles.

Earl Scruggs: b. 1924, Flint Hill, North Carolina, worked in textile mill during World War II, member of Bill Monroe's Blue Grass Boys.

Arthur Smith: b. 1921, Kershaw, South Carolina, father was loom fixer in Spring Mills plant and the director of a mill brass band, worked in Spring Mills plant, leader of Arthur Smith and the Carolina Crackerjacks.

Jimmie Tarlton: b. 1892, Chesterfield Co., South Carolina, worked at Little Hanna Pickett mill, East Rockingham, North Carolina, 1930-32.

Wilmer Watts: b. ca. 1896, Mount Tabor, North Carolina, loom fixer in mills around Belmont and Gastonia, fiddler and leader of Lonely Eagles.

Brenda McCallum

The Gospel of Black Unionism

Introduction

Set within the historical context of the vitalization of black unionism in the New Deal era and against the background of racial and social stratification in Birmingham, Alabama, this essay examines expressive culture as an agent for social change. Many black workers in Birmingham during this period had rich associational lives as gospel singers, and their interconnected contexts for alliance—at the workplace, in company towns and industrial communities, in the union hall, and in the church—provided alternative arenas, modes, and levels of communication and expression. The discourse, narratives, and songs that emerged from these overlapping social networks served as analogous channels for black workers' response to the prospects for profound economic and social reform brought about by black unionism.

By drawing on and reinterpreting traditional religious speech and song, black miners and industrial workers in Birmingham helped give unionism "an extraordinary cultural and ideological vitality" (Grossberg 1986:54–55). This essay investigates the practice, among some Birmingham black workers and gospel singers, of transforming religious songs to union songs which commemorated and canonized labor leaders, sanctified labor organization, and praised the gospel of black unionism. Performed in a quasi-sacred style and empowered by the unifying ideologies of evangelical Protestantism and democratic unionism, these pro-labor songs provided an active mode in which black workers could articulate an emerging consciousness and a new collective identity.

Historical background

Established in 1871, because of its proximity to iron ore, coal, and limestone deposits, Birmingham became the New South's leading industrial city, with an economy based on mining and heavy industries such as iron and steel manufacture. By 1900, Birmingham's phenomenal growth made it a commercial-industrial center second only to Atlanta in the region, with some 3,398 manufacturing establishments, including hundreds of iron ore and coal mines, limestone and dolomite quarries, coke ovens, foundries, furnaces, mills, and factories (Taft 1981:95). In the 1910s, boosters' literature promoted Birmingham as "The Magic City" and "The Pittsburgh of the South" (Brownell 1972:48; Northrup 1943:27). Production continued to boom in the World War I decade, in the 1920s, and again during World War II, when the Birmingham District was the region's largest source of primary steel (White 1981:95).[1]

By 1890, rural black migrants had generally displaced eastern and southern European immigrants as the majority of the Birmingham District's industrial common laborers. By 1900, more than three-quarters of the iron and steel workers and half of the coal and iron ore miners in the state were black. From 1900 to 1910, Birmingham reported the largest increase in Negro population (215.6 percent) of any city in the United States. By 1920, blacks made up some 40 percent of Birmingham's population, the highest percentage of blacks to the total population of any major American city. Through the 1930s, black laborers dominated Alabama's workforce in coal and iron ore mining as well as in iron and steel production. Many of the black miners and industrial workers in the Birmingham District came from rural areas in south Alabama, or the adjacent states of Florida and Georgia. The migration of blacks from the rural Deep South—which had begun in the Reconstruction era, peaked in Alabama from the 1910s to 1930s, and continued through World War II—has been likened to a refugee movement, or an exodus. In addition to many conditions that pushed people out of sharecropping and tenant farming, urban life and industrial work had considerable appeal for southern blacks. Production boomed in the companies of the Birmingham District, and the industrial labor agents who recruited black workers promised superior housing, schools, and health care, and, most of all, a regular paycheck.

In 1926 the Birmingham Jubilee Singers—the first of scores of black all-male vocal ensembles called "jubilee and gospel quartets" to develop within the District's black industrial communities and to go on to record commercially and achieve widespread recognition outside of the area— released a 78-RPM recording entitled "Birmingham Boys."[2] The text of this song provides a cultural frame of reference for this critical era when blacks uprooted themselves from the country to secure wage work and the material prosperity promised by the city. The migration from an agrarian to an urban environment voiced in the song "Birmingham Boys" represented the early experiences of many local black workers, who viewed jobs in the District's mines and mills "as a means to another way of life" (Gutman 1968:97, 1977:173). Musically, "Birmingham Boys" typified the widely-imitated early Birmingham gospel quartet style, an egalitarian blend of four or more a cappella voices in close and complex harmony. Although approached in a light-hearted secular manner, much in the idiom of nineteenth-century minstrel and medicine show songs, a new urban male collective identity is the cause for jubilee:

> Birmingham boys are we,
> Jolly as can be.
> Rolly, jolly, Birmingham boys are we.
> You can tell without a doubt,
> When the Birmingham boys are out,
> Rolly, jolly, Birmingham boys are we.
> I was tired of living in the country,
> So I moved my wife to town,
> And there I bought a cottage,
> And then I settled down. . . .
> Birmingham, Birmingham, Birmingham Boys are we.
> If you could hear those Birmingham boys,
> How happy you would be (oh, you would be).[3]

While the city lured rural blacks and wage labor offered black men a point of entry into the industrial world, their subordinate status continued in the New South as in the old and their progress was severely restricted. Despite the optimism expressed in the song's lyrics, before the 1950s settling down in Birmingham for a black worker and his family seldom meant being able to buy a house. Nor was migration to the city, in the early years, a move toward unlimited occupational mobility and economic advancement. Birmingham's black workers were bound between the legacies of slavery, their memories of sharecropping, and the realities of black working class life in the city's mines and mills. Barriers of racial and social stratification continued to defend the American dream against any inroads made by southern black industrial workers.

By the 1880s, segregated company housing—built by the District's coal, iron, and steel companies for their workers—became the usual pattern of geographic development in the Birmingham District, and welfare capitalism became the dominant means of maintaining social and economic relations. Tennessee Coal, Iron and Railroad Company (TCI), the District's largest employer, alone once operated some twenty-two separate company towns, ranging in size from a few hundred to 3,500 families. By the early-twentieth century, many of the local companies had begun to provide a variety of social welfare programs, in addition to company housing and commissaries, for their employees. At one end of the spectrum, after it became a subsidiary of U.S. Steel Corporation in 1907, TCI "implemented one of the most elaborate systems of welfare capitalism of any industrial concern in the United States" (Rikard 1983:37). TCI established "model" company "villages" with well-built houses, schools, churches, social halls, transportation systems, bathhouses, clinics, parks, and ball fields. Following TCI's example in the District, some local companies, like Republic Steel and ACIPCO (American Cast Iron Pipe Company), also began in the 1910s to upgrade their workers' housing and sanitation facilities, to provide medical care, and to sponsor a wide range of welfare programs for employees and their families. Still others continued to supply little more than rudimentary company housing and a commissary (Fitch 1912).

The effect of such corporate paternalism on black workers and their families was not entirely beneficial, however. Life in the District's industrial company towns was incompatible with the tenets of self-determination and self-governance. The extensive authority and influence of the employer extended even to non-work life (Gutman 1977:172). In fact, those aspects of culture that Raymond Williams has termed " 'reserved' or 'resigned' areas of experience and practice and meaning"—like religion, recreation, and enter-tainment—were often appropriated and exploited by the employers as a means of social control (Williams 1977:126). Companies like TCI employed social workers and "colored community supervisors" to conduct dramatic, dance, art, music, athletic, and other recreational programs for their work force, and built churches for black residents in their company towns (Rikard 1983:263). Industrial employers, through such extensive social welfare activi-ties, attempted to thwart unionization and to tie their black work force to the company town and to company models of appropriate working-class behav-ior. While some Birmingham industrialists did provide relatively progressive social welfare programs, they also implemented "a system of political, social, and economic segregation" and strictly controlled and regulated their com-pany towns and their black work force (Jaynes 1986:314). Armed guards, company police and sheriffs, fences, and locked gates often accompanied the amenities of the company towns. A severe and manifold system of both customary and legally-codified restrictions and controls, which included vagrancy laws, poll taxes, violent anti-unionism, and vigilante terrorism by the Ku Klux Klan and other groups, firmly maintained the old order of social and racial relations (Harris 1977; Brownell 1975; Lewis 1987).

In the mines and mills, as in the company towns, Birmingham's in-dustrialists perpetuated the South's long-standing racial hierarchy by relying on the influx of black migrants as low-paid, untrained, mostly unskilled laborers. A surplus labor pool and paternalistic employment relations were created that intensified competition for employment, obviated the need for modern labor-saving machinery and improved work conditions, exacerbated racial divisions among workers, facilitated on-the-job discrimination, kept wages low, and suppressed unionization activities (Norrell 1986). Rigidly segregated, the local iron and steel industry strictly segmented labor into "white" and "black" jobs (Cayton and Mitchell 1939:331; Northrup 1943:38). Blacks were the "last hired and first fired," given only the less desirable, lower paying, menial jobs, where they worked as "helpers" under whites who often had less experience. In industrial tasks in the iron and steel industry, black workers were organized into labor gangs or "pit crews" reminiscent of slavery, where they did extremely hard manual work—breaking apart and loading pig iron, stoking the blast furnace, loading coke ovens, or pouring molten metal (Kulik 1981). The oral tradition of black workers contains many references to employers' practices of racism and discrimination, to white workers' protection of their control over the workplace, and to whites' lack of regard for black men's intelligence, or ability to do any but the most menial common labor. "Good, old, dumb common labor" was the term one retired white supervisor used to describe what he looked for when he hired a black man to work in his iron furnace.[4] Retired iron worker George Brown remarked, "I was hired from my shoulders and [the white worker] was hired from the tip of his toes to the top of his head."[5] Particularly in the Depression years, industrial employers also used the threat of unemployment— the warning of job hunters at the factory gates—to intensify workers' fear and insecurity and to mitigate complaint or protest. Frank Sykes, a retired ACIPCO pipe shop worker and gospel quartet singer, relates one version of this warning:

> Well now, if you worked there, you had to be pretty good because they didn't mind showing you that gate. . . . I've heard them tell fellows, "I see a whole lot of those barefooted niggers coming to that fence out there. If you want your job, you'd better straighten up."[6]

A racially based job hierarchy also existed in the District's iron ore and coal mines, but black and white miners worked together more closely and on a more egalitarian basis than in other Birmingham industries (Northrup 1943:38). Nevertheless, Birmingham operatives also manipulated black and white miners and exploited the prevailing segregationist sentiment in an attempt to curtail District blacks' persistent union activism.

Set apart from white workers, a special camaraderie often existed among black co-workers in the mines and industrial plants of the Birmingham

District. In part, this inward orientation was a constraining, defensive reaction to racism and inequalities on the job and to the intricate web of legal and customary power and authority that regulated blacks in Birmingham in the era of segregation. However, it was also an assertive action—a "positive desire for independent cultural expression" and a means of attaining collective strength and expressing allegiance to one another (Genovese 1976:235; Williams 1958:334–35). Black workers' expressive culture in Birmingham developed within and grew out of what Archie Green has described as a "traditionalizing circle" and was demonstrated through a complex of oral narratives about associational life—camaraderie on the job, solidarity in the union, and fellowship in the church (Green 1978:76). Black workers' expressive culture in the Birmingham District was also propagated through songs of work and songs of worship.

Birmingham's black workers and jubilee gospel quartets

Birmingham served, in the first half of the twentieth century, as a center for the development and diffusion of jubilee gospel quartet music, both a style and form that evolved from indigenous traditions within the District's black industrial communities. During the early years, only Norfolk and the Virginia Tidewater region became a similar cultural hearth for black quartet singing.[7] The formative period of the jubilee gospel quartet tradition in Birmingham coincided with the period of greatest industrialization and unionization and the largest migration of rural blacks to the District. From the 1910s through the 1930s each black industrial community in Birmingham seemed to have one or more quartets associated with it. New groups formed with ever-changing personnel; as new quartets were established, they drew singers from veterans of earlier groups as well as recruits from churches in the District's company towns and industrial neighborhoods. Birmingham's black gospel tradition is significant for the number of quartet groups organized by or composed of coworkers from a particular mine site, industrial plant, company town, or union hall.[8]

Company towns and corporate welfare programs, especially company-built churches and schools and company-sponsored social affairs, also affected the evolution of the black gospel quartet tradition in the Birmingham District. While literally hundreds of area quartet groups developed and performed autonomously within black communities, local companies often appropriated indigenous musical traditions for their own purposes. The L&N (Louisville and Nashville) Railroad, for example, sponsored the Old Reliable Choral group, one of the city's most popular (Atkins 1981:139). ACIPCO sponsored segregated bands and vocal groups to entertain employees at holiday picnics and baseball games and on founder's day. The segregated "welfare societies" of the Alabama Fuel and Iron Company and the DeBardeleben Coal Company organized many social affairs featuring programs by the company string band, "Negro Song Leaders," and other musical groups ([Debardeleben] 1937:10; Lewis 1987:70). As well as sponsoring instrumental groups like bands, TCI and ACIPCO also sponsored company quartets and male choruses. Made up entirely of employees and often taught and directed by trained musical instructors hired by the company, these segregated musical groups performed for entertainment at special company holiday events and served as advertising and public relations vehicles for the industrial employers.

TCI's social welfare programs for its workers included musical instruction and the encouragement and sponsorship of performing groups. King Chandler, Jr., bass singer with the Shelby County Big Four, earlier with the Missionary Four and the Five Silver Kings quartets, says that he first received musical training in pitches, scales, arrangement of notes, and the "minor, major, and off chords" at the age of fifteen at the TCI company school in the Muscoda mining camp where his father was employed as an iron ore miner.[9] He organized his first group, the TCI Youth Quartet, at the company-sponsored school. Charles Bridges from Pratt City also recalls training an early quartet group from the TCI mining district, but its personnel and activities are unknown. The Docena Four and the Dolomite Jubilee Singers, who sang together briefly in the early 1920s, may also have been organized by TCI miners in these company towns. Three a cappella black musical ensembles (the TCI Sacred Singers, TCI Women's Four, and TCI Section Crew) recorded for Paramount in 1927 in Chicago, and probably included employees from TCI's Birmingham enterprises, possibly under the company's sponsorship.[10]

In the New Deal era as well, other gospel quartet groups began their musical activities because of their associations at the industrial workplace. In 1936 a group of singers from the Southern Coal and Coke Company mining camp in Boothton, just southeast of Birmingham, organized the Shelby County Big Four. Jobie Thomas, of the Bessemer Big Four and the Shelby County Big Four quartets, and George Bestor and Cleveland Smith, of the Bessemer Big Four and the Sterling Jubilee/CIO Singers, worked together at U.S. Pipe and Foundry Company in Bessemer. Freeman Farris, of the Blue Eagles Quartet and the Four Eagle Gospel Singers, and Henry Holston, of the Sterling Jubilee/CIO Singers, describe the "bathhouse singing" at the workplace that led to their membership in gospel quartets:

Farris: The Blue Eagles was already singing when I got with them. One of the fellows heard me singing in the bathhouse on the job [at U.S. Steel's Fairfield, Alabama Sheet Mill] one day and had me to meet them, and that's how I got with them.[11]

Holston: They'd just hum on the job [at the U.S. Pipe Shop in Bessemer, Alabama] and when they'd get to the washhouse a bunch of them would be in there and maybe a guy would hit a tune over here and you'd join in with him and like that, you know, and it'd sound pretty good and, well, sometimes they'd form a group right there.[12]

Alfred Rutledge, Jr., a member of the Delta-Aires gospel quartet, who for many years worked as an iron ore miner at TCI's Muscoda mining camp, also recalls the power of song in the workplace, and how he, too, first learned to harmonize in the quartet style. For a brief period Rutledge worked at the U.S. Steel plant with Tom Lacey, of the Sterling Jubilee/CIO Singers, and Rufus Beavers, of the Dunham Jubilee Singers:

We used to be sitting down there [in the rail fastening department at the steel plant], I would be working with them, and we'd just go to singing. That was really an inspiration. Looks like work would just pass by much faster if you sang. Time would just move fast, see, and you know the shift is almost over, when you . . . just sing and go on like that. We used to do it for many days. Somebody would be always wanting to hit a song. You know, we'd be sitting around and when you love singing—and me, I was just a boy considered to them—and they would go to singing, and I'd find me a tune too, and we'd just go to singing.[13]

The Birmingham black gospel quartets, while they often took the name of their employer because of their associations at the workplace, and some-times performed at semi-official functions such as company social events, were usually recruited and paid on a temporary basis, if they received any monetary compensation at all. They were rarely accorded any special status by their employers during the regular work day, although quartet singers have always been highly regarded within the black community. As Heilbut states, they functioned as "an institution of black working-class life akin . . . to athletic teams or fraternal lodges" (1982:105). The close relationship of the gospel quartets to the District's mines and mills was well-founded: a group of men who worked together decided to form their own group and often selected its name from their primary associations together. Sharing in hard daily work, often members of the same union local and the same church, frequently living in the same community, these men interacted regularly on a number of levels. Together these factors formed a strong group identity, a bond that grew out of shared life experiences, and their music expressed deeply felt emotions about their common condition.

The early period of the development of jubilee gospel quartet music coincided with a major transfiguration of southern black culture—migration from the country to the city in search of industrial wage work. The quartet songs expressed religious faith and other-worldly emphasis in "a society filled with inequities and in the midst of a profound economic and social transformation" (Gutman 1968:89, 1977:164).[14] Through their music, Birmingham's quartet singers kept alive a continuity with the religious traditions of the rural South; their music provided spiritual solace in a time of social stress. Although the gospel quartet songs commented only implicitly on secular life in the city and in the workplace and rarely overtly protested or criticized it, the mines and the mills of the Birmingham District were invisible yet ever-present backdrops. In addition, the jubilee quartet groups (also called "families," "fellowships," and "clubs") provided an important social network for the singers, an adjunct to the community, the church, the workplace, and the union, yet autonomous and self-controlled. The quartets, like black fraternal organizations, provided a surrogate setting for black men to vote, hold office, administer funds, wield power, and gain status and prestige, options withheld by white society in the segregated South (Levine 1979:268). In many cases, the quartet group was, simultaneously, an extended social and familial network, a brotherhood or fraternal organization, a beneficial society and mutual aid association, and a convocation for spiritual fellowship.

As an "adaptive strategy," Szwed has discussed Afro-American religious song as a group phenomenon paralleling the organizational structure of church and community and functioning to symbolize and reinforce social behavior (1969:113).[15] The classic pre-World War II period of jubilee gospel quartet music that developed in Birmingham generated a stylistically distinctive school of singing—an egalitarian style of broad, extended chords of deep four-part harmony. Rather than spotlighting the individualistic lead singer, emphasis was placed on the evenness and equality of all voices collectively striving for a cohesive, blended sound. Tom Lacey, a retired steelworker who sang with area quartet groups for more than fifty years, described the aesthetic of equal participation in jubilee gospel music: "When you're keyed up right, nobody's off chord. You're all working right in a solid chord just like one big voice . . . ."[16] Harmony—as both a spiritual and a musical concept—was the credo of the quartets. Freeman Farris, bass singer with the Four Eagle Gospel Singers, comments:

> Peace and harmonizing kind of holds you together. If you're harmonizing, why, it sounds like one. When you make close music, you can't tell who's singing what voice. You can get so close 'til you don't know who's singing lead, or who's singing bass, or who's singing baritone, and that helps keep you together.[17]

Jubilee gospel song, as a collective artistic expression, functioned, in part, to articulate a major social value of the group—that of social equality and spiritual concord. The Sterling Jubilee Singers' tenor, Henry Holston, also describes this sense of companionship: "Our fellowship is so close, that sometimes when the group doesn't get together for a few weeks we get lonesome for each other."[18] L. T. Smoot, of the Four Eagle Gospel Singers, agrees that to be a successful quartet, its members must have a special relationship: "Harmony and love amongst the group, that's the main object. If you get that to work, then you can hold on, with God to help."[19]

Black Unionism in the Birmingham District

Membership in an overlapping circle of association was shared by many of the jubilee gospel quartet singers in the Birmingham District, especially after the advent of federal sanctions for labor organization and the massive union reorganization campaigns that occurred during the 1930s.[20] The Great Depression had forced most industrial employers in the Birmingham District to drastically reduce or abandon the welfare capitalism programs begun in the 1900s and had begun to break down the longstanding paternalistic system of control and regulation of the black work force (Brody 1980:103–104,134). The upsurge of New Deal era unionization provided an analogous context for black gospel singers' collective response to social change. While the gospel quartet groups were essentially spiritual, normative, and conservative in their orientation, the labor unions were materialistic, oppositional, and radical. The gospel of unionism served as a legally and culturally sanctioned basis for social action and reform and provided relatively safe and noncombative strategies and modes of protest that were particularly effective in the Jim Crow South. It was within the image of a Christian and democratic mission of unionism that the seemingly dichotomous values of spiritual fellowship and hope for material gain could be merged. Southern black workers' narratives and songs began to address social problems as well as spiritual problems; they were used to praise the gospel of unionism, with an implicit message of social protest. Pro-labor gospel songs thus served, concurrently, functions that were both oppositional and conservative .

A sense of the dual function, as both belief and strategy, of the ideologies of Christianity, egalitarianism, unionism, and social reform is especially critical in a study of the expressive culture of Birmingham black workers in the New Deal era (Gutman 1968:58, 1977:131). Many Birmingham blacks carried over the ideas and values of evangelical Christianity in their belief that labor organizations like the United Mine Workers (UMW) were "a secular church" (Gutman 1977:131). Using religious metaphors common to older black workers in the Birmingham District, Jobie Thomas, member of the Bessemer Big Four and Shelby County Big Four gospel quartets and former coal miner and steelworker, places equality for black and white workers within the biblical context. Thomas draws on both Old Testament and antebellum history to sanctify black unionism as a means for the collective deliverance and emancipation of the black wage slave:

> All the rest of the time [before unionization] we were the little horses that was following the white horse across the pastures, across the hills. We was grazing on what was left, and that would be a penny. . . . We sing a song that a way, "Tell Old Man Pharoah To Let My People Go." We had been bound down and didn't have a chance and that [the union] opened up the way.[21]

Particularly after passage of Section 7a of the National Industrial Recovery Act (NIRA) in 1933, which UMW-CIO leader John L. Lewis called "the emancipation proclamation" of the union movement, collective bargaining and the "religion of brotherhood" seemed to offer hope for a new order of social, and racial, relations (Sitkoff 1978:175; Gutman 1968:76, 1977:150). Organizing drives were often promoted as a holy cause (Cowley 1980: 212). Southern black workers drew traditional and ritually powerful elements from the Bible and religious song and, perceiving the union as a "collective democratic institution," saw a means for "equality and brotherhood among men on earth" (Williams 1958:346; Gutman 1977:90). Legendary narratives of southern blacks beatified both black union activists and certain white labor leaders. Among others, Cleveland Perry, of the Capstone mining camp in the Birmingham District, sang praises to John L. Lewis, who was well-supported by black miners (Lewis 1987:176–77):

> John L. Lewis is our leader,
> He's a mighty man.
> He made the NRA contract,
> Union people going to let it stand.[22]

The gospel of unionism and social reform also spread to the area's black iron and steel workers because of the national leadership of the Steel Workers Organizing Committee (SWOC), an early CIO affiliate that entered the District in 1936. UMW vice-president Philip Murray headed the SWOC and personally "brought to the union movement a concern for civil rights rooted in the religious teachings of his faith" (Sitkoff 1978:181). Murray's widely-publicized activities on behalf of racial equality endeared him to southern black industrial workers, and his powerful progressive image provided an effective medium through which the gospel of industrial unionism could be spread to black workers in the Jim Crow South. Borrowing from biblical texts and the language of the black Christian church, the discourse and narratives of black workers in Birmingham contain "a common and deeply felt set of images, analogies, and metaphors" to express their belief in the role of unionism in social reform (Gutman 1977:164). Herman Taylor, a retired steelworker who continues to be active in union committee work, speaks of the emancipatory function of organized labor, and its sacred importance to black workers in the Birmingham District:

> The greatest thing that happened to me, it was the union. That's true. Because if it hadn't been for the union, I'd have been gone a long time ago. And that is—ought to be—the salvation of any man, the union.[23]

Black labor songs in the Birmingham District

The coal mines of the Birmingham District have been known since the United Mine Workers' campaigns of the 1890s for both biracialism and for the pro-union songsters among their workers. Labor songs from the area that date from the late-nineteenth and early-twentieth centuries have been documented in the *Birmingham Labor Advocate, United Mineworkers Journal,* and other labor publications of the time.[24] Under the sponsorship of the UMW, George Korson toured the bituminous coal regions of the United States, including Alabama and other southern states (Tierney 1973:4; Gillespie 1980:75). In 1940 he recorded Uncle George Jones, "the Negro bard and folk minstrel" of the Trafford coal camp just northeast of Birmingham, who laid his life "on the altar of the union" in 1894 and who "throughout his career . . . sang church hymns and Negro spirituals. He sang in church choirs, down in the mines, and on the picket line." The UMW commissioned many of his ballads, like "This What The Union Done," which honors President Franklin D. Roosevelt and white labor leaders as it chronicles the passage of the NIRA:

> In nineteen hundred an' thirty-three
> When Mr. Roosevelt took his seat
> He said to President John L. Lewis,
> "In union we must be.
> Come, let us work together,
> Ask God to lead the plan,
> By this time another year
> We'll have the union back again."
>
> Chorus:
> Hooray! Hooray!
> For the union we must stan'
> It's the only organization

Protect the living man.
Boys, it makes the women happy,
Our children clap their hands,
To see the beefsteak an' the good po'k chops,
Steamin' in those fryin' pans.

When the President and John L. Lewis
Had signed their decree
They called for Mitch an' Raney—
Dalrymple make the three:
"Go down in Alabama,
Organize ev'ry living man,
Spread the news all over the lan':
We got the union back again!"[25]

George Korson recorded Charles Langford and the Marvel Quartet from Alabama singing "Union Boys Are We" in Columbus, Ohio in 1940, at the "golden-anniversary convention" of the UMW (Korson 1943:46). "Union Boys Are We" was an unmistakable reworking of the 1926 song, "Birmingham Boys," which conveyed the aspirations of black migrants during the period of early settlement in the Birmingham District. The text of this musical transformation more than a decade later reflected the developing consciousness of black industrial workers as they rejected their subordinate role and redefined their collective identity as independent workers and union members, joined in struggle against the company and its agents:

Union boys are we, happy as can be,
Rolly rolly, jolly, jolly,
Union boys are we.
Progressives in de valley go bow-wow-wow,
Scabs in de pen go wee-wee-wee,
An' snitchers in de barn go hee-haw-hee,
Popsicles on de fence go cock-cockle-do-do-do . . .
Union boys, union boys, are we,
If you could live a union life,
How happy you would be.[26]

Other little known Birmingham gospel quartet singers also demonstrated their union affiliations and propagated their political beliefs through the medium of labor-oriented, semi-religious song. In 1940, for example, at the SWOC's Second International Wage and Policy Convention, held in Chicago, a black "quartette" from Bessemer accompanied southern region directors William Mitch and Noel Beddow and performed before the assembled delegates (Foner and Lewis 1983:109). Anderson Underwood, Bessemer iron ore

Courtesy Samford University

Courtesy W. S. Hoole Special Collections Library, University of Alabama

miner and bass singer with the Volunteer Four quartet, recalls the singers' role as proselytizers for the unionization movement in the region:

> We belonged to [the International Union of] Mine, Mill and Smelter workers. "Mine, Mill," that's what we were . . . Lawyer Lipscomb—his name was Jim Lipscomb—he'd get up in a truck somewhere out there and about five or six hundred folks [would be] there and he'd be just like a preacher up there, talking about the working conditions. And folks went to joining the union just like everything . . . we'd sing at the union meetings, we'd just be singing for the union. There'd just be a crowd of folks there, and we'd just sing and have a big time . . . I was singing in a quartet then, the Volunteer Four. . . . And we'd sing and the folks would be out there by the hundreds. . . . We kept that club [quartet] for twenty-three years. All of us was working in the mine.[27]

In 1941, Library of Congress collectors recorded the Bessemer Big Four Quartet, organized from a 1920s youth quartet, the West Highland Jubilee Singers. The Bessemers is one of two known local groups that sang in advocacy of the CIO. Jobie Thomas, the only living member of the group, describes the early organization of the Bessemer Big Four out of family and occupational associations:

> 'Way back there in '28 or '29 we started right out here [in the Pleasant Grove community just west of Birmingham] as just little bitty boys singing. . . . Four of us first cousins that was reared in the same house by my auntie. Some of us was in the mines then. We started in the mines on Thanksgiving Day 1928. I was thirteen years old. . . . About dark we'd gather back by an oak tree—it's still sitting in the yard there—and sing half the night. There wasn't nothing else to do. We'd practice . . . that's the way we started off.[28]

The group was later reorganized by George Bestor and renamed the Bessemer Big Four Quartet. The group affiliated with the SWOC and the CIO during their early organizing drives in the Birmingham District in the late 1930s and early 1940s. One of the two extant recordings of the group espouses its union affiliation. This disc became a theme song on local radio broadcasts for the CIO. "Good Evening Everybody" features lead Jesse Thompson, first announcing the group and its employer, the U.S. Pipe Shop in Bessemer. Then Thompson introduces each group member and his voice part in a variant of the "come-all-ye" greeting of earlier labor ballads. The song confirms and celebrates new membership in the CIO:

> Spoken introduction:
> Good evening, ladies and gentlemen. We are the Big Four Singers of Bessemer, Alabama, employed by the big Pipe Shop, U.S. Coming to you, doing a number about "Good Evening Everybody."

Refrain:
Good evening everybody, how are you? (Lord, how are you?)
Now is there anything that we can do for you? (Do for you?)
I said, we want you to know we belong to the CIO.
Great God, good evening everybody, how are you?
(Lord, how are you?)[29]

In 1940 George Korson also recorded Cleveland Perry, who had earlier been "drafted by his company to sing spirituals at company union brotherhood meetings." His UMW song, "Got My Name on De Record," attests to the kind of solemn rite that signing one's name was for southern blacks, and its opening line echoes the Bessemer Big Four's CIO song:

Good evenin', ev'ry body,
Do you belong to dis union?
I'm a thoroughbred union [man]
Yes, Lord, I done went to dat office
An' I sho' done signed,
Got my name on de record
An' sho' have jined. . . .
Oh, we thank Walter Jones,
Oh, we thank Mr. Mitch,
Dey have put us on de main line.
Yes, Lord, den we went to dat office
An' we sho' done signed,
Got our name on de record,
An' we sho' have jined. . . . [30]

In 1929 local quartet master Charles Bridges first organized and trained the Sterling Jubilee Singers of Bessemer. The group included several employees of the U.S. Pipe Shop in Bessemer, in addition to workers from TCI and the L & N Railroad. In the 1940s Perry L. "Tiger" Thompson, ex-prize fighter and local WJLD radio disc jockey, who worked at the Pullman-Standard Plant in Bessemer, managed the group. Thompson was an early black CIO organizer, vice-president of USWA Local 1476 for twenty-three years, and vice-president of the Bessemer CIO Council. The group appears to have been renamed the CIO Singers by Thompson when they began appearing weekly under that name on his CIO-sponsored Sunday morning radio program, singing during break time after he talked about union affairs. During this period the group also sang for other CIO functions at banquets, meetings, and conventions in Gadsden, Montgomery, and elsewhere.[31] Thompson promoted the group until the early 1950s and issued a recording by them on a local private label in 1952. Two topical gospel-union ballads, "The Spirit of Phil Murray" and "Satisfied," composed by lead Roscoe MacDonald as memorials to the late union leader, were recorded at WJLD radio studios and released as Tiger 100 at a USWA-CIO convention in Montgomery, Alabama in 1952.[32] Henry Holston, a former member of the CIO Singers, reflects on the strong sacred foundation of these songs:

> Roscoe MacDonald made that in the form of a spiritual song . . . to where we could sing it for the CIO because he [Murray] was a great labor leader and he did so much for the CIO, for the working people, that we made it up in a song for him.[33]

"The Spirit of Phil Murray" eulogizes the labor leader and lends an "aura of sacredness, thus further legitimizing the authority" of his leadership and "the sanctity of his cause" (Denisoff 1972:56–57):

> Chorus:
> Let the spirit of Phil Murray live (on and on)
> Just let his spirit (live right on)
> Let the spirit of Phil Murray live (on and on)
> God has called Mr. Murray home.
>
> (Verse 1)
> Well, in nineteen-hundred and forty-two
> Labor leaders didn't know exactly what to do.
> Mr. Murray smiled, "said I'll be your friend,
> I'll fight for the rights of the working men."
>
> (Verse 3)
> Well, in nineteen-hundred and fifty-two
> God called Mr. Murray, say, "Your work is through.
> Your labor on earth have been so hard,
> Come up high and get your reward."
>
> (Verse 5)
> The Congress Industrial Organization assembled.
> The whole world began to tremble.
> Men, women, and children cried,
> When they heard the sad news Mr. Murray had died.
>
> (Verse 6)
> He was the CIO's loss, but he's Heaven's gain.
> In the Day of Resurrection we'll see him again.
> Good God Almighty our best friend is gone.
> I want you boys to help me, just sing this song.[34]

"Satisfied," on the record's reverse side, makes an extended statement on the origins of unionism in biblical scripture and on salvation through union solidarity:

Chorus:
Satisfied, satisfied with Jesus
Satisfied, my soul's been satisfied.
God said he would be my compass,
God said he would be my guide.

(Verses 2–4)
Well you read in the Bible,
You read it well.
Listen to the story,
That I'm bound to tell.
Christ's last Passover,
He had his Communion.
He told his disciples,
Stay in union.
Together you stand,
Divided you fall.
Stay in union,
I'll save you all.
Ever since that wonderful day my soul's been satisfied.[35]

Black industrial workers in the Birmingham District expressed the importance of the unions through the medium of gospel music. Like some earlier British and American labor songs, these gospel pieces held a strong ideological commitment grounded in Christian theology. Birmingham singers proclaimed unionism as a holy cause. Empowered by evangelical principles and performed in a quasi-religious style, these area labor songs were couched in terms of biblical scripture, transferring the roles of union leaders like John L. Lewis, Philip Murray, and others to those of Old Testament redeemers. While the labor movement's ultimate aims were secular, its ideologies—affirmation of the dignity of working people and their right to economic freedom, advocacy for black and white workers as the children of God together in a collective struggle, and commitment to social justice—assumed sacred meaning to Birmingham's black workers, and to those singers who celebrated it in song. Culturally, such songs are complex phenomena, developed within an historically evolving social matrix of associations of work and worship, as expressions of praise and protest.

These songs united black workers' belief in the Bible as "the ultimate authority for social change" and God as "the primary agent of liberation" with their perception of NIRA Section 7a as a civil sanction for political and economic reform and unionism as a correlative strategy for emancipation (Wiggins 1987:89–90). As a medium of expressive culture, gospel music in Birmingham functioned to negotiate a balance between continuity with the past, the discontinuities of the present, and prospects for the future. Structurally and musically, these pro-labor gospel songs were rooted in the traditions of southern black sacred music, while the texts articulated black workers' new collective identity and heightened response to the industrializing secular world. They provide us with aesthetic and ideological documents of the emergence of southern black workers' new political consciousness and the resurgence of unionism as a powerful social movement, offering potential solutions to both economic and social inequities.

The advance of democracy for southern blacks—emancipation first by the Union Army, then by the United Mine Workers and other labor unions—was frequently proclaimed in late nineteenth-century songs and in the press as a "jubilee" (Foner 1975:95–96, 165–66, 178, *et passim*). Black Birmingham jubilee gospel quartet singers continued the theme of union emancipation. Within this tradition their music coalesced with the "jubilee" celebrations of antebellum work-related festivals and with the "jubilee spirituals" of Emancipation Day (Foner 1975:88, 146; Wiggins 1987:86–92). The coming of unionization in the New Deal era to the Birmingham District's black industrial workers was sanctified in their songs, expressing anticipation of a new day of material prosperity, social dignity, and spiritual fulfillment, the promise of freedom and enfranchisement prophesied in Leviticus 27:24:

> In the day of atonement shall ye make the trumpet sound throughout all your land. And ye shall hallow the fiftieth year, and proclaim liberty throughout all the land unto the inhabitants thereof: it shall be a jubilee unto you; and ye shall return every man unto his possessions, and ye shall return every man unto his family. . . . For it is the jubilee; it shall be holy unto you: ye shall eat the increase thereof out of the field.

Bowling Green State University
Bowling Green, Ohio

Editor's Note. Brenda McCallum died on August 25, 1992, in Bowling Green, Ohio. In our last telephone talks, we looked ahead to this publication. Brenda had wanted to send "thank-you" copies to friends in the Birmingham District, veteran miners and steelworkers who had shared songs and stories with her. Sadly, she did not read her article in its closing form. Thus, Maria Hetherton and I have collaborated in its final editing.

MaCallum's study appeared originally in *New York Folklore* (Winter-Spring, 1988) titled "Songs of Work and Songs of Worship: Sanctifying Black Unionism in the Southern City of Steel." We reprint it, in altered form, with the kind permission of the *NYF* editors. Brenda had selected the shortened title ("The Gospel of Black Unionism") to reflect changes within her article from 1988 to 1992, as well as to note her move from the University of Alabama to Bowling Green State University.

During 1985, National Public Radio broadcast "Working Lives," a thirteen-part series on black workers' culture in the Bir-mingham District. McCallum's documentary stands out among the most sophisticated presentations in the field of occupational folklife. Brenda did not shrink from asking how she might best "repay" the folk from whom she drew strength. Before her death, she had projected a CD recording on Alabama work songs. When released, it will mark the connection of her ethnographic endeavor to the expressive treasures in mine and mill, juke-joint and tabernacle.

Notes

Primary data for this paper are drawn from over 300 hours of tape-recorded interviews conducted in 1980 to 1984 in Jefferson County, Alabama, with more than 150 black first- and second-generation iron ore and coal miners and iron and steel workers, as well as union activists, ministers, gospel singers, and others. The author would like to acknowledge partial support for this field research from the National Endowment for the Arts, Folk Arts Program, to tape record interviews and musical performances in preparation of the LP phonograph record and accompanying booklet, "Birmingham Boys": Jubilee Gospel Quartets from Jefferson County, Alabama (1982), and the documentary radio series, "In The Spirit" (1986); and from the National Endowment for the Humanities, Humanities Projects in Media, to tape record interviews for production of the thirteen-part documentary radio series "Working Lives" (1985). I particularly wish to thank my colleague on the "Working Lives" project, Cliff Kuhn, and Archie Green and Mia Boynton, who read early versions of this essay. Unless otherwise noted, all unpublished interview quotations have been excerpted from the original field recordings which are on deposit at the Archive of American Minority Cultures, William Stanley Hoole Special Collections Library, The University of Alabama, Tuscaloosa, Alabama.

1. The term "Birmingham District" has been used since the nineteenth century to include Jefferson, Walker, Bibb, and portions of Tuscaloosa and Shelby counties, the location of Alabama's richest coal and iron ore deposits and most extensive mining operations, as well as the highest concentration of iron and steel manufacturing in the state. In this study, the "District" includes the metropolitan city of Birmingham, the neighboring industrial towns of Bessemer, Ensley, and others, several separately-incorporated industrial satellites, like Fairfield, and many smaller outlying communities that originated as company towns, like Westfield, Pratt City, Dolomite, Docena, and Muscoda.

2. "Birmingham Boys" and other recordings by area jubilee gospel quartets have been reissued on *Birmingham Quartet Anthology* (Clanka Lanka, CL–144, 001002), *All Of My Appointed Time* (New World, NW224), *Brighten the Corner Where You Are* (John Edwards Memorial Foundation, JEMF 108), and *Jubilee to Gospel* (Library of Congress, Folk Music in America, Vol. 8, LBC–8). Recordings made by the author of contemporary area gospel quartets can be heard on *"Birmingham Boys": Jubilee Gospel Quartets from Jefferson County, Alabama* (Alabama Traditions, 101).

3. This transcription of "Birmingham Boys" is taken from Doug Seroff's jacket notes for *Birmingham Quartet Anthology*. Attributed to the Birmingham Jubilee Singers' lead singer and one of the area's best-known quartet trainers, Charles Bridges, this was the quartet's theme or introduction song and was also performed in Birmingham by many other quartet groups. Its popularity became widespread outside the area after the release of the 1926 recording (Columbia, 14547–D), and other gospel quartets, both

locally and outside the area, frequently substituted their name or their location in variants of the song. The opening greeting of "Birmingham Boys" is textually similar to the first lines of traditional Anglo-American miners' songs with late nineteenth-century popular music hall origins, such as "Down In A Coal Mine" ("I am a jovial collier lad, as blithe as blithe can be") and "Six Jolly Miners" ("six jolly wee miners, and miners' lads are we"). See Korson (1938:277–78), Lloyd (1978 [1952]:36–37, 126–27, 347), and Green (1972:48, 447).

4. J. B. Oliver, interview with author, Birmingham, Alabama, 11 May 1983.

5. George Brown, interview with author, Birmingham, Alabama, 11 May 1983.

6. Frank Sykes, interview with Cliff Kuhn, Birmingham, Alabama, 3 August 1984. See also Norrell (1986:676) and Charles Stephenson's discussion of the threat of unemployment in "'There's Plenty Waitin' at the Gates': Mobility, Opportunity, and the American Worker" (Stephenson and Asher 1986:72–91).

7. Doug Seroff estimates that from 1890 to 1960, "approximately 10,000 sides" of black gospel quartet songs were recorded in the United States, and by 1946 strong quartet traditions had developed in "New York, Philadelphia, Baltimore, all through the Carolinas, Florida, Texas, and California" (*Program in Black American Culture*, 1981:9, 14–16). Birmingham's distinctive quartet style dominated in the Deep South, Southeast, and Midwest, while Virginia's dominated on the East Coast.

8. In the jacket notes to *Birmingham Quartet Anthology*, Doug Seroff has exhaustively surveyed the histories and personnel of many early Birmingham jubilee gospel quartet groups. The author also traces the work histories and workplace connections of many of the District's quartet groups in the booklet that accompanied the LP phonograph record *"Birmingham Boys": Jubilee Gospel Quartets from Jefferson County, Alabama.*

9. King Chandler, Jr., interview with author, Bessemer, Alabama, 19 October 1981.

10. Norm Cohen, in *Long Steel Rail*, discusses these TCI groups and the 1927 Paramount recordings, which may have been re-creations arranged by black musicologist Willis Laurence James (1981: 646–47). The author also relies on information from telephone conversations with Joe Wilson, 26 January 1981, and Richard K. Spottswood, 2 July 1981. For discographic details, see Godrich and Dixon (1969:175, 680).

11. Freeman Farris, interview with Brenda McCallum and Doug Seroff, Birmingham, Alabama, 11 October 1980. The Four Eagle Gospel Singers were first named the Blue Eagle Singers in part after the official emblem of the National Recovery Administration (NRA), the federal agency created in 1933 to establish and enforce codes of fair competition and labor in trade and industry. In addition to the quartet's symbolic association with the bird that carried the United States out of the Great Depression, the name probably made reference to a highly popular Birmingham gospel group that recorded commercially, the Famous Blue Jay Singers.

12. Henry Holston, interview with Brenda McCallum and Mike Williams, Bessemer, Alabama, 16 August 1981.

13. Alfred Rutledge, Jr., interview with author, Bessemer, Alabama, 2 February 1983.

14. The jubilee gospel quartets' sacred repertoire included adaptations of spirituals ("Steal Away To Jesus," "Ezekial Saw The Wheel," "The Old Ship of Zion"), jubilees ("When They Ring Them Golden Bells," " 'Low Down Chariot," "Roll, Jordan, Roll"), hymns ("Shine On Me," "Just As I Am," "Come to Jesus"), religious ballads ("Brother Jonah," "Blind Barnabus," "Noah"), and composed gospel songs ("We'll Understand It Better By and By," "[Just A] Little Talk With Jesus," "When Folks Around You Prosper").

15. Following Szwed's analysis, gospel quartets exhibit a particular adaptational strategy because of the community of black Christians' group-sacred-conservative

orientation (1969:113). This particular strategy has been opposed to but has co-existed in the same time and place with those of other members of the community, such as blues singers with an individual-secular reactionary orientation (see also Keil 1966). Levine also discusses the cultural complexity of the historical development of these musical forms (1979 [1977]:223). On the concept of the musical, religious, and cultural community of black gospel quartet singers, see also the booklet notes by Kip Lornell accompanying the LP phonograph record, *"Happy in the Service of the Lord"* *Memphis Gospel Quartet Heritage—The 1980's* (High Water, 1002) and Lornell's book of the same title (1988).

16. Tom Lacey, interview with author, Bessemer, Alabama 13 March 1981.

17. Freeman Farris, interview with Brenda McCallum and Doug Seroff, Birmingham, Alabama, 11 October 1980.

18. Henry Holston, interview with author, Bessemer, Alabama, 13 March 1981.

19. L. T. Smoot, interview with author, Birmingham, Alabama, 7 December, 1980.

20. I do not mean to attribute either cultural or political homogeneity to black industrial workers in the Birmingham District. As Raymond Williams states, "a common culture is not, at any level, an equal culture" (1958:336). Nor do I mean to imply historical constancy. Certainly not all black workers were performers, or even audiences of black gospel quartet music, nor did black unionism, particularly in the early years, win their unanimous support. Rather, both sacred gospel quartet and sacralized pro-union songs were key aspects of a larger "conditional expressive repertoire" that derived from parallel associational networks within a complex social field, and from which a variety of individual responses were articulated to meet the demands of changing conditions (Límon 1983:40). See also Williams (1958:343), Bauman (1972:38), Shils (1981:26–27), and Conrad (1988:179–201).

21. Jobie Thomas, videotape-recorded interview with Judy Stone for University [of Alabama] Television Services, Bessemer, Alabama, October 1981.

22. Korson 1943: 309.

23. Herman Taylor, interview with Cliff Kuhn, Birmingham, Alabama, 17 July 1981.

24. See, for example, Foner (1975:212–13), and Foner and Lewis (1980:174–75).

25. Korson's 1940 recording of Uncle George Jones singing "Dis [This] What The Union Done" was included in *Coal Dust on the Fiddle* (1943:301, 445–46) and was also issued in 1965 on *Songs and Ballads* of *the Bituminous Miners* (Library of Congress, AFS–L60). This transcription of the song's lyrics is taken from the album notes (pp. 10–12). In June 1933, after the passage of Section 7a of the NIRA, William A. Mitch, who had been an officer of the Indiana district of the United Mine Workers since 1915, was sent to the Birmingham District by John L. Lewis to begin reorganizing miners in the state. An appeal to miners to join the union and help reorganize UMW's District 20 (Alabama) was published in the Birmingham *Labor Associate* on June 10, 1933, and was signed by William Mitch and William Dalrymple. Another labor official, Sherman H. Dalrymple, was president of the United Rubber Workers of America (URW) and was also active in the mid-1930s in Alabama on behalf of the URW and the CIO (Taft 1981:84–85, 116–17, 195). Mitch was president of UMW District 20 (Alabama) from 1933 to 1946 and was appointed director of the southern region of the SWOC in 1936. See Foner and Lewis (1983:625), Taft (1981:103), Mitch (1960:16), Painter (1979:377–78), and Norrell (1987:673). In an interview with William E. Mitch, Jr., by Cliff Kuhn (Birmingham, Alabama, 29 September 1985), Mitch states that William Rainey [Raney] was an international UMW representative who worked in the coal miners' reorganizing campaign in the Birmingham District in the mid-1930s (see also Taft 1981:90). Jones's ballad is related in narrative technique and structure to earlier

Anglo-American broadsides and occupational ballads as well as to Afro-American disaster "ballets" and topical gospel songs (see also n. 34 below.) The emphasis on food in this song's chorus and in other songs excerpted in this paper suggests continuity with nineteenth-century black minstrel, medicine show, and vaudeville songs like "The Sounds of Chicken Fryin' In The Pan" and lines like "Ham fat, ham fat, frying in de pan." See Dennison (1982:275, 364) and Oliver (1984:51, 99).

26. Korson (1943:46, 307–308). A reference tape of "Union Boys Are We" as furnished by the George Korson Folklore Archive at King's College, Wilkes-Barre, Pennsylvania, courtesy of Rae (Mrs. George) Korson. The common barnyard animals —dogs, cats, pigs, and roosters—of the final verses of "Birmingham Boys" have become, in this transfiguration, the antagonists of the labor movement: "progressives" refers to corporate social reformers; "scabs" is an epithet for company-hired strike-breakers; "snitchers" are company-planted and paid informants; "popsicles" are bogus company-sponsored unions.

27. Anderson Underwood, interview with Cliff Kuhn, Bessemer, Alabama, 23 May 1984. According to Horace Huntley (1977:48), Jim Lipscomb was a former miner who had been blacklisted in the 1920s, but returned to Birmingham after passage of the NIRA in 1933 to practice law and assist in launching the organizing drive of the International Union of Mine, Mill and Smelter workers.

28. Jobie Thomas, interview with Brenda McCallum and Mike Williams, Bessemer, Alabama, 23 August 1981.

29. Recorded 3 July 1941 in Bessemer, Alabama. Reference tape (LC–5042–A and B) furnished by the Library of Congress, Archive of American Folk Culture.

30. Korson (1943:306–307) Hired and sent to Alabama by the national UMW office (Lewis 1987:103), Walter W. Jones was one of the most widely-respected black UMW organizers in the Birmingham District from the 1910s until his untimely death in the 1930s. His bravery, evangelical spirit, and oratorical skills are well remembered by older black workers in the District (see n. 25 above on William A. Mitch).

31. Henry Holston, Bessemer, Alabama, interview with author, 13 March 1981; with Brenda McCallum and Mike Williams, 16 August 1981; and with Brenda McCallum and Cliff Kuhn, 26 April 1983. I am grateful to Archie Green for providing photocopies of two articles about Tiger Thompson published in *Steel Labor* (October 1972:16 and September 1973:n.p.).

32. "The Spirit of Phil Murray" has been reissued on *Songs of Steel & Struggle* (United Steelworkers of America, no issue number; Collector 1930), *Songs of Labor & Livelihood* (Library of Congress, Folk Music in America, vol. 8, LBC–8), and *Birmingham Quartet Anthology* (Clanka Lanka, CL–144, 0011002).

33. Henry Holston, interview with Brenda McCallum and Mike Williams, Besse-mer, Alabama, 16 August 1981.

34. Four verses and the chorus have been excerpted from "The Spirit of Phil Murray" as reissued on *Birmingham Quartet Anthology* and transcribed in the jacket notes by Doug Seroff. Such gospel labor songs are textually and generically related to other topical gospel songs of the period, like Otis Jackson's ballads ("Why I Like Roosevelt," in particular) popularized by the Soul Stirrers, Dixie Hummingbirds, and other groups (Reagon 1974:170–84 and Hayes 1973:14, 52). They also share a stock of formulaic phrases and floating lines with both these topical gospel songs as well as with black religious and disaster ballads ("The Wreck of the Titanic" and "The 1927 Flood," for example), circulated on broadsides beginning in the late-nineteenth century and on blues recordings since the 1920s (Courlander 1963:75–79; Levine 1979:171–74, 258–59; Oliver 1984:174, 195, 222–23, 226–27).

35. "Satisfied" has been excerpted from Doug Seroff's transcription in the jacket notes to *Birmingham Quartet Anthology*. For other examples of the celebration of emancipation through song, see Lloyd (1978 [1952]), Greenway (1953), Denisoff (1972), Foner (1975), Dennison (1982), and Wiggins (1987).

References Cited

Atkins, Leah Rawls. 1981. *The Valley and the Hills: An Illustrated History of Birmingham and Jefferson County*. Woodland Hills, Calif.: Windsor Publications Inc., for the Birmingham-Jefferson County Historical Society.

Bauman, Richard. 1972. "Differential Identity and the Social Base of Folklore." In *Toward New Perspectives in Folklore*, edited by Américo Paredes and Richard Bauman, 31–41. Austin: University of Texas Press, for the American Folklore Society.

Brody, David. 1980. *Workers in Industrial America*. New York: Oxford University Press.

Brownell, Blaine A. 1972. "Birmingham, Alabama: New South City in the 1920s." *Journal of Southern History* 38:21–48.

———. 1975. *The Urban Ethos in the South, 1920–1930*. Baton Rouge: Louisiana State University Press.

Cayton, Horace R., and George S. Mitchell. 1939. *Black Workers and the New Unions*. Chapel Hill: University of North Carolina Press.

Cohen, Norm. 1981. *Long Steel Rail: The Railroad in American Folksong*. Urbana: University of Illinois Press.

Conrad, Charles. 1988. "Work Songs, Hegemony, and Illusions of Self." *Critical Studies in Mass Communications* 15:179–201

Courlander, Harold. 1963. *Negro Folk Music U.S.A.* New York: Columbia University Press.

Cowley Malcolm. 1980. *The Dream of the Golden Mountains: Remembering the 1930s*. New York: Viking.

[Debardeleben]. 1937. "The Debardeleben Oasis—Unionism's Last Frontier." *Alabama: The Newsmagazine of the Deep South* 2/13:9–10.

Denisoff, R. Serge. 1972. *Sing A Song of Social Significance*. Bowling Green, Ohio: Bowling Green University Popular Press.

Dennison, Sam. 1982. *Scandalize My Name: Black Imagery in American Popular Music*. New York: Garland.

Fitch, John A. 1912. "The Human Side of Large Outputs." *The Survey* 27/14:1527–1540.

Foner, Philip S. 1975. *American Labor Songs of the Nineteenth Century*. Urbana: University of Illinois Press.

Foner, Philip S., and Ronald L. Lewis. 1978–1984. *The Black Worker: A Documentary History from Colonial Times to the Present*, 8 vols. Philadelphia: Temple University Press.

Genovese, Eugene D. 1976. *Roll, Jordan, Roll: The World the Slaves Made*. New York: Random House, Vintage Books

Gillespie, Angus K. 1980. *Folklorist of the Coal Fields: George Korson's Life and Work*. University Park: Pennsylvania State University Press.

Godrich, John, and Robert M. W. Dixon. 1969. *Blues and Gospel Records, 1902–1942*. London: Storyville Publications.

Green, Archie. 1972. *Only A Miner: Studies in Recorded Coal-Mining Songs*. Urbana: University of Illinois Press.

———. 1978. "Industrial Lore: A Bibliographic-Semantic Query." In *Working Ameri-*

cans: Contemporary Approaches to Occupational Folklife, edited by Robert H. Byington, 71–102. Los Angeles: California Folklore Society, Smithsonian Folklife Studies, no. 3.

Greenway, John. 1971 [1953]. *American Folksongs of Protest.* New York: Octagon Books.

Grossberg, Lawrence, ed. 1986. "On Postmodernism and Articulation: An Interview with Stuart Hall." *Journal of Communication Inquiry* 10:45–60.

Gutman, Herbert G. 1968. "The Negro and the United Mine Workers of America." In *The Negro and the American Labor Movement,* edited by Julius Jacobson, 49–127. Garden City, N.Y.: Doubleday, Anchor Books.

———. 1977 [1976]. *Work, Culture, and Society in Industrializing America.* New York: Random House, Vintage Books.

Harris, Carl V. 1977. *Political Power in Birmingham, 1871–1921.* Knoxville: University of Tennessee Press.

Hayes, Cedric J., comp. 1973. *A Discography of Gospel Records 1937–1971.* Denmark: Karl Emil Knudsen.

Heilbut, Anthony. 1982. "The Secularization of Black Gospel Music." In *Folk Music and Modern Sound,* edited by William Ferris and Mary L. Hart, 101–15. Jackson: University of Mississippi Press.

Huntley, Horace. 1977. "Iron Ore Miners and Mine Mill in Alabama: 1933–1952." Ph.D. diss., University of Pittsburgh.

Jaynes, Gerald Davis. 1986. *Branches Without Roots: Genesis of the Black Working Class in the American South, 1862–1882.* New York: Oxford University Press.

Keil, Charles. 1966. *Urban Blues.* Chicago: University of Chicago Press.

Korson, George. 1938. *Minstrels of the Mine Patch.* Philadelphia: University of Pennsylvania Press.

———. 1943. *Coal Dust on the Fiddle.* Philadelphia: University of Pennsylvania Press.

Kulik, Gary. 1981. "Black Workers and Technological Change in the Birmingham Iron Industry, 1881–1931." In *Southern Workers and Their Unions, 1880–1975,* edited by Merl E. Reed, Leslie S. Hough, and Gary M. Fink, 23–42. Westport, Conn: Greenwood Press.

Levine, Lawrence. 1979 [1977]. *Black Culture and Black Consciousness: Afro-American Folk Thought from Slavery to Freedom.* New York: Oxford University Press.

Lewis, Ronald L. 1987. *Black Coal Miners in America: Race, Class, and Community Conflict 1780–1980.* Lexington: University Press of Kentucky.

Límon, Jose E. 1983. "Western Marxism and Folklore: A Critical Introduction." *Journal of American Folklore* 96:34–52.

Lloyd, A. L., comp. 1978 [1952]. *Come All Ye Bold Miners: Ballads and Songs of the Coalfields,* 2d ed. London: Lawrence and Wishart.

Lornell, Kip. 1988. *"Happy in the Service of the Lord": Afro-American Gospel Quartets in Memphis.* Urbana: University of Illinois Press.

Mitch, William. 1960. "Labor's Depression Recovery." *Journal of the Birmingham Historical Society* 1:18–19.

Norrell, Robert J. 1986. "Caste in Steel: Jim Crow Careers in Birmingham, Alabama." *Journal of American History"* 73:669–94.

Northrup, Herbert R. 1943. The Negro and Unionism in the Birmingham, Alabama Iron and Steel Industry. *Southern Economic Journal* 10:27–40.

Oliver, Paul. 1984. *Songsters and Saints: Vocal Traditions on Race Records.* Cambridge: Cambridge University Press.

Painter, Nell Irvin. 1979. *The Narrative of Hosea Hudson: His Life as a Negro Communist in the South.* Cambridge, Mass.: Harvard University Press.

Program in Black American Cultures: Black American Quartet Traditions. 1981. Washington, D.C.: Smithsonian Institution, Smithsonian Performing Arts.

Reagon, Bernice. 1974. "'Uncle Sam Called Me': World War II Reflected in Black Music." *Southern Exposure* 1:170–84.

Rikard, Marlene Hunt. 1983. "An Experiment in Welfare Capitalism: The Health Care Services of the Tennessee Coal, Iron and Railroad Company." Ph.D. diss., University of Alabama.

Shils, Edward. 1981. *Tradition.* Chicago: University of Chicago Press.

Sitkoff, Harvard. 1978. *A New Deal For Blacks.* New York: Oxford University Press.

Stephenson, Charles. 1986. "'There's Plenty Waitin' at the Gates': Mobility, Opportunity, and the American Worker." *In Life and Labor: Dimensions of American Working-Class History,* edited by Charles Stephenson and Robert Asher, 72–91. Albany: State University of New York Press, SUNY American Labor History Series.

Szwed, John F. 1969. "Musical Adaptation among Afro-Americans." *Journal of American Folklore* 82:112–21.

Taft, Philip. 1981. *Organizing Dixie: Alabama Workers in the Industrial Era.* Revised and edited by Gary M. Fink. Westport, Conn.: Greenwood Press.

Tierney, Judith, comp. 1973. *A Description of the George Korson Folklore Archive.* Wilkes-Barre, Penn.: King's College Press Publications of the D. Leonard Corgan Library, Wyoming Valley Series No. 1.

White, Marjorie Longenecker. 1981. *The Birmingham District: An Industrial History and Guide.* Birmingham, Ala.: Birmingham Publishing Company (for the Birmingham Historical Society).

Wiggins, William H. 1987. *O Freedom! Afro-American Emancipation Celebrations.* Knoxville: University of Tennessee Press.

Williams, Raymond. 1958. *Culture & Society 1780–1950.* New York: Columbia University Press.

———. 1977. *Marxism and Literature.* Oxford: Oxford University Press.

John Cowley
Shack Bullies and Levee Contractors: Bluesmen as Ethnographers

Protest in African-American song has always held a fascination, certainly from the time that texts to nineteenth-century spirituals could be interpreted as freedom songs in disguise. Using song lyrics as a means of historical interpretation, therefore, is not a new technique. Paul Oliver in his influential analysis *Blues Fell this Morning* (1960) used this theme, but in recent years it has almost been ignored. Most contemporary blues writers base their findings on performer biographies or discussions of musical and lyrical form. While we now generally accept that the lyrics of nineteenth-century spirituals can be understood on two or more levels, the existence of more overt songs of protest in African American society during the last seventy or more years is hardly documented and often denied. My discussion is a contribution to putting that record straight.

Using black folklore material, most of which was obtained in the 1930s and 1940s by white folklorists in the employ of the Library of Congress (principally Alan Lomax), I shall present the texts of this orally collected evidence as an historical source, quoting in full to establish both a substantive record where little other evidence exists and to maintain aesthetic value. In order to explain the context of these performances, I shall first examine black protest songs in general, and the historical reasons for the existence of "shack bullies" and "levee contractors."

In his book devoted to *American Folksongs of Protest,* John Greenway identifies two reasons for the lack of such songs in folksong collections. First, these songs can be short lived, their sometimes spontaneous nature making them ephemeral. Second, there are the ideological attitudes of uninformed and intolerant scholars, who have often ignored protest songs because of their "unpleasant" and "disturbing" connotations (1960:3).

For blacks the existence of ethnic hostility has been a further inhibition. They are reluctant to disclose such positive reflections of disaffection, especially in a society where, until recent years, open racial discrimination was rife. Folklorist and novelist Zora Neale Hurston admirably sums up the tactics employed by her fellow blacks: "The white man is always trying to know into somebody else's business. All right I'll set something outside the door of my mind for him to play and handle. He can read my writing but he sho' can't read my mind. I'll put this play toy in his hand and he will seize it and go away. Then I'll say my say and sing my song" (1978:4-5).

Thus, the twentieth-century collector of black protest folksongs has had to overcome the prejudices of his informants (as well as, perhaps, his own) and the problem of the ephemeral nature of some of the songs themselves. Small wonder, therefore, that there are few examples of black protest song in the body of oral material collected by folklorists during the first half of this century.

The most successful early collector of black protest songs, Lawrence Gellert, printed some of his findings (mainly chain-gang songs) in two collections: *Negro Songs of Protest* (1936) and *Me and My Captain* (1939). Indeed, so successful was Gellert that his unique material has been called into question because others less skilled or politically committed than he have not made similar discoveries. There are, however, a few protest songs in the black folksong studies of Howard W. Odum and Guy B. Johnson and in the unpublished field recordings held by the Library of Congress Archive of Folk Culture—some of which concern us here—but in quantity they do not match Gellert's findings. To these can be added a few commercial recordings made for the "race" market both before and after the Second World War and a small number of post-war field recordings.[1]

For reasons examined already, few of the known black protest songs are about individual whites, with the exception of Lawrence Gellert's recording of an unidentified vocal/guitarist singing about one "Mr. Tyree," almost certainly an official at Bellwood Prison Camp, Atlanta, Georgia, who was also the subject of a 1934 John A. Lomax recording made at the same camp: "I Promised Mr. Tyree" (AFS 254 B1), sung by a group of black convicts.[2]

Another exception is Lightnin' Hopkins's commercially recorded blues about "Tim (Tom) Moore's Farm" (Gold Star 640), which over the years has focused attention on the farming Moore brothers of Texas and the blacks who have worked for them. Other songs recorded by Texans—Mance Lipscomb, Billy Bizor, Joseph "Chinaman" Johnson—testify to the use of the theme in that state. Indeed a June–July, 1933, cylinder recording, "Tom Moore's A

Good Man" (AFS CYL 10 4), made in Texas during John and Alan Lomax's first Library of Congress field recording trip, may be the first to chronicle the Moore family.[3]

During the same field trip, the Lomaxes discovered and recorded (11 July 1933) Henry Truvillion, a foreman working for the Wier Lumber Company, Wiergate, Texas. Truvillion recalled several songs from his Mississippi past of twenty years before and one, "Shack Bully Holler," contains one of the first documented references to another less well known family who feature in recordings—the Lowrence brothers, Mississippi River levee contractors. This family and its involvement with levee construction provides the primary focus for the black protest content of my discussion.

At this point, however, in order to establish an historical background to the principal folk material featured, I summarize the development of levee construction along the Mississippi River and the part black laborers have played in this endeavor. The *Oxford English Dictionary* shows that from 1718 to 1720 the New Orleans settlers used the French-American word "levee" to describe their (artificial) river embankments; that meaning has gradually become commonplace in the United States.

To protect their settlement from flooding, the French, under Sieur Le Blonde de la Tour, constructed the first recorded artificial levee in America. With the land, both up- and down-stream, cleared for cultivation, the protection these embankments afforded to the fertile alluvial lands on either side of the Mississippi River encouraged their gradual but sporadic extension. Together with the more obvious unsnagging and dredging of channels, it was subsequently discovered that the building of levees greatly reduced the river's navigational hazards, thus helping increase riverboat trade. The draining of adjacent swamp lands, including canal construction, also helped improve water flows as well as increase land availability. These incentives greatly encouraged such works.

As the plantation owners extended the levees, they became responsible for the maintenance of their individual water frontages and used slave labor for the bulk of this construction work. In order to keep costs at a minimum, various state authorities purchased slaves for levee and other river work (Starobin 1970:31–32). For example, in 1856 the Louisiana state engineers "were allowed to use, for the space of a year, all the runaway slaves in the Baton Rouge depot" (Gould 1889:327).

In the aftermath of the Civil War, the southern states suffered great social, economic and political unrest, one result of which was the fixing, in the South, of the brutal convict lease system. The emancipated blacks who, in general, had previously been controlled and punished by their owners became subject to civil and criminal law and prime Jim Crow targets for convict lease. Prisoners were leased (in virtual bondage) for heavy manual labor, including onerous levee construction and maintenance and, often, under these despicable conditions blacks continued with this work.[4]

The Civil War had left the existing levee system greatly weakened, both by lack of maintenance and by flooding. Efforts to reconstruct and improve it were hampered by the post-war unrest. Neither did the obvious solution of strengthening and extending the levees meet with much wanted success, for in endeavoring to prevent one of the world's largest rivers from using its flood plain when in spate, man has been no match for the river. From the earliest period of European settlement until well into this century, contemporary witnesses recorded and described a succession of devastating and costly floods.

Federal concern with the problem led to the establishment by Congress, in 1879, of the Mississippi River Commission to work out a unified plan of flood control and navigation. They cooperated with the Army Corps of Engineers to extend the levee system—it now stretches for just over two thousand miles—and raise it to an arbitrary grade height based on the highest previous flood level. This one-sided policy ended with the catastrophic flood of 1927.[5] Over a long period the Commission has built on its experience but, even so, until recent years floods have continued to disrupt the lower Mississippi valley.

State legislatures gradually abandoned the convict-lease system by the first quarter of this century but, for all practical purposes, it was superseded by an equally iniquitous arrangement that had developed alongside it—that of peonage.[6] In levee work, the U.S. Corps of Engineers subcontracted a construction program to white-run earthwork businesses and, arguably, these levee contractors held their black employees as peons. The employers were, in consequence, not squeamish about who worked for them and, sometimes, prisoners continued to be used, particularly in times of flood. It is not surprising, therefore, that black workers at levee camps gained an evil reputation such as that graphically described by John L. Mathews in the story of his 1901–02 voyage down the Mississippi in a houseboat: *The Log of the Easy Way.* His period description is worth quoting in full:

> We had been very fortunate, so far, in avoiding the "levee" camps along the river. Work on the enormous earthen dams which restrain the flood waters is continually going on. At intervals along the way are camps where Negro laborers are housed in tents. To these camps commonly drift the ugliest and most criminal of their race—graduates from the convict camps being numerous in them. Gambling and drinking and quarreling pass away the idle hours, and murders are common occurrences. We had an experience this Sunday morning which amazed us and showed us what they might be like; for the fog held us to

the Arkansas bank which did not happen to be channel side, and we went down behind a towhead, and from the bank the Negro men and women reviled us, shouted curses and taunts and threats and unprintable things at us and gave us very good reason to be glad that we were afloat on our own boat and quickly to be hidden in the fog. (1911:180–81)

Convict laborers filling sandbags, Hymelia Crevasse, 1912. *Courtesy Roy Samuel*

Convict laborers reinforcing levee, Hymelia Crevasse, 1912. *Courtesy Roy Samuel*

Conditions in the levee camps, situated at isolated locations along the riverbank, had not changed significantly by the late 1920s and early 1930s. In 1929, at the request of state health officers in Arkansas, Illinois, Kentucky, Louisiana, Mississippi, Missouri, and Tennessee, the U.S. Public Health Service commissioned H. N. Olds, a sanitary engineer, to conduct surveys "to determine whether these camps may be a factor in the interstate spread of disease and if so the measures of prevention most adaptable" (Bureau Orders, 18 September 1929).[7] There were sixty-five camps (none in Illinois) and Olds visited fifty-six of them. Blacks made up sixty-three percent of the population of 2,427 in the camps he inspected.

Olds's subsequent *Report* covers the conditions both in the camps and on quarter-boats, noting that the boats seemed to have better accommodation than the land-based tents and cabins.[8] Camps employing blacks invariably allocated them inferior accommodation; for example, "At many of the Negro tent camps no excreta disposal facilities were provided with a result that probably requires no elaboration on the part of the writer." And, although Olds did not find a need for closing the camps nor think they posed a threat to interstate disease—due, probably to what he believed to be the "robust" nature of the laborers—he considered, in most cases, that the camps were insanitary and putrid.

At least two of the camps Olds inspected concern this study specifically: one in Mississippi County, Arkansas, near Wilson and Joiner, where V. A. Long was foreman for the levee building contractors, the Lowrence Brothers of Memphis; the other in DeSoto County, Mississippi on a setback levee near Memphis, where one Forrest Jones was the superintendent for Rogers and Jones, the contractors.

The Lowrence Brothers' camp, when visited on 20 November 1929, was populated by four whites, forty-six blacks, and twenty-seven "others" (possibly black women?) quartered in about forty-five tents with one large tent used as a commissary. The whites used a common kitchen and mess hall, the blacks ate in several "boardinghouses." The black workers' tents were generally in bad shape and poorly maintained with ineffective screening. The camp also contained about fifty horses and mules, corralled about twenty-five feet from the black workers' quarters. Its most flagrant unsanitary features were an unprotected pump well, open back privies, lack of adequate manure and garbage disposal, and the ineffective screening of living quarters. Olds noted that the foreman had "no desire to consider sanitation as essential to camp."

Forrest Jones's camp, visited on 27 November 1929, was populated by twelve whites and sixty to seventy blacks. Here, too, they ate in poorly maintained "community boarding-tents" while the whites' kitchen and mess tent were in "good shape." Similarly, the thirty tents used to accommodate them were in poor condition. The camp held two cows, twenty-two hogs, and fifty horses and mules.

Refuse was "thrown to the hogs surrounding the tents." Olds noted that the "camp is in most filthy condition"—the main sanitary problems being potentially dangerous well water supply; open back unsanitary privy for whites; no toilet facilities for about seventy Negroes; piles of garbage, refuse, manure and human fecal matter (scattered) all over camp; and lack of screening for Negro tents. The camp manager's attitude was "affable but quite indifferent towards sanitation at the camp."

The Olds report gives one perspective on levee camp life and the peonage system. Further views can be obtained from an article by Roy Wilkins in the New York-based black radical journal *Crisis*. Writing on "Mississippi Slavery in 1933," he described working conditions for black levee laborers in that low, flat, northwestern portion of Mississippi known as the Delta—bounded by the Mississippi River on the west and the Yazoo and Tallahatchie Rivers on the east—in which Forrest Jones's camp was located (Wilkins 1933:81). Wilkins's findings support assertions of peonage and bad working conditions and his indignant exposé stands as its own testimony:

> In the four months between crops some of the farmers seek employment on "public works" as they call road building and levee construction. But the levee work, while it promises the much desired cash money, actually delivers no more than the plantation owner. It is no exaggeration to state that the conditions under which Negroes work in the federally-financed Mississippi levee construction camps approximate virtual slavery.

Wilkins noted the financial and physical mechanics of labor control. Once a job had been secured, a worker

> would be promised $1.00 a day for common labor, perhaps $1.25. If he could drive a tractor he would be promised $1.50 or, in rare cases, $2.00 a day. He would work from 5:30 a.m. until 5:30 p.m., with a "snatch" lunch on the job at noon. Or if he was on a night crew, he would work from 5:30 p.m. until 5:30 a.m. under flood lights. In some camps he would work on the day shift from 4:30 a.m. until 6:30 p.m. with no overtime.

A caterpillar tractor driver told of a contractor who had forced him to work *eighteen hour shifts*. An essential feature of this extended shift system was the "shack bully." A hated character, used by employers to keep order in the quarters and wake workers at the appropriate time for their shift, he was always armed and carried himself arrogantly. Describing his function, one worker told Wilkins: "Sometimes they come and rousts you out at 3:30 in the morning, telling you it's too cold to work the night crew any longer. You go to get up and hit it."

Another pernicious characteristic of peonage is withholding and/or making deductions from workers' pay. Again Wilkins's angry and detailed description serves as damning evidence:

> This system is a great one for the contractor. The longer the pay days are withheld, the more food and clothes the men buy at the camp commissary at the high prices in vogue there. Then, too, there is the money lending business which all foremen carry on at twenty-five cents interest on the dollar. If pay days are dragged out two and three months apart, with commissary prices at the pleasure of the contractor, a workman has only a dollar or two cash money coming in at the end of three months.
>
> Then there are those other deductions: a lump sum, three or four dollars a week for commissary, whether one uses that amount or not; fifty cents for drinking water, fifty cents for the cook (single men pay this); fifty or seventy-five cents tent rent. . . .

Wilkins had heard "of at least two contractors who had paid off in December for the first time since August and September respectively."

Wilkins's privilege to such sensitive information came because he too was black and could share the confidence of the laborers with whom he stayed in Mississippi. Also he was a member of the National Association for the Advancement of Colored People (publishers of *Crisis*), on whose behalf his "slavery" investigation was conducted. His summary of complaints about working conditions defines succinctly the peonage system operated in the levee construction camps:

> While there is complaint from workers on all the forms of exploitation, the greatest wail is against the irregular pay day system. The men grumble over the small pay, the long hours, the cursing, the beating, the food, the tents, the commissary fleecing, but they reserve their greatest bitterness for the contractor who "won't pay you even that little you got coming."

The findings of Olds and Wilkins are supported by further contemporary evidence, gathered in 1934 for a social anthropological study of caste and class, *Deep South*. This again describes the levee camp system, adding that a further control was the contractor's "organization of extensive facilities for gambling and prostitution." In addition, the intimidation used to establish subordination by fear is spelled out:

> The use of physical violence by white contractors and foremen in "driving" colored levee workers was frequently reported by workers. One foreman made a practice of beating each new colored worker. Sometimes serious in-jury, or even death resulted. (Davis, Gardner, and Gardner 1941: 439–41)

As Olds had already discovered with respect to accommodation differences, the subordination of blacks was also effected by the less oppressive treatment received by whites employed in this construction work.

Having summarized the reasons for levees and the evolution of the "slave"-labor system used for their building and maintenance, before discussing the folklore material relating to this work, it is necessary to explain something of the mechanics of the construction process. The building of river and canal bank levees involved moving large quantities of ballast to provide fill for the sloped embankments on either side of the watercourse. Before mechanization, great teams of men took up such building and maintenance work. These teams constantly used "wheelers" (wheelbarrows). Teamsters called "muleskinners" transported ballast to the levees and handled mule-driven carts and scoop scrapers. "Lumpers" filled the carts with clay and rubble; "dumpers" unloaded the rubble for use by "graders." Teamsters themselves dumped the filled scrapers mechanically.[9]

The manufacture of willow cane reinforcement hurdles or mats became an important aspect of levee maintenance. In order to curb wear from currents, these were weighed down and placed at strategic positions along the levee/riverbanks to form revetments. Groups of small boats in the ownership of the U.S. Corps of Engineers/Mississippi River Commission were often used for this work and came to be known as the "U.S. Government Fleet."[10]

The evolution of black levee camp songs has received scant written attention, despite certain of their verses having appeared in collections (including recordings) since the beginning of this century. An exemplary exception, however, is Archie Green's discourse on the origins of the "roll on buddy" stanza of the hammer worksong "Nine Pound Hammer" which points to a fascinating corpus of levee songs (1972:329–69).

In his discussion, Green establishes that the term "levee camp" has gradually become applicable not only to riverbank but also to general construction sites. He also points out that the word "roll" in "roll on buddy" was originally used to describe hand propulsion of wheelbarrows carting building materials and that this meaning was later extended to other construction aids, probably by muleskinners and members of workgangs, after the introduction of mechanical graders, scrapers, and draglines (339–40).

From these descriptions, it can be seen that the existence of "shack bullies," "levee contractors," and their like, are in direct relationship to the labor system operated in the Southern United States. An interwoven progression of controls, ranging from slavery and convict lease to chain gangs and peonage by labor contractors, kept black manual workers in "servitude" as cheap and expendable labor for onerous construction projects. The means by which this was effected is reflected in black folklore, and in particular folksong.

Tractors and trailors, Vicksburg.   *Courtesy Mississippi River Commission*

Revetment of levee, Vicksburg.   *Courtesy Mississippi River Commission*

As with most construction work using black labor, supervision on the job fell to the hated section or "Walking" Boss—so called because he walked the section he controlled. Also called a "Straw" Boss and epitomized in numerous black work songs as "Captain," he usually carried a watch, and often a gun, to keep laborers in subordination: a fact testified to in the well known work song stanza, which exists in several variants such as that quoted by Odum and Johnson in "Captain I'll Be Gone" (1926:100):

> Captain, captain, what time o' day,
> Captain, captain, what time o' day,
> Say he look at Waterbury,*
> Throw his watch away.
>   [*make of watch]

This motif also appeared on a commercial record by Texas Alexander in his "Section Gang Blues" (Okeh 8498; 12 August 1927):

> Oh, captain, captain, what time of day,
> Oh, he looked at me, and he walked away.

Mention of Texas Alexander, one of the most important "rural" blues singers from the first phase of "race" recordings, highlights the fact that these songs were not peculiar to the Mississippi River and its tributary. Alger Alexander, as his nickname indicates, was a Texan, and the reverse of Okeh 8498 is another work holler, "Levee Camp Moan Blues," as is his "Penitentiary Moan Blues" (Okeh 3640; 16 November 1928). The primary focus of my discussion—Mississippi River levee camps—is not the place for an analysis of Alexander's fascinating lyrics. However, his songs serve to emphasize the links between the prison-peonage work regimes and the construction gangs. They also provide the link to introduce the archetypal levee camp song, also recorded by a Texan, Gene Campbell. His "Levee Camp Man Blues" (Brunswick 7154: c. May 1930) is a prime oral history documentary description of the system:

> These contractors, they are getting so slack,
> These contractors, they are getting so slack,
> They'll pay you half of your money, and hold the other half back.
>
> There ain't but two men, that gets paid off,
> Ain't but two men that gets paid off,
> That's the commissary clerk and the Walkin' Boss.
>
> I see somebody coming, down to the water trough,
> I see somebody coming, down to the water trough,
> I know it ain't the contractor, it's that doggone Walkin' Boss.
>
> A levee camp mule, and a levee camp man,
> A levee camp mule, and a levee camp man,
> They works side by side, and it sure is man for man.
>
> A levee camp man, ain't got but two legs you know
> A levee camp man, ain't got but two legs you know
> But he puts in the same hours, that a mule do on four.

I wouldn't drive no four-mule team,
I wouldn't drive no four-mule team,
For no doggone contractor, I ever seen.

Men on the levee hollerin', "Whoa and gee"
Men on the levee hollerin', "Whoa and gee"
And the women on the levee camp, hollerin', "Who wants me?"

From the foregoing description of the levee camp system and construction work, most of this song's imagery will be understood readily. Worthy of note, however, is the protest against men being forced to compete, as 'beasts of burden' with mules. "Whoa haw gee" are muleskinner cries, though Campbell seems to sing "and" rather than "haw" in this song. Levee camp prostitution also receives mention, the women "hollerin' 'Who wants me?'"

As Archie Green points out, it must be remembered that construction firms used contract labor throughout the South, and "levee" camps, therefore, existed in Texas and elsewhere on non-river projects. In the context of Texas Alexander's and Gene Campbell's songs, however, according to John A. Lomax, at least one Texas levee was built in a Brazos River reclamation project, for which black laborers (along with their women) were imported from Memphis, Tennessee—on the Mississippi (1917:143; Lomax and Lomax 1934:193). And, of course, the Red River, which rises in Texas, is a Mississippi tributary. The maintenance of site embankments, therefore, forms part of the flood-control responsibility of the Mississippi River Commission and the specific contract-labor system which I shall now discuss.

It is likely that Johnny Ryan, a contractor mentioned in Texas Alexander's "One Morning Blues" (Vocalion 02192; 30 September 1934) was associated with Red River/Mississippi River Commission levee work. This is suggested by a further reference to Ryan in the important levee-camp song "Honey I'm All Out and Down" (Melotone M13226; 23 January 1935), recorded by famous black songster Huddie Ledbetter.[11] Leadbelly, to use his more familiar nickname, was born only a few miles from Shreveport, Louisiana, a town situated on the Red River. He knew the north Louisiana-Texas borderlands well. Incarcerated in the Louisiana State Penitentiary, Angola, Leadbelly was discovered by John and Alan Lomax on their pioneering folksong collecting field trip in 1933. On the same expedition, they found Henry Truvillion and obtained his "Shack Bully Holler," learned twenty years before, with its reference to one of the levee-contracting Lowrence brothers. At this point, it should be noted that Peetie Wheatstraw's commercial recording "Shack Bully Stomp" (Decca 7479; 1 April 1938) is one of the few instances I know where this particular expression is used, with the exception of work by the Lomaxes.

The song's significance is diminished, however, by the fact that the lyrics (by Giles Jones) do not touch further on the subject.[12]

Starting with Truvillion's song, I shall now examine the Lowrence folklore material in chronological detail. The Lomaxes printed "Shack Bully Holler" in their collection of *American Ballads and Folk Songs* (Lomax and Lomax 1934:45–46) with a brief preface:

> 'Early in de mornin', Charley Diamon's levee camp, long about three, four clock, you can hear Mr. Isum Lorantz (killed mo' men up an' down de Mississippi dan de influenzy) knockin' on de ding-dong wid his nigger punchin' 44. Nigger by de name o' L. W. Simmons hollers way down end o' de quarters"
> —Henry Trevelyan, former levee worker, Wiergate, lower Texas.[13]

> Who dat knockin' on de fo'-day dong?
> Mus' be Isum Lorantz, 'cause he don't knock long.
> Den Mr. Isum Lorantz spoke up his own se'f says,
> Raise up, boys, raise up, raise up—
> Breakfas' on de table, coffee's gettin' col',
> Ef you don't come now, goin' throw it outdo's.
> Aincha gwine, aincha gwine, boys, aincha gwine?
> Den ol' shack bully Simmons 'gin to holler same way.
> Ol' nigger Shakleton in bed yit,
> Here I am smokin' my third cigaritt.

> Little bell call you, big bell warn you.
> If you don' come now, I'm gonna break in on you.
> Aincha gwine, aincha gwine, boys, aincha gwine?

Judging by the title, Truvillion's cylinder recording of the song is "Who's Dat Knockin' On De Old Ding Dong" (AFS CYL 12 5). Embodied in these lyrics are the "folk" values by which whites achieved black subservience—the addressing of the white levee contractor as "Mister"; the contractor's use of force, by killing on occasion, to achieve a reputation of fearsome authority; the use of a "trusted" black "shack bully"—bought off to maintain a further split in a work force separated already by "color"—to reinforce the expectation of especially severe punishment by whites; and the substandard working conditions. Yet, at the same time, the lyrics also act as a catalyst for protest: criticizing the conditions and personalities responsible for them—witness the recalcitrant attitude of "Ol' nigger Shakleton." Other songs and stories relating to the Lowrence brothers reinforce their family's reputation as feared levee contractors and it is the warnings and protestations reflected in this folk material that form the oral history evidence that follows.

Alerted by Truvillion to the existence of the Lowrence brothers, the Lomaxes continued to seek information and songs about them: Alan Lomax pursued the subject on at least four more occasions, one of his most fruitful sources being Sampson Pittman, whom Lomax recorded in Detroit, Michigan during October–November, 1938. Pittman had resided in Blytheville, Arkansas, before moving north to Detroit and, on the evidence of the two recordings featured here, had almost certainly worked on the Arkansas levees. He probably moved north with the Frazier family, possibly late in 1936. The Fraziers came from Memphis, Tennessee, and one of the family, Calvin Frazier, recorded with Pittman; both were excellent guitarists. Judging by their repertoires, Sampson Pittman was about ten years older than Frazier.[14]

The Pittman-Frazier guitars are heard to good effect on Pittman's "I Ain't No Stranger, I Been Down in The Circle Before" (AFS 2477 A). [15]

> Pittman (spoken): Boys, ain't no need to try to tell me nothing, you can't tell me nothing about the circle because, not Laconia Circle, 'cause I work for every contractor up and down the line and I know just exactly what they'll do and how it is . . . That's why you hear me say I ain't no stranger, you can't tell me nothing, I've been down there lots of times.
>
> (verse)
> I worked on the levee, long time ago,
> And ain't nothing about the levee camp boys that I don't know,
> Partner, partner, partner, don't you think I know,
> Say now I ain't no stranger, been down in the circle before.
>
> No there ain't but the one contractor on the levee that I fear,
> Your Bullyin' George Hulan, they don't 'low him back here,
> Partner, partner, partner, don't you think I know,
> Say now I ain't no stranger, I been down in the circle before.
>
> Now there's Mr. Forrest Jones, ain't so long and tall,
> He killed a mercy man and he's liable to kill us all,
> Partner, partner, partner, don't you think I know,
> Say now I ain't no stranger, I been down in the circle before.
> (spoken) Play it one time, play it.
>
> (verse)
> Now Mr Charley Lowrence is the mercy man,
> The best contractor, partner, that's up and down the line,
> Partner, partner, partner, don't you think I know,
> Well I ain't no stranger, I been down in the circle before.
>
> Now when you leave out [West] Helena, on Highway 44,[16]
> The first camp that you get to it is called "Rainymo,"[17]
> Partner, partner, partner, don't you think I know,
> Said I ain't no stranger, been down in the circle before.

I ain't gonna criticize, I ain't gonna breakdown,
Breaking down and wheeling 'll get a man all down in his back,
Partner, partner, partner, don't you think I know,
Said I ain't no stranger, I been down in the circle before.

Now I have a friend in Arkansas, tell me what to do,
I told him to come to Arkansas, I told him no, no, no,
Partner, partner, partner, don't you think I know,
Say now I ain't no stranger, I been down in Arkansas before.
(spoken) Goodbye.

Immediately following this performance, Lomax interviewed Pittman:

L: Tell us about the Lowrence brothers, who they were; who the Lowrence brothers were?
P: The Lowrence brothers is seven companies of 'em, each seven brothers; one Charley Lowrence, Lawrence Lowrence, Eddie Lowrence, Clarence Lowrence, and Blair Lowrence, Ike Lowrence, levee contractors.
L: Where do they live?
P: All throughout the states of Arkansas, Louisiana, Mississippi, and Georgia.
L: ...
P: They were given pretty tough ... Charley was given pretty.... [18] Charley Lowrence is the best of all, he owns a farm in "Garders" Arkansas.
L: Why are they called "Pickhandle Slims"?
P: He's the man that pleads for the labor daily when they were so cruel to the mens on the levee. Yon was the time when Pickhandle Slim was walking his beat.

The warning theme of this text is apparent immediately. Several details, however, require further explanation, first of all, the establishment of geographical context. In the spoken introduction, Pittman's reference to Laconia Circle is to a circular levee that encloses Snow Lake (at the end of Arkansas Highway 85) and Laconia. It is positioned on a bend of the Mississippi River between the river and White River Bottom, just above the confluence of the White and Mississippi rivers. In verse five, Highway 44 is the Arkansas designation for the road that runs south from West Helena through Wabash, Elaine, Ratio (where it nears the Mississippi River), Mellwood, and Crumrod. To the north its route goes away from the river and ends at Marianna. And, in the interview, the reference to "Garders," Arkansas, where Charley Lowrence ran a farm, may be to Girder, just below Osceola, on U.S. Highway 61.

This is the territory of H. N. Olds's *Report* and it is not surprising, therefore, that two of the contractors mentioned, Forrest Jones and the Lowrence brothers, were encountered in his labor-camp sanitation survey. Pittman's "circle" is probably a cabal of levee contractors also referred to as "the line" or, less likely, a particular camp/contractor. "Wheeling"—wheelbarrowing—in

"Wheeling."   *Courtesy Roy Samuel*

verse six has been explained already, and the reference to "breakingdown" in the same verse, is almost certainly to rock-breaking with a heavy hammer. The lyrics allude to both forms of hard labor as punishment for "criticism"— further evidence of coercion. It is possible that the man called "Pickhandle Slim" in Pittman's interview is synonymous with the "Shack Bully," although it seems more probable that this was yet another name for the "Straw" or "Walking" Boss.

Pittman's other levee camp piece, his ironical "Levee Camp Story" (AFS 2477 B) is just as intriguing, and the tale may be based on an actual event, his irony serving both to entertain and, as with the "Circle" song, warn his listeners.[19] Apart from two verses relating to the "Circle" performance, both sung in the style of a work holler, at the beginning and end respectively, this is a recitation, accompanied by Calvin Frazier's guitar playing.

(verse)
Pittman
Mr Charley, Mr Charley, what's the matter with you, Although I have done everything, partner, you asked me to do.

(spoken)
Now look here Slim, they tell me that you is known to be the baddest shine that lives on the line. Is it true about you carrying two .45s around and is it a fact that every time you kill a man that you puts a notch on your gun? Let me look at your gun Slim. Mmm, mm-mm, pretty tough guy. There's one place that I don't see—what is that? That's a kind of flash—what kind of man is that? Mmm.

Now Slim I'll tell you, I'm an official in the camp. I'm going to try to buy everything to suit you, to try to please you. I don't want no trouble out of you and I guess you is the same by me. Now do you know this is Mr. Lawrence Lowrence talking to you Slim?

Yeah, I don't care nothing about Mr. Lawrence, no more than I do no one else.

Well Slim, tell me what do you call this flour bread that I got here? I bought the best flour that could be bought and you tell me to my face that when the biscuit is made from the best cook, that they are [cackied], strictly [cackied].[20]

What are you going to do about it then?

Not a thing Slim.
Slim, I went to Memphis and bought the best Arbuckle coffee that the Arbuckle Company could afford to make and they tell me you call it Java. Is that true Slim?

Yes, Java, what can you make out of that?

Nothing Slim, that's OK.
Now Slim, they tell me that you call every mule that I've got on my job a shaving tail. What do you mean by shaving tail Slim?

They are no good, they're [plugs].[21]

All right Slim.
Now Slim, there is one thing that I would like for you to do, and that is, this morning, I want you to go down to the river with me. I wants to see what kind of marksman you is and if you is a pretty good marksman, I want to take you on my hunt. I'm going out for a hunt and I want real good marksman.

All right, we pitch the barrel out in the creek. First I take my shots. Look out there Slim, I missed six clear shots. Now let's see can you hit the barrel while she floats. One, two, three, four—oh yeah you hit it. All right Slim, I want to pitch one more and see can you hit it. Here we go. All right Slim, one, two, you missed it. Now Slim do you have another gun or anything? Oh no there's no need to—er load another revolver, you have another one. Let's see what you have in that revolver. All right, let's go—one, two, three, four, five, six. Oh Slim, you hit it in the sixth. Now Slim, let's see have you got another revolver?

No, that's all.

No other revolver?

I can reload.

No, no need to reload. Slim, is you quite sure that's your last cartridge and that's the onliest revolver you have?

Yeah, that's all I have.

Well look here Slim, here's what I want to tell you. Do you know this is Mr Lawrence, Mr Lawrence Lowrence? Slim, I didn't like your look when you first walked in the camp and I told Bullwhippin' Shorty to tell you that I want to see you this morning and this is what I want to tell you Slim. Out of all the flour that I could buy you call it, Java—[cackied], coffee, Java, you call the best mules costing me 250 dollars each, you call them shaving tails. Slim, I don't like that. Now listen Slim, you get on the Government Ridge and talk long green, stand on the Government Ridge and let you feet run away with your body. Let's get moving, on time.

(verse)
Partner, partner, now don't you think I know,
Well I ain't no stranger, partner, partner,
I've been down in the camp before,
Partner, down in the camp before.

Again, the discriminatory practices designed to keep "uppity" black workers in their place are emphasized in this text. It is "Mr." Lawrence Lowrence who gains the upper hand, the story serving as a signal to listeners of the perils of crossing any of the Lowrence brothers or others in the "line" of levee contractors. The Government Ridge is almost certainly the levee itself, maintained as it was by federal funds. What, however, Pittman meant by "talk long green" (if it has been correctly transcribed) is not clear, unless it refers to money—"greenback" dollar notes—but this seems unlikely. Perhaps the singer meant "take the long green" in reference to a path through green grass, cane, or foliage. By implication its meaning may be much more sinister, probably death.

In May, 1939, and September–October, 1940, John A. Lomax again located Henry Truvillion who was still living and working near Wiergate, Texas. Lomax recorded Truvillion's repertoire in full and on 3 October 1940 obtained three more of Henry's levee camp pieces: "Wake Up Calls" (AFS 3985 A1), "Mule Skinner's Holler" (A2), and "Sub-Contractors Song" (A3). Unfortunately for the purposes of these studies, Truvillion makes only a brief, minor reference to one "Isum Lorando": this in the latter song.

Lomax also obtained details of Truvillion's career which adds a description of an individual's varied levee work experience to this oral history documentation:

He has done all kinds of railroad work in his time, and he can tell them off on his fingers: "First, gradin' in th' levee camp, now called 'gradin' camp'; then up and down the river on a cotton boat, cuttin' willow an' makin' mats for holes in the levee, an' placin' 'em. Made a dollar a day cuttin' willow—a mean tedious job." After that he did "river work— a little killin' too," he said. "Spent twelve years with the shevil [shovel]." (Lomax 1947:254–55)

Together with earlier spells in farming and in railroad work, and later employment in railroad track laying for the Wier Lumber Company, Truvillion's broad-based manual experience gave him a wide repertoire of work songs; this attracted the Lomaxes to record him.

Levee and interrelated cornfield (work) songs were also an aspect of black folk music which Fisk University and the Library of Congress collected during their joint 1941–42 "Folk Culture Survey In Coahoma County, Mississippi." Black Mississippian Lewis W. Jones, a researcher involved in this project, in an undated (Spring 1942) "Memorandum" described one of his field trips to Dr. Charles S. Johnson (Fisk) and Alan Lomax (Library of Congress). Jones notes:

> Concentration was made on secular music on this trip. The following lines indicate what might be secured:
>
>> I. T. Clark gave a pay day, Idaho gave a drag,
>> _____ went wild on a Nigger's ass.
>
> The fellow giving this said, "You know Idaho's a big man round here now." In the same vein is the song beginning:
>
>> Ever since I been born
>> I been dodging that man Forrest Jones.[22]

Forrest Jones is, almost certainly, the levee camp contractor mentioned in the sanitation *Report* of H. N. Olds and in Sampson Pittman's "Circle" song.

In July, 1942, during another Fisk-Library of Congress field trip, Alan Lomax recorded Charley Berry at Stovall, Mississippi, singing two unaccompanied "Cornfield Holler(s)" (AFS 6629 A4, B5). Both are available in a Library of Congress album, AFS L49, and some of Berry's stanzas contain possible references to two of the Lowrence brothers.

> [Didn't] you hear Mr Charley, [about] Mr Blair,
> Mr Charley paid off, Mr Blair gave a drink,
> Where I bound, no, woman, would you want to be?
> I be workin' for Mr Charley, I go to Mr Blair.

In two more "Levee Camp Holler(s)" (AFS 6667 A2, B1), probably made at the same session, Berry also sings and speaks about Forrest Jones.

> I'd rather meet a forkey tailed devil, than to meet [Tom Paine],
> Well ain't nothing but a bully travellin' through the land.
> Well, every Monday, oh Lord, in the mornin',
> I can't hear a thing but that long chain man.
> Well, I said, oh, to myself, It must have been nobody,
> but old Bullyin' Forrest Jones.

The "long chain man," equated with "Bullyin" Forrest Jones [and Tom Paine], is a feared name for the chain-gang official who transferred convicted prisoners from court to penitentiary and elsewhere.

Charley Berry had worked on the levees for three years but was now farming on Mr Howard Stovall's plantation. There he recorded with McKinley Morganfield (Muddy Waters), his brother-in-law, also employed by Stovall.[23] Berry's second "Levee Camp Holler" (6667 B1) again has two verses about Mr. Charley and Mr. Blair (Lowrence):

> Old man, old man Charley buying more
> western wagons [than] Mr Blair have teams,
> Mr Charley got more western wagons [than]
> Mr Blair got teams.
> Old man Charley, old man Charley, I don't
> want no more Bear brand molasses with the cub
> on the can,
> Oh Lordy, with the cub on the can.

Western wagons may be mechanical earth moving equipment that replaced the carts hauled by mule teams.

When asked by Alan Lomax, in an interview following this recording, "Do you know any verses about the Lowrence brothers?" Berry replied, "No sir, I don't." He, therefore, may not have consciously referred to the Lowrences at all, Mr Charley and Mr Blair being just symbolic names in his repertoire of verses ("Mr. Charley" is a well-known black synonym for a white "bossman"; or, probably he was being especially cautious). Questioned about Mr Forrest Jones, Berry described him as "a pretty bad man" who operated a "big [timber] farm camp down in Arkansas, just . . . spur, down there in White River Bottom," stating that he would not work for Jones until he was dead![24] Berry recalled a time when he and his brother had been seeking levee work and "looking over" Jones's camp, when Jones "whipped [a] nigger's ass" with a root.

Once more the oral history/folklore evidence, collected during the Fisk University-Library of Congress Coahoma County "Folk Culture Survey," details the system of coercion used to maintain a cheap, expendable, segregated work regime in the South and adds to our understanding of the detail of its operation, both on the plantations, where "discipline" was often less overt and, more particularly, in the contract labor camps, where brutality ruled the day. In turn this points up the occupational links between forms of black work song, whether individual hollers or gang choruses for collective manual labor. This applies wherever the location, penitentiaries and prison farms included.

To return to the Lowrence brothers specifically, the musicians discussed so far, with the exception of Sampson Pittman, cannot be considered to have been professionals in the strict sense of the word. This was not the case with the three informants Lomax next interviewed on the subject: Big Bill Broonzy (Natchez), Memphis Slim (Leroy), and John Lee "Sonny Boy" Williamson (Sib). Although their roots were in the South, all were established blues recording artists and Chicago club performers. Probably recorded in New York in 1947, parts of these interviews were included in Lomax's classic documentary album "Blues in the Mississippi Night," but he used more complete versions in his summer 1948 article for *Common Ground*: "I Got the Blues" (Dundes 1973: 471–86).[25] Omitted from the record but fortunately included in the article is the Lowrence brothers discussion:

> "Look here Leroy" [Natchez said]. "Did you ever work for the Loran brothers?" "You mean those guys that built all the levees up and down the river from Memphis? Sure, man, I've worked for the biggest part of the Loran family— Mister Isum Loran, Mister Bill Loran, Mister Charley Loran—all of them. I think them Lorans are something like the Rockefeller family. When a kid is born, he Loran junior. They got Loran the second, Loran the third. Now—Loran brothers—some of them big business mens in town, some of them running extry gangs and levee camps and road camps. And they were peoples wouldn't allow a man to quit unless they got tired of him and drove him away."

The text speaks for itself in identifying yet more members of this feared levee-contracting family and the scope of their operations. A discourse follows on the term "Mr Charley," already noted as the black slang for a white "bossman," which was used commonly in work hollers. Alan Lomax speculates that in Charley Lowrence, he has, at last, discovered the identity of the elusive "Mr Charley," although it is unlikely that this generic name for a white man originated with Charley Lowrence himself. Indeed, Alan Dundes, in a footnote to the reprint of Lomax's article, observes that Mr Charley "would appear to date from antebellum times" (Dundes 1973:482). It seems unarguable, however, that when "Mr Charley" was used in hollers and work songs up and down the Mississippi, it is likely to have been sung with Charley Lowrence in mind.[26]

> "Mister Charley was one of them *real* Southerners," [said Leroy, gently ribbing Lomax] "had a voice that would scare you to death whenever he would come out with all that crap of his. Always in his shirt sleeves. I don't care how early in the mornin' and how cold it was. Night or day," Natchez began to chuckle with him. "Didn't make no difference to Mr Charley what time it was."
>
> "Don't care how early he'd get up, you gonna get up too. He'd holler —'Big bell call you, little bell warn you. If you don't come now I'm gonna break in on you.' And he *meant* it."
>
> "Sho he did," laughed Natchez. "He the man originated the old-time eight hour shift down [t]here. Know what I mean? Eight hours in the morning and eight more in the afternoon."

Having, once more, substantiated the Lowrence work regime, Lomax asked a further question, based on his previous Charley Lowrence findings:

> "I'd always heard of this Mr Charley in the song as 'the mercy man.' Is he the same as Charley Loran?"
>
> "Naw, man, that's Mr Charley *Hulen,* the best friend we had down in [that] part of the country, really a friend to our people. He was the man we all run to when somebody mistreated us," Natchez told me.
>
> "Otherwise known as 'the mercy man,'" Leroy added. (Dundes 1973:477–78)

A fact made clear from this, and earlier references, is that workers used a special symbolic language to describe levee contractors, a "mercy man" being the black man's friend, and "bullyin" describing someone who was otherwise. Charley Lowrence, it seems, may have received both titles. In this context, one wonders whether Charley Hulen and the "Bullyin" George Hulan of Sampson Pittman's "Circle" song were related?

Finally, Alan Lomax elicited a description of the barrelhouses and honkytonks operated in the levee camps by contractors, the haunts of many blues players—presumably Big Bill Broonzy, Sonny Boy Williamson, and Memphis Slim included. He also secured yet more details of the harrowing conditions used to force men to work on the levees; maintained as "peons" by debt and fear of death, at the behest of each contractor:

> "Toughest places I *ever* seen," said Natchez, "were some of them honkytonks, call them barrel-houses, in Charley Loran's camps. Negroes all be in there gamblin', you know, and some of them short guys couldn't quite reach up to the crap table—and I've seed them pull a *dead* man up there and stand on him."
>
> "Yeah, stand on 'em. I've seed that," Leroy said.
>
> But Natchez had more to tell. "Down in them barrel-houses in Loran's levee camps I've seed them stand on a dead man and shoot craps all night long; and I've heard Loran come around and say, 'If you boys keep out the grave, I'll keep you out the jail.'" Yeah, and I've heard him say, "Kill a nigger, hire another. But kill a mule and I'll have to *buy* another."
>
> "That's just what he believed Natchez," Leroy said, in anger and at the same time with curious pride. "Peoples like him had another word, too. On those camps, when the fellows were wore down from carrying logs or doing some kind of heavy work, the bosses used to say, *'Burn out, burn up. Fall out, fall dead!'* That was the best you could do. You had to work yourself to death or you proved that you were a good man, that's all."
>
> "Main thing about it is some of those people down there didn't think a Negro ever get *tired!*" Natchez's ordinarily quiet voice broke with sound that was half sob, half growl. "They'd work him —work him till he couldn't work see! You couldn't *tell* 'em you was tired."
>
> "Why couldn't you?" I asked.
>
> "They'd crack you 'cross the head with a stick or maybe kill you. One of those things. You just had to keep on workin' whether you was tired or not.

From what they call 'can to can't.' That mean you start to work when you can see—early in the mornin'—and work right on till you can't see no more at night." (Dundes 1973:477–78)

In the mid 1950s, Big Bill Broonzy recalled a folk tale concerning another of the Lowrence brothers—Lawrence. In a text recovered from the Broonzy biographical files of the late Yannick Bruynoghe and published in *Living Blues* (1982:20), Lawrence Lowrence is outsmarted in a tale by a black policeman:

> —I do remember once I was working on levee camp for the Lorand brothers, the baddest men in White River Bottom. So the one we called Mr Lost Lorand, he went to a town not far across the Mason-Dixon line. They had negro police there and they didn't allow nobody to carry a pistol. But Mr Lost Lorand had two .45s, one on each side.

> This Negro police walked up to Mr Lorand and said to him:

>> "It's against the law to carry a gun in this town. Did you know that?"
>> So Lorand said to the Negro police: "Say, Negro, do you know who I am?"
>> "No I don't," said the Negro police, "so tell me who is you?"
>> "I'm Lost Lorand."
>> Pulling out his big 38.40 pistol and cocking it in Lorand's face, the Negro police said: "Mr Lorand, you once was lost, but now you're found."
>> He handcuffed Lorand, took his two .45 guns and took him to jail.

> The news traveled all over the South and North because that Negro was the first to arrest a bad white man and there was Negro police in all Southern towns and in the North too, but they just arrested other Negroes, because white people don't break the law, they make it. You had to be black to break the law.

> So when Mr Lorand came back to White River Bottom he was better to Negroes, and at the meeting one day he got up and told all of us this story just like it happened. He said he had never thought a Negro could or would ever have nerve enough to attempt to arrest one of the Lorand brothers.

The contrast between this positive text and the warnings inherent in Sampson Pittman's "Levee Camp Story" is significant. It signals changing racial attitudes, with a gradual demise of the use of peonage, occasioned probably by altered labor requirements as levee maintenance became more and more mechanized after the Second World War.[27]

Another commercially recorded blues singer-guitarist, Big Joe Williams, worked for Charley Lowrence too. His testimonies, printed in an interview with David Mangurian (1963:15) and recorded in his "Levee Camp Blues" (Bluesville BVLP 1083) are the concluding oral history evidence in this collection of folklore and folk music that protests the working conditions in the Mississippi River levee-construction camps. Williams told Mangurian:

> I left home run off to the levee camp. I was about twelve years old then. I went to a camp in Greenville, Mississippi—Captain Charlie Lawrence. I went out there and I was a willow driver. Yeah, popped lotsa mules out there—mule driver. I did that for a long time.
>
> The life was hard. The men worked from sunrise to sunset. At night, they slept in filthy tents on rotten mattresses with a couple of blankets to crawl under. The food just about kept a man alive— we had black-eyed peas for supper . . . for breakfast for dinner; an' what you call cornbread, an' salt pork meat. That's all we had to eat. He'd just throw it in the pot, you know, and yell 'Come an' get it,' that's all.
>
> The pay was $1 to $1.50 a day and that went on Saturday-night drinking and women.

As with previous evidence, this description adds to our detailed knowledge of the coercion employed in levee work, expanding on both working activities and living conditions.

Little or no pay and the hazards of mule poppin'—hour after hour driving sickly mules hauling carts of earth, by force with a "loaded nine" whip—is the subject of Joe's "Levee Camp Blues." The graphic description in his verses provides the final folk song of protest under consideration:

> (verse)
> Well good morning, captain, well, well, my lead mule won't go 'long,
> Well good morning, captain, well, well, my lead mule won't go 'long,
> Well she won't drink water, you know my lead mule won't eat corn.
>
> Well my backband's poppin', yes you know my collar cryin',
> Well you know my backband's poppin', you know Big Joe's workin' collar cryin'
> Well you don't need a doggone thing, whoa but a loaded nine.
>
> Yes I been workin' on the levee, oh I been workin' both night and day,
> Yes I been workin' on the levee, oh I been workin' both night and day.
>
> (spoken) That's somewhere around Greenville, Mississippi.
>
> (verse)
> Yes, every Saturday night I went to Clarksdale, Mississippi,
> Charley Lowrence tells me, 'Big Joe Williams you ain't go no pay.'
>
> My lead mule cripped and my off-mule blind,
> My lead mule cripped and my off-mule blind,
> How can I drive her, buddy, when I ain't got me a loaded nine.
>
> (spoken) Bring me a loaded nine.
>
> (verse)
> Hmmm, I ain't gonna work both night and day.
> (spoken) I hate to tell you Captain Charley,

(verse)
Hmmm, I ain't gonna work both night and day,
(spoken) I hate to tell you Captain Charley,

(verse)
Hmmm, I ain't gonna work both night and day,
I can't help you build your levee, ooh well,
and you won't give me no pay.

I conclude with the history and genealogy of the Lowrence family. Oral documentation demonstrates that they operated along both sides of the Mississippi River, upstream and downstream from Memphis, Tennessee. Just one of the brothers, Isum, is associated with Henry Truvillion's song. Sampson Pittman, however, recalled seven brothers but mentions only six—Charley, Lawrence, Eddie, Clarence, Blair and Ike (presumably the seventh was Isum?). Memphis Slim (Leroy) mentions three brothers by name, Isum, Bill and Charley, Bill making the total we know about, eight. A little extra information concerning three of them can be gleaned from entries in the *Memphis City Directory*. Edward M. Lowrence resided in Memphis between 1928 and 1931, his occupation listed as either "levee contractor" or, simply, "contractor." Lucy D. Lowrence, as his widow, has an entry in 1933. Blair Lowrence lived in Memphis between 1929 and 1935. Designated "levee contractor," except in 1930 when he is shown as a "planter"; in 1931 no occupation is stated. William Tate Lowrence, listed as a "levee contractor" in 1925, does not appear again until 1928, when he also is shown as a "levee contractor." He is designated as a "contractor" in 1929 and 1930, the latter year, his final entry.

As has become evident by its presentation, oral evidence admirably supports and complements the levee camp documentation of such as Olds and Wilkins, and the *Deep South* findings of Davis, Gardner and Gardner. Together, they paint a vivid picture of life and conditions in the Mississippi River levee camps, particularly during the late 1920s and early 1930s.

In addition, this black folklore demonstrates that repressive conditions were not accepted passively, but became the subject of pragmatic overt protestation within the folk community as well as outside of it, whenever circumstances permitted commentary without reprisal in the form of torture or death. Sometimes, workers took this risk despite the consequences. Integrity is shown, both in historical accuracy and communal solidarity. And, above all, these protests define the aesthetic yardstick by which such folklore must be judged—maintenance of humanity whatever the odds. It stands in judgment against oppressors and doubters alike.

Hertfordshire, England

Notes

During research for this article, I have received information and other forms of encouragement from a number of friends—in particular Pete Daniel, David Evans, Archie Green, Bob Groom, and Paul Oliver. Kip Lornell and John Barnie kindly checked the Memphis City Directory for me and supplied data on levee contracting Lowrences recorded there. To all these, and others not named, I am especially grateful. Needless to say, all views expressed are my own. This is a revised and expanded version of an article first published in the JEMF Quarterly *16/60 (Winter 1980) and in two parts in* Juke Blues *3 (December 1985) and 4 (March 1986).*

1. For an overview of "Protest and Irony in Negro Folksong," see Russell Ames's article, reprinted with a useful editorial introduction in Dundes (1973). See bibliography for works by Odum and Johnson. Oliver (1960) discusses some of the commercial recordings.

2. Issued in the LP record "Negro Songs of Protest," Rounder 4004. The singer identifies Bellwood in his first verse, although the notes (4) wrongly transcribe the word as "here Lord" and "their work." Tyree is also the subject of a verse of "Negro Got No Justice" in the same album.

3. For comprehensive details of songs and stories about the Moore brothers, Tom in particular, see Mack McCormick, "Tom Moore's Farm," insert notes to "A Treasury of Field Recordings," Vol. 2, 77–LA–12–3, London, 1960 and "Three Moore Brothers," Jackson, 1972; 53–61. Lipscomb's recording (by "Anonymous") is in 77–LA–12–3 and Blues Classics LP 16, Bizor's in Arhoolie LP 1017, and Johnson's in Elektra LP EKS 7296.

4. For a period description of convict lease, see George W. Cable's exposé, "The Convict Lease System in the Southern States" *Century Magazine* (February 1884): 582–99. An historical overview is Fletcher Melvin Green's "Some Aspects of the Convict Lease System in the Southern States," in Green (1949): 112–23. Sellin (1976) has a contemporary view of the links between slavery and the penal system.

5. Aspects of nineteenth-century river conditions and a brief résumé of the setting up of the Mississippi River Commission are in Twain (1883, 1962). For a documentary account of the 1927 Mississippi River flood, see Daniel (1977).

6. The extent of peonage has been examined by Daniel (1973); the economic and legal system that still maintains it in some forms, by Novak (1978).

7. U.S. National Archives, Record Group 90, United States Public Health Service Files for 1924–35, Box 43.

8. Ibid. H. N. Olds, *Report of Preliminary Sanitary Surveys of Labor Camps Maintained by Contractors Engaged in Mississippi Flood Control Operations, 1920–29.*

9. For general details of levee work, see Alan Lomax, insert notes to "Murderers' Home," Nixa NJL 11, London, 1957, p.3; Oliver (1960):26–27; Walter Cline, "Levee Camp Recollections," Green (1972):368–69.

10. Certain background information on levee/riverbank revetment is described in Moore (1972):58, and *Arkansas* (1941):328. The "U.S. Government Fleet," about which Son House recorded his AFS 4780 B1 "Government Fleet Blues" (issued in Flyright FLY LP 541), is so defined in *Mississippi* (1938):277.

11. For a fuller version of the song and a reference confirming Ryan's levee-contractor status, see Lomax and Lomax (1936):131–35.

12. The lyrics and an analysis of their meaning are in Peel (1972):19.

13. John A. Lomax's notes for his 1939 field recording expedition show that Truvillion is the correct spelling.

14. For further details on these performers and their recordings, see John H. Cowley, sleeve notes to "I'm in the Highway Man," Flyright FLY LP 542, Bexhill-on-Sea, 1980.

15. Issued in Flyright FLY LP 542.

16. "[West]": Pittman's enunciation is indistinct.

17. "Rainymo" is a phonetic interpretation.

18. Pittman's word may be "mens."

19. For an annotated collection of black American folk tales, see Dorson, 1967; he includes a chapter on "Protest Tales," 300–20.

20. "Cackied" is a phonetic interpretation.

21. "Plugs" is a phonetic interpretation.

22. Copy in my files.

23. Berry's relationship with Waters is established in O'Neal, "Muddy Waters," *Living Blues* 64 (March–April 1985):23. It is presumed that he was Waters's brother-in-law by Muddy's first wife.

24. Possibly either Catron Spur or Mosby Spur, both of which are situated on the high land between the Mississippi River and White River Bottom.

25. Memphis Slim (Leroy) gives this location and date for these recordings (Jim O'Neal, letter to author, 20 January 1978) and they are confirmed by the fact that all three performers were in New York for a "Music at Midnight" concert in the Town Hall in 1947—see Harris (1979). This is contrary to my suggestion (*Blues Unlimited* 121 [October 1976]:26–27) that a 1942–43 Chicago date seemed logical.

26. It is interesting to observe that in Texas the black folksong "Uncle Bud" became similarly associated with one individual, prison transfer officer Uncle Bud Russell. See Mack McCormick, "The Bawdy Song" (1960b:6–7).

27. For a useful, though now somewhat dated, analysis of the changes in racial attitudes as reflected in Southern folklore, see James M. Lacy (1964).

References Cited

Ames, Russell. 1950. "Protest and Irony in Negro Folksong." Reprinted in Dundes, ed., *Mother Wit from the Laughing Barrel*, 487–500.

Arkansas, A Guide to the State. 1941. New York: Hasting House.

Boatright, Mody C., Wilson M. Hudson, Allen Maxwell, eds. 1964. *A Good Tale and a Bonnie Tune.* Dallas: Southern Methodist University Press.

Bruynoghe, Yannick, and Big Bill Broonzy. 1982. "In Chicago with Big Bill & Friends: 'Truth about the Blues.'" *Living Blues* 55:15–20.

Cable, George W[ashington]. 1884. "The Convict Lease System in the Southern States." *Century Magazine* 27:582–99.

Cline, Walter. 1972. "Levee Camp Recollection." In *Only a Miner,* edited by Archie Green, 368–69.

Cowley, John. 1976. Review of *Murderers' Home/Blues in the Mississippi Night,* Vogue (UK) VJD 515 (two record set). *Blues Unlimited* 121:26–27.

———. 1980. Sleeve notes to *I'm in the Highway Man.* Flyright FLY LP 542. Bexhill-on-Sea.

Daniel, Pete. 1973. *The Shadow of Slavery: Peonage in the South, 1901–1969.* New York: Oxford University Press.

———. 1977. *Deep'n As It Come: The 1927 Mississippi River Flood.* New York: Oxford University Press.

Davis, Alison, Burleigh Gardner and Mary R. Gardner. 1941. *Deep South*. Chicago: University of Chicago Press.

Dixon, Robert M. W., and John Godrich, comps. 1982. *Blues & Gospel Records 1902–1943*. Chigwell: Storyville Publications.

Dorson, Richard M. 1967. *American Negro Folktales*. Greenwich: Fawcett Publications.

Dundes, Alan, ed. 1973. *Mother Wit from the Laughing Barrel*. Englewood Cliffs, New Jersey: Prentice Hall.

Gellert, Lawrence. 1936. *Negro Songs of Protest*. New York: Carl Fisher.

———. 1939. *Me and My Captain*. New York: Hours Press.

Gould, E. W. 1889. *Fifty Years on the Mississippi*. St. Louis: Nixon-Jones.

Green, Archie. 1972. *Only a Miner*. Urbana: University of Illinois Press.

Green, Fletcher Melvin. 1949. "Some Aspects of the Convict Lease System in the Southern States." In *Essays in Southern History,* edited by F. M. Green, 112–23. Chapel Hill: University of North Carolina Press.

Greenway, John. 1960 [1953]. *American Folksongs of Protest*. New York: A. S. Barnes.

Harris, Sheldon. 1979. *Blues Who's Who*. New York: Arlington House.

Hurston, Zora Neale. 1978 [1935]. *Mules and Men*. Bloomington: Indiana University Press.

Jackson, Bruce, ed. 1972. *Wake Up Dead Man: Afro-American Worksongs from Texas Prisons*. Cambridge, Mass.: Harvard University Press.

Jones, Lewis. [1942]. "Memorandum re: Field Trip to Coahoma County Mississippi in Connection with the Folk Culture Study." Washington, D.C.: Library of Congress, Archive of Folk Culture.

Lacy, James M. 1964. "Folklore of the South and Racial Discrimination." In Boatright, ed., *A Good Tale and a Bonnie Tune,* 101–11.

Lomax, Alan. 1948. "I Got the Blues." Reprinted in Dundes, ed., *Mother Wit from the Laughing Barrel,* 469–86.

———. 1957. Insert notes to "Murderer's Home." Nixa NJL 11, London.

Lomax, John A. 1917. "Self Pity in Negro Folk-Songs." *Nation* 105:141–45.

———. 1939. Field notes to Library of Congress Archive of Folk Song recording trip. Washington, D.C.: Library of Congress, Archive of Folk Culture.

———. 1947. *Adventures of a Ballad Hunter*. New York: Macmillan.

———, and Alan Lomax. 1934. *American Ballads and Folk Songs*. New York: Macmillan.

———. 1936. *Negro Songs as Sung by Lead Belly*. New York: Macmillan.

McCormick, Mack. 1960a. Insert notes to "A Treasury of Field Recordings." Vol. 2, 77–LA–12–3. London.

———. 1960b. Insert notes to "The Unexpurgated Folk Songs of Men." Raglan 51. Berkeley.

Mangurian, David. 1963. "Big Joe Williams." *Jazz Journal* 16/2: 15–17.

Mathews, John L. 1911. *The Log of the Easy Way*. Boston: Small, Maynard and Co.

Memphis City Directory. 1925, 1928, 1929, 1930, 1931, 1932, 1933, 1934, 1935.

Mississippi, A Guide to the Magnolia State. 1938. New York: Viking.

Moore, Norman R. 1972. *Improvement of the Lower Mississippi River and Tributaries, 1931–1972*. Vicksburg: Mississippi River Commission.

Novak, Daniel A. 1978. *The Wheel of Servitude: Black Forced Labor after Slavery*. Lexington: University Press of Kentucky.

Odum, Howard W., and Guy B. Johnson. 1925. *The Negro and His Songs*. Chapel Hill: University of North Carolina Press.

———. 1926. *Negro Workaday Songs*. Chapel Hill: University of North Carolina Press.

Olds, H. N. *Report of Preliminary Sanitary Surveys of Labor Camps Maintained by Contrac-*

tors Engaged in Mississippi Flood Control Operations, 1920–1929. U.S. National Archives, Record Group 90, United States Public Health Service Files for 1924–35, Box 43.

O'Neal, Jim, and Amy O'Neal. 1985. Interviews with Muddy Waters. *Living Blues* 64: 15–40.

Oliver, Paul. 1960. *Blues Fell this Morning.* London: Cassell & Co.

Oxford English Dictionary. 1933. Oxford, Clarendon Press.

Peel, David. 1972. *The Peetie Whitstraw Stomps.* Burlington, Ontario: Belltower Books.

Sellin, J. Thorsten. 1976. *Slavery and the Penal System.* New York: Elsevir.

Starobin, Robert S. 1970. *Industrial Slavery in the Old South.* New York: Oxford University Press.

Twain, Mark. 1962 [1883]. *Life on the Mississippi.* London: Oxford University Press.

U.S. National Archives, Record Group 90, United States Public Health Service Files for 1924–35, Box 43.

Wilkins, Roy. 1933. "Mississippi Slavery in 1933." *Crisis: A Record of the Darker Races* 40: 81–82.

Neil V. Rosenberg

"An Icy Mountain Brook": Revival, Aesthetics, and the "Coal Creek March"

The awareness of folklore as a special kind of human behavior began with the rise of the Romantic Movement in the eighteenth century. Percy, the Grimms, Scott, and others collected and published aspects of their native lands' folk culture—language, story, song—because they saw in it the means for a revival or revitalization of national culture. Essentially, they viewed the material they collected as a resource for the artist—like painters viewing nature and creating landscapes—and because these men wrote, they interpreted and interpolated with their own art the folklore they published. By the present standards of folklore studies, all would be found guilty of tampering with the material they collected. Indeed, we now know that some of what the eighteenth-century writers presented as authentic folk stuff was in fact totally spurious; the most notable example is James MacPherson's *Ossian*. And yet, we remember that because of MacPherson (a faker) and Percy (a tamperer), Herder found inspiration to preach the awareness and study of *das Volk*. Is it too ahistorical to say that in this sense fakelore (the stuff) created folklore (the study)? Whether we agree or not, it seems clear that the revival and scholarly study of folklore are often linked.

In the following pages I present a case study of the folk tune "Coal Creek March" and consider how its roles as an object of artistic revival and folkloric study intertwine. Although this tune grew out of labor strife, its significance to folksong revivalists was not as an example of folk protest song but as an aesthetic object. From the perspective of contemporary folklore and folklife studies, occupational lore has many dimensions; the aesthetic one has received relatively little attention. I focus upon the unquestioned assumptions about aesthetic values that have influenced the thinking of those engaged in American folklore research and the folksong revival alike, during the decades between 1930 and 1970. These values can be seen in the work of individuals who stated primary goals as education, entertainment, or both. And they are shared by individuals holding theoretical perspectives as comparativist, functionalist, populist, and social activist. It is my contention that while these people may have differed explicitly about means, they agreed implicitly about ends. And finally, I will suggest that from this era's folksong revival emerged a new generation of scholars and entertainers imbued with a different aesthetic.

I became interested in the history of the "Coal Creek March" within the folksong revival because of a question raised by Charles K. Wolfe in his detailed case history of this piece. He discusses Alan Lomax's 1938 Library of Congress field recording of banjoist Pete Steele playing the "March" (issued for sale to the public on a phonograph recording in 1941 and in print ever since) and comments "how influential it was outside of the folklorist community is unclear" (1976:2). Wolfe's provocative statement advances the term "folklorist community." It connotes a group extending beyond the confines of academic researchers and teachers to include interested amateurs. Such a perception of folklore (the study) is widely held by those outside it; but insiders do not like it any more than academic historians like being identified with romantic historical novelists. Folklorists and folk revivalists often perceive themselves as being on opposite sides of issues. Ultimately, though, as Wolfe suggests, they form a community. I will return to this point later; first an examination of the evidence is in order.

The "Coal Creek March" lives as part of a complex of folklore clustering around the memory of events that occurred at Coal Creek, Anderson County, on the Cumberland Plateau of eastern Tennessee. In 1891 members of the Knights of Labor struck against the Tennessee Coal Mining Company, operators of the Coal Creek mines. This led the company to hire as scab miners a group of black convicts through Tennessee's convict-lease system. The Tennessee Coal, Iron & Railroad Company, popularly known as the TCI, had originally leased the men from the state. On July 14, 1891, some 300 striking miners, many of them Civil War veterans, stormed the stockade at nearby Briceville and, after a bloodless victory, marched the guards and convicts off to a freight train which took them to Knoxville. This precipitated a struggle that lasted for two years and involved the state legislature, as well as the sending of the national guard. The strike and the issue of convict labor have been discussed in detail in Archie Green's *Only a Miner* (1971) and need not be retold here.

Green documented one song composed specifically about these events: "Coal Creek Troubles," supposedly written by J. W. Day, the blind fiddler whom Jean Thomas romanticized as "Jilson Setters." Another song that Green discusses, "Buddy Won't You Roll Down the Line," deals with convict labor and, in at least one version, has been tied to Coal Creek events. Pete Steele performed a third song, "Pay Day at Coal Creek," for Alan Lomax at the same time as his "Coal Creek March."

The "March" is the fourth musical piece connected with the events. Charles Wolfe shows that during the early decades of this century, many of the men who learned to play the five-string banjo in the Appalachians, particularly in southeastern Kentucky, played the piece. It was, as Wolfe says, popular "on the ground," that is, locally within the region (1976:4). Indeed, since his article appeared, at least three more commercial recordings of the tune by Kentucky banjo pickers have surfaced: two by the late David "Stringbean" Akeman of his "Cold Creek March," which includes a single song verse as well as the tune; and one by the Skinner Brothers, an unissued Gennett recording from the early thirties.[1] No doubt other examples exist unreported in private collections, as was the case of my own recording of a performance by the late Oscar "Shorty" Sheehan, an East Tennessee native, which I will discuss later.

These performances, like those documented by Wolfe, reinforce his conclusion that this tune became popular locally. Its popularity can be explained in several ways. First, it had a lasting topical connection with an important regional occupation, coal mining. Even when, as happened with several of the documented performances (including Steele's), the musician no longer knew of the convict-labor issue, the tune was associated with a narrative about an unusual event at the mines, like an explosion. Usually it was not connected to the topic through song lyrics (though several versions of the March do include them) but through the narrative, which served to explain the title and the sound effects often included in the tune.

These sound effects constituted a second factor which helps to explain the tune's popularity: as a "program piece," it included musical sound effects—drums, gunshots, etc. Program pieces are often more popular with audiences than other instrumental types because they use the instrument to produce concrete (albeit musical) sounds instead of semantically abstract melodies. Fiddlers succeed with the train-like "Orange Blossom Special," harmonica players with the "Fox Chase," trumpeters with "The Flight of the Bumblebee."

A third factor in the tune's popularity derived from its use as a learning piece for novice banjoists. Like many program pieces it sounds more difficult to perform than it really is. Such pieces are often played in public by neophyte musicians striving to demonstrate their competence. I base this conclusion on the East Kentucky (and adjacent) regional traditions from which the tune sprang and also on my own observation of "Coal Creek March" in the folksong revival during the fifties and sixties.

Wolfe demonstrated a fourth factor: the piece continued in the repertoire of several itinerant professional entertainers in the East Kentucky region, thereby gaining popular currency in tradition through its performance in assembly events—fairs, school concerts, contests, and open-air busking type venues. Again, the role of professionals in spreading the song has parallels in the folksong revival, as we shall see.

The American folksong revival

The revival of folksong has been traced as a historical movement in the U.S. back to the 1930s (though its historical roots lie deeper than that). Viewed diachronically it is a complex phenomenon about which much has been written. Viewed synchronically at any point between about 1940 and the mid-sixties various elements can be perceived in it. Some would call it a music business "boom" in which economic exploitation, denounced as commercialism by purists, perverted the original goals of the movement. Others, stressing social rather than economic aspects, might use the terminology of anthropologists who advocate the ethnoscientific approach, deeming it a "cultural scene." However seen, there is no doubt that it represented a diversity of musical tastes and individual personalities. How are we to make sense of it in intellectual terms?

In 1966 Kenneth S. Goldstein wrote: "Urban singers of folk songs and professional folklorists refer to the present popular interest in folk songs as a folk music revival. It is, however, far from a revival of any kind. . . . It is a *new* experience. . . ." Goldstein, who spoke from personal experience as one of many who had made the move from revival enthusiast to scholar, illustrated his point with hypothetical examples:

> A Jewish adolescent of Eastern European parentage who resides in the Bronx and sings English and Scottish ballads is not reviving anything from his own cultural background; the Italian-American boy from Chicago whose parents came to this country from Genoa and who specializes in singing Negro blues is reviving nothing from his cultural heritage. . . . (1966:47–48)

Close analysis might reveal elements of revival through syncretism in examples like those given by Goldstein, but his point is clear: for most people the folksong revival consisted of acquiring other peoples' old traditions. We might interpret this as a form of assimilation under the guise of cultural pluralism. It is, however, most common to follow the perspective of Roger Abrahams (like Goldstein, a revivalist before he became a folklorist) in describing the activity of his peers as an example of the way in which " . . . we have repeatedly raided the arts of our country neighbors in our incessant attempts to renew our sapping cultural vitality." Abrahams makes this statement by way of introducing a study of two female singers which shows how their contrasting repertoires reflect their different life histories and personalities. He argues that such studies are needed because " . . . we have voraciously seized and only partially digested the arts of other cultures" (1970:5–34). In arguing in favor of understanding rather than consumption, Abrahams articulates the contemporary aesthetic concerning folk arts: educated middle class urbanites, he would argue, should know about this topic because it tells them about other humans and how they organize their lives. As we will see later, this stance differs from that of the folk revival of 1930 to 1965.

In one sense the term "folk revival" is not as inaccurate and misleading as it might seem. Those most deeply involved in this movement approached it with the missionary zeal of religious revivalists, motivated by their belief that folk music was meaningful and accessible in a way that other forms of music were not. A corollary to this belief states that music is a transcendent language, a means of understanding and communication. By listening to and performing folk music one avoided the tasteless and wasteful commercialization of popular music. More accessible than classical music or modern jazz, both of which required a knowledge of apparently rigid and arcane music theory, this was music of the people, free and easy. Through the experience of listening to and performing it one could learn about and appreciate other classes and cultures, thus discovering alternative values. By supporting the music of people whose artistic expressions they believed to be threatened by the homogenizing (and, therefore, deracinating) effects of mass culture, the revivalists hoped to rejuvenate—revive—such music by giving the underprivileged and isolated a voice: a kind of armchair activism focused on the artistic products of other cultures.

Behind these beliefs in the efficacy of folk music and the universality of music lay a faith in the power of popular education. Most students of the American folksong revival have viewed it as an urban intellectual movement with its roots in left-wing political action and theory of the 1930s and its flowering in the popular culture of the 1960s. However it can also be viewed from a broader perspective, as part of an older indigenous intellectual tradition, one which persists today. Its beginnings lie in the nineteenth-century middle-class traditions of the Lyceum and the Chautauqua. Based on the idea that mass education (essential in a democratic state) is best accomplished through a forum that combines entertainment with instruction, the tradition continues today in public broadcasting concepts, college and university extension courses, and a host of other popular educational institutions and concepts. Folklorists in America have been involved in this tradition for a long time.

At the end of the nineteenth century, the study of folksong in America blossomed at Harvard under Francis J. Child and his successor George Lyman Kittredge. Within a few decades, graduates of this elite institution brought the message to the public in the entertainment-with-instruction format. John Lomax started giving illustrated lectures following the publication of his *Cowboy Songs* in 1910 (Lomax 1947:82–84). In the twenties Robert W. Gordon used his column "Old Songs Men Have Sung" in the popular monthly pulp magazine, *Adventure,* as a vehicle that entertained readers by answering questions about old songs while at the same time educating readers as to the songs' significance.[2] Others participated, but these two were especially important because of their role in bringing folksong into the domain of governmental support of culture, through the Archive of Folksong at the Library of Congress.

Gordon founded and served as the first head of the Archive (1928–1933). Although involved in efforts to combine popular and scholarly approaches, he thought of himself primarily as a scientific scholar and directed his work at the Library accordingly. Gordon's successors, John Lomax and his son Alan, saw their role differently. Speaking in 1978 at the Fiftieth Anniversary Symposium of the Archive of Folksong at the Library of Congress, Alan Lomax emphasized the mandate that he and his father perceived when they came to the Archive. They were not there to please the scholars by collecting new examples; rather they were to give the hitherto voiceless folk a means of communicating to the nation. The Lomaxes did this by bringing charismatic folk entertainers like Huddie Ledbetter (Leadbelly) and Woody Guthrie to educated middle-class urban audiences, often in schools.

Alan Lomax maintains that unless scholars use mass media in order to act as advocates for folk cultures, such cultures will be overwhelmed by mass culture and the assimilation processes it embodies. For both Lomaxes, as for Herder, Scott and many others, folksongs became symbols of autochthonous cultures. Preserving and reviving the symbols would help to preserve such cultures. Both Lomaxes attended Harvard and knew of the science of folksong study; but as self-conscious Texans and southerners, their views were colored by a commitment to the preservation of a way of life they saw threatened with change through external forces.

The two Lomaxes shared this view, but lived a generation apart in their political interpretation of cultural data. The elder Lomax had the populist perspective of the early twentieth-century American South; he saw the cowboy as the "knight of the plains," a romantic folk figure who reified the image of a culture, giving dignity and validity to a region struggling against the sweeping changes imposed (it seemed) by industrialization and urban hegemony from other regions. The younger Lomax shared this perception but added to it a new radical perspective, acquired during his education at Harvard in the early thirties; for him, class and race oppression played a part in the struggle.

The Lomaxes did not serve alone; Charles Seeger, Ben Botkin, and others shared their concerns and helped articulate the theories which animated their actions. At the Library of Congress during the New Deal years, the Lomaxes (particularly Alan) sought to educate the American people about the folk music of their various regions and ethnic groups. Alan believed that by putting the symbols of folk culture on display in the mass media, they would be introduced to the urban peoples who had lost or never known of such traditions. The airing of folk culture in the media would also facilitate communications between members of threatened groups, giving them a sense of the validity of their own lives and encouraging them to revitalize their cultures.

Alan Lomax articulated these ideas with characteristic eloquence in his 1968 introduction to the system of musical analysis he calls cantometrics. Speaking of "The Cultural Grey-Out," he stated:

> ... big government, national education, information networks and a worldwide marketing system kill off cultures whose ways do not conform to those of the power center. Our western mass-production and communications systems are inadvertently destroying the languages, traditions, cuisines and creative styles that once gave every people and every locality a distinctive character—indeed their principal reason for living. (1968:4)

This he asserted to be bad because humanity lost a valuable resource, one which added genetic variety to the seed of human creativity:

> Folk and primitive arts, their flinty structure tested at the fireside across the centuries, have always strengthened the more effete traditions of the city. Though somewhat more narrowly dimensioned, these simpler traditions have a germinal vitality and staying power that much cosmopolitan art lacks. (1968:5)

In this statement we can see that, in addition to populist, radical, and evolutionist ideas, Lomax expressed aesthetic values: these arts are flinty, narrowly dimensioned, simple.

Ironically, Lomax believed folk and primitive arts could be saved through the use of the very communications and information networks then killing off the cultures that produced these arts:

> Every culture has a mature and ripened heritage of speaking and singing styles that can immediately find a place on records, radio, film, and television. An "underdeveloped" people feels a renewed sense of significance when its own artists, communicating in genuine style, appear on the powerful and prestigious mass media or begin to use them for their own purposes. Experience teaches that such direct feedback of genuine, uncensored native art to its roots acts upon a culture like water, sunlight, and fertilizer on a barren garden; it begins to bloom and grow again. (1968:9)

The "experience" to which Lomax alludes is his own; he served as one of the principal architects of the process whereby field recordings and folk singers entered the mass media as part of a folksong revival. Indeed, as we will see presently, Pete Steele's "Coal Creek March" represents an early example of this process. But let us note first that—to follow Lomax's verdant metaphor—when the garden blooms anew, it always shows the hand and mind of the gardener. In utilizing mass media as a feedback system, Lomax played an important role in shaping the message, as did all the others who followed his example. The Lomaxes approached the folksingers they recorded with preconceived ideas about folk culture, folksong style and repertoire, and with their own perceptions of audience taste.

At the Library of Congress celebration, Alan Lomax spoke of the months following their first meeting with the black convict singer Leadbelly. Leadbelly's favorite song was Gene Autry's then-recent hit "That Silver Haired Daddy of Mine," and, Lomax noted, it took months to sort out Leadbelly's repertoire so that he was playing the right kinds of song. Bill Ferris reports that black singers in Mississippi have different repertoires for black and white audiences (1970:439–49). Was Leadbelly giving the Lomaxes his "white" songs when they wanted his "black" ones?

Blues enthusiasts, speaking of Afro-American folksingers whose repertoires include much non-blues material, call them "songsters." Did the Lomaxes mold Leadbelly to their ideal of black folksinging? In both cases, preconceptions exist: the singer performs that which he believes the listener wants, and the listener requests that which he believes the singer knows and does best.

In deciding what his informants should sing for the radio, record, and schools, Lomax acted in the manner and spirit of commercial recording company men like Ralph Peer and Art Satherly, radio station men like John Lair and George D. Hay, and the others who, during the twenties through the forties, told working-class black and white southerners what to sing (and frequently also what to wear and say in public) if they wanted to make money.

Lomax spoke of his 1942 Library of Congress recording session with McKinley Morganfield—whom he remembered as a ragged farm boy. The next time Lomax saw him, he was Muddy Waters, driving a Cadillac "a block long." Lomax implied that the Library of Congress recordings had put him on the road to stardom. Robert Palmer's careful tracing of Morganfield/Waters's career demonstrates the inaccuracy of this assertion of cause and effect by Lomax (1981). Waters became a star by working within the rough and tumble world of commercial blues music during the post-war years when it became rhythm-and-blues. Eventually many would share Lomax's perception of Waters as a folk star, but this happened after Waters had paid his dues and become a blues star.

Regardless of the validity of his example, Lomax makes an important argument. He recognized the value of "stardom"—an entertainment category which occurs in the world of mass communications, not in the universe of folk culture—in promoting his method of revival using the mass media. But the kind of feedback Lomax hoped for did not happen very frequently. Why? For one thing, feedback systems which utilized folk music traditions already existed. The blues/rhythm and blues system in which Waters worked, country music, norteño music, polka music, cajun music—each drew folk musicians into a professionalized commercial milieu through which they marketed their music to their own culture. Although he was slow to identify them in print for what they were, Lomax did pioneer at bringing performers from these systems into the elite media—as in 1944 when he brought Brownie McGee and Sonny Terry, Mainer's Mountaineers, The Coon Creek Girls, Woodie Guthrie, and Burl Ives to play together on the BBC. But even at the height of his influence during the forties, when he was working first for the federal Office of War Information and then for Decca Records, he really had little access to or control over these commercialized feedback systems.

Actually, Lomax placed field recordings in the elite and middle-class-oriented educational broadcast and record media. Hence, some of the performers he discovered and recorded (like Guthrie and Leadbelly) became commercial "folk" stars for young, middle-class, urban, college-educated people. Even more frequently specific songs became "hits" when issued on record. Often this hit process occurred when these young people recorded their own performances of folksongs they had learned from the field recordings issued on such educational record labels as those of the Library of

Congress and Folkways, and other labels that followed these during the fifties with the advent of the LP album. These young revivalists copied field-recorded folk music the way Pat Boone copied the rhythm and blues record-ings of Fats Domino. Just as rock and roll developed from rhythm and blues, country, and other earlier forms, a new feedback system emerged within the folk revival. Like rock and roll, it soon grew beyond its models into a complex system, combining entertainment with education. The folk revival commodified already existing folk music, created its own new popular musi-cal and lyrical forms, and stimulated intellectual activity that led to further collection and research. It is from this perspective that we turn to the Pete Steele recording of "Coal Creek March" to see where it fits into this system.

The two Petes—Steele and Seeger

In 1958 Pete Seeger wrote in the notes to his Folkways *Carnegie Hall* album, "I heard the record [Steele's 'Coal Creek March'] twenty years ago, and tried unsuccessfully to play the number.[3] Since the recording was made in 1938 but was not issued by the Library of Congress until 1941, Seeger probably heard Alan Lomax's field recording soon after it was made. In the late thirties Seeger, a Harvard dropout and son of composer, musicologist, and pioneer ethnomusicologist Charles Seeger, was the first to work as a volunteer (and, briefly, as a paid assistant) at the Library's Archive of Folk Song. He had been exposed to the five-string banjo and had travelled extensively in the rural South learning how to play it from old-timers. At the time he pioneered; many followed. We can imagine Lomax and Seeger—the dynamic young field collector and the enthusiastic young musician—listening to the newly made field recording (did they make a working dub?) the way Ralph Peer and his cohorts at Victor listened to their new Carter Family and Jimmie Rodgers recordings in the fall of 1927. By 1941 Seeger had even participated in some field recording trips with Lomax.

During the 1940s Seeger became well-known and popular within the small group of urbanites, mostly in New York City, who followed "folk songs." As a member of the Almanac Singers and the Weavers he introduced old-time five-string banjo to a new generation, region, and social class. Even though he was unable to play "Coal Creek March," his aesthetic response to the Steele recording was communicated to and shared by his disciples. In 1949 one young revivalist banjo player, a Chicagoan named Fleming Brown, recorded a version of "Coal Creek March" performed by Doc Hopkins. A native of Harlan County in Eastern Kentucky, Hopkins had learned the piece between 1908 and 1924 from local musicians. At the time Brown recorded him, Hopkins had just retired from a long career as a country musician; he is best known as a member of the Cumberland Ridge Runners on the National Barn Dance broadcast from WLS in Chicago.

Hopkins, like his WLS compatriots John Lair and Bradley Kincaid aware of and interested in the traditional elements in his repertoire, presented the "Coal Creek March" as a song about a strike conflict which involved troops; he did not in his spoken introduction to the tune make reference to convict labor. Subsequently, Brown played for Seeger his recording of Hopkins' version, which contains sound effects (drums, bugle calls, barking dogs), a running commentary, and several verses of song. In the notes to the 1958 Folkways album mentioned previously, Seeger compared Hopkins' performance with Pete Steele's. He called Steele's version ". . . but a folk fragment, since others play a much more extended version (not necessarily any better!)."

Two ideas are discernible in Seeger's reaction to Doc Hopkins's version of "Coal Creek March": 1) the common tendency to regard the version of a folkloric item (game, song, story) that one learns first as the "correct" or "best" one, valued as original and, perhaps, more authentic and, 2) the aesthetic value judgement embodied in Seeger's statement that Steele's version is a "fine folk fragment, clean and high, reminding one of the waters of an icy mountain brook," while Hopkins' additional segments (closer in many ways to the typical programmatic folk versions) are "rather pretentious virtuoso sound effects" (1962:18). Value here is placed on imagined simplicity of style and presentation.

A similar repertoire and style evaluation motivated the Lomaxes to wean Leadbelly away from "That Silver Haired Daddy of Mine." Just as a sentimental, subjective, newly-composed song by a white singing cowboy from Oklahoma was not considered appropriate in the repertoire of a black folksinger from Louisiana, so a Kentucky banjo picker was not supposed to be using musical techniques associated with nineteenth-century middle-class pop music. The conventional wisdom regarding "sound effects" had been stated by ethnomusicology pioneer George Herzog: "Folk music in general appears to be abstract in this sense; it is very rarely programmatic or representative . . . authentic folk singing does not use our hackneyed expressive devices" (1950:1040).

While we rightly regard Herzog as one of the first scholars to advocate functional or contextual approaches to folk song and music, in this instance he incorporates aesthetic values into his definition. Let us look at his statement closely. He articulates, in a few pejorative words, an underlying assumption of the intellectual tenets of early twentieth-century art criticism. Like the New Critics in literature, Herzog says that we need look no further than the content and form of the genre in order to recognize authentic examples. Essentially Richard M. Dorson did the same in his coinage of "fakelore": he contrasted the cute, folksy, and inauthentic with the raw, folk, and authentic. To be sure, Dorson stressed the scholarly distinctions between the social grounding of folklore and the individualistic (and commercialized) dimensions of popular culture to which fakelore belonged. But his reiteration of pejorative descriptors "cute" and "folksy" in connection with fakelore maintained a strong covert aesthetic value dimension in his definition. The trained mind, he seemed to say, can distinguish fakelore from folklore merely by hearing or looking at a text. Dorson, like Herzog and Lomax (whose cantometrics also strives to define folk culture in terms of content and form), saw folkloric authenticity embodied in flinty, simple, raw stuff.

This critical stance involves two elements, both common to twentieth-century perceptions of art: 1) the tendency to separate the artist from his or her product. Truly authentic art speaks for itself, goes the argument; we need not bother to ask how the personality of the artist speaks through it. Folklore fit well into this frame of reference since it was thought to have a strong communal dimension: the folk artist spoke for the community; 2) the post-Victorian reaction against the sentimental, the subjective, and the complex in all forms of art, and a consequent valuing of the non-sentimental, objective and simple. Hemingway's terse dialogue and bold description; Picasso's flat, stark surfaces: both served as artistic models of the time. Both turned to exotic folk culture for reinforcement—Picasso to the art of Africa, Hemingway to the outdoor life in the Caribbean, Spain and Africa.

Those who led the way in specializing in folklore studies in the 1930s and 1940s brought to the discipline their own aesthetic values—often expressed, as we have seen, in a covert or unexamined manner—which shaped their ideas about the aesthetic dimensions of the materials they studied. Pete Seeger, an educated enthusiast and, like Lomax and Dorson, a Harvard student during the thirties, found such ideas easy to understand and accept because they were the common coin of the time in intellectual circles. That folk music ought to be "abstract" and simple no doubt seemed proper to Seeger also because he grew up in the family of a composer and musicologist at a time when post-romantic and baroque music held sway. His preference for a "fine folk fragment" over "pretentious virtuoso sound effects" reveals something of the aesthetic which enabled urban intellectuals to "appreciate" exotic folk arts. However, as we shall see presently, Seeger assigned his own programmatic valuation to Steele's piece when he described it as "clean and high, reminding one of the waters of an icy mountain brook."

Clearly, by 1958 for Seeger and his emulators, fans, and folksong enthusiasts in general, Steele's version of "Coal Creek March" was the standard one. Why was this so? For one thing, although an early hillbilly recording of the tune existed, it soon went out of print. For many years Steele's performance was the only one available on record. When Tom Paley, one of the first young urban banjo virtuosos to follow in Seeger's path, recorded the tune in 1953 for Elektra Records, his version basically repeated that of Steele.[4] Paley's record, though not a big seller, became important in the revival, containing a number of instrumental and vocal pieces which were much copied at the time. Recently Roy Berkeley recalled the impact of that record: ". . . [it] immediately became a classic, a textbook for the small-but-growing community of the urban folksong revival" (1978:28).

Lee Haring, another member of the community at that time, recalls seeing Paley perform "Coal Creek March." Lee noted that in order to play the piece in the key of E (Steele's recording is slightly above E) Paley had to capo his banjo high up the neck at the ninth fret and play in the key of E using G tuning. Rarely do banjoists use a capo that far up the neck; in this instance Paley tried to copy Steele and did not know the proper tuning for the piece.[5]

Thus, in spite of the fact that the proper tuning for the piece could not be deciphered from the recording, it was still popular enough to be copied and recorded. This reflects aesthetics of the time already discussed: the product (the sound of the recording) and not the style (the details of performance practice) emerged as primary. Very likely, during the fifties Paley's recording sold more copies than Steele's. Seeger and Paley and the other revivalists served as translators, agents of acculturation, and salesmen of the fashionable exotic. Indirectly, they extended the impact of Steele's Library of Congress recording.

Other revivalists also extended the impact of that record. In Indianapolis, Art Rosenbaum, teenage son of a doctor, became interested in the five-string banjo. Influenced by Pete Seeger on records with the Almanac singers, Tom Paley's album, and various albums which reissued hillbilly and blues recordings as folk music, he began playing the five-string banjo: "Actually, I didn't start in earnest until I began college in the East; Columbia University in 1956. I heard Pete Seeger give a concert and he talked about Pete Steele" (Brislin 1982:5).

The following summer Rosenbaum and Ed Kahn, a high school classmate from Indianapolis, went to Hamilton, Ohio, and looked up Steele. Steele had sold his banjo recently and had not played in months. Once he had Kahn's banjo in his hands, the first tunes he played for his visitors were ". . . the in-

strumentals that had won him fame through his Library of Congress recordings." On a subsequent visit Kahn recorded Steele; Folkways, in 1958, released
an album of Steele and his wife. In the notes to this record, Kahn refers to
Steele's "Coal Creek March"as "this fantastic instrumental."[6] It was through
the "rediscovery" of Steele by Rosenbaum and Kahn that Seeger, in 1958,
could write: "Finally last year I met Mr. Steele. . . . The visit also permitted
Seeger to describe the tuning and picking style that Steele used in performing
the song.[7]

As soon as he learned the tune, Seeger added it to his concert repertoire.
He introduced it much as he does in notes to his Folkways *Carnegie Hall*
album, telling about how he had heard the record, wanted to learn the tune,
and had been unable to figure it out until recently when he met Steele.
Seeger's introduction to the tune served to validate the authenticity of his
performance while testifying to the tune's exotic qualities. It also reiterated a
theme central to his ideas about folk music as set forth in his concerts: go to
his sources rather than copy him. Both Kahn and Rosenbaum followed this
message and subsequently became active collectors and scholars of folk music
and song.

While urging his passive audience members to become active field
researchers, Seeger at the same time made it unnecessary for his banjo-playing
followers to actually go to Steele, or even to Steele's recordings, to learn the
"Coal Creek March."[8] He published a banjo tablature to the piece in two
places—the notes to his 1958 Folkways *Carnegie Hall* LP and his 1962 Hargail
Press publication, *The Goofing-off Suite.*[9]

And although Seeger made a point of saying that he had modeled his
performance of the tune on that of Steele, it differed from Steele's on a
number of levels. When musically active, Steele performed the piece at his
home and the homes of friends, in a context reflecting the oral/aural mode in
which he had learned it.[10] Seeger presented the song from the concert stage,
on commercial records, and in a music book, using mass media techniques for
purposes of entertainment and education. In introducing the song, Steele set
it in context with a narrative about a coal mine explosion and the deaths
which resulted. Steele had heard a traditional legend with the song, one
which conveyed a sense of danger and tragedy, part of the consciousness of all
who lived and worked in the eastern Kentucky coalfields. Seeger's narrative
introduction associated it with the events surrounding the 1891 strike and the
convict-labor issue. He knew of these events through his reading knowledge
of the history of the American labor movement. Such reading, linked to his
vision of the bloody struggle in which oppressed miners responded in magnificent music, made the tune an ideological metaphor for him. Finally, in

To the left, Pete Steele, with banjo and wife, Lilly, in front of their Hamilton, Ohio, home in 1958. Ed Kahn's photograph appeared in the brochure to the album of their music he edited for Folkways Records. To the right, above, professional photographer Allan W. Kahn posed icons of labor, home, and music in his studio to capture succinctly the major themes in the album produced by his son Ed.

terms of the performance itself, Seeger's version was, as he himself stated, in "fingering and arrangement, not exactly [Steele's]."[11]

In his instructions accompanying the tablature in the Folkways brochure, Seeger suggests that although the tune is played with the banjo's strings in a D tuning, "it sounds better if the capo is moved up . . . so that the piece actually sounds in the key of F or F#. The higher key gives it the feeling of an icy mountain brook." Playing the tune in this higher key accentuated the tune's contours—a series of descending arpeggios in the first section and of ascending and descending arpeggios in the second part. It is easy to hear where Seeger gets the aural image of an icy (high pitched) mountain brook (descending and ascending arpeggios). Such an art-music programmatic metaphor, an interpretation involving a knowledge of musical notation and theory, probably had the same vividness for him that "pretentious sound effects" had for Kentucky banjo players. Whatever the case, the fact remains that Seeger adapted the piece to his intellectual tradition, altering both the musical form and the narrative imagery that accompanied it. His alterations reflect a conscious aesthetic, based on a viewpoint that places the tune in an art-music milieu. Also, "Coal Creek" sounds like "Cold (Col') Creek," another way of saying "Icy . . . brook." Did Seeger make a programmatic pun?

If Seeger had only recorded the song and published his version in a book of banjo-tune tablatures, his contribution to its popularity would have been limited. But by 1958 he toured and gave concerts extensively and this tune became a regular part of his repertoire. The Weavers' commercial success had been cut short in 1951, when major radio and television networks blacklisted the group. The group disbanded until 1955, and Seeger turned to solo concerts and recordings as a means of livelihood. Most of his concerts took place in big cities or college and university towns, mainly in the northeast, upper midwest and far west. His political reputation, reinforced by the blacklist, precluded wide acceptance but it also enhanced his appeal to those whose political sympathies lay left of center; he symbolized opposition to HUAC and the McCarthyites. By the end of the decade he had a growing audience of folk music fans who liked him in spite of, as well as for his politics. One of Seeger's fans, Dick Reuss, made his life work the study of "left" music. As fellow graduate students in Folklore at Indiana University we spent many hours outside of class discussing revival issues.

Seeger marshalled considerable abilities as an entertainer, but his performances always included a didactic element. He presented songs and tunes as having not only artistic but also social values. He often contrasted items in his repertoire with contemporary popular music, which he characterized as sentimental, romantic, and not dealing with the realities of everyday life as did folksongs. In doing so he maintained the aesthetic stance discussed earlier.

It is in this context that Seeger offered the story and tune of "Coal Creek March." His presentation, on the several occasions when I saw it in 1958 and 1959, was essentially similar to what he wrote in the notes to *Pete Seeger at Carnegie Hall*. He talked about the strike, described the "March," alluding briefly to the more complex versions of the tune. Then he spoke of hearing the Library of Congress recording and of being unable to figure out the tune until he met Steele recently. Remarking that people should not copy him but should go to the people he copied, he made this an example: if you want to learn the tune properly, go to Hamilton, Ohio. Seeger made field workers out of those who took him seriously, especially the banjo pickers.

And Seeger made Pete Steele's "Coal Creek March" a popular tune, we might even say a hit, within the folk revival. In 1961 Elektra Records produced an album of performances by urban revival five-string banjo virtuosos. The LP included Art Rosenbaum's dazzling performance of "Coal Creek March." In the liner notes to the album, folklorist Lee Haring called the tune "celebrated." A decade later Archie Green echoed Haring's evaluation in a note on the tune in the brochure accompanying Doc Hopkins's album. Green called the tune "a 'folksong revival' favorite," and stressed the role of performers like Pete Seeger, Tom Paley, Fleming Brown, and Art Rosenbaum in creating this popularity.[12]

The popularity had two results. In the short term, it led to the currency of the tune within the repertoires of folk revival banjo players. Seeger's tablature and his concert rhetoric about folk music as home-made stuff accessible to all encouraged people to try it. From my own experience as a college-student revivalist during the late fifties, I recall that all of us who were learning banjo played "Coal Creek March." The second result of this popularity emerged more slowly but had in the long run a greater impact. It came from Seeger's urging his followers to seek out the originals. Not every folk revival banjo picker became a field researcher. Only those most committed to the ideology and the aesthetics of the movement, like Rosenbaum and Kahn, took up the mantle.

Henry Glassie suggests persuasively that our perception of variation in Anglo-American folksong has been skewed because of collectors' persistent efforts to force half-forgotten ballads from the memories of singers who had such songs in their inactive repertoire (1970:32–33). Such was the result of the influence of the Child collection on folksong study in the early years of this century. A similar process occurred when folksong revivalists like Kahn and Rosenbaum revisited Steele.

Likewise, Pete Seeger's younger half-brother Mike stumbled onto Doc Boggs's version of the tune while recording Boggs's life history. Boggs, a native of southwestern Virginia who had worked in the mines and performed on hillbilly records in the late twenties, retained the tune, but as an inactive part of his repertoire, "one of the first chording pieces." It was of great interest to Mike Seeger, who is, like Pete, an entertainer but also a serious student of American folk music who has done field research in a number of regions and has occasionally taught workshops and full-length folk music courses at colleges. Archie Green says Boggs responded to "Seeger's interest in the piece during 1963" by boning up on its "history" from his relatives, and several months later, recording it. It became part of his concert repertoire. As Green points out, this would not have happened if Seeger had not stimulated Boggs' interest in coal-mining lore (1971:49–51).

A further example comes from my own research. In 1961, I met Shorty Sheehan, a native of Johnson City, Tennessee, living in Franklin, Indiana. Shorty, well-known in central and southern Indiana as a fiddler and country music bandleader, had played the five-string banjo in his youth. I persuaded him to record what he remembered of his banjo repertoire. Of all the tunes he played, he recalled "Coal Creek March" with the most difficulty. He had been reminded of it because recently he had met Art Rosenbaum and heard Art play the tune. When he mentioned this to me I excitedly recalled what I knew of the tune and its story from the Seeger and Steele recordings. Being an eager folklore student doing his first "collecting," I urged him to play it for my recorder. Shorty performed the imperfectly remembered fragment, using my banjo, after first making me turn off the recorder so he could practice. Like Boggs with Mike Seeger, and Steele with Kahn and Rosenbaum, this was a recording situation in which the performer attempted to adapt to a new and special audience whose requests could only be met with items from the inactive repertoire. It is not coincidental that in each of the foregoing examples, the collectors were "revival" banjo players themselves.

These examples help to explain why we know so much about "Coal Creek March" today, but they also illustrate the way in which the most committed of the young revivalists began to move toward a new aesthetic perspective. In searching for song and music, they found singers and musicians. Their aesthetic involvement underwent a shift of focus from appreciation of the artistic product to fascination with the life of the producer. Developing skills as field workers, those who followed seriously Pete Seeger's advice to take to the field increasingly found the product to be secondary and the producer primary. This new set of aesthetic values is not so much articulated as exemplified in the work of this generation, whether folklorist, entertainer or artist.

In the early sixties Ed Kahn began graduate studies in the Folklore and Mythology Program at UCLA, where he completed a dissertation on the famous country music group, the Carter Family. His focus was biographical; he emphasized how these individuals, functioning as producers in a new medium, received, shaped, and retransmitted tradition.

Art Rosenbaum became a painter and completed a master's degree in Fine Arts at Columbia. He continued to be active as a musician, performing on records and at festivals. At the same time he did field work and acted as a presenter of his informants at folk festivals. After teaching in the Fine Arts department at the University of Iowa, he moved to the University of Georgia where, in his own words:

> I've worked out a project where I've been . . . pulling my art out of the field work. I've been doing paintings of people like the Yeller brothers and other musicians whom I've recorded, worked with and presented. (Brislin 1982:7–8)

This has resulted in gallery shows which present his field recordings and paintings, and his wife Margo's photos of informants. In 1983 the University of Georgia published a book version of the shows, entitled *Folk Visions and Voices*.

Mike Seeger's career has been more directly in the field of entertainment but, like Rosenbaum, Seeger has emphasized his informants in various ways. Not only has he acted as a presenter at festivals, he has also collected and edited albums of documentary recordings of a number of folk performers. Indeed his Dock Boggs album was one such activity. Even in his activities as a performer, Seeger has stressed the importance of various personal performance styles he recreates, tying these to the individuals for whom he is a self-styled advocate "fighting to regain an audience for lots of traditional musicians" (Hatlo 1979:15).

Finally my own research as a folklorist has been in the realm of establishing and documenting certain aspects of the relationships between folk and country musics by showing how such musics operate within the lives of individuals. To do this I have worked with models of individual behavior based on biographical data. A number of other folklorists with revival backgrounds—Ellen Stekert, Roger Abrahams, Sandy Ives, Dick Reuss, and Barre Toelken come to mind—have also worked extensively in the biographical mode, but other folklorists who were not active revivalists have also worked in this domain.[13]

To the extent that biography and the study of the individual now take precedence over the study of the folkloric product, the old aesthetic values have been turned upside down. *Humanitas* has replaced *communitas* as the focus. In academic folklore study the personal experience narrative has become one of the most studied forms. Similarly "oral history" has made proletarian and ethnic biography a popular commodity. The arts in general have turned away from the abstract and simple: representational paintings (like those of the Pre-Raphaelites) are in fashion; fiction is dominated by non-fictional models with a heavily biographical slant. Explanations of broad trends such as this are never simple, but surely this turning away from the product reflects the impact of modern media technology. If we can't purchase an art work we can (it seems) xerox, tape record, videotape or otherwise copy it. Because so many artistic products can be easily reproduced, we tend to seek artistic values not in products but in their producers. The contemporary approach reflects a suspicion of materialism and seeks authenticity in human character.

The evidence I have presented shows that the folksong revival in the U.S. during the period from 1930 to 1965 shared with other art-oriented movements an aesthetic perspective that shaped its perception of culture. Intellectuals—scholars and revivalists alike—chose from folk culture that which best fit their preconceptions of art. Now a later generation of intellectuals, though inspired by the earlier revival, has developed a different perception of artistic values in folk culture. And like the older one, the new biographical aesthetic is shared by academics and revivalists. I mean not to denigrate such facts, but just to point out that it is important for us to be aware of our own perspective.

If we think of historical processes in dialectical terms then the emphasis on biography is but the new orthodoxy and surely the next generation is shaping a response to it which will lead to new perspectives gathered to illustrate a different aesthetic. If this is indeed happening then we would do well to reflect on the way in which Seeger's metaphor of the icy mountain brook served as a catalyst in the shaping of a new aesthetic. Was there a cause-effect relationship? That I can't say, but I have no doubt that the "Coal Creek March" has taken us a long way from the minehead in Tennessee in the name of art.[14]

Memorial University
St. John's, Newfoundland

Notes

1. The recordings by Stringbean include a 45-RPM single, Cullman 335, and an album, *Going to the Grand Ole Opry,* Ovation 1926. The latter was first listed in *Country Sales Newsletter* 91 (Jan. 1978). Jimmie Skinner and his banjo-playing brother Esmer, born in Madison County, Kentucky, and living in Hamilton, Ohio (home since 1937 for Pete Steele, a key figure in this tune's history) when they recorded in the early thirties for Gennett, learned their version of the song from Marion Underwood. See Ivan M. Tribe, "Jimmie Skinner, Country Singer, Bluegrass Composer, Record Retailer," *Bluegrass Unlimited* 11/9 (March 1977):34.

2. Gordon's "popular-scholarly approach" is described in Debora G. Kodish, *Good Friends and Bad Enemies: Robert Winslow Gordon and the Study of American Folksong.* (Urbana: University of Illinois Press, 1986).

3. Notes, *Pete Seeger at Carnegie Hall, with Sonny Terry.* Folkways FA2412, 1958.

4. Paley included it in a medley entitled "The Banjo Pieces," saying "The 'Coal Creek March' . . . commemorates the great mine disaster in Coal Creek, Tennessee which killed 900 miners." Elektra EKL–12, *Folk Songs from the Southern Appalachian Mountains,* produced by Kenneth S. Goldstein.

5. Personal communication from Lee Haring, Salt Lake City, 14 October 1978.

6. Brochure, *Banjo Tunes and Songs.* Folkways FS3828, 1958.

7. Notes, *Pete Seeger at Carnegie Hall.* Folkways FA2412, 1958.

8. Pete Seeger, *How to Play the 5-String Banjo,* 3rd ed. (Beacon, New York: The Author 1962). In the third edition, Seeger refers to "Coal Creek March" three times. The reader is told of the Hargail *Goofing-Off Suite* tablature for it in the section on D-tuning (22); and in Appendix 7, "Phonograph Records" (72), it is listed with "top choices" along with other Library of Congress Recordings. Here he also mentions the Steele Folkways album.

9. The transcription and tablature for the piece given in the Hargail book differ from those presented in the Folkways notes in that the "B" and "C" sections are transposed.

10. Steele made at least one concert appearance, at Indiana University in 1965. It was not very successful; see Paul R. Pell, "Pete Steele: A Concert Review," *Blue Yodel* (Indiana University Folksong Club Newsletter) 3/4 (April 1965):11. A recording of the concert is on deposit at the Indiana University Archives of Traditional Music, accession number 65–217–F.

11. Notes, *Pete Seeger at Carnegie Hall.* Folkways FA2412, 1958.

12. Brochure with Birch 1945, *Doc Hopkins* 1965:2. Incidentally, although the recording was made in 1965, as Wolfe indicates, the LP (and notes) were not issued until ca. 1969–70.

13. The popularity of the biographical approach is recognized and analyzed in Jeff Todd Titon's "The Life Story," *Journal of American Folklore* 93 (1980):276–92.

14. Thanks to Archie Green, Debora Kodish, Martin Lovelace, Sandy Paton, Bob Pinson, and D. K. Wilgus.

References Cited

Abrahams, Roger D. 1970. "Creativity, Individuality and the Traditional Singer." *Studies in the Literary Imagination* 3:5–34.

Berkeley, Roy. 1978. Review of "Tom Paley, Hard Luck Papa" (Kicking Mule KM 201), *Old Time Music* 28:28.

Brislin, Richard W. 1982. "Art Rosenbaum." *Banjo Newsletter* 10/2:5.

Ferris, William R., Jr. 1970. "Racial Repertoires among Blues Performers." *Ethnomusicology* 14:439–49.

Glassie, Henry. 1970. "'Take That Night Train to Selma': An Excursion to the Outskirts of Scholarship." In *Folksongs and their Makers,* edited by Henry Glassie, Edward D. Ives, and John Szwed, 32–33. Bowling Green, Ohio: Bowling Green University Popular Culture Press.

Goldstein, Kenneth S. 1966. "Robert 'Fiddler' Beers and His Songs: A Study of the Revival of a Family Tradition." In *Two Penny Ballads and Four Dollar Whiskey,* edited by Kenneth S. Goldstien and Robert H. Byington, 47–48. Hatboro: Folklore Associates.

Green, Archie. 1971. *Only a Miner.* Urbana: University of Illinois Press.

Hatlo, Jim. 1979. "Mike Seeger: Cherishing His Music and Its Traditions." *Frets* 1/1:15.

Herzog, George. 1950. "Song: Folk Song: And the Music of Folk Song." In the *Standard Dictionary of Folklore, Mythology and Legend.* New York: Funk and Wagnalls.

Lomax, Alan. 1968. *Folk Style and Culture.* Washington: American Association for the Advancement of Science.

Lomax, John A. 1947. *Adventures of a Ballad Hunter.* New York: Macmillan.

Palmer, Robert. 1981. *Deep Blues.* New York: Viking.

Rosenbaum, Art. 1983. *Folk Visions and Voices.* Athens: University of Georgia Press.

Seeger, Pete. 1962. *The Goofing-Off Suite.* New York: Hargail Music Press.

Wolfe, Charles K. 1976. "New Light on 'The Coal Creek March.'" *JEMF Quarterly* 12:1–8.

Rebecca B. Schroeder and
Donald M. Lance

John L. Handcox: "There Is Still Mean Things Happening"

In 1979 H. L. Mitchell, co-founder of the Southern Tenant Farmers Union, dedicated his autobiography to "John Handcox . . . the young black share-cropper, union organizer and composer of folk songs of the Southern Tenant Farmers Union in 1935–37," and took his title from one of Handcox's songs:

> *Mean Things Happening in This Land* is dedicated to John L. Handcox and the hundreds of other black, brown and white sharecroppers and farm workers who laid their lives on the line in making their real contributions to this movement of theirs only to disappear later into the barrios and ghettos of the cities. . . . (Mitchell 1979:v)

Later in the book Mitchell reports that one day in 1935 Handcox, at that time living in St. Francis County in eastern Arkansas, had appeared in the office of the Southern Tenant Farmers Union (STFU) in Memphis with a four-line poem written "in pencil on ruled tablet paper," and asked him to print it in "our paper," *The Sharecroppers' Voice:*

> When a sharecropper dies
> he is buried in a box
> Without any necktie,
> and without any sox.
> (Mitchell 1979:111–12)

In the STFU the thirty-one-year-old Handcox had found a cause in which he could believe and one to which he could devote his talents in song and verse. He had learned about the union from a friend, who had heard about it at a local cotton gin. "I said, 'Man that's the thing we need!'"[1] He wrote to the STFU for information and began to go from house to house, and plantation to plantation, trying to organize, finding inspiration for his songs in the conditions and events of the time. Born on the family farm in Monroe County, Arkansas, about two miles southwest of Brinkley on the road to Clarendon,

February 5, 1904, Handcox got interested in poetry when he was about twelve and his father brought home a book of poems by Paul Lawrence Dunbar. John started writing poems about the kids in school—"Something to make people laugh" (Miller 1985:6). But he had not found much to laugh about as he grew up on the forty acres of land south of Brinkley that his father and uncle had purchased. They cleared some of the home place and farmed it, but his father also farmed other land in the area, not as a sharecropper but as a renter who owned his own mules and tools. Handcox's father died in 1921 or 1922 after suffering a broken back when his team of mules panicked and threw him off the wagon. He was wedged between the wagon and a stump and died within a short time.

John had to quit school in the ninth grade to take care of his mother and his younger brothers and sisters. The year after his father's death, the family moved to St. Francis County, where he rented some rich bottom land on the St. Francis River about twelve miles southeast of Forrest City. Having learned from his father's frugal practices, he did not accommodate to the prevailing custom of living on credit advanced by the landowner. He asked for itemized bills for his few purchases and receipts for payments. At the end of the year, he had to use these statements and receipts to prevent the landlord's bookkeeper from cheating him. The result of these unorthodox practices was that after only one year on the plantation the manager told him: "Handcox, you all are good workers and everything. But we can't make no money off of you. You don't trade enough" (RBS 10-17-89). Handcox then rented 150 acres nearby and began to make home brew to sell. Fishing, growing vegetables, buying in bulk—flour in barrels and lard in forty-five pound cans—as his father had done during World War I, he made a clear crop that year. But he knew that some of his neighbors, who had been there longer than he was old, had never been out of debt. The union seemed to offer a way to help them.

Encouraged by Mitchell to continue song writing and organizing, Handcox composed songs about the problems facing the sharecroppers and sang them at meetings in churches and homes:

> The songs I wrote was to try to tell the laboring people, the ones where I was trying to organize, to try to reveal to them the things that they was doing, you know, and it was forced on them. It wasn't because they had asked for it but it was being forced on them by the landlords. And to show that they deserve a better life than what they were getting. They were producing everything and getting nothing. (RBS 10-17-89)

Remembering those days in Arkansas on a 1989 visit to Columbia, Missouri, Handcox conceded that it was a mission that required the courage of his convictions. The hostility toward black sharecroppers who joined the union or wrote to Washington about the plight of the plantation workers was so great that Roosevelt administration officials in Washington felt it necessary to take precautions in replying to letters from the South. According to Cedric Belfrage, when Claude Williams visited the Relief Administration's black director in the mid-1930s he found:

> [He] had a mountain of protest letters from Arkansas Negroes. He did not have to be told that each letter represented the risk of death taken by the writer. He said that when he replied to them he wrote on plain stationery because he knew it was not healthy for a Southern Negro to receive mail from the meddling Yankee authorities. (Belfrage 1941:217)

Handcox says, "You've got to believe in what you're trying to do. That brings about the courage." Meetings had to be "kind of covered up":

> . . . because the landlord hisself didn't have to do the dirty work. All they had to do was tell some of their people that was on their place and they would do it for them.
> Q: Black people as well as white people?
> A: Black people as well as white people.
>   (RBS 10-17-89)

He found some of those he was trying to help "on both sides of the fence." And then there were some "that wouldn't let they shirttail touch they back until they go to the old boss and tell him what was going on. That was the worst part of it."

Handcox's activity as a labor organizer in Arkansas came to an end in the spring of 1936 during a large strike that spread over three counties in the southeastern part of the state. The spring had been dry, weeds and grass didn't grow, and consequently there was less need for hoe-hands than usual. On May 18 the STFU called a strike; union members began marches through the plantation area to call attention to the plight of the workers without jobs, and J. Marion Futrell, governor of Arkansas, sent the National Guard to break up the strike (Mitchell 1987:37). Anti-unionists found out which tenant farmers and laborers were members of the union or union sympathizers and went into their homes and "rolled up their belongings and put them beside the road." The sight of people being evicted from their homes was the image in Handcox's mind when he wrote "There Is Mean Things Happening in This Land" (DML 8-1-89; 8-9-89).

His own situation became perilous. A white friend warned his wife and mother that there were plans to hang him:

> I was in the river, fishing, and my momma and my wife come running down, hollering for me. Their voice was so distressful I just knew something happen

with the kids. But my momma said, "John. You better get away from here." You see, a friend of mine, a white fellow, he'd been up at the store and overheard them say, "That nigger John Handcox, we gonna hang him. We got the rope and we got the limb, all we want is him." (Miller 1985:1, 1986:17)

At first he wanted to stay and fight on, but was persuaded to leave so his family would not get into trouble. The threat of "the rope and the limb" remained strong in Handcox's memory; he recited the rhyming summation of the story in two of the telephone interviews and on several occasions during his visit to Columbia. He said he knew that if he didn't leave a lot of [black] people would be killed (RBS 10-17-89).

I went over on the highway. At that time they just had a gravel road. Two lanes, one going, one coming. I caught a Greyhound. I caught that puppy to Memphis. (Miller 1985:1, 1986:18)

Though he dedicates *Mean Things Happening in This Land* to Handcox, Mitchell actually writes only briefly of the organizer whom he calls one of the "great voices of the disinherited," probably because Handcox for a number of reasons discontinued his association with the STFU in the late 1930s. Mitchell numbered Handcox among those who "had laid their lives on the line" for their cause, "only to disappear later into the barrios and ghettos of the cities." Chapter 8 of *Mean Things*, "Voices of the Disinherited," is mainly comprised of letters Mitchell received in 1935–1936 but is introduced by a four-line stanza from a Handcox song:

> Hungry, hungry are we
> Just as hungry as hungry can be
> We don't get nothin' for our labor
> So hungry, hungry are we.

The chapter closes with a three-paragraph tribute to "The Sharecropper Troubador" and includes the four-line verse Handcox first brought him for publication in *The Sharecroppers' Voice* (Mitchell 1979:111–12). The book has altogether three songs or poems by Handcox and fragments of other songs are quoted. We are left with a powerful but sketchy impression of "The Sharecropper Troubador" and his work in the book for which his song-poem provided the title.

In telephone and personal interviews with Handcox, half-century-old memories of the chronology of his escape from Arkansas to Memphis, his journey to Missouri, and other travels after leaving Arkansas (1936–1939) remained elusive. However, Handcox recalled many aspects of those days very vividly. He stayed in Memphis for "about a month" and then went to Charleston, Missouri, to the plantation of Thad Snow (1881–1955). Most land owners were hostile to the Tenant Farmers movement, but Mitchell reported that Snow, who owned a large cotton plantation in southeast Missouri, actually invited the union to send an organizer.

According to Mitchell, Handcox was chosen to go (Mitchell 1979:349). In the first telephone interview, Handcox did not recall specifically being sent by the STFU, but he did remember that Mitchell had asked him if he wanted to go to Missouri to get farther away from Arkansas. While there he could help in the organization of local chapters of the union. In a 1990 interview, he mentioned that J. R. Butler had also asked him whether he would go to Missouri. He recalled that he was in Charleston from June 1936 until the early spring of 1937 (DML 9-30-90). During that time he wrote a poem to Thad Snow. In a prefatory note to "Out on Mr. Snow's Farm," which he included in a collection of "Songs and Verses from the Movement" in his autobiography, Mitchell said that Handcox sent him the poem with a request to "Please fix this up and send Mr. Snow a copy":

Out on Mr. Snow's Farm

or

The Kind of Man We Like to Meet

Early the second Monday in June
I walked up to Mr. Thad Snow's Home, all alone
And introduced myself to Mr. Snow
One of the best men in SE-MO I know.
 He says to me, something for labor ought to be done
And you are perfectly welcome to go on my farm,
He pointed me out some of the hands in the field,
Told me to talk with them and see how they feel
Then he asked me what else he could do
To help put our labor movement thru
I told him his help would be much if he didn't object
For the labor on his farm to join our union as such.
I walked over Mr. Snow's farm in all ease
For I knew that Mr. Snow was well pleased.
I sang, I talked and rejoiced as I went,
For I knew I had gotten Mr. Snow's consent.
This is the kind of men we need you know.
Men that are in sympathy with their labor, like Mr. Snow.
      (Mitchell 1979:349)[2]

Snow, a native of Indiana and a successful alfalfa farmer there, had pioneered in the southeast Missouri Delta, or as he soon began to call it, "Swampeast Missouri," in 1910, when, as he said, "it was the last frontier in the Midwest," a raw and untamed swampland (1954:2). About 1924, the

Above, John L. Handcox, 1988. Photograph by Steve Castillo. Left, Thad Snow (seated), with Owen Whitfield, ca. 1955, at book signing for *From Missouri.*

"cotton culture" of the South began to move toward Missouri, which was thought to be above the "boll weevil line," and with the cotton came the black "cotton croppers." In *From Missouri,* his autobiography, published in 1954, Snow describes the changes that occurred when the black workers came into the area and some of the farmers of southeast Missouri became "rarin' back" planters. As he had noted early in his book, it was necessary "to know how rich we are in order to understand why we have so many more very poor people than other areas of the Midwest" (4).

According to a letter of October 20, 1934, to Victor Anderson, special attorney for the Agricultural Adjustment Act, Snow was at that time growing three- to four-hundred acres of cotton and had twenty sharecroppers, all black. In *From Missouri,* Snow describes a variety of difficulties suffered by farmers in the Missouri Delta, including droughts, floods, the planters' diversions of government payments intended for the sharecroppers, short-lived cotton picker strikes, and the hardships and injustices that led to the Sharecroppers' Roadside Demonstration in southeast Missouri in 1939 (227–32). However, he does not mention John Handcox's visit to his plantation. Snow's wife died in the spring of 1937, and he himself became seriously ill; when he did not improve after a year, he was advised to travel to a better climate and spent over a year in the Southwest and Mexico with his younger daughter.

As Snow travelled, he carried with him his concern about what was happening to the tenant farmers and black sharecroppers. On his way back to Missouri, he took the opportunity to talk with farmers and county Agricultural Adjustment committeemen in several states:

> I . . . satisfied myself that the landowners of the Delta had merely followed a pattern of behavior in respect to their tenants and croppers that had become widespread and accepted practices in every commercial farming area I knew. In my view it amounted to a national scandal. I have talked with very few county, state or national administrators of the farm control law who do not feel that the miscarriage of the tenancy policy of the law amounted to a national scandal. Yet there was little mention of it in the press until after the roadside-sit-down-strike of January 1939, and most of what was written then was sketchy and confused. (230)[3]

Snow returned to Mississippi County in 1938, finding that the situation there had not improved in his absence:

> My own sharecroppers had a lot to tell. . . . They knew which planters were toting fair with their croppers and which were not, because the Negro croppers from all over the Delta had been getting together in an organized way for the purpose of talking over their affairs and exchanging information. I asked them, of course, if they had joined the union, and they said they had and that they were having lots of meetings. It was plain to see that their union meant a good bit to them and that they were mightily enthusiastic over something or other. . . . I did find out that their union was really a unit of the Southern Tenant Farmers Union, which had been launched several years before with headquarters in Memphis but had not to my knowledge ever ventured up into our part of the Delta in an important way. (232)

"In an important way" seems to be the key phrase in this passage. Snow mentions that two years before "there was a rumor that the union had designs on our part of the Delta," but he associated this activity with Owen Whitfield, the black preacher and labor activist, who was for a time the local leader for the STFU.

Since a copy of "Out on Mr. Snow's Farm" is not among the Thad Snow Papers at the University of Missouri Western Historical Manuscript Collection in St. Louis, it is possible that he never received the poem John Handcox wrote about his visit to the Snow farm. Handcox recalls that he saw Snow "only a couple of times," but was welcomed to his farm in the summer of 1936 by Mr. Snow himself and stayed with a family on the plantation "for six to eight months" (DML 8–1–89). In his account of farm labor activities in 1936, Snow describes a "brief cotton picker's strike" in 1936, a precursor to the more serious strike in southeast Missouri in January 1939, but no mention is made of either Handcox or an STFU representative from Memphis as being associated with the early strike (232–36, 239).

However, a letter of April 15, 1937, to Snow from William R. Amberson of the University of Tennessee in Memphis indicates that the officers of the Southern Tenant Farmers Union were aware of the support that Snow was then giving their people in Missouri.[4]

> The union office tells me that you have taken the lead in your community in aiding the organization of a local of the Southern Tenant Farmer's union. This is indeed a courageous step for which I think you deserve great credit. I know of several other men of your group who have come to see that the Union can furnish an educational drive which may do much to lift the workers from their present depths. I can only hope that your example will soon be followed by other landlords.

Some Missourians appreciated Snow's concern for the injustices he saw around him and reported in letters to the St. Louis *Post-Dispatch*. On April 28, 1937, Cyril Clemens, president of the International Mark Twain Society, wrote to offer Snow the honorary membership in the society once held by Will Rogers, in recognition of the "outstanding contribution to the honor of America by your conversation and writings."[5] Most of Snow's neighbors, however, were bitterly antagonistic. Snow noted that an incident related to the 1936 strike made him "the big devil of the big strike in January, 1939." He had asked the circuit court judge to look into the wrongful arrest and conviction of three blacks who had gone rabbit hunting rather than pick cotton on the day of the 1936 incident. The judge freed the three from their 140-day sentence when Snow asked the arresting officer and the prosecutor to state what had actually happened. This incident and "a few others comparable to it put me on the wrong side of what we often called the Negro problem"; consequently, when the 1939 strike occurred "and the mass hysteria swept over the land all my sins were recalled and brought out to support the satisfying conviction that I was the devil behind it all" (236, 239).

By early 1938, Snow had certainly become well aware of STFU activity in the area. In a letter of January 2, 1938, to Charles G. Ross, who had sent him a copy of a St. Louis *Post-Dispatch* editorial of December 30, 1937, about the plight of the sharecroppers, he wrote:

> Our local relief officers are helpless and panicky. They have even quit telling the niggers to get the hell out, and are trying to explain to them that it is necessary for them to starve because there are no funds available.
>
> Of course negroes starve very slowly and are supposed to do so silently, while hoping for an early spring to provide greens which are wholesome if unsatisfying. But we have a new factor this winter in the existence of a real live organization, the STFU. Several hundred negroes are gathered together in a certain school house this moment (8:30 p.m.) debating the advisability of staging a preliminary semi-riot or demonstration before they get too weak to make it realistic. The leadership is pretty level-headed, so I doubt if there will be any disorder at this time.

Strickland (1987) and Greene (1987) do not mention Handcox in their articles on the 1939 Missouri Highway Sit-Down Strikes, but there is some persuasive evidence, in addition to his own remembrances, that John Handcox had a hand in organizing the sharecroppers of southeast Missouri during his stay on Mr. Snow's farm. Just prior to the Missouri Roadside Demonstration of January 1939, Snow attended a sharecroppers' meeting in a black church and reported the experience to Mitchell.

> We expected Whitfield to gravely exhort his people to be steadfast, to try to bolster up their courage for the danger and hardships ahead. But Whitfield went to the pulpit and spoke: "The Hebrew children had to leave someplace, had to get someplace better. [That's right!] When they went they couldn't go back. And old Boss Pharaoh and his riding bosses in their shiny chariots couldn't catch 'em. [No!] Couldn't catch 'em then, ain't gonna stop us now! [Amen!] 'Cause the time is come we too must make an exodus. [Cheers] Would you rather starve to death like an old hound wandering from door to door, or make a stand? Then if we're gonna starve, let's starve right out on the highway so the whole world can see!" [The entire crowd leaped to its feet!] (Mitchell 1987:46–48)

One of the songs reportedly sung at this meeting was an appropriate verse from a Handcox composition:

> Homeless, homeless are we
> Just as homeless as homeless can be
> We don't get nothing for our labor
> So homeless, homeless are we.
>   (Mitchell 1987:46)

By this time, however, John Handcox had left Missouri. Early in 1937 members of the STFU had gone on a fund-raising tour to Washington and New York. Handcox remembered that there were several carloads in the group, recalling that Mitchell was in one car and J. R. Butler in another. At each stop on the tour a collection would be taken, and Handcox would be able to send money to his family, who were still living near Forrest City, Arkansas. By this time he had composed a number of songs inspired by conditions and events in Arkansas and Missouri, and Mitchell suggested that when the others returned to Memphis he take a train from New York to Washington and record his songs at the Library of Congress.[6]

As Archie Green has noted, it is because of this historic recording, made on March 9, 1937, for the Library of Congress Archive of Folksong by Charles Seeger and Sidney Robertson, that so many know of John Handcox today:

> What would have been John Handcox's role had he not recorded any songs in Washington, D.C.? How could we have come to an appreciation of his contribution? Literally, his discs—"field" recordings in a public-agency studio— became the mechanism that shaped our attention to Handcox, the sharecroppers' voice. (Green 1990:11)

Certainly these recordings made his songs known long before the composer was rediscovered.

A Library of Congress listing indicates that Handcox recorded "3 discs containing . . . labor organizing and political songs." He announced the title of each song or composition himself on the recording, sometimes noting that it was "composed by" John Handcox, sometimes making no attribution:

> "Raggedy, Raggedy Are We," composed by John Handcox; "We're Gonna Roll the Union On," sung by John Handcox; "Join the Union Tonight," by John Handcox; "In My Heart"; "No More Mourning"; "There is Mean Things Happening in This Land," composed and sung by John Handcox; "The Planter and the Sharecropper," by John Handcox; and "Landlord, What in the Heaven Is the Matter With You?" by John Handcox.[7]

In the last two selections he sometimes seems to be reading the text rather than reciting from memory. The verse that he took to the STFU office in 1935 constitutes two lines in "The Planter and the Sharecropper," a forty-line composition in the Library of Congress recording. The poem as read had been published in the March 1936 issue of *The Sharecroppers' Voice* under the pseudonym "John Henry"!

As he worked to organize the sharecroppers, Handcox had found it easier to express his feelings in songs than to make speeches, and fifty years later he was to say "Some people don't know how bad things really are unless they hear somebody talking or singing about it" (McLaren 1989:B4). In what Delvecchio (1988:B5) has called "a few timeless phrases from the heart," John Handcox told people how bad it really was.

One of his best songs and one which depicts the plight of the sharecropper in a few timeless and poignant phrases is "Raggedy Raggedy Are We," whose many variations in published versions suggest that it was one of his most popular songs. As we have noted, a verse from this song introduced Mitchell's chapter on "The Voices of the Disinherited." Another verse was sung at the sharecroppers' meeting Snow attended. Mitchell published a four-stanza version, "Hungry, Hungry Are We," with the first two stanzas in reverse of the order of stanzas in the Library of Congress version. The latter has eight stanzas, beginning with "Raggedy, Raggedy Are We," each with four lines. The second and fourth lines repeat the key word of the first line:

> Raggedy, raggedy are we,
> Just as raggedy as raggedy can be.
> We don't get nothing for our labor,
> So raggedy, raggedy are we.

The subsequent three stanzas follow the same pattern and have the same third line as the first stanza:

> Hongry, hongry are we,
> . . . .
> Landless, landless are we,
> . . . .
> Homeless, homeless are we,
> . . . .

In the next three stanzas, the third line refers to practices that made it impossible for sharecroppers to raise farm animals or food for their families. Many landowners planted cotton or other crops to the front and back steps of the sharecropper cabins.

> Cowless, cowless are we,
> Just as cowless as cowless can be.
> The planters don't allow us to raise them,
> So cowless, cowless are we.

> Hogless, hogless are we,
> . . . .

> Cornless, cornless are we,
> Just as cornless as cornless can be
> The planters don't allow us to raise it,
> So cornless, cornless are we.

In the last stanza the third line returns to the form of the first stanza:

> Pitiful, pitiful are we,
> Just as pitiful as pitiful can be.
> We don't get nothing for our labor,
> So pitiful, pitiful are we.

In *American Folksongs of Protest,* John Greenway printed the song as Handcox had sung it at the Library of Congress (1953:219–20), but Peter Seeger and Bob Reiser, in *Carry It On,* replaced Handcox's final stanza, "Pitiful, Pitiful Are We," with a verse by Lee Hays, "Union, Union Are We" (1985:128).

Handcox's most famous song is "Roll the Union On," which according to H. L. Mitchell "ranks third" among "America's labor songs," behind "Solidarity Forever" (of the Industrial Workers of the World) and "We Shall Not Be Moved" (sung by West Virginia miners in their 1929 strike) (1987:37). Pete Seeger, in an interview with Marjorie Miller, called it "a great picket line song," and once told Handcox, "If you'd gotten $25 for every time 'Roll the Union On' had been printed in a songbook during the last several years you'd have several thousand dollars" (Miller 1986:19). The part of the song that has become "a great picket line song" has the repetitious structure of a gospel hymn. The version that Handcox sang for the Library of Congress has six six-line stanzas, each with the same structure: the first, second, and fourth lines are exactly the same in all verses, and the sixth is the same except for the absence of "Gonna" in verses two through four. The third line in each stanza, each listing one of the "enemies" of the union, is repeated verbatim in the fifth line.

> We gonna roll, we gonna roll, we gonna roll the union on.
> We gonna roll, we gonna roll, we gonna roll the union on.
> If the planter's in the way, we're gonna roll it over him.
> Gonna roll it over him, gonna roll it over him.
> If the planter's in the way, we're gonna roll it over him.
> Gonna roll the union on.
> . . . .
> If the boss is in the way, we gonna roll it over him.
> . . . .
> If the merchant's in the way, we gonna roll it over him.
> . . . .
> If the banker's in the way, we gonna roll it over him.
> . . . .
> If Peacher's in the way, we gonna roll it over him.
> . . . .
> If Governor Futrell's in the way, we gonna roll it over him.
> Gonna roll the union on.[8]

Though Handcox did not indicate in his Library of Congress recording that he composed the song, Mitchell, Seeger, and others attribute it to him (Seeger and Reiser 1985:173). Today it is generally attributed to him, although *Songs for Labor,* prepared by the AFL-CIO Department of Education in 1983, credits Claude Williams and Lee Hays with "Roll the Union On" (Shields 1983:29). Greenway includes a version of the song, noting that it is an adaptation of the gospel hymn "Roll the Chariot On." He also notes that he had taken it from a "Bulletin of the Original Southern Tenant Farmers Union" and that "it was made up in 1937 by a Negro woman in Little Rock, Arkansas, a student in the New Era schools" (1953:223). However, Handcox had left Arkansas in 1936, and he obviously knew the song by that time.

Alan Lomax, Peter Seeger, and Woody Guthrie (1967:268–69) make the same attribution as Greenway, but Edith Fowke and Joe Glazer credit John Handcox and Lee Hays and substitute "Boss, Scab, Sheriff" for Handcox's "Planter, Banker, Merchant, Deputy Peacher, and Governor Futrell" (1973:44–45). In a telephone interview, Handcox said he remembered well that he composed both "Roll the Union On" and "Mean Things Happening in This Land" when he fled from Arkansas to Memphis in 1936 to escape lynching; he was "sitting outside in the yard, in the sun" (DML 1989 interviews). Greenway's printed version and that of Lomax, Seeger, and Guthrie in *Hard-Hitting Songs* substitute "the preacher" for "Peacher," thereby losing a reference that would have been very important to Handcox in 1936. Both also have a final stanza listing "Wall Street" as an enemy of the union. Paul D. Peacher, Deputy Sheriff and City Marshall of Earle, Arkansas, was tried and convicted in 1936 for holding thirteen union members in slavery (Mitchell 1979:92). Peacher had taken part in an attack on a "union march," had arrested some of the men, and had them sentenced to jail by a justice of the peace. Then he held them in a stockade to work on his own plantation. Thus, in addition to Handcox's own statement, internal evidence would suggest that his version of "Roll the Union On" predates the one printed by Greenway and attributed to the woman in Little Rock.

Mitchell's published versions of "Roll the Union On" include two introductory stanzas that Handcox did not sing at the Library of Congress. The first gives an erroneous date—June 9—for the May 18 strike (Mitchell 1979:348). The date was corrected in *Roll the Union On* (Mitchell 1987:93).

> It was nineteen hundred and thirty six
> And on the 9th of June
> When the STFU pulled a strike
> That troubled the planters on their thrones.
>
> The planters they all became troubled
> Not knowing what 'twas all about
> But they said "One thing I'm sure we can do
> That's scare them sharecroppers out."

With some textual changes, these stanzas are included as verses five and six of "The Man Frank Weems," published in *American Songs of Protest* (Greenway 1953:221). Apparently, Handcox wrote one or both of these stanzas when he composed "Mean Things" and "Roll the Union On" while staying at the STFU in Memphis, for he used a variant of the first stanza as an introduction to "Mean Things Happening in This Land":

> On the 18th day of May
> The union called a strike,
> But the planters and the bosses
> Throwed the people out of their shacks.
>   (Greenway 1953:218)

It is difficult to reconstruct an exact chronology of Handcox's travels from his songs and poems. He commented that he had stayed in Memphis for a month after escaping from potential lynching after the strike activity had already started in Arkansas; and in his poem to Mr. Snow, he indicated that he arrived in southeast Missouri on the second Monday in June, which was June 8, the date of the march in Earle, Arkansas, in which Frank Weems was beaten. It is possible, however, that Handcox arrived in Missouri on the Monday following the Frank Weems incident.

A number of Handcox poems and songs have been published by various researchers and anthologists interested in labor movements. In addition to "Raggedy, Raggedy," Greenway included "There Are Mean Things Happening in This Land" and Handcox's eloquent prose account of the attack on Weems (220). *Hard Hitting Songs for Hard-Hit People* included "There Is Mean Things Happening," "No More Mourning" ("the Negro spiritual sung by John Handcox in sharecroppers' union meetings all over the South"), "Raggedy Raggedy Are We," "The Planter and the Sharecropper," and a fragment they call "Landlord, What in the Hell Is the Matter with You?" (Lomax, Guthrie and Seeger 1967:260–63, 265–66). In one of his 1989 interviews, Handcox said that he never used this title: "Some people did, but I didn't" (RBS 10-17-89). "Landlord, What in the Heaven Is the Matter with You?" was published in *The Sharecroppers' Voice,* May 1, 1936, attributed to "John Henry, negro poet and organizer, STFU."

Although his songs and poems became known throughout the English-speaking world, undergoing the changes and adaptations commonly occurring in oral transmissions, and were frequently published, "The Sharecropper Troubador" lived out of contact with other song writers and labor leaders for four decades. Pete Seeger and Woody Guthrie tried without success to locate him when they were compiling material for *Hard Hitting Songs for Hard-Hit People,* but it was not until the 1980s that Joe Glazer finally located him through H. L. Mitchell.[9] According to Seeger, a friend of Handcox's had seen Mitchell's *Mean Things Happening in This Land* in a bookstore, and thus was reminded that Handcox had written a song by that title. "John contacted the publisher, got in touch with Mitch, and among other things there was a little reunion in Memphis of various people who worked on the job of organizing Southern tenant farmers in the mid-30's" (Miller 1986:17).

The songs and poems Handcox wrote for the STFU have an immediacy that brings back the hardship and danger of the times in which he and other organizers lived and worked. "The Planter and the Sharecropper" effectively contrasts the life of the planter and his family with that of the sharecropper and his family:

> A lot of good things the planter have to waste,
> But the sharecropper knows not how it taste.
> The sharecropper wife go to the kitchen, wash tub, and fields

> While the planter's wife enjoys herself in an automobile.
> The planter's children dresses up and goes to school
> While the sharecropper's puts on rags and follow a mule.
> If you ask the planter for your rights,
> You might as well to spit in his face and ask for a fight.
> The planter says he inherits his wealth from birth,
> But it all come from the poor man who tills the earth.

The poem concludes with this couplet:

> And if anyone thinks that this ain't the truth
> He can go through the South and get proof.[10]

"Landlord, What in Heaven Is the Matter with You?" focuses on the situation that arose when the planters found ways to keep from having to share government payments with farm tenants by forcing them to become day workers or evicting them from the farms altogether. The Agricultural Adjustment Act remained ambiguous in its provision that tenant farmers get a share of the cotton plowed up in 1933 and not grown in the following years. Gardner Jackson, who was fired by the Department of Agriculture for his efforts to see that the sharecroppers were treated fairly, estimated that in almost half the cases the sharecroppers "didn't get a nickel of the money" (Mitchell 1979:42). In his fifty-six-line litany of the wrongs suffered by the sharecroppers Handcox wrote:

> In 1933 when we plowed up cotton
> Some of that money your labor have never gotten
> You pledged the government your labor you would pay
> You put it in your pocket and you went your way.
> And in the AA contract in 1934
> You chiseled your labor out o' some more
> And in 1935
> The parity money your labor you deprived,
> And in the AA in 1936
> You are all trying to fix.
> We hope that it'll be so;
> You'll get yours and no more.
> Your labor you've always robbed.
> . . . .
> You say move away from landlords who treat you unfair.
> You must want us to live up in the air.
> . . . .[11]

"In My Heart" recalls those who were enemies and those who were friends, those against the sharecroppers, and those for them. "I don't want to be like the planters," Handcox sang, "like Deputy Peacher, like Governor Futrell, like Senator Robinson." Instead:

> I want to be like Norman Thomas
> . . . .
> I want to be like Howard Kester
> . . . .
> I want to be like J. R. Butler,
> . . . .
> I want to be like Gardner Jackson
> In my heart, in my heart
> I want to be like Gardner Jackson
> In my heart, in my heart
> I want to be like Gardner Jackson
> In my heart.[12]

"In My Heart" evoked a time that was still alive for John Handcox, one he saw replaying in 1989 when he visited Columbia. The list of villains and heroes that Handcox included in this song attests both to his deep sense of the injustices he saw and to the national scope of his awareness of political and labor issues in the United States. The actions of the planters and the infamous deputy sheriff of Earle, Arkansas, not only illustrated the need for laborers to organize and build political strength but also touched the hearts of anyone sensitive to the conditions of the poor during the depression. Joe T. Robinson, U.S. Senator from Arkansas, was majority leader of the Senate and chairman of the Convention Resolution Committee for the Democratic National Convention in 1936. He was nicknamed "Greasy Joe" by Mitchell. Among Handcox's heroes were Norman Thomas, Howard Kester, and J. R. Butler. Thomas, Socialist party candidate for President each election year from 1928 to 1948, was attacked in 1935 by angry "riding bosses" in Birdsong, Mississippi County, Arkansas (Mitchell 1979:69–70). Kester and Butler were early supporters and workers for the STFU. Kester helped organize the South's first interracial student movement, served as an investigator of lynchings for the NAACP, and founded the Fellowship of Southern Churchmen. He was threatened with lynching himself in 1936 when a sharecroppers' meeting was "raided by a mob of plantation riding bosses and deputy sheriffs" (Mitchell 1979:116–17). Butler, a chief organizer for the STFU and President of the Union in 1942, wrote the first constitution. Gardner Jackson was a Department of Agriculture spokesman for the sharecroppers, a commitment which cost him his job (42).

"King Cotton" and "Strike in Arkansas," two additional Handcox song-poems published by Mitchell in *Roll the Union On*, further demonstrate the

"Sharecropper Troubador's" powerful talent for evoking the plight of the South's disinherited—and of those who tried to help them:

> Oh! King Cotton, today you have millions of slaves
> And have caused many poor workers to be in lonesome graves,
> When Cotton is King of any nation,
> It means wealth to the planters—to the laborer starvation.
> (Mitchell 1987:87)

"The Strike in Arkansas" is a chilling account of violence in Earle, Arkansas, when Peacher threatened "Miss Evelyn Smith and Mrs. Clay East" . . . [who] went out to take pictures of the Union people he had in the stockade":

> If you go through Arkansas, you better drive fast.
> How the labor is being treated, you better not ask.
> (Mitchell 1987:88)

In remembering the four-and-a-half decades between his visit to the Library of Congress to record his songs and his reunion with Mitchell, Handcox reported that shortly after he returned to Charleston from the STFU tour in March 1937, the union members met in Memphis. He did not attend the meeting, but Owen Whitfield was there. When Whitfield returned, Handcox asked him whether the STFU could provide him with an allowance to help with organizing in Missouri, as both Mitchell and J. R. Butler had asked him to do earlier. The response was negative. He recalled Whitfield saying that Handcox's name was never mentioned at the meeting but that he himself was to receive $200 a month to continue his own work in southeastern Missouri.

Mitchell had from the beginning resisted the idea of paying STFU organizers. In an interview with Jeff Sutter of Washington University, he stated: "Every man became an organizer. We had no paid organizers. We didn't have any paid organizers until maybe 1937, somewhere along there, about the time we started thinking of joining the CIO."[13] In his account of his "two-year wrangle with Donald Henderson" and the United Cannery, Agricultural, Packing and Allied Workers of America, Mitchell reported that he was the only "regular hired hand" in the STFU. In 1937 the convention had voted to pay him $25 a week provided he could raise the money (Mitchell 1979:156). J. R. Butler of the STFU was paid $200 a month as vice-president of the UCAPAWA after his election in Denver in 1938 to that office (166). At the fifth annual convention of the STFU in 1938, Owen Whitfield was elected second vice-president of the union. However, when Mitchell led his supporters out of UCAPAWA in 1939, Whitfield remained with the CIO, believing that it had provided more aid for the sharecroppers during the demonstrations than had the STFU (Strickland 1987:406). His financial support probably came from the former rather than the latter organization.

There seemed little chance that Handcox could obtain sufficient financial support in Charleston, so he went to St. Louis in search of work. He had some Socialist party brochures and knew of people who might help him. He was told that there were few jobs in St. Louis, but that there was to be a meeting of the Socialist party in Chicago the following evening and he might be able to get financial support there. He said, "The bus let me out right in front of the place where the Socialist Party was meeting, so I didn't have to wait long for help in Chicago."

Handcox sang at party meetings in Chicago for a short time and then decided to go to Detroit, where an uncle lived. After his father's death he had continued the tradition of sending pecans, cured hams, and sorghum from Arkansas to the family in Detroit and thought his uncle might be able to help him. But he attended a Socialist party meeting on his first night in Detroit, and the next morning overheard his aunt expressing some reluctance to help him. His uncle took him to another section of the city where he was able to find accommodations and financial assistance. He lived for a time in a house owned by the Socialist party, but after staying in Detroit for about two months, he knew he had to move elsewhere to make a living for himself and his family.

When his mother and other members of the family moved to Bartlesville, Oklahoma, where his mother's "baby sister" lived, he decided to join them and to try to make a living in Oklahoma. There, he worked at various jobs, including that of a butcher's helper and carpenter. While in Bartlesville, the family had bought a lot on Virginia Street, and he built four rock houses: one for his mother, one each for two brothers, and one for himself. One fall he worked for "a lady who was a millionaire." When the work season was over, she laid him off and asked him to return in the spring. When he returned, she told him she could use him but that she would have to reduce his pay. She was not willing to pay enough for him to live on, so he refused the job.

For a couple of months in 1942, Handcox worked at a "soldiers' camp" under construction in Salina, Kansas. There he heard from a fellow-worker that the climate in California was very good, so he decided to move. "The best day in my life," he said, "was November 28, 1942," when he arrived in San Diego. The climate proved all he desired; he found work. At first he worked as a laborer with a white carpenter "who couldn't saw a straight line but was making fifty cents more per hour." The carpenter would ask Handcox to do the work that required carpentry skills. Rather than continue doing another man's work for less money, he decided to join the Carpenters Union to get better pay. His family joined him in San Diego, starting a migration to California—"more people than followed the Pharaoh." After World War II, he contracted to take cottonpicking crews to the area around Bakersfield, California, in the summers. This type of business lasted until the machines came in. "Labor had a kick in the rear," he said, "when the machines came in and replaced people."[14]

After his work for the STFU in 1936–37 and his brief effort to earn a living singing at socialist gatherings, Handcox had stopped writing poems and songs. When located in 1980 and recognized for his earlier work, he renewed his interest in song writing, updating his old songs and writing new ones. He sang a new stanza of "Roll the Union On" at a meeting in Columbia, October 15, 1989, and later recorded it for the authors:

> We're Gonna Roll the Union On (October 1989)
>
> We gonna roll, we gonna roll, we gonna roll the union on
> We gonna roll, we gonna roll, we gonna roll the union on
> If Bush is in the way we're gonna roll it over him
> Gonna roll it over him, gonna roll it over him
> Gonna roll the union on.
> We're gonna roll, we gonna roll, we gonna roll the union on
> We're gonna roll, we gonna roll, we gonna roll the union on.

"Raggedy, Raggedy Are We" provided images and themes for a new song:

> In the U.S.A.
>
> Jobless, jobless in the U.S.A.
> Millions are searching for work every day
> Machines have taken their jobs away
> Jobless in the U.S.A.
>
> Hunger, hunger in the U.S.A.
> People without a bit to eat
> People without a place to stay
> Machines have taken their jobs away
> Hunger in the U.S.A.
>
> Homeless, homeless in the U.S.A.
> Millions are searching for work every day
> Machines have taken their jobs away
> Homeless in the U.S.A.
>
> Suffering, suffering in the U.S.A.
> Many people are sleeping in the streets

Not a penny in their pockets, not a bit to eat
Machines have taken their jobs away
Suffering in the U. S. A.

Working, working in the U.S.A.
Working toward a better day
Where bosses want to take our jobs away
Working in the U.S.A.

Changing, changing in the U.S.A.
Changing things until we have our say
Listen, friend, there's gonna be a new day
We're gonna make some changes, in the U.S.A.
We're gonna make some changes, in the U.S.A.[15]

The "machines that have taken their jobs away" concerned him most. "With all the machinery and mechanisms, when one person has displaced thousands—What's going to happen? No answer. That's the thing that worries me today." Still the revolutionary, whose voice for the disinherited was as strong at the end of his life as it was in the 1930s, Handcox warned of trouble ahead: "Maybe one of these days the poor people will wake up. Of course it may cost thousands and thousands of lives to do it. I think we'll have a revolution. I think it's going to be forced on us. I can't get it figured out. Sometimes I wake up at night and try to figure it out" (RBS 10-17-89).

After his re-discovery by the labor movement in 1980, Handcox again became one of the movement's great troubadours. He attended the Labor Heritage Foundation Great Labor Song Exchange in Washington in 1985 and made another recording for the Library of Congress.[16] In 1987 he sang at the Western Workers' Labor Heritage Festival, and on his eighty-fourth birthday, February 5, 1988, he was featured in the *San Francisco Chronicle*. In 1987 he told a reporter that he had written more in the previous five years than he had written in all the years from 1936 to 1980. In 1989 the Labor Heritage Foundation awarded him the first annual Joe Hill Award for his more than fifty years of support for labor. The plaque given to Handcox lists some of the achievements that won him the award:

Poet of the Southern Tenant Farmers union in the 1930's
Composer of "Roll the Union On" and Other Labor Classics
An Eloquent Voice for Workers' Rights for More than 50 Years
85 Years Young and Still Going Strong![17]

After his 1989 visit to Missouri, he performed at the Vancouver Folk Festival, the largest in North America. He made his twelfth trip to Washington, D.C., in 1991. And, shortly before his death on September 18, 1992, he was looking forward to more opportunities to sing.

The new and reworked songs and poems—like those recorded for the Library of Congress in 1937 that provide a history of the 1930s more troubled than most Americans care to remember—present an unflinching look at "Mean Things Still Happening." The new "Machines Have Taken Our Jobs Away" speaks powerfully for the unemployed and homeless:

> I was talking with a group of people the other day.
> They say I'm not working—machines have taken my job away.
> One with a machine can do more than a thousand men can do in a day.
> What else can you say—machines have taken their jobs away.
> Jobless, jobless in the U.S.A.
>
> Many were born on a farm and thought that they were there to stay,
> Machines came along and taken their jobs away.
> Jobless, jobless in the U.S.A.
>
> There are million of people out of work today,
> Because machines have taken their jobs away.
> Jobless, jobless in the U.S.A.
> Go down town you see people sleeping on the street
> With no home to go to an nothing to eat.
> Jobless, jobless in the U.S.A.
>
> In this land of plenty and home of the brave
> Machines are taken jobs every day,
> We are sleeping on the streets and eating out of garbage cans.
> We live our lives from day to day,
> Machines have taken our jobs away.
> Jobless, jobless in the U.S.A.
>
> You go to the employment office and what do they say?
> Sorry we have no work today,
> Come by tomorrow an try again,
> Machines have taken our jobs away.
> Jobless, jobless in the U.S.A.

As long as he had voice, John Handcox spoke for the poor, the homeless, and the hungry of the land. His will, written September 15, 1986, donating his body to the School of Medicine, University of California at San Diego, reflected and explained his dedication to the cause to which he devoted his life:

> I donated my life to the workers of America. There are many who want to know why. I've tried to answer that question on many occasions. I knew that I was risking my life when I began to try to organize the poor workers against the opposition of the plantation owners, who wanted their workers to be submissive and ignorant. It is the workers who have produced the wealth of the world.

No one ever came to me and asked me to join the union, or try to organize for the union. I did it on my own inspiration, on account of all the injustices that I had seen, and I determined to change things that I felt were wrong. . . .

If my body can be used to make this a healthier world to live in, I'll be happy to know that. Let it be said that I not only donated my life to helping others, but my death too. I know that if my brain were transferred to someone else, they would be singing "We Are Gonna Roll the Union On," and "There Are Mean Things Happening in This Land." If my heart could be transferred to someone else, it would be full of love for the workers of the world.

John Handcox's life, spanning most of the twentieth century, reflected his love for the disinherited workers of his time; his songs reflect a desire to right the injustices he saw. As Archie Green (1990:11) has said, "How can one add to his eloquence?"

Missouri State Library, Jefferson City
University of Missouri–Columbia

Notes

An early version of this article, "John L. Handcox: The Sharecropper Troubador," appears in the Missouri Folklore Society Journal, *8/9 (1986–87):123–42. The authors express their appreciation to the following scholars for providing valuable information for this article: Laurel Blaydes, Labor Heritage Foundation, Washington, D.C.; Archie Green, San Francisco; Joseph C. Hickerson, Head of the Archive of Folk Culture, Library of Congress; Tony Holland, Professor of History, Lincoln University, Jefferson City, Mo.; Michael Honey, University of Washington, Tacoma; David Roediger, Professor of History, University of Missouri– Columbia; and Arvarh E. Strickland, Professor of History, University of Missouri–Columbia.*

1. John Handcox. Interview with Rebecca Schroeder, October 17, 1989. Information on Handcox's personal history was obtained in six interviews with Donald M. Lance (July 26, August 1, October 9, 1989; September 30, 1990; March 17, 1991; July 14, 1992) and with Rebecca B. Schroeder (October 17, 1989). Material quoted from these interviews is cited by interviewer and date in parentheses. Typescripts of the interview notes by Lance and an audiotape of the interview by Schroeder are included in the John Handcox Papers in the University of Missouri Western Historical Manuscript Collection, Columbia.

2. This poem is also published in Denise Franklin, "Workin', Travelin', Singin', Writer Strives for Better World," *Santa Cruz Sentinel,* January 19, 1987.

3. Snow devotes several chapters (pp. 227ff) to the demonstration and ensuing mass hysteria. Mitchell describes "The Missouri Highway Sit-Down" in *Mean Things,* pp. 171ff. See also Arvarh E. Strickland's "The Plight of the People in the Sharecroppers' Demonstration in Southeast Missouri," *Missouri Historical Review* 81 (July 1987): 403–16, and Lorenzo Greene's "Lincoln University's Involvement with the Sharecropper Demonstration in Southeast Missouri, 1939–1940," *Missouri Historical Review* 82 (October 1987): 24–50.

4. Information on Snow's activities and his views relating to farm labor conditions in the 1930s and 1940s is included in the Thad Snow Papers, University of Missouri Western Historical Manuscript Collection, St. Louis.

5. Thad Snow Papers.

6. The 1937 recording made by John L. Handcox is available as Library of Congress recording AFS 32/37–39. A copy of the recording and a typescript of the songs are included in the John Handcox Papers in the University of Missouri Western Historical Manuscript Collection, Columbia.

7. "Missouri Field Recordings in the Archive of Folk Culture," Library of Congress, May 4, 1992.

8. Library of Congress Recording 32/37A2.

9. From *Art Works* (Newsletter of the Labor Heritage Foundation, 1982), p. 6. Additional information provided in telephone interview by Lance, August 1, 1989, with Laurel Blaydes.

10. John Handcox, "The Planter and the Sharecropper," Library of Congress Recording 32/39A 1. The version printed in *The Sharecroppers' Voice* has minor variations in the text and concludes, "If anyone thinks this ain't the truth/ he can go thru Arkansas and get the proof."

11. John Handcox, "Landlord, What In The Heaven Is The Matter With You?" Library of Congress recording 32/39B 1.

12. "In My Heart," Library of Congress Recording 32/37B 2.

13. Undated typescript, provided by David Roediger, University of Missouri–Columbia.

14. This account of Handcox's activities between March 1937 and November 1942 is a composite derived from all the interviews.

15. Typescript from John Handcox.

16. Interview with John Handcox, conducted by Joe Glazer and Michael Honey at the Library of Congress, May 15, 1985.

17. Laurel Blaydes provided a copy of the tribute.

References Cited

Belfrage, Cedric. 1941. *South of God.* New York: Modern Age Books.

Delvecchio, Rick. 1988. "Last of Legendary Labor Poets." *San Francisco Chronicle,* February 5, B5.

Fowke, Edith, and Joe Glazer. 1973. *Songs of Work and Protest.* New York: Dover Publications.

Franklin, Denise. 1987. "Workin', Travelin', Singin' Writer Strives for Better World." *Santa Cruz Sentinel,* January 19.

Green, Archie. 1990. "Let Us Now Praise John Handcox." *Tradition, Newsletter of the University of Missouri Cultural Heritage Center* 6:11.

Greene, Lorenzo. 1987. "Lincoln University's Involvement with the Sharecropper Demonstration in Southeast Missouri, 1939–1940." *Missouri Historical Review* 82:24–50.

Greenway, John. 1953. *American Folksongs of Protest.* Philadelphia: University of Pennsylvania Press.

Lomax, Alan, Woodie Guthrie, and Pete Seeger. 1967. *Hard Hitting Songs for Hard-Hit People.* New York: Oak Publications.

McLaren, John. 1989. "Labor Troubador Still Inspires." *San Diego Tribune,* January 2, B4.

Miller, Marjorie. 1985. "Socialist Gains Belated Recognition: Efforts to Organize Poor Farmers Led to Inspirational Music." *Los Angeles Times,* San Diego Edition, April 14, San Diego County Section, 1, 4–7.

———. 1986. "Footprints: John Handcox, Songwriter." *Southern Exposure,* January-February, 17–22.

"Missouri Field Recordings in the Archive of Folk Culture." 1982. Library of Congress, May 4.

Mitchell, H. L. 1979. *Mean Things Happening in This Land: The Life and Times of H. L. Mitchell, Cofounder of the Southern Tenant Farmers' Union.* Montclair, N.J.: Allenheld, Osmun.

———. 1987. *Roll the Union On: A Pictorial History of the Southern Tenant Farmers' Union.* Chicago: Charles H. Kerr.

———. n.d. Interview at Washington University c. 1989. Typescript in University of Missouri Western Historical Manuscript Collection, Columbia.

Seeger, Pete, and Bob Reiser. 1985. *Carry It On, A History in Song and Picture of the Working Men and Women of America.* New York: Simon and Schuster.

Shields, Dorothy, ed. 1983. *Songs for Labor.* AFL-CIO Publication No. 56. Washington, D.C.: AFL-CIO Pamphlet Division.

Snow, Thad. 1954. *From Missouri.* Boston: Houghton Mifflin.

Strickland, Arvarh E. 1987. "The Plight of the People in the Sharecroppers' Demonstration in Southeast Missouri." *Missouri Historical Review* 81:403–16.

Archie Green
Woody's Oil Songs

A few union songs hold wide appeal and wield great power. "Joe Hill," "Solidarity Forever," and "Which Side" continue to move beyond organized ranks to reach general audiences. Indeed, these classic compositions often carry the labor movement's values to the large American public. By contrast, many labor songs remain in the shadows—hidden from the vision of the most dedicated union members and neglected by libraries and archives.

Two of Woody Guthrie's offerings, "Boomtown Bill" and "Keep That Oil A-Rolling," composed in 1942, have rested in limbo for five decades (see fig. 1). Joe Klein, in a biography of Guthrie, does not mention either number. David Dunaway, in a biography of Pete Seeger, briefly mentions "Boomtown Bill." No editor has re-issued either piece in LP or CD form. Woody's oil songs deserve new audiences in the 1990s—unionists, folksong fans, labor historians, popular-culture critics. In this study, I call fresh attention to these songs and speculate on their obscurity.

Early in 1941, Pete Seeger and several friends in New York City formed the Almanac Singers, a group of young radicals who used folksong to further political cause. A few of the Almanacs knew Communist Party life from within the movement; others, in the parlance of the day, "traveled" on the fringes. Some individual Almanacs attributed "progressive" properties to folksong; accordingly, they connected performance to radical posture. Hence, they were caught by wrenching twists in Communist position—from isolationism to win-the-war activism; from sectarian exclusivity to Popular-Front unity.

The Almanac Singers wished their efforts to serve working people, particularly to help organize unions. However, the core politics embraced by the Almanacs often came between the group's enthusiasm and desired audience. In the tension generated by contradiction between the inherent limits of folksong and the party's overarching line, much Almanac material failed to reach intended workers. Essentially, Guthrie's oil songs did not catch hold in oil patch or refinery town.

We do not always comprehend and continue to puzzle over a given song's path into tradition's maze. Why does one spring ahead as others lag behind in acceptance? Many songs are composed; few are treasured by folk audiences. We can sense something of the different trails particular numbers leave by noting four representative Almanac recordings.

In May, 1941, as part of the Almanacs' first Keynote labor album, the group recorded "Talking Union," a durable friend that has remained embedded in union tradition for a half century. On the other hand, the sprightly "Ballad of Harry Bridges," recorded in the summer of 1941, is unavailable and unknown to present-day longshoremen. Two months after Pearl Harbor, the Almanacs issued a wartime album including

Fig. 1 Photographed from private collection of Ron Cohen

"Reuben James," honoring sailors lost on our first torpedoed ship of World War II. Contemporary "folksong revival" audiences still prize "Reuben James." By contrast, an earlier disc, "The Ballad of October 16," remains an unsung and embarrassing reminder of sectarian attacks on Franklin Delano Roosevelt.

Based in New York City, the Almanacs traveled throughout the land to sing for discrete radical audiences, as well as for subway motormen, steel puddlers, meat packers, and other industrial workers. Readers who wish to pursue the Almanac story will find useful the biographies of Guthrie (Klein:1980) and Seeger (Dunaway:1981)), and Richard A. Reuss's Indiana University dissertation (1971).

During the war, the individual Almanacs moved in many directions: army, merchant marine, defense plant, political activity, show business. As they dispersed from Manhattan, Detroit became a second and concluding home. In 1941, the Almanacs had helped Ford workers come together in a massive union rally at Cadillac Square. In 1942, the young singers returned to the Square for a "Conversion-to-War-Production" rally. Shifting from auto making to tank building, the auto-work force turned the city into an "Arsenal of Democracy." In June, four of the Almanacs took up Detroit residence, singing to lift war-production morale.

Previously, in March, 1942, the Oil Workers International Union (OWIU-CIO) had commissioned the Almanacs to write two songs for an intended phonograph recording combining union-building strategies with win-the-war sentiments. Edwin S. Smith, the Oil Workers Organizing Campaign's director, visited Manhattan to enlist Guthrie and Seeger in this task. Decades later, Pete Seeger (in a letter to me) recalled the assignment. Smith came to the Greenwich Village apartment of the Almanacs and requested two songs. Pete stated, "Woody immediately hopped to the typewriter and within a few days had several songs."

Before joining the OWIU staff, Smith had served on the New Deal's two early labor boards created in 1934 by Congressional Resolution 44, and in 1935 by the Wagner Act. Smith favored industrial over craft unions. President Roosevelt, faced with management hostility to the NLRB and internecine labor conflict, ended Smith's term in 1941. Living in Washington and partisan to the CIO, Smith had encountered the Almanacs; he admired their mixture of egalitarian and militant messages cast into folksong modes.

The OWIU assignment calling for a pair of oil songs fell mainly to Woody Guthrie, probably because of previous familiarity with production-field practices. As a native Oklahoman, Woody had seen rigs on the horizon and knew something of roughneck culture. On trips in the Southwest, he had sung to roustabouts and to refinery hands.

Dipping into his rhetorical treasure chest for a brawny "Boomtown Bill," Woody called up the traditional railroader's tune, "Wabash Cannonball." The new song shaped itself immediately and he submitted the text to Smith. The latter, in a letter of acceptance (March 27, 1942), noted that O. A. "Jack" Knight, international president, liked it but felt it to be burdened by technical terms. Knight suggested that Guthrie's infatuation with terminology lessened the ballad's spontaneity.

For a second number, Smith—then engaged in a crucial campaign to organize Standard Oil—asked for a song on company unionism linking memories of John D. Rockefeller's role in the infamous Ludlow Massacre to the then-current OWIU drive. Smith wrote to Guthrie remarking on a 1913 coal strike in which Colorado state militiamen had burned the miner's tent colony, killing women and children. Rockefeller had responded to the tragedy, not by recognizing the United Mine Workers of America, but by setting up a company union throughout his vast industrial empire.

For the recording's second song, Smith wanted a rousing chorus in which new unionists could voice, "We'll smash the company union and join the CIO." Apparently, this Ludlow piece did not jell in Guthrie's mind as readily as had "Boomtown Bill." Woody cobbled together a tune reminiscent of "Salty Dog Blues" and "Bye, Bye Blackbird," and typed out his opening lines:

> I'm gonna tell you something, maybe you don't know
> Your company union was born at old Ludlow.

In the interplay between the various Almanac songwriters, Baldwin "Butch" Hawes helped alter Guthrie's basic text for "Keep That Oil A-Rolling." The Ludlow reference vanished as the revised song opened :

> You oilfield workers, come listen to me
> I'm goin' to tell you a story about old John D
> That company union made a fool out of me.

Receiving the new songs, Smith printed both in the *CIO News* (OWIU edition, May 25, 1942). Additionally, he wrote a feature column, "Songs for a Second Front," tying the new Almanac numbers to the European war. Smith made explicit the political setting for Guthrie's oil songs in a period when Reds had hardly recovered from their "Yanks are not coming" disasters during the Hitler-Stalin pact. There is no evidence that great numbers of oil workers accepted Communist party positions; nevertheless, Smith felt it necessary to certify the patriotic content of Guthrie's new oil songs.

Some time in June, 1942, the Almanacs entered a Manhattan studio to record their oil compositions for Keynote Records. We know little today of this firm. Eric Bernay, who combined roles as *New Masses* treasurer and record-store proprietor of the Music Room, had started this label in 1940. During the War, it served with other specialty labels to bring together a "folksong revival" audience: urbanites, academicians, leftists, New Dealers, and a sprinkling of jazz, "race," and "hillbilly" disc collectors.

Apparently, the firm pressed 1,000 copies of Keynote 5000 for shipment to OWIU headquarters at Fort Worth, Texas. Subsequently, the Union priced these discs at 60 cents each (postpaid). On September 21–25, 1942, the OWIU held its thirteenth convention at Fort Worth. In the published *Proceedings*, Smith noted two cultural achievements geared to the organizational drive at Standard Oil:

> By means of a grant of $1,000 from the Robert Marshall Foundation, we held a poster contest open to CIO artists and three winning posters have been widely displayed. We also had two songs composed for the campaign by the Almanac Singers and put on records. The playing of these records at union meetings and elsewhere has created a lot of enthusiasm for the Union (33).

I have been unable to learn how many copies of Keynote 5000 the OWIU sold. Some could have been stored and overlooked as the War effort came to dominate CIO strategies. Other copies may have been broken in transit. Today, this 78-RPM disc is extremely rare; I know of no sound archive holding a copy.

Fortunately, knowledge of the Almanacs' oil songs did not vanish entirely at the close of World War II. During 1942, the OWIU had printed a little green-covered songbook holding a three-stanza text for "Boomtown Bill." Next, Moses Asch, proprietor of Folkways Records, gathered Woody's best poems into an inexpensive booklet, *American Folksong* (1947). It included nine stanzas for "Boomtown Bill" as well as the tune transcribed with labeled guitar chords. Editing *Woody Guthrie Folk Songs* (1963) for Ludlow Music, Pete Seeger used a seven-stanza text and tune for "Boomtown Bill." Also, Tom Glazer included this text/tune in *Songs of Peace, Freedom, and Protest* (1970).

"Keep That Oil A-Rolling" seems to have had a shorter life in print than its companion number. "Keep . . . " circulated briefly on the OWIU's Keynote record. Additionally, the Almanacs issued typescript broadsides of Woody's original text and subsequent revision. Finally, the Highlander Folk School (Monteagle, Tennessee) distributed a series of mimeographed song texts, during 1943, including "Keep That Oil A-Rolling."

I had first encountered the Almanac Singers in 1941–1942 through their albums *Talking Union* and *Deep Sea Chanteys*. Intrigued by the mix of traditional and union songs, I sought to learn the group's history. Working in San Francisco, and subsequently away for Navy service, I could not purchase a copy of Keynote 5000 when it was available. In 1983, undertaking an oil-song discography, I corresponded with Dick Reuss, Bob Pinson, Gene Earle, and other collectors. None had found the Almanacs' oil disc.

In 1985, my search for "Boomtown Bill"/"Keep That Oil A-Rolling" eventually led me to Jerry Archuleta in the Denver office of the Oil, Chemical, and Atomic Workers Union (successor to the OWIU). As Archuleta cast a wide net for the disc—by then lost in union memory—he hit the jackpot with an appeal to Harvey and Jessie O'Connor. Harvey had worked for the OWIU after World War II and had written a comprehensive history of the Union. The O'Connors had retained a single worn copy of the Keynote disc without being aware of its rarity or recalling the identity of the performers. Willingly, Harvey and Jessie O'Connor taped the songs for the OCAWU with copies for use by scholars. We are reminded again that laborlore artifacts slip away, but, luckily, devoted individuals do save emblems commenting upon occupational culture. Harvey O'Connor died at the age of 90 on August 29, 1987, his life marked by attention to the chain of labor tradition.

With the Keynote tape at hand, I transcribed each song text:

Boomtown Bill

Come all you oilfield workers and listen to my tale,
I worked for Drake in '59, way back in Titusville.
The state called Pennsylvania in the Allegheny field;
I've chased the oilfields ever since. My name is Boomtown Bill.

I've worked in wind and weather of rain and sleet and snow;
Yes, I done all the work, folks, but John D got the dough.
I don't like them company unions and, you know, I never will;
I'm CIO from head to toe. My name is Boomtown Bill.

Chorus:
I got my CIO card of which I'm mighty proud;
Whatever I believe in, I like to holler loud.
I don't like your company union 'cause it just don't fill the bill;
I'm USA and CIO, and my name is Boomtown Bill.

(instrumental break)

I've polished bits in Texas from the ocean to the plain;
Worked every field in the 48 states, and half way back again.
And now we're fighting in a war, the oil has got to flow;
And the best way to beat Hitler is to join the CIO.

Across the rolling ocean, the whole wide world around,
There's union workers fighting to tear old Hitler down.
Yes, I'm an oilfield worker and a soldier in my field;
I'll fight to save our oilfields. My name is Boomtown Bill.
(chorus)

I've got a lot of work to do and great big war to win;
I'll take my pipewrench back to work and see you all again.
The CIO's the best I know from the wildcat to the still,
So work and fight for what is right, and remember Boomtown Bill.
(final chorus)

Keep That Oil A-Rolling

You oilfield workers, come and listen to me,
I'm goin' to tell you a story about old John D.
That company union made a fool out of me.
That company union don't charge no dues,
But it leaves you singing them Rockefeller blues.
That company union made a fool out of me.

Chorus:
Takes that good ole CIO, boys,
To keep that oil a-rollin', a-rollin' over the sea;
It takes that good ole CIO, boys,
To keep that oil a-rollin' over the sea.

Drilling oil to beat Japan,
But the company union don't give a damn.
That company union made a fool out of me.
The oilfield workers and the NMU
Are going to beat Hitler, and damn quick, too.
That company union made a fool out of me.
(chorus)

Old Berlin to Tokyo,
The tanks can't roll if the oil don't flow.
That company union made a fool out of me.
Canada to Mexico
Is joining up with the CIO.
That company union made a fool out of me.
(chorus)

CIO is the place for me;
When this war is over, I want to be free.
That company union made a fool out of me.
I'm a union man in a union war,
It's a union land I'm a-fighting for.
That company union made a fool out of me.
(final chorus)

Receiving the tape copy of Keynote 5000, I could establish that Pete Seeger had sung lead on "Boomtown Bill" during the 1942 recording session. Several other Almanacs joined on the chorus. Pete played banjo; Woody, harmonica; Josh White may have been the guitarist. For "Keep That Oil A-Rolling," Guthrie sang lead as he switched from harmonica to mandolin. I cannot identify the chorus singers.

During years of shared inquiry with Dick Reuss, I felt his deep interest in Woody Guthrie. Reuss' bibliography on Guthriana and his challenging article on the Okemah bard for the *Journal of American Folklore* remain fine scholarly tools. In 1986, I did not know that my letters and phone calls to Dick in search for "Boomtown Bill" would close out our joint exploration in the laborlore wilderness. Happily, I had sent him a tape copy of the Keynote songs prior to his death.

In Dick's last letter to me (January 21, 1986), he suggested a fine interpretive frame for "Boomtown Bill." Within several epic-like ballads, such as "Hard Traveling," Guthrie portrayed a set of super workers. Composing two intertwined songs set to the tune of "John Hardy" ("The Ballad of Jackhammer John," "The Girl in the Red, White and Blue"), Woody placed four suitors in a gambling den/brothel, The Rising Sun. John Henry, Paul Bunyan, Edwin "Driller" Drake, and Jackhammer John vie for the girl's hand by touting their job exploits. The heroine, who can be seen as Miss America, ends their squabbling by sending them out to work in the forty-eight states.

Reuss believed that "Boomtown Bill" came from Guthrie's period of greatest vitality when he viewed national issues through the experience of brawny, virile, rambling workers. These legendary toilers metamorphosed from song to song as Guthrie shifted their scenes from hobo camp to river-dam construction site to wartime assembly line. Such progression reveals itself in placing "Boomtown Bill" side-by-side with Woody's "East Texas Red." In this latter song, a "double tough" brakeman becomes a railroad "bull" harassing bums. Red's victims are itinerant workers. Among them, some "boys" seek oilfield and pipeline jobs. In time, the wanderers return to the jungle where the "bull" had "dumped their last stew pot." The "boys" dispatch Red to his final ride.

In "East Texas Red," Guthrie's workers achieve private justice in ending the "bull's" life. In "Boomtown Bill," workers achieve public justice by joining the CIO to defeat Nazis. The latter theme emerged strongly in a July, 1942, NBC network radio broadcast, "Labor for Victory." In this program Woody offered songs and stories about CIO blue-collar giants fighting Hitler.

The poet's restless imagination merged fictive Boomtown Bill—roustabout, ruffneck, coke knocker—with historical Edwin Drake and mythic Paul Bunyan. Guthrie was not alone by invoking the spirit of Olympian workers. In the 1930s, coal miners used John L. Lewis' words and deeds to spark the CIO's initial drive. John L. could drop a mine mule with a single blow; John L. could bamboozle the glibbest politician; John L. could comfort the grieving widow.

Strangely, despite Guthrie's popularity, no singer has chosen to re-record either of his two oil numbers. Thus, I return to speculation on the obscurity of "Boomtown Bill" and "Keep That Oil A-Rolling." In seeking to explain the loss of a particular item of industrial expression, whether or not indigenous to the workplace, we raise interconnected matters of aesthetics and ideology. Consequently, we question the labor movement's direction as well as the conscious value choices of its activists.

No single factor doomed Guthrie's oil songs. The Oil Workers International Union faced a thousand compelling problems after World War II, among them, sorting out the allegiance of members and officers. When Edwin Smith lost his OWIU post in the spring of 1943, no one remained in union headquarters with special attachment to the Almanac Singers' recording. By 1948, 78-RPM discs faced competition (and eventual extinction) at the hands of 45-RPM singles and LP albums.

Matters of union survival, ideological adjustment, and changes in sound-recording technology combined to push Keynote 5000 down the memory hole. Further, as unionists broke with Communists in the 1950s, the former jettisoned considerable sectarian as well as Popular-Front expression. Some Almanac energy moved into a successor singing unit, The Weavers. However, the latter group lacked a direct bond to the labor movement.

Current performers know Guthrie's iconic labor songs but not his ephemeral material. In attempting to bring "Boomtown Bill" or "Keep That Oil A-Rolling" to contemporary union activists, we face the possibility that listeners may find Guthrie's poetry dated, with its blend of blue-collar chauvinism, job nomenclature, old-fashioned unionism, and wartime patriotism. "Boomtown Bill"'s stanza four (1963 printing) illustrates these conjunctions:

> Them walking beams and rotaries,
> I know my rigs by heart;
> I put your Kelly in your Rathole,
> Take your Christmas Tree apart.
> Gotta war ta lick them fascist rats,
> This black oil's got to flow;
> Best way t'beat these nazis
> Is t'join the C.I.O.

Not all labor educators, today, have need to or wish to resurrect Almanac imagery or trace the group's seesaw positions. A few students in the late 1980s looked back at radical culture through the lens of *glasnost*. We can anticipate that ties between the Almanac Singers, Marxist aesthetics, and organized labor will be examined critically in the decade ahead. Folklorists have a special responsibility to reopen assumptions that girded "People's Songs" phenomenon, to untangle the authoritarian and libertarian impulses within Popular-Front appeals.

Guthrie fans have not found it easy to deal with his contradictory politics invoking Franklin Roosevelt and Joseph Stalin. Many who have guarded Woody's memory have also avoided questions about his sexual drives. I have noted above two of his songs placing heroic workers in a gambling den/brothel. Among his many unpublished texts at the Smithsonian Institution, the "Boomtown Gallyhouse" narrates a pipeliner's erotic adventures after pay day at Borger, Texas.

Although Guthrie's typescript is undated, folklorist Guy Logsdon suggests that it reports a scene in the 1930s, but was composed in 1942, perhaps in conjunction with Woody's oil-union songs. We can only speculate that the OWIU commission stimulated buried memories. The bawdy number holds a cryptic footnote:

> I saw this song happen several hundred times during my several years as an odd job cleanup man around five or six oily boom towns. (I was never an officer on the public payroll.)

Presumably, in the parenthetical statement, Guthrie certified his proletarian authenticity by distinguishing himself from revenue agents, red-light district inspectors, or police informants.

Readers may wish to keep in mind Woody's intended tune, "The Jolly Roving Tar," for the "Boomtown Gallyhouse." The text follows:

Boomtown Gallyhouse

The first good job of work I got
When I struck old Borger town
Was digging a ditch on a pipeline gang
Of wild and rowdy men.
I grabbed my pay that thirty first day
And I drunk till I was soused,
They rolled my clothes and got my dough
In a boomtown gallyhouse.

Chorus:
She wiggled and jiggled and smiled at me
And she lit my black cigar
She showed me all the ins and outs
Of her boomtown gallyhouse.
She showed me all the ups and downs
Of her boomtown gallyhouse.

She'd traveled with a circus once,
And a carnival, too, she said.
I combed my fingers through her hair
While sitting on her bed.
She told me how she fed the cops,
The beddy bug and the louse,
She fed her mule and landlord, too,
Of the boomtown gallyhouse.

I seen her tatooed bumbledy bee
Somewhere above her knee,
I fought and scratched, I puffed and blowed
To scare that bee away.
I pooched my lip, I licked my mouth,
Then I blew from north to south,
And the bee was gone when the daylight come

To my boomtown gallyhouse.
My clothes was gone from that old nail
That she did hang them on,
Nobody but me was there to see
Them stinky bugs climb that wall.
I pulled a towel around my hips,
I clumb a sewer pipe down,

> I didn't come back for thirty one days
> To the boomtown gallyhouse.
>
> When I walked in, I bumped a man
> That weighed two hundred pounds,
> I asked him about my bumbledy bee,
> Ohh, is she still around?
> I married her last night, he says,
> And he kicks me in the mouth,
> I lost my pocketbook on the stairs
> Of my boomtown gallyhouse.

Conscious that some folklorists, union educators, and feminists will be uncomfortable with the "Boomtown Gallyhouse," I present it to indicate one obvious aspect of occupational culture. Cowboys, miners, loggers, oil-field hands, and other workers in the "boondocks" used bawdy material variously to comment on isolation, to indulge in fantasy, and to relieve tension. Labor-song partisans find it disturbing that many more workers are familiar with off-color lore than with union classics.

While focusing upon the circumstance of composition and political message in Guthrie's two commissioned oil songs, I have put aside other contextual areas: oil-union history, oilfield tradition. A few references will guide students. Three authors have treated oil-union history: Harvey O'Connor (1950), Melvin Rothbaum (1962), Harry Seligson (1960). A large backdrop of black-gold tradition stands behind Woody's oil songs. From the discovery of Pennsylvania's Allegheny fields in the 1850s, some occupational pieces have circulated in the oil patch and in appropriate trade journals. Readers will find Mody Boatright's books a useful guide into the songs and stories, customs and beliefs of oil workers.

Curiously, sound-recording firms did not turn to oil balladry with the same vigor in which they presented railroad, coal mine, and textile songs. We find only a handful of oil items before the Almanacs recorded Keynote 5000. I cite four discs preceding "Boomtown Bill": Blind Lemon Jefferson's semi-bawdy "Oil Well Blues" (1929); Dennis McGee's Cajun "Valse de Puit d'Huile" (1929); Jesse Rodgers' country-western "Roughneck Blues" (1934); Moon Mullican's honkytonk "Pipe Liner's Blues" (1940).

In retrospect, Guthrie's oil songs hold discographical significance beyond their temporal message or their use of folk melody. Keynote 5000 can be placed in sequence with the records of Jefferson, McGee, Rodgers, and Mullican. These disparate artists—with roots of varying depths in folk communities—pioneered in capturing oil song in living dimension. Sound recordings hold the walking beam's pulse and the gusher's roar.

Perhaps a history-oriented performer involved in union education or connected to a petroleum museum will now record a full-length "Boomtown Bill." This song and "Keep That Oil A-Rolling," whether considered worthy musically or conceptually, represent the first two oil-union compositions recorded in the United States. Woody Guthrie's roustabout pair remain a window to one feature of labor's past.

American workers display superb skill in building and staffing schools, museums, archives, libraries, or film centers. In these institutions, workers accept proper roles as maintenance hands, cafeteria cooks, seminar teachers, bibliographers, or computer programmers. However, the men and women who build and staff cultural institutions are not always certain of the appropriate "shrines" in which to place their own expressive artifacts. Who gathers the banners, buttons, ballads, and blues that constitute laborlore?

We find it difficult to confront the erosion of occupational tradition and puzzle over past functions in our songs and stories. We struggle to assess meaning in lore stemming from the workplace. To lose a single phonograph disc seems a minor loss. To neglect a recorded capsule of workers' creativity diminishes strength in future paths. "Boomtown Bill" and "Keep That Oil A-Rolling" deserve to come out of limbo.

San Francisco

Author's Note. David Samuelson and Ronald Cohen include Woody Guthrie's two Keynote oil songs within a multi-CD reissue set of American protest/political music: Bear Family BCD 15720, forthcoming (1994).

References Cited

Almanac Singers. 1942. "Boomtown Bill/Keep That Oil A-Rolling." 78-RPM disk. Keynote 5000.

Archuleta, Jerry. 1985–86. Correspondence with author.

Boatright, Mody. 1963. *Folklore of the Oil Industry*. Dallas: Southern Methodist University Press.

———, and William Owens. 1970. *Tales from the Derrick Floor*. Garden City, New York: Doubleday.

CIO News, OWIU edition. 1942a. "Songs for a Second Front." May 25:7.

———. 1942b. "Ballad Heroes Join CIO Fight to Beat Hitler." July 20:5.

Dunaway, David. 1981. *How Can I Keep from Singing: Pete Seeger*. New York: McGraw-Hill.

Glazer, Tom. 1970. *Songs of Peace, Freedom, and Protest*. New York: McKay.

Guthrie, Woody. 1947. *American Folksong*. New York: Disc Company of America.

———. 1963. *Woody Guthrie Folk Song*. New York: Ludlow Music.

Highlander Folk School. 1943. "Keep That Oil A-Rolling." Monteagle, Tenn.: The School. (Mimeographed songsheet).

Klein, Joe. 1980. *Woody Guthrie: A Life.* New York: Knopf.

Logsdon, Guy. 1991. Letter to author, January 8.

O'Connor, Harvey. 1950. *History of the Oil Workers International Union.* Denver: The Union.

OWIU. 1942a. *Songs for Labor.* Fort Worth, Tex.: Oil Workers International Union.

———. 1942b. *Thirteenth Convention Proceedings.* Fort Worth, Tex.: Oil Workers International Union.

Reuss, Richard A. 1970. "Woody Guthrie and His Folk Tradition." *Journal of American Folklore* 83:273–303.

———. 1971. "American Folklore and Left-Wing Politics: 1927–1957." Ph.D. diss., Indiana University.

———. 1986. Letter to author, January 21.

Rothbaum, Melvin. 1962. *The Government of the Oil, Chemical and Atomic Workers Union.* New York: Wiley.

Seeger, Pete. 1986. Letter to author, November 26.

Seligson, Harry. 1960. *Oil, Chemical and Atomic Workers: A Labor Union in Action.* Denver: University of Denver Press.

Smith, Edwin S. 1942. Letter to Woody Guthrie, March 27. (In David Dunaway files.)

Michael Heisley

Truth in Folksong: A *Corridista's* View of Singing in the California Farm Workers' Movement

On September 16, 1965, the National Farm Workers' Association (NFWA) called an urgent meeting of its membership at the largest available hall in Delano, California. Eight days earlier Filipino farm workers in the Agricultural Workers' Organizing Committee (AWOC) struck ten vineyards near this southern San Joaquín Valley town. They demanded $1.40 per hour for the arduous work of harvesting table grapes, the prevailing wage elsewhere in the state for this work. The Delano growers offered $1.20 per hour, the previous year's wages. Many of the predominantly Mexican American members of the NFWA were employed at nearby vineyards not affected by this strike, but the organization had to decide on a course of action. Although César Chávez and other NFWA leaders felt that their group was unprepared for a prolonged strike, ignoring the efforts of the Filipinos would be tantamount to scabbing (London and Anderson 1970:151).

At the NFWA's September 16 meeting Chávez explained the risks of a strike, but NFWA's sympathies were clearly with the Filipino strikers. The Mexican American farm workers voted overwhelmingly to join the strike or *la huelga* as it is known in Spanish. Not only did they refuse to cross AWOC's picket lines, but they walked off their jobs as well. This vote precipitated the merger of the NFWA and AWOC into the United Farm Workers (UFW).[1] More importantly, coming as it did in the midst of the rising tide of expectations engendered by the civil rights movement of the 1960s, the farm workers' decision marked the opening of a new era in farm labor history.

The United Farm Workers, through strikes, boycotts, and other public protests, brought national, even international attention to the problems and injustices faced by farm workers in the United States. This movement eventually inspired not only farm workers, but also people outside of farm labor, including Mexican American workers in other industries, students and youth in the emerging Chicano Movement, and idealistic volunteers from the urban middle class.

Like the Industrial Workers of the World (IWW), the United Mine Workers of America, and African American civil rights struggles, the UFW is a movement for social justice in which song and singing traditions play an important role. The singing of this movement is perhaps best known to non-farm worker audiences through the performances and recordings of El Teatro Campesino (The Farm Workers' Theater), a theatrical troupe begun among UFW strikers. El Teatro Campesino fused elements of commedia del'arte, agit-prop, *carpas* (travelling tent shows featuring entertainers from Mexico), and everyday experiences of farm workers into a dramatic educational tool equally effective in rural farm worker towns and on college campuses. There also is a local tradition of songmaking among Mexican and Mexican American farm workers that plays a significant role in the singing of the union and served as a basis for much of El Teatro Campesino's music (El Teatro Campesino 1966; Heisley 1977, 1983).

Of particular importance in the repertoire of farm worker singers is the *corrido*, a ballad tradition with roots in Spain, Mexico, and the Texas-Mexican border. *Corridistas* (composers or singers of corridos) in the farm workers' movement used this genre to comment on local events in the union's development. As with other movements for social justice, songs and singing helped define and sustain the farm workers' cause by giving voice to the ideas, emotions, and experiences that form the roots of social protest. These traditions may be as essential to a movement's survival as the practical everyday actions of organizers, for they give expression to the subjective sense of ethnic and class identities that move people from acceptance of the status quo to direct action. Indeed, the organizers of the UFW understood this well and incorporated songs, theater, graphic arts, and Mexican Catholic traditions into the union's strategies in order to mobilize farm workers as well as outside supporters.

In 1973 while working as a boycott organizer for the UFW in Washington, D.C., I began recording corridos sung by rank and file members of the UFW. I was moved by the seriousness and intensity of these songs. Part chronicles of particular strikes and appeals to the conscience, these songs also seemed to me to be powerful comments on the meaning of the hardships and changes individual strikers endured in order to build a successful union. Like the songs of social struggle brought to northern cities by Aunt Molly Jackson in the 1930s or the Freedom Singers in the 1960s, farm worker corridos symbolized to me the dignity, strength, and vitality of the cultures of oppressed people.

The singers I recorded in the East were rank and file union members who, after going out on strike, volunteered for work on the union's grape and lettuce boycotts. Through these boycotts the UFW gained the economic leverage necessary to bring growers to the bargaining table and sign contracts. After moving to California in 1974, I recorded farm worker singers who drew upon a variety of sources for their corridos, including compositions made popular by El Teatro Campesino, songs by Mexican American recording artists, and ballads from the United States-Mexico borderlands. Their corridos celebrated key events in the movement's early development, events also recounted in oral narratives told by strikers and featured in the union's newspaper (Brown 1972; Heisley 1983).

Corridos and the individual singer

Writing about the Texas-Mexican corrido, Américo Paredes noted a similar connection between ballads and stories about heroes of border conflict such as Gregorio Cortez and Jacinto Treviño (1958, 1976). Elaborating on these findings, John McDowell indicated that "the purpose of the corrido is not, as some scholars have supposed, to convey news. News travels readily enough through less formal channels such as gossip, anecdote, etc. Generally, the corrido depends on a prior transmission of news; its purpose is to interpret, celebrate, and ultimately dignify events already thoroughly familiar to the corrido audience" (1981:47). In short, most people already know of events in their communities from spoken or written sources; songs rarely serve as an oral newspaper. If this is true, why did farm workers find songs about local events so appealing?

Pablo Saludado, a UFW member and corridista, residing in Earlimart, California, suggested an answer. During an interview in his home, we discussed a corrido about César Chávez, the UFW's well-known leader. He likened the sentiments expressed in this song to a proverb used in his family: "*La mentira dura mientras de que la verdad no llega.*" He translated this saying as "Lies will last only until the truth arrives." Like many corridos about the UFW and farm labor strikes, this song and two other ballads considered in this essay touch on specific events and people in the union's history. As Pablo's proverb suggests, however, these corridos express a point of view about events rather than simply recounting them. It is this point of view, the selective portrayal of events and heroic images of César Chávez, and the associations evoked by tunes and symbols used in his songs, that make them an effective way of communicating his thoughts and feelings.

Ballad scholars have long considered the individual singer's view of *truth* as expressed in songs. Cecil Sharp, writing in 1907, noted that for the ballad singer "there is no tale like the true tale; and to heighten the sense of reality, he will often lay the scene of his story in his own locality" (quoted in Ashton 1977:12). Likewise William J. Entwistle noted in *European Balladry* that "Ballads are to be accepted as true. Truth is, perhaps, not a quality demanded by the aesthete, but it is the necessary leaven of traditional narrative poetry, whether epic or ballad" (1939:114–16).

In an article published in 1939 entitled "Truth in Folk-Songs—Some Observations on the Folk-Singer's Attitude," Herbert Halpert sought to illuminate the "problems of the human relationships to the song" by examining how singers in New York and New Jersey conceived of British ballads in their repertoires as being "true songs." Drawing in part on the work of Sharp, Phillips Barry, and George Herzog, Halpert cited, for example, the singer's "intense emotional participation in the song narrative" and the well-known practice of localizing songs to familiar places or personages as evidence of traditional singers' attraction to songs that they conceive to be true (Barry 1961; Herzog 1938, 1949; Sharp 1907).

For the most part, these scholars focused on questions of the persistence of versions or variants of old ballads among contemporary singers. Their work also presaged an attempt now more common in folksong scholarship to understand narrative songs in terms of the ideas, experiences, and attitudes of individual singers and specific audiences. Their efforts and those of recent researchers represent a move among folksong scholars away from the stereotypical view of folksingers as inherently conservative and folksongs as relics from the past and toward an understanding of the singer's view of the personal and social uses of song.

Scholars of the Mexican and Mexican American corrido have shown a parallel but distinctive interest in a singer's attitudes toward historical events and personages expressed in ballads. Adopting a view of folksong as a reflector of culture, several scholars have interpreted this genre as a barometer of popular sentiment, especially feelings about a group's identity in situations of social upheaval and cultural conflict. Américo Paredes's classic studies of Texas-Mexican corridos provide a vivid illustration of the use of folksong in the protracted cultural conflict between Anglos and Mexicans along the lower Río Grande border. Texas-Mexicans celebrated heroes of cultural conflict such as Gregorio Cortez in both prose narrative and corrido. Through Paredes's writings we see how these heroes reach their apotheosis as epic figures defending their rights as Mexicans and symbolically reversing Anglo stereotypes.

Merle Simmons views the corrido as an historical document reflecting popular attitudes of the Mexican *pueblo* (Simmons 1957). While he notes that corridos express a wide range of human concerns, Simmons primarily considers this form of Mexican balladry as it relates to major historical events. For example, during the Mexican Revolution (1910–1917) the corrido, in Simmons's view, informed people of current events in this struggle. More importantly corrido singing helped sustain morale by entertaining the troops and reminding them of the ideals for which they were fighting (1957: 34–35).

The two streams of folksong scholarship described above share many concepts and preoccupations, including an interest in the ways singers and their audiences express perceptions of historical events through songs. They also conceive of traditional song from differing perspectives. Anglo-American folksong scholarship—with important exceptions such as those noted earlier—has tended to view truth as lodged in a static and outmoded view of the world supposedly held by traditional singers. In contrast, corrido scholarship has been especially sensitive to historical change in a particular group's outlook or interests. For the most part, researchers of Mexican balladry have conceived of folksong as group expression and the corridista as a composer whose songs reflect the views of a particular historical era and/or a more or less homogeneous audience. Rarely have scholars of Mexican or Mexican American balladry been concerned with an individual singer's attitudes toward particular songs and conceptions of the role of corridista.

In recent years scholars have devoted renewed attention to songmakers and singers and consequently researchers have begun to explore the role of individuality in traditional singing (e.g., Glassie, Ives, Szwed 1970; Heisley 1983; Porter 1986). Roger D. Abrahams, for example, suggested that the role of the individual (and of individuality) in the development of repertoire is an important area of folksong scholarship that promises to increase our understanding of how a singer's choice of materials expresses his or her personal and social identities (Abrahams 1970:9). In a similar vein Kenneth Goldstein argued that understanding the status of particular items of folklore in an individual's repertoire is an important task for scholars. Reflecting on his experiences recording traditional songs he wrote: "Each song had its heyday in the informant's repertory, some serving continuously for perhaps as long as half a century, others for only a couple of months. And every one of them is associated in the memory of the singer with a particular time or place, one or more of his friends or relatives, a meaningful experience, or some combination of these" (Goldstein 1971:66). In sum, we must turn to individual singers to understand how and why these performers find traditional songs appealing and meaningful.

Truth and the singer's conception of corridos

By looking at corrido singing from an individual singer's perspective, I wish to consider this seldom explored approach to this expressive form.[2] Pablo Saludado's selection of subjects as appropriate for songs, his attitudes toward specific compositions and the personal and social uses of singing are fundamental to understanding the meaning of this song tradition to him. We also gain insights into how and why, as a participant in a social justice movement, he found the corrido to be an appropriate means of expression.

For Pablo Saludado, I believe that his view of truth as expressed in corridos is a key factor influencing his decisions about which songs from the farm workers' union to learn and sing. As John Ashton has noted, "the singer's view of the term 'truth' is eminently flexible and . . . a song need not necessarily be documentary or ethical in its application to be considered true" (1977: 13). Ashton indicated that singers also may consider songs which invoke a common affective response derived from past experience to be true songs, particularly if these songs serve to illustrate or reinforce the singer's sense of morality (Ashton 1977:15). Pablo has a similar attitude toward sentiments of truth expressed in his songs. Like many corridistas, Pablo learns songs that mirror his attitudes and feelings about local events (Paredes 1971–1972; McDowell 1981). This aspect of corrido singing makes it an especially appropriate medium for understanding the ways that singing may excite and sustain participants in social movements and not just recount events.

I first met Pablo Saludado in the spring of 1975 through the UFW office in Delano, California. Like the singers I had previously recorded in the East, he sang songs that friends and fellow strikers composed in response to their experiences as *huelguistas* (strikers). For most of his life he had sung corridos, but the songs about the UFW were the first ones that commented on events in his own community. Neighbors who composed corridos brought their songs to him to sing and Pablo actively sought corridos from workers from other parts of California whom he met at union rallies. His daughter Juana, who as a student worked for the union after school, encouraged him to learn songs from El Teatro Campesino. In short Pablo's role as a corridista revolved around existing social networks, but his singing also helped him create new social relations during the turbulent years of the strike.

Pablo performed mainly corridos and other Spanish-language union songs for farm worker audiences, but our conversations revealed that he was a versatile musician from a family that valued singing and instrumental music. His father, Secundino Saludado, was a trained musician who had a strong influence on Pablo's commitment to singing. He emigrated to the United

States from Mexico in 1910. While playing in an orchestra in Ciudad Juárez along the Texas-Mexican border, Secundino had heard talk about the *peso cuate* (literally, double *peso* or higher wages) and employment opportunities north of the border. Secundino, his wife, and nine musicians from the orchestra crossed the border to find work in El Paso, Texas.

Soon afterwards, the Saludados settled in the copper mining town of Morenci, Arizona, where they worked in the mines and participated in strikes by Mexican miners. These workers received lower wages than Anglo miners for performing some of the most difficult and dangerous tasks in the mines. In Morenci, where Pablo was born in 1914, Secundino organized an orchestra among the miners and taught music when not working as a *minero*. Moving to California in the 1920s, the family settled in East Los Angeles. There Pablo enrolled in a music school in addition to his regular schooling and began to play the violin.

Seeking better opportunities, Pablo's father left construction work in Los Angeles; during the remainder of the 1920s, the Saludados migrated to various parts of California as Secundino worked for the railroads and did farm work. For a short time, the family ran a small grocery store in the San Joaquín Valley. All the while Pablo learned music and songs from his father, and he took up playing the guitar, his preferred instrument. During this period of migration, Pablo and his father often performed together for neighborhood dances with Pablo providing guitar accompaniment to his father's violin.

As father and son, they became recognized musicians in each of the communities in which their family settled. Pablo and Secundino frequently volunteered to perform for public celebrations, especially on Mexican patriotic holidays and in support of the *Comisión Honorífica*, a self-help and patriotic society affiliated with the Mexican consulate that sought to protect the rights of Mexicans in the United States. Secundino's support of the *Comisión Honorífica* indicated his political and cultural loyalties; although he resided in the United States for over forty years, he chose to remain a citizen of Mexico.

After losing their small store in the Depression, the Saludados turned to farm work in the San Joaquín Valley. Respecting the picket lines of striking farm workers in the valley's cotton fields during the 1930s, the Saludados often drove many miles to find work outside of strike zones. In these years, Pablo began learning new songs from farm workers who travelled from other states and elsewhere in California. Early morning radio broadcasts from Los Angeles by such groups as Pedro J. González's *Los madrugadores* (The Early Risers) and *carpas* (travelling tent shows) featuring performers such as the Texas-Mexican singer Lydia Mendoza, also influenced Pablo's playing in the years immediately before World War II. In many respects the songs and singing styles Pablo learned in the 1930s along with those his father taught him earlier served as the principal backgrounds for his singing before UFW audiences during the 1960s and 1970s.

In 1934 the Saludados settled in Earlimart, a small farm worker town about ten miles north of Delano on state highway 99. In addition to the large cotton and wheat farms that then formed the mainstay of agriculture in the area, a number of small farms produced fruits and vegetables. Japanese growers operated many of these farms. Pablo found work after settling in Earlimart within this network of growers.

In order to maintain a stable and skilled work force, the Japanese hired local residents, trained them, and kept them working on several of the local farms. Pablo recalled, "They had real small places, but they wouldn't even let me rest on Sundays . . . or I couldn't afford to rest on Sundays because, see, I don't know, they always seem to like to work you on Sundays." Others who refused to work Sundays were often not rehired, Pablo pointed out. "And then, see, they had such small patches," continued Pablo, "that I used to work for one of them, maybe two or three weeks or maybe a month at most and then his work was over. But he used to tell me, 'You go with so-and-so and I'll let him know that you're going up there.' So that's the way they kept me working all the time, just all the time."

Working for the Japanese growers required handling teams of mules and horses, a skill Pablo had previously acquired. It also involved learning the farming skills particular to growing fruits and vegetables. As Pablo put it, the Japanese growers he worked for "were real good farmers. They took real good care of their crops. Well, everything that I know about farming, about raising fruits or vegetables and grafting and budding and whatever, I learned it off the Japanese. They were something special for agriculture." On another occasion Pablo commented:

> These Japanese, they used to really want you to work hard and no rest, no nothing. One thing, though, I was always very pleased with them [for] they always used to treat me very nice even though they wanted me to do a lot of work for them. But what I really liked . . . that's probably why I used to didn't mind to work so hard with them because I was *learning* so much.

The Japanese growers worked closely with those they hired. In addition to teaching specific skills related to planting, cultivating, and harvesting, they noted and carefully set the pace of work. When Pablo first began working, they observed his ability to pace his work with horses in order not to tire them during a long day's work. "I didn't hurry myself so much, and the work would go far because I had a lot of experience with the team, mules and the horses."

Pablo recalls that many Japanese growers worked in the fields alongside the hired workers, doing the same tasks while exercising control over the work crews. For example, Pablo remembered the rest periods during the cantaloupe harvest on Mr. Kono's farm:

> Once in a while he knew we were working real hard and especially when he had some cantaloupes ready, some cantaloupes ripe. He wouldn't—you know most of them, you ask them for a cantaloupe or something and they'd go give you culls—and he used to go and pick the best ones. The best ones for his work-ing men. And then we was working maybe ten o'clock or so, and the sun was real hot in the cantaloupe season, real hot . . . gets real hot. He goes and picked up a real nice cantaloupe. Some of the first class, no culls or nothing, the *best*.

These breaks provided a needed rest for the grower and worker alike, but kept control in the grower's hands. As Pablo commented, "He knew we were working hard, and that we needed a rest, but he wouldn't say to take a rest."

During the eight years between his first employment on Japanese farms and the wartime relocation of the Japanese on the West Coast in 1942, Pablo came to think of himself as "a specialist for their work . . . for their vegetable plants and fruit plants." Although the work was demanding and the pay was low, Pablo felt that the employment he found with local farmers had a number of advantages, especially during the Depression. Primarily it meant steady work without having to go through a labor contractor—a middleman between grower and farm worker who often cheated workers out of their pay. In contrast, the smaller growers, while paying the same wages and also demanding long hours on the job, hired workers in person and worked alongside them in the fields. The hierarchy characteristic of the large corpo-rate farm was absent or differed substantially on the smaller farms. Only a few years earlier many Japanese farmers had been farm workers themselves.

Although not directly related to his corrido singing, Pablo's service in the U.S. Navy in World War II also contributed to his view of himself as a performer during the years of the farm workers' movement. In training at Treasure Island Naval Base near San Francisco, Pablo found new audiences and learned new songs. He was in demand as a singer and guitarist in the barracks, and he often sang Mexican patriotic songs such as "Soy puro mexicano" ("I Am All Mexican") for the sailors. "Even the white boys would sing with me," recalled Pablo. "Some of them could pronounce the words and some of them couldn't. But they went ahead and sang with me all of the time. They hardly didn't let me rest at all."

The singing in the barracks included popular songs of the time, in English as well as Spanish. Pablo remembers singing "Paper Doll" and "Mistress at the Saturday Dance" and at the request of others he accompanied Anglo country songs. Referring to these experiences, Pablo said, "And, you know, that would lift my spirit. That's why I could just keep on playing and playing with them. I didn't think I could play that much, but I could." This experience in the military prepared him for singing in later years for audiences outside of farm worker communities.

Like many Mexican-American servicemen of the G.I. generation, Pablo returned home from his wartime experiences with a sharpened awareness of the low social and economic status of farm workers. In California agriculture, Mexicans along with Chinese, Japanese, Filipino, and other immigrant workers built and sustained the state's industrialized farms. Farm workers occupied a place at the bottom of an ethnically stratified labor force in which growers recruited immigrants to do the hardest jobs often under extremely poor conditions and for little pay. His awareness of the contradictions between the promises of United States democracy and the reality of his life as a farm worker served as a background for his participation in the UFW.

Returning to Earlimart after the Second World War, Pablo found employment at a large vineyard. He worked as an irrigator, harvest worker, and in the winter as a tender of smudge pots. During the fifteen years that he was employed by the same grower, Pablo was expected to work long hours and be on call to protect the crops during floods and freezes. Recalling his music and singing during this period, Pablo said, "For this fifteen years that I worked there for [the] Pandols, I never did play [in public] at all. I used to play here in my house just by myself. Once in a while I'd get the guitar and sing just a little bit by myself, but I wasn't playing at all outside. I didn't have no time for that."

In the early 1960s, Pablo suffered a serious job-related injury. After working all day lifting heavy bundles of wet lumber, he returned home and paralysis struck his arm. He feared that he had suffered a stroke. "When I was paralyzed, I couldn't practice [the guitar]," Pablo explained. "I couldn't move my hand, I couldn't move my fingers or anything. So that's one time that I really went back on my music."

Referring to his disability, Pablo commented, "That's one time that I can see the difference between when we didn't have a union contract and now that we have a union." His employer, unwilling to incur the expenses of medical treatments or disability benefits, kept him working. As Pablo explained, "I couldn't get no insurance; I couldn't get no benefits because I was working. Even if I couldn't work, they had me out there working, you know."

Pablo contrasted this experience with a later accident he had while working for Bill Stewart, a small grower in Earlimart:

> Afterward I got injured in my other arm, and I then was working here for Bill Stewart right here across the tracks, and he had me go to this little doctor here in Earlimart. And this little doctor, he treated me fast as he could, just a fast little treatment because my arm was awful; and then he sent me right away to a specialist. I had to have an operation on that arm, you know. He sent me right away, he cleaned me up, he washed me a little.

Pablo nearly lost his arm in the accident at Bill Stewart's farm. The prompt medical care he received through the efforts of Mr. Stewart, and the assistance with disability benefits provided at the farm worker clinic in Earlimart, contrasted with the lack of concern and eventual loss of employment he had experienced earlier when injured on the large farm.

Following his second injury, Pablo had considerable difficulty playing his guitar, but he refused to give up his music. Playing guitar was essential to his recovery:

> I couldn't get that guitar. I couldn't move it with my fingers. I used to get it and scratch it with my right hand. . . . I could move my right hand, but I couldn't move my left. But still I used to get it and little by little. . . . Then I kept on with home remedies. I used to massage it myself, and if I had a friend come over [I would tell him]: "Here, massage my arm with mineral oil or something." And I was always moving it. And if I would try and push, why, heck, my arm just wouldn't hold.

Gradually Pablo made progress in regaining the use of his hands. He said, "I just kept on, kept on, and massaged my arm, and made a little exercise, especially with my guitar. A group of friends gave him a new Gibson guitar. "When they give me this guitar, boy, I used to see this guitar, and I wanted to get ahold of it so bad. This probably helped, too. And then right after that, my cousin came [from Mexico]."

His cousin Lorenzo encouraged Pablo to play in a *mariachi* with him. "I told him," Pablo said, "'Why, you see that I can't even move my hand.' And he said, 'Why, oh, just keep time for us.' And I didn't want to play at all, and he just kept on. And I told him, 'I'll try and keep time for you, but you look for somebody to play guitar with.'"

Remembering these sessions playing with his cousin's mariachi, Pablo recalled:

> I used to go and keep time for him, and I wasn't even putting my hands on the strings where they should be, but I kept time for them. And little by little my hands started to move more, and I kept on massaging them and exercising them and moving them on the guitar.
>
> I was in a heck of a fix, but I just kept on going, kept on going. I didn't stop even if I knew that I wasn't doing anything nice [on the guitar], but it was doing a lot. . . . I was getting a lot of benefit out of those exercises like that with the guitar.

His persistence and the encouragement of others eventually paid off. By the early 1960s, Pablo regained the use of both hands and was able to work and play the guitar again.

Singing and social commitment

Pablo was among the first members of the National Farm Workers' Association (NFWA), an organization of year-round resident farm workers primarily of Mexican descent founded in 1962 by César Chávez. This organization joined Filipino strikers in the Agricultural Workers Organizing Committee to form the UFW in the early weeks of the strike that Filipino workers began in September 1965. Although Pablo did not work on a farm affected by this dispute, he attended union meetings in Delano and was sympathetic to the strike.

Not long after picketing began in September 1965, Pablo's neighbor, Juan D. Tavena, composed *"Huelga y violencias"* ("Strike and Violences"). He taught this corrido to Pablo, and the two of them rehearsed it at Pablo's house and later sang it at a Friday night strikers' meeting at Filipino Hall in Delano. At these weekly events, huelguistas shared news of the strike, and union members made important decisions concerning strategy. After a long week of picketing, strikers also gathered at these meetings for morale boosting activities such as corrido singing. Following their performance one Friday evening, Señor Tavena and Pablo distributed mimeographed broadsides with the lyrics to *"Huelga y violencias."*

This corrido was the first song that Pablo sang for the fledgling farm workers' union. It portrays the major events of the early weeks of the picketing, a period when many strikers were unsure of their union's ability to win the strike. Growers recruited strikebreakers to harvest the grapes, some huelguistas returned to work, and the local police enforced a court-ordered ban on the use of loudspeakers on the picket line (Brown 1972; Nelson 1966). This latter development became a major rallying point during the initial phase of the strike and is an important theme in the corrido.

Huelga y violencias
Words by Juan D. Tavena
Tune: *"Corrido de los Hermanos Hernández"*

Un día ocho de septiembre	One day, the eighth of September,
Del año sesenta y cinco	In the year of sixty-five,
Comenzó a según se entiende	There began, or so it is said,
Una huelga contra los ricos.	A strike against the rich.
Todos los trabajadores	All the workers
De sus trabajos salieron	Walked off their jobs

Pidiendo sueldos mejores	Asking for better wages
Y en huelga se levantaron.	And went out on strike.
Por ahí nos dijo un ranchero,	Around there a grower said,
"De hambre los voy a matar;	"With hunger I am going to kill you;
No tienen mucho dinero	You do not have much money,
Muy pronto se van a dar.	Very soon you are going to give up."
Pero se han equivocado,	But they were mistaken,
Todo les salió al revés;	Everything turned out differently;
Comida les ha sobrado	They had more than enough food
Y dinero cada mes.	And money every month.
Ay, ay, ay, ay	*Ay, ay, ay, ay,*
Aguilita ve volando	Fly away little eagle;
Avísale al mundo entero	Tell the entire world
Que algo serio está pasando.	That something serious is happening.
A todos los Filipinos	All the Filipinos
De sus campos los echaron;	Were thrown out of their camps;
Afuera hacia los caminos	Out on the highways their clothes
La ropa se las tiraron.	Were thrown out after them.
Con unos pistoleros	With armed goons
Les quitaron las cabinas	They were made to leave the cabins,
Porque fueron los primeros	Because they were the first ones
Que abandonaron las viñas.	that left the vineyards.
Con máquinas de polvear	With dusting machines
Ya los andaban ahogando;	They tried to choke them;
Con azufre querían ahogan	With sulphur they wanted to choke
A la gente organizando.	The people who were organizing.
Fue uno de los rancheros,	It was one of the growers,
Provocativo y valiente,	Provoking and a bully,
De tantos fue el primero	Of all of them he was the first
Que ataca cobardemente.	To attack cowardly.
Ay, ay, ay, ay,	*Ay, ay, ay, ay,*
Virgencita ten piedad	Dear Virgin take pity
De los que piden justicia;	On those who ask for justice;
Merecen tu caridad.	They deserve your charity.
Cuarenta y cuatro arrestaron	Forty-four were arrested
Sin cometer violación;	Without committing a crime;
Nomás porque le gritaron	Their only offense was to yell
"¡La huelga!" a un patrón.	"Strike!" to a boss.
Entre ellos iban señoras	Among them were women
Y también nueve ministros.	And also nine ministers.
Pasaron sus largas horas	They spent long hours
Encerrados sin delito.	Imprisoned without having commited a crime.

Con armas peligrosas	With dangerous arms
En el rancho Sierra Vista	In the ranch of Sierra Vista
Golpearon a Manuel Rosas	They beat up Manuel Rosas,
Al mero gallón huelguista.	A true leader of the strikers.
Lo llevan al hospital	They take him, badly wounded
Muy mal herido y sangrando.	And bleeding, to the hospital.
La suerte fue fatal,	He had bad luck,
Lo fueron encarcelando.	They put him in jail.
Ay, ay, ay, ay,	Ay, ay, ay, ay,
Cuánta pena y sufrimiento,	So much pain and suffering,
Nomás por la mucha gente	Only because there are so many people
Que hay sin entendimiento.	Who do not understand.
Peor caso le sucedió	Something worse happened
Al señor Manuel Rivera.	To Mr. Manuel Rivera.
Cuando un troque lo aplastó	When he was hit by a truck
Le quebró pierna y cadera.	He broke his leg and hip.
El jefe de policías,	The chief of police,
Que también es mexicano,	Who also is Mexican,
Muy conforme se retira	Very conveniently left the scene
Porque así lo había planeado.	Because he had planned it that way.
A pesar de tanta infamia	In spite of such infamy
La huelga va caminando.	The strike marches on.
Y por todo California	And now throughout California
El águila anda volando.	The eagle is flying.
Aconseja el director	The director advises
Que no provoquen violencia,	Not to provoke violence,
"Sé que nos sobra el valor	"I know that we have more than enough courage,
Pero hay que tener paciencia."	But we must be patient."
Ay, ay, ay, ay,	Ay, ay, ay, ay,
Y con ésta me despido.	With this I take my leave.
En la huelga de Delano	This is what happened
Esto es lo que ha sucedido.	In the strike in Delano.

In this corrido, Señor Tavena portrays the numerous hardships and dangers that farm workers encountered when they went on strike, and he emphasizes one of the early dilemmas of the farm workers' efforts to organize. The strikers faced a major problem communicating with workers harvesting grapes in vineyards located far away from the roadside property lines. Each morning car caravans of strikers left Delano to find harvest crews and set up roadside picket lines. Picketers needed loudspeakers and bullhorns in order to address workers in the fields.

Huelga y violencia

Growers constantly harassed picketers and succeeded in getting a local judge to issue an order banning shouting and the use of amplified sound on the picket lines. Although the injunction violated the workers' rights and eventually higher courts overturned them, growers easily obtained such rulings from sympathetic local judges. Further inflaming the situation, a sheriff arbitrarily decided that the picketers' public reading of Jack London's labor classic, "Definition of a Strikebreaker" (indicated by *"nomás porque gritaron '¡La huelga!'"* in the corrido), was grounds for arrest. In addition, local law enforcement officers, including a police chief who was Mexican American, refused to intervene to stop violence against strikers. The union's leadership seized upon these events to stage a confrontation and create a test case to challenge the court orders from local judges. This strategy also was useful in generating publicity favorable to the union and in garnering support among urban liberals and unions from outside of the San Joaquín Valley.

During this period of the strike, Pablo experienced the polarization within the community that divided not only growers and workers but also segments of the Mexican and Mexican American community that had different feelings about the strike. Pablo recalled,

> When the strike first started, I wasn't too much involved on the picket line. I used to sing only in the union halls or maybe some parties where the farm

> workers were at. I always used to sing there. But I really didn't do very much singing out in the public on account of so many enemies that we had.

In this context, he perceived singing corridos in support of the union as a potentially dangerous act. Indeed, *"Huelga y violencias,"* in addition to reflecting the strategic problem of freedom of speech on the picket line, also conveys the climate of fear and uncertainty many strikers felt at the time. The corrido brings into relief the violence done to neighbors, the David and Goliath fight between the powerful and powerless in agribusiness, and the very concrete fears strikers had of losing their homes and belongings, not to mention their jobs. Given this social environment, Señor Tavena's corrido focuses attention on shared experiences and the emotions stirred by the strike.

By singing this ballad before union audiences, Pablo and Señor Tavena hoped to inform their listeners about the violence and denial of civil rights suffered by the strikers, but they also sought to accomplish other ends. This corrido expresses their perception of the strikers' action as justified resistance to the growers' legal and illegal efforts to break the strike. In Tavena's words, he composed this song *"para decirle al campesino"* ("in order to tell it to the farm worker"). By this he implied that the corrido form was to him the best way of communicating to fellow farm workers the meanings of recent local events. He accomplished this end by drawing upon traditional techniques and thematic associations with older songs.

In recounting the strike in *"Huelga y violencias"* Señor Tavena selectively presents events showing strikers as peaceful and law abiding people who suffer verbal abuse from a grower and unconscionable acts of violence on the picket line. These depictions do not simply narrate events, they dramatize them and point to their importance in a manner typical of other corridos. Choruses break the narrative after every four verses and allow the corridista to comment on the events portrayed in the previous set of verses. The choruses also inject additional devices of traditional Mexican balladry including the dove (here transformed into an eagle, the symbol of the union) and the Virgin of Guadalupe, the patron saint of Mexico. The eagle replaces the dove used in other corridos as a messenger relaying important news to the outside world.

By invoking the intercession of the Virgin of Guadalupe, the song reflects another element of Mexican folklore characteristic of corrido tradition, the benevolent figure of the Virgin Mary as protector of the poor and oppressed. In this role she is a symbol of the justice and moral correctness of the cause (Herrera-Sobek 1990). Within Mexico and in Mexican American communities, the Virgin of Guadalupe is both a religious figure and a powerful social symbol of the Mexican people. Her apparition in 1531 to Juan Diego, a recently converted Indian, on Mount Tepeyac outside of Mexico City, was an event of great symbolic significance in the formation of the Mexican nation.

In 1810 followers of Miguel Hidalgo in Mexico's War of Independence from Spain carried her image into battle as did Emiliano Zapata's army in the Mexican Revolution a century later (Wolf 1958:34–39). Her image is ubiquitous in Mexican American homes and churches throughout the United States where, as in Mexico, her feast day (December 12) is celebrated with a special mass and festivities in homes. In the farm workers' movement, her religious and political aspects are evident on banners heading marches, in roadside shrines on picket lines, and in political proclamations, poetry, and songs.

Juan Tavena composed his ballad to the tune of *"Corrido de los hermanos Hernández,"* a composition recorded in the 1930s (Sifuentes 1982; Sonnichsen 1975). The earlier song related the story of two Mexican prisoners who were the first persons Arizona authorities executed in the gas chamber. This ballad portrays the Hernández brothers as victims of Anglo injustice and a cruel form of punishment. Like the ballad about the Hernández brothers, *"Huelga y violencias"* depicts the victimization of Chicanos at the hands of Anglos. In this regard it is similar to the pattern of corridos Manuel Peña points out as popular in Mexican American communities in the post-World War II era. Corridos of this period, according to Peña, "portray Mexicans as helpless victims of Anglo injustice" and suggest "a diminishing need for symbolic status reversal [typical of earlier corridos of border conflict] in favor of more direct action." In place of dramatic heroes single handedly defending their rights against Anglos, the corrido of victimization portrays the collective power of the Mexican American community (Peña 1982:36).

The thematic thread of injustice faced by Mexicans at the hands of local authorities linking these two ballads may not be appreciated by all listeners. Pablo did not know the older ballad that served as Tavena's model until he learned it from his neighbor, but the mood elicited by the tune and musical style of the older ballad complement his feelings about the events that the corrido recounts.

Pablo learned *"Huelga y violencias"* and many of his corridos about the UFW from fellow farm workers soon after the events that these songs recount and comment upon. Pablo's attraction to corridos about the strikes, however, is not solely dependent upon the events to which they allude and how soon after them he learns or performs the song. A good example of a contrasting appeal of corridos about events during the strike is *"Corrido de César Chávez,"* a song that Pablo learned in 1972. Lalo Guerrero, a popular entertainer at that time working in Los Angeles, composed *"Corrido de César Chávez"* in 1968 and recorded it the same year on a 45-RPM record (Guerrero 1968). In this song Guerrero recounts Chávez's twenty-five-day fast of rededication to nonviolence that concluded with a Mass in Delano Park that hundreds of farm workers and their supporters attended.

Although Guerrero's song did not come to Pablo's attention until five years after the entertainer recorded it, Pablo was immediately attracted to this corrido by the melody for which he and his daughter Juana have worked out a special harmony. Pablo also was attracted to this song by the identity of the composer, for he had long admired Guerrero as a performer. As an "outsider" who composed the ballad using information from a newspaper account of Chávez's fast, Guerrero showed great understanding, according to Pablo, of the farm workers' cause.

Corrido de César Chávez
Words and music by Lalo Guerrero

Deténte mi corazón,	Stop, my heart,
En el pecho no me cabe	In my breast there is no room
El regocijo y orgullo	For the joy and pride
Al cantarle a César Chávez.	Of singing of César Chávez.
Inspiración de mi gente,	Inspiration of my people,
Protector del campesino	Protector of the farm worker,
El es un gran mexicano	He is a great Mexican;
Ese sería su destino.	This would be his destiny.
De muy humildes principios	From very humble beginnings
Organizaste a la gente;	You organized your people;
Y a los hacendados ricos	And against the rich ranchers
Te paraste frente a frente.	You stood face to face.
Injustamente te acusan	Unjustly they accuse you
Que intentaste usar violencia	Of intending to use violence.
Ayunaste veinticinco días	You fasted for twenty-five days
Pa' probar tu inocencia.	In order to prove your innocence.
El estandard que lleva	On the standard that carries
Mi Virgen de Guadalupe,	My Virgin of Guadalupe,
Que viniste ante a alabar,	In whose presence you came to worship,
De bendiciones te tuve.	I esteemed you with my praise.
A los veinticinco días	After twenty-five days
El ayuno terminó	The fast ended;
En el parque de Delano	In the park in Delano
Una misa celebró.	A Mass was celebrated.
Junto con ocho mil almas	Together with eight thousand souls
Bobby Kennedy *asistió;*	Bobby Kennedy attended;
Admiración y cariño	Admiration and affection
Nuestra gente le brindó.	Our people offered him a toast.
Vuela de aquí de me seno,	Fly from my breast,
Paloma, vete a Delano;	Dove, go to Delano;
Y por si caso no sabes	And if perhaps you don't know,
Allí vive César Chávez.	There lives César Chávez.

Pablo considers this song one of the most important corridos about the union that he sings, and yet few of his fellow unionists ask him to sing it. I have not heard other singers in the movement sing it. Pablo's preference for this song suggests the role of individuality in defining one's repertoire even within the restraints of singing for union audiences. In discussing Guerrero's composition in an interview, Pablo related its meaning to the family proverb mentioned previously, *"La mentira dura mientras de que la verdad no llega"* ("Lies will last only until the truth arrives"). He perceived the song as a statement countering accusations growers made prior to Chávez's fast in 1968 about the union's alleged use of violence and arson. His reasons for learning it, however, extend beyond the events and tensions of that period of the strike. Guerrero's corrido expresses for Pablo the deeply felt admiration that he has for Chávez.

> Then this other one that Lalo Guerrero composed [*"Corrido de César Chávez"*], oh, that really hits my heart. That's a beautiful song, just beautiful. I think that's a . . . since he's not even a *campesino*—you know he's not a farm worker—that came out of his feelings toward the poor people and the farm workers. I think that was . . . he felt, ah . . . he felt almost just like we do over this cause and especially over César Chávez, you know. We admire, we like him, well, we can say we love him, and we think a lot of him. And so since the words that are on this corrido are. . . . I think they are really nice . . . are really something, you know. So that really inspired me to learn this corrido.

As an expression of Pablo's admiration of Chávez, this song portrays the union's director not just as a dedicated labor leader but also as a heroic fighter for justice. In this regard it has affinities with the symbolic expression of older corridos and with more recent songs prevalent in the Mexican American community in the early 1960s celebrating President John F. Kennedy as a fighter for civil rights. The most prominent parallel with older corridos is the song's evocation of the Virgin of Guadalupe in relation to Chávez. "The Virgin," a formulaic element found in many corridos, symbolizes in Pablo's ballads the strong sense of ethnic identity of Mexicans in the union. In this corrido, the Guadalupe symbol is also a comment on the nature of Chávez's commitment to the farm worker's movement. Well before the strike began, Pablo had the opportunity to observe from first-hand experience Chávez as a leader.

Unlike many union organizers, Chávez remained personally very close to the workers' social and cultural roots. A devout Catholic, Chávez sacrificed his personal and family life for the union's cause (Brown 1972). His twenty-five-day fast in 1968 further demonstrated what many had already observed—that Chávez put the principles of the strike before his comfort and well being. In light of Chávez's reliance on his religious faith and willingness to suffer for the cause, the image of the Virgin of Guadalupe is a most appropriate cultural idiom for expressing the tenor and emotion of the respect farm workers hold for their union's leader.

This song's resemblance to Mexican American corridos about John F. Kennedy indicates another aspect of its appeal to Pablo and his listeners. In a study of corridos composed about Kennedy, Dan William Dickey examines twenty-two compositions portraying the slain president in a heroic light. These compositions, like Guerrero's song about Chávez, circulated in Mexican American communities primarily on recordings produced by small regional record labels. Unlike the impersonal and objective tone of the corrido of earlier periods, these recent compositions often are told from a first person perspective with a decidedly emotional attitude toward the song's subject. In *"Corrido de César Chávez"* the corridista addresses Chávez in the familiar verb form indicating affection for him and elsewhere in the song he characterizes the union's leader as *"un gran mexicano"* ("a great Mexican") who heroically confronts the rich and powerful on behalf of the farm workers.

Guerrero's characterization of Chávez also suggests the influence of corridos about John F. Kennedy. The latter group of ballads portray the former President as a fighter for equal rights who greatly respected Mexico and Mexicans living in the United States and who courageously sacrificed his life for a noble cause. Many Mexican Americans closely identified with President Kennedy; as an Irish Catholic, he became a symbol of resistance to the ethnic and religious discrimination faced by Mexican Americans. In addition to the thematic affinities of Kennedy and Chávez as heroic figures in corridos of the 1960s, the name of Senator Robert F. Kennedy in the corrido by Guerrero alludes to the younger Kennedy's interest in the farm workers. Mention of his presence at the end of Chávez's fast in *"Corrido de César Chávez"* is an additional association linking this song with the positive feelings aroused among many Mexican American farm workers by the memory of the martyred president and his family.

The first strike at a ranch where Pablo worked occurred in 1972. This strike began two years after the historic signing of contracts with Delano area grape growers following the union's successful boycott of table grapes. White River Farms refused to renegotiate a contract with the United Farm Workers, bringing in undocumented workers from Mexico to replace strikers during the harvest (Taylor 1975:275–88). County sheriffs arrested Pablo and other UFW members on the picket line as the farm workers attempted to convince strikebreakers to leave the vineyards.

In jail, the strikers composed *"El Corrido de Schenley,"* so named because Schenley Industries originally owned the White River Farms vineyards. Schenley was one of the first growers to sign a contract with the UFW in the 1960s. Pablo explained that the huelguistas composed this corrido as a way of passing the time in jail. For most it was their first time to be arrested. Like the arrest of the forty-four strikers and their supporters on the picket line in 1965 mentioned in *"Huelga y violencias"* and Chávez's fast in 1968, farm workers told stories about the White River Farms strike. While I recorded a long-playing record album of Pablo's singing in 1976, he recalled this strike in the following words:

> Bueno, primeramente, yo soy Pablo Saludado y resido en Earlimart, Califor-
> nia. Yo soy un trabajador campesino que he trabajado toda mi vida en la
> agricultura, y compusimos una cancioncita una vez por cuestión de que yo
> trabajaba con la compañía de Schenley. Pero resulta de que vino una compañía
> petrolera que se llama Buttes Gas and Oil Company y compró este rancho en
> donde tenemos un contrato nosotros allí por la unión de campesinos. Y cuando
> esta compañía compró este rancho de seis mil acres, ella misma dijo que lo que

ella quería era desbaratar nuestra unión. De modo es que cuando se cumplió el contrato que tuvieron que renovarlo ella dijo que, que, pos iba, iba a desbaratar nuestra unión. Y pos no pudieron negociar el contrato, no, no se pudo arreglar y entramos en huelga en 1972. Anduvimos como quince días haciendo huelga y no hubo ningún problema, pero como a los quince días vinieron los quebrahuelgas guiados por los policías. Iban, iban los policías, venían enfrente y los, los contratistas hicieron a un lado a los huelguistas y se metieron a trabajar. Entonces, andábamos nosotros haciendo demostración alrededor de las viñas cuando el 25 de septiembre empezaron a ir. Los policías y nomás porque andábamos con nuestras banderitas [nos] subieron a los carros y nos llevaron a la cárcel a Bakersfield. Pos, pasando el tiempo, para pasar el tiempo, un poco allí en la cárcel nos juntamos entre todas, unos . . . pusimos uno, dos tres palabras, otros un verso y compusimos el corrido que le nombramos "Corrido de Schenley." Y en este tiempo ya era el White River Farms, pero pusimos "El Corrido de Schenley" porque antes allí era donde trabajamos.

Well, first, I am Pablo Saludado and I live in Earlimart, California. I am a farm worker and I have worked all my life in agriculture, and once we wrote a little song about an incident that occurred when I worked for the Schenley Company. It turned out that an oil company called Buttes Gas and Oil Company bought this six thousand acre ranch, bought this ranch where we, the farm workers' union, had a contract. And when this company bought this six thousand acre ranch, the same company said that it wanted to break up our union. The fact is that when the contract expired and they [the company] had to renew it, they said that they were going to break up our union. And they couldn't settle the contract; they couldn't agree, and we went on strike in 1972. We were on strike about fifteen days and there had been no problems. But after fifteen days the strikebreakers, led by policemen, came. The police came and went at will in front [of the strikebreakers], and the contractors moved the strikers aside and they [the strikebreakers] entered to work. Then we were demonstrating around the vineyards when, on the twenty-fifth of September, the police started to come just because we were marching with our flags; and they put us in the cars and took us to jail in Bakersfield. Well, in order to pass the time there in jail, we all got together; some added one, two, or three words, others a verse, and we wrote the ballad that we call "The Ballad of Schenley." And at that time it was already called White River Farms, but we called it "The Ballad of Schenley" because that was its name when we worked there before.

This narrative, although elicited by an outsider for the purpose of introducing "*El corrido de Schenley,*" reveals something important about this song's meaning to Pablo. As the "audience" for this story, I was impressed with Pablo's ease in recounting his experiences under the pressure of recording. He surely drew upon earlier experiences speaking about the White River Farms strike to strangers when he served as a boycott organizer in Wisconsin in 1973 and 1974. Although undoubtedly differing in some ways from his narrating on the boycott, Pablo later told me that this narrative preserved important elements of the stories told among White River Farms strikers at home and on the boycott.

Principal among these elements was the anger farm workers felt as Schenley Industries transferred its vineyards to Buttes Oil and Gas Company, an enterprise with little interest in agriculture and a strong desire to break the union. The White River Farms walkout also struck a chord with strikers because it protested the actions of growers who, no longer under the pressure of a grape boycott, refused to deal with the union and instead imported strikebreakers. The union's hard-won victories of a few years earlier appeared lost.

This strike and its corrido mark an important change in Pablo's thinking about his relationship to local authorities. Prior to this experience, Pablo had not felt first hand the anger and disillusionment conveyed in the stories he heard about the arrests of peaceful picketers, even when these stories came from his daughter. "I wouldn't believe her," Pablo explained, "because I had a lot of respect for the law. But it happened that when I went on strike, then is when I had a different way of thinking. Some of the officers will take advantage [of you]. Because I was walking up there on the picket line and all of a sudden here comes the police car and took me to jail. So from there on I went full force [for the union] on account of the law."

"*El corrido de Schenley*" has a special personal significance for Pablo because of his direct involvement in the strike and the circumstances under which the song was composed. He sang it in cities for audiences who came to learn about the boycott, though many of these listeners, like his Navy audiences during World War II, may not have understood Spanish. He also sang it for workers from other areas of California who were involved in similar strikes.

El Corrido de Schenley
Words by White River Farms Strikers
Tune: "*El contrabando de El Paso*"

Señores voy a cantarles	Gentlemen, I am going to sing to you
Lo que en Delano ha pasado	About what happened in Delano,
Que en los ranchos del White River	That on the White River Ranches
Fuimos varios arrestados.	Several of us were arrested.
Nos llevaron de Delano	They took us from Delano
A la cárcel del condado	To the county jail
Porque quebramos la orden	Because we violated the order
Que el juez nos había dado.	That the judge had given us.
Fue en septiembre 25	It was on September 25
Que todos recordarán	That everyone will remember
Decidimos los huelguistas	We, the strikers, decided
A esos files entrar.	To enter these fields.

Nosotros lo que queríamos	What we wanted was
Con esquiroles hablar,	To talk to the scabs,
Que no quebraran la huelga	To ask them not to break the strike
y fueran a otro lugar.	And to go to another place.
Pablo López empezó	Pablo López began
A meterse con la gente,	To mix with the people.
Y dijo llegando allí,	And upon arriving there, he said,
"Les encargo que se sienten."	"Let's sit down."
Llegamos a ese lugar	We arrived at that place
Que Pablo nos indicó,	That Pablo indicated to us,
Cada quien con su bandera	Each one with his banner
Que nunca la separó.	With which we never parted.
Al pie de nuestra bandera	At the foot of our flag,
Símbolo de nuestra unión,	Symbol of our union,
Decíamos, "¡Viva la Causa	We said, "Long live the Cause
Por todita la nación!"	Throughout the whole nation."
Como las dos de la tarde	About two in the afternoon
Del día antes mencionado,	Of the day already mentioned
En los carros del Cherife,	They took us away handcuffed
Nos llevaron esposados.	In the sheriff's cars.
Las mujeres son valientes	The women are brave
Y grandes de corazón;	And of great heart
Gritaban, "¡Qué viva Chávez,	They shouted, "Long live Chávez,
El líder de nuestra unión!"	The leader of our union!"
Les pedimos su criterio	We ask your judgment
Y gracias por su atención;	And thank you for your attention
Estos versos compusimos	We composed these verses
Adentro de la prisión.	Inside the prison.

Arrested strikers, Pablo among them, composed *"El corrido de Schenley"* in the Kern County jail in Bakersfield using the tune to *"El contrabando de El Paso."* While in part an aid for composing under less than ideal conditions, the huelguistas found this song to be an appropriate model for other reasons as well. *"El contrabando de El Paso"* is a lament expressing an arrested smuggler's emotions upon his journey to prison. As Paredes notes, this song comes from the Texas-Mexican border where, "Smuggling occupied a much higher position than other kinds of activities proscribed by law because, in the traditional scale of values, the smuggler was seen as an extension of the hero of intercultural conflict" (Paredes 1976:43). The strikers viewed themselves as unjustly arrested and used the associations evoked by this corrido to decry their treatment by local authorities.

Following his arrest on the picket line in 1972, Pablo dedicated all of his energies to the UFW. He volunteered to go to Wisconsin to work on the union's boycott of grapes from White River Farms. As a boycott organizer, he traveled to towns throughout the state talking to church groups, students, labor unions, and consumers at supermarkets about the union's cause. In the process he gained the admiration of many farm worker union supporters. He returned to Wisconsin in 1975 to visit the people who helped with the boycott. His collection of photos, letters, and newspaper clippings attests to the friendships he made in that state and the acclaim he received as an organizer. This prestige was accorded to many huelguistas in the 1960s and 1970s who demonstrated an unusual degree of commitment by volunteering for the boycott and going wherever the union needed them (Brown 1972:180–86).

Shared experiences and meanings

Pablo Saludado's corrido singing expresses many of the concerns of Mexican American farm workers during the seven years in which the UFW moved from a fledgling movement of rural workers to an organization able to challenge the power of California agribusiness and win contracts from growers in several regions of the state. While his songs open a window into the hearts and minds of rank and file farm workers, they do so through the prism of Pablo's individual experiences and emotions. As his participation in the union increased and his commitment to the farm workers' movement deepened, Pablo drew upon corridos as a personal resource to express and redefine his sense of himself as a farm worker and *mexicano*.

Many of the obstacles Pablo confronted as his participation in the union increased are ones he shared with other farm workers and are alluded to in his corridos: violence, going to jail, denial of one's rights, the deeply felt divisions within the community that made even singing a potentially dangerous act. Through his corrido singing Pablo expressed ideas and emotions about these happenings that did not simply mirror local events and union strategies. Pablo's singing, to paraphrase Clifford Geertz, is a vehicle of meaning and this meaning arises from the uses of songs and singing in expressing his concerns to his various audiences (1983:118).

To understand the dynamics of this meaning, I focus not on a fixed truth underlying Pablo's choices of songs but on the process of change that he underwent. In the context of the strike and boycott, Pablo used singing traditions to both anchor his actions in a useable past evoked by corridos and to suggest a subjective environment in which to come to terms with new social identities. His comparison of the meaning of his union songs to the family proverb mentioned earlier suggests that to Pablo and many of his listeners, corridos expressed feelings they have long held about being farm workers. Oral historians note a similar tendency of narrators to focus on psychological and subjective truths about events when telling stories of important happenings in their communities. Paul Thompson goes so far as to claim that a narrative taking this approach can become "a historical force of immense power in its own right" (1990:140). Through his proverb, Pablo metaphorically suggested that similar psychological or emotional truths are symbolized in his songs about the UFW.

As with most good singers, Pablo does not take lightly the process of song selection. In learning corridos he considers factors other than the events that inspired a particular song. For example, *"Corrido de César Chávez"* appeals to him primarily because of the sentiments it expresses about a heroic leader, its melody, and the identity of its composer, a well-known Mexican-American recording artist. He also developed a special arrangement of this song with his daughter, and they sang it together perhaps more frequently than Pablo performed it for union members. Noting the multiple appeals of songs about local events, Edward D. Ives makes a similar point about local songs from another region of the United States. Ives argues that "A song might be *commentary* on the news for those who knew the principals involved, and it may have drawn some sustenance from the general acceptance of its extrinsic truth (*"Them songs was all true"*); but for the most part it had to make its way on its intrinsic worth (*"I always liked that song"*) just like any other work of art" [emphasis in the original] (Ives 1978:404). Pablo's corridos, like the songs mentioned by Ives, have multiple appeals and this is part of the reason that they are able to successfully convey his ideas and feelings in various contexts such as family and neighborhood gatherings, union meetings in Delano, and before unfamiliar audiences on the boycott.

Pablo's corrido singing displays a considerable range of sensibilities in expressing his views. His song choices are not rigidly conditioned or limited by a single approach to corrido singing. Rather, Pablo selected songs influenced by three diverse strands of the corrido tradition: songs from the 1930s commenting on the victimization of Mexicans in the United States, ballads of cultural conflict from the Texas-Mexican border, and contemporary corridos similar to those recorded about President Kennedy. Often scholars of this genre seem to suggest that a single type of corrido dominates a given historical era. Looking at Pablo Saludado's choices, one can see that he selected three songs from as many distinctive strands of the tradition. Pablo found all to be appropriate during the relatively short span of the struggle to establish the UFW.

Given this diversity of approaches to the corrido in Pablo's singing, there are also similarities in the ways his songs appeal to listeners. On the one hand, his songs indicate the importance of certain events and celebrate leaders such as Chávez in concrete and readily discernable ways. On the other hand, his songs are subjective and call to mind past associations related to specific corridos and invoke symbols and images from Mexican balladry in general. These latter elements suggest a less literal and more emotional meaning and evaluation of local events and personages.

Taking the concrete or more literal appeal of his songs first, this aspect is exemplified by the frequency with which Pablo's corridos focus on specific injustices strikers suffered and the celebration of those who confront these injustices. By highlighting beatings and jailings, for example, his songs reflect a grass roots rhetoric that sees justice as rooted in very concrete experiences rather than as an abstract construct. By choosing songs about local events such as these, Pablo also points out the meaning of the mistreatment of strikers as they stand up for their rights, and he underscores the long-standing social divisions in Delano that the strike brought into relief.

The specific injustices Pablo mentions in his corridos serve the social and psychological functions of challenging the legitimacy of local laws used against the union's organizing and pointing to the sources of injustices in his community. These facets of his songs are manifestations of cognitive and emotional reorientations that many individuals experience as participants in movements for social justice (Arce 1981). As Pablo learned about the growers' tactics from trusted friends, his daughter, and eventually as a striker himself, he had to rethink his relationship to his job and community and make increasing personal commitments to challenge the powerless position of Mexican farm workers in California agribusiness. The three songs considered above suggest the emotional contours of Pablo's personal reorientation as he became active in the union. *"Huelga y violencias"* portrays strikers as victims of injustice, *"Corrido de César Chávez"* celebrates a courageous role model who fights for justice, and given the social context in which it was composed and sang, *"El corrido de Schenley"* affirms the importance to Pablo of direct action in the White River Farms strike.

Pablo's corridos convey a strong sense of right and wrong that, in the context of the farm workers' struggles, suggested the values of the movement in contrast to those of the growers. For this reason his singing played a role in the moral discourse that was as much a part of the strike as economic issues and working conditions. Rarely are the specific demands of the strikers (e.g., contracts, increased wages, hiring halls, protection from pesticides) mentioned in corridos about the strike. Rather the songs tend to emphasize the moral issues and the social identity of farm workers as mexicanos that underlie and define the struggle. Just as African American labor and the civil rights movements borrowed from spiritual and gospel traditions to "sanctify" their struggles and underscore the moral authority of their positions, so Mexican American farm worker singers such as Pablo Saludado turned to the secular corrido tradition to make a similar point about the justice of their cause (McCallum 1988).

In addition to indicating the meaning of specific injustices, a second appeal of Pablo's corridos is found in the associations with the past and the symbols and images his songs and singing bring to mind. The images of the Virgin of Guadalupe, the Hernández brothers, the Kennedys, and the lament of a border smuggler evoke subjective responses in Pablo's listeners. These responses, suggested by melodic and/or thematic affinities of Pablo's corridos with other compositions, bring to mind past experiences of listening to corridos. The experience of hearing Pablo sing about the strike may also evoke a variety of associations and emotions that reinforce traditional standards of justice suggested by corridos one has heard before. These subjective responses link the experiences of huelguistas in Delano with a sense of historical continuity as mexicanos, a key element in Mexican American farm workers' sense of ethnic identity.

Besides evoking historical continuity, Pablo's songs also indicate the role of social change in Mexican American farm workers' participation in the UFW. For example, Pablo's songs show the influence of the civil rights struggles of the 1960s by portraying Chávez as a leader of a nonviolent movement. This movement differs in its tactics, issues, and leaders from earlier efforts to organize farm workers. In the 1930s the Saludado family encountered unions concerned primarily with wages rather than the broad civil rights agenda of the UFW.

Further indicators of change within the Mexican American farm worker community are the generational and ideological differences illustrated by Pablo's father's allegiance to the *Comisión Honorífica* in earlier decades and Pablo's more recent support of the UFW. The former organization was oriented to the concerns of Mexican immigrants; the latter sought solutions for the problems of resident workers. The one appealed to nationalistic sentiments and the other embraced the diversity of cultural groups in the work force and, at least officially, eschewed the nationalism of Chicano militants of the 1960s. In short, the UFW represents a new basis for grassroots activism for farm workers, and Pablo's songs capture some of the excitement and hope that these developments stirred among the rank and file.

Pablo's new attitude toward his job is another sign of social change in his corridos. As a lifelong farm worker, he endured many situations requiring him to face injustices with little realistic hope of challenging them. Researchers such as Ernesto Galarza and Patricia Zavella have argued that Chicano and Chicana agricultural and cannery workers in California developed an ability to endure [*aguantar* in Spanish) on-the-job problems in order to survive and support a family (Galarza 1977; Zavella 1987). This attitude is implicit in Pablo's comments quoted earlier about his long hours and injuries on the job. Far from being a passive resignation, this endurance represents a choice that, as the composers of *"El corrido de Schenley"* demonstrated, can be reversed given the right conditions.

Active resistance is not always a possibility, and few farm workers made the decision to go on strike without reflecting on its costs to their families. Nevertheless, for workers such as Pablo and his fellow strikers at White River Farms in 1972, the threat of losing their union contract combined with the solidarity generated during the UFW's first seven years made direct action both a realistic possibility and an emotionally attractive option. In part the "arrival" of the truth Pablo mentioned in his proverb may be a metaphor for the meaning to him of his new attitude toward farm work inspired by the union.

Twenty years have passed since the White River Farms strike, and Pablo now finds fewer occasions for singing his songs about the UFW. This situation should not obscure our appreciation of his singing during the union's formative years. It is the nature of corridos that new events and heroes arise to replace earlier ones as subjects of ballads. As I have suggested, corridos are symbolic expressions of both continuity and change in the social identities of farm workers.

As a corridista in the farm workers' movement, Pablo found a new use for his traditional role as a performer. His individuality in defining this role can be seen in the variety of corridos he chose to express his personal feelings and to address new situations and audiences as they arose. Pablo was one of many singers in the movement, yet his choice of songs spoke to his specific situation as a farm worker and the expressive needs he felt were important in interpreting the movement to others. Pablo's songs connect his individual experiences and perceptions with those of others by mentioning shared injustices and evoking the feelings and memories that many farm workers recall from their experiences in the union's struggle. In a small but important way Pablo's singing helped nurture and express the meaning of the farm workers' movement to others. The continuity within change in Pablo's role as a corridista affirms the importance of expressive traditions such as corrido-singing in remembering and recreating who we are as human beings. The strike was an occasion for Pablo Saludado to do just that.

University of California
Los Angeles

Notes

I wish to thank Pablo, Carmen, and Juana Saludado for their warm hospitality and cooperation during our many interviews and recording sessions. For their patience and love throughout my research and writing I thank my wife Suzanne and son Reed. Grateful acknowledgements go to Patricia West Harpole for the musical transcriptions of the three songs in this essay. I am also grateful to the Chicano Studies Research Center, University of California, Los Angeles for a Rockefeller Foundation Fellowship in the Humanities during which time I completed this essay. I also received funding from the Folk Arts Program, National Endowment for the Arts, the UCLA Institute of American Cultures, and the Office of Folklife Programs, Smithsonian Institution, for my field recordings of farm workers' corridos.

1. Following the merger of AWOC and NFWA the union was officially known as the United Farm Workers' Organizing Committee (UFWOC) and later the AFL-CIO recognized it as a full fledged union now known as the United Farm Workers of America. Throughout this essay I refer to the union as the United Farm Workers (UFW) for the sake of brevity and to indicate the organization's continuity throughout its various name changes. For background on the UFW's development within the context of California farm labor history, see Galarza (1977), Levy (1975), Meister and Loftis (1977), and Taylor (1975).

2. Much of corrido scholarship is grounded in a concept of ballads as indices of "group" consciousness, but scholarly writings reflect a range of views on the importance of individuality in the corridista's role. For example, T. M. Pearce, writing about a New Mexican singer, argued that "his individuality as a poet is submerged in the stream of group or community feeling which animates all his compositions" (1953:248). On the other hand Bess Lomax Hawes considered possible individual motivations and rewards of corrido singing in her study of a local ballad composed in California (1974).

References Cited

Abrahams, Roger D. 1970. "Creativity, Individuality, and the Traditional Singer." *Studies in the Literary Imagination* 3:5–34.

Arce, Carlos H. 1981. "A Reconsideration of Chicano Culture and Identity." *Daedalus: Journal of the American Academy of Arts and Sciences* 110:177–91.

Ashton, John. 1977. "Truth in Folksong: Some Developments and Applications." *Canadian Folk Music Journal* 5:12–17.

Barry, Phillips. 1961. "The Part of the Folk Singer in the Making of Folk Balladry." In *The Critics & the Ballad,* edited by MacEdward Leach and Tristram P. Coffin, 59–76. Carbondale: Southern Illinois University Press.

Brown, Jerald Barry. 1972. "The United Farm Workers' Grape Strike and Boycott, 1965–1970: An Evaluation of the Culture of Poverty Theory." Ph.D. diss., Cornell University.

Dickey, Dan William. 1978. *The Kennedy Corridos: A Study of the Ballads of a Mexican American Hero.* Austin: Center for Mexican American Studies, University of Texas at Austin.

Entwistle, William J. 1939. *European Balladry.* Oxford: Oxford University Press.

Galarza, Ernesto. 1977. *Farm Workers and Agri-business in California, 1947–1960.* South Bend, Indiana: University of Notre Dame Press.

Geertz, Clifford. 1983. "Art as a Cultural System." In *Local Knowledge: Further Essays in Interpretive Anthropology,* 94–120. New York: Basic Books.

Glassie, Henry, Edward D. Ives, and John Szwed. 1970. *Folksongs and Their Makers.* Bowling Green, Ohio: Bowling Green University Popular Press.

Goldstein, Kenneth S. 1971. "On the Application of the Concepts of Active and Inactive Traditions to the Study of Repertory." *Journal of American Folklore* 84:62–67.

Guerrero. Lalo. 1968. *Corrido de César Chávez.* Colonial 597.

Halpert, Herbert. 1964 [1939]. "Truth in Folk-Songs—Some Observations on the Folk-Singer's Attitude." In *Traditional Ballads and Folk-Songs Mainly from West Virginia,* edited by John Harrington Cox, 13–20. Publications of the American Folklore Society, Bibliographical and Special Series, 15.

Hawes, Bess Lomax. 1974. "'El Corrido de la Inundación de la Presa de San Francisquito': The Story of a Local Ballad." *Western Folklore* 33:219–30.

Heisley, Michael. 1977. Insert notes to Las voces de los campesinos: *Francisco García and Pablo & Juanita Saludado Sing Corridos about the Farm Workers and their Union.* FMSC–1.

———. 1983. "*Corridistas de la huelga*: Songmaking and Singing in the Lives of Two Individuals." Ph.D. diss., University of California, Los Angeles.

Herrera-Sobek, María. 1990. *The Mexican Corrido: A Feminist Analysis.* Bloomington: Indiana University Press.

Herzog, George. 1938. "The Study of Folksong in America." *Southern Folklore Quarterly* 2:59–64.

———. 1949. "Song: Folk Song and the Music of Folk Song." In *Funk and Wagnalls Standard Dictionary of Folklore, Mythology, and Legend,* edited by Maria Leach, 1033–50. New York: Funk and Wagnalls.

Ives, Edward D. 1978. *Joe Scott: The Woodsman-Songmaker.* Urbana: University of Illinois Press.

Levy, Jacques. 1975. *César Chávez: Autobiography of* La Causa. New York: W. W. Norton.

London, Joan, and Henry Anderson. 1970. *So Shall Ye Reap: The Story of César Chávez and the Farm Workers' Movement.* New York: Thomas Y. Crowell.

McCallum, Brenda. 1988. "Songs of Work and Songs of Worship: Sanctifying Black Unionism in the Southern City of Steel." *New York Folklore* 14:9–33.

McDowell, John Holmes. 1981. "The *Corrido* of Greater Mexico as Discourse, Music, and Event." In *"And Other Neighborly Names": Social Process and Cultural Image in Texas Folklore,* edited by Richard Bauman and Roger D. Abrahams, 44–75. Austin: University of Texas Press.

Meister, Dick, and Anne Loftis. 1977. *A Long Time Coming: The Struggle to Unionize America's Farm Workers.* New York: MacMillan.

Nelson, Eugene. 1966. Huelga!: *The First Hundred Days of the Great Delano Grape Strike.* Delano, California: Farm Worker Press.

Paredes, Américo. 1958. *"With His Pistol in His Hand": A Border Ballad and Its Hero.* Austin: University of Texas Press.

———. 1971–1972. *"El concepto de la médula emotiva aplicado al corrido mexicano: Benjamín Argumedo." Folklore Americano* 19/20:139–76.

———. 1976. *A Texas-Mexican Cancionero: Folksongs of the Lower Border.* Urbana: University of Illinois Press.

Pearce, T. M. 1953. "What Is a Folk Poet?" *Western Folklore* 12:242–48.

Peña, Manuel. 1982. "Folksong and Social Change: Two *Corridos* as Interpretive Sources." *Aztlán: International Journal of Chicano Studies Research* 13:13–42.

Porter, James. 1986. "Ballad Explanations, Ballad Reality, and the Singer's Epistemics." *Western Folklore* 45:110–25.

Sharp, Cecil. 1907. *English Folksong, Some Conclusions.* London: Sempkin.

Sifuentes, Roberto. 1982. *"Aproximaciones al 'Corrido de los Hermanos Hernández ejecutados en la Cámara de Gas de la Penitenciaría de Florence, Arizona el día 6 de julio de 1934.'" Aztlán: International Journal of Chicano Studies Research* 13:95–109.

Simmons, Merle E. 1957. *The Mexican Corrido as a Source for Interpretive Study of Modern Mexico 1870–1950.* Bloomington: Indiana University Press.

Sonnichsen, Philip. 1975. Insert notes to *Texas-Mexican Border Music, Vols. 2 & 3, Corridos, Parts 1 & 2.* Folklyric 9004–9005.

Taylor, Ronald B. 1975. *Chávez and the Farm Workers.* Boston: Beacon Press.

Teatro Campesino, El. 1966. *Songs and Sounds from the Delano Strike.* Thunderbird 00001.

Thompson, Paul. 1990. *The Voice of the Past: Oral History.* 2nd ed. Oxford: Oxford University Press.

Wolf, Eric R. 1958. "The Virgin of Guadalupe: A Mexican National Symbol." *Journal of American Folklore* 71:34–39.

Zavella, Patricia. 1987. *Women's Work and Chicano Families: Cannery Workers of the Santa Clara Valley.* Ithaca, New York: Cornell University Press.

James P. Leary and Richard March

Farm, Forest, and Factory: Songs of Midwestern Labor

You ask me to sing, so I'll sing you a song;
I'll tell how in the marshes they all get along,
Bohemians and Irish and Yankees and Dutch,
It's down in the marshes you'll find the whole clutch.

Knee deep in bogs all day, bedded in makeshift shanties at night, the nineteenth-century cranberry pickers of Jackson County, Wisconsin, were a mixed lot, a babble of tongues, a bazaar of tastes:

The Bohemians are drinkers—good soup they like best.
The Irish, the red men, bad whiskey will test.
The Yankees eat dainties and never grow stout,
  But the Dutch they will eat of the best sauerkraut.

Besides the Bohemians, Irish, "red men" (Winnebagos), Yankees, and Dutch (Germans) enumerated above, the cranberry pickers who traded their labor for seasonal cash were also Norwegians, Poles, and Welsh. Their "Cranberry Song" was a typical workers "catalogue," a sung genre that functioned like a photo album or yearbook from the "school of hard knocks." With a consistent tune and verse structure, but no set verses, it presented shifting characters and events: "At each marsh every year, new verses are composed about the workers present at that season. Romances, accidents, humorous incidents are incorporated so that every new year the song changes."[1]

Throughout the Upper Midwest other workers in other places at other occupations have drawn upon traditional patterns to compose new verses—witty, celebratory, bitter, or satirical—about their experiences. These songs may be grounded in immediate experience or borne by currents of ideology. Some have circulated entirely in oral tradition, others have found their way in and out of print, while still more have been issued as commercial recordings. Sometimes in a foreign tongue, sometimes in English, sometimes in a hybrid dialect, these songs chronicle the labor of midwestern agricultural workers, loggers, miners, factory hands, and tradesmen.

Apart from the Anglo-Celtic traditions of the lumbercamp, so rich a body of expressive culture has attracted curiously little scholarly attention.[2] While students of labor songs have been few within the world of American folksong scholarship, students of foreign songs have, until very recently, been almost entirely absent from that world.[3] And almost no one has considered foreign labor songs. This essay, consequently, attempts to survey a single American region, including both English and foreign examples, in the hope that subsequent researchers might explore the territory.

Just as immigrants introduced jokes and anecdotes about the crafty hired man who tricks a greedy farmer out of a warm bed and a good meal, or magic tales of the woodcutter whose ax chops by itself, they also brought songs reminiscent of the triumphs, complaints, and aspirations of Old Country workers. The bulk of transplanted songs of work predictably concerned peasant toil, but Scandinavians and workers from alpine central Europe sang of the woods, Italians and Croatians from Dalmatia retained their songs of fishing and seafaring, Poles and Czechs sang of tradesmen like the shoemaker (*"Dratewka"*) and the tinker (*"Dratenik"*), and German socialists carried "48ers" anthems of urban labor.

Fig. 1 Jerry Novak

Jerry Novak (1895–1981) of Moquah, Wisconsin, the grandson of a serf, traveled from Podebrady near Prague to rural Wisconsin in 1902 (see fig. 1). His family and neighbors possessed a full repertoire of Czech and Slovak songs. Jerry learned dozens of these, many of which regarded peasant life. *"My Jsme Sedlaci"* grieved that "we are peasants in our village, like dogs." Mistreated workers sometimes tempered rage with humorous defiance. A pair of verses from *"Sedlacku Kdye Nejsi Pak"* reckons:

> It's hard to work for the farmer
> Because he's very mean.
> He gets up in the morning
> And asks if the feed is chopped.
> "You're lazy," he says.

And the hired man gets up
And swings around his hat.
He says, "Farmer, you are dumb.
Cut your own feed, we'll see how you cut it.
I'm going to see my girlfriend."
(Leary 1981:5–7,30)

These songs must have sustained Novak's father, Josef, as he struggled to clear cutover land, a logging company's detritus, to establish a farm. Despite a multitude of stumps and rocks, the poverty of the soil, and the short growing season, Josef Novak had no boss to dictate when he cut his feed.

Alice Everson of Blair, in the coulee country of Wisconsin's Trempealeau County, was born in 1891 of Norwegian parents. Their *"Husmanden's Klagesang"* despaired of the lot of Old Country tenant farmers: the crofter worked on a yearly lease, and there would always be another crofter to replace him if the proprietor was dissatisfied with his work. This bleak portrait was balanced, however, with *"Solung Vise,"* a song about farmer/loggers from Solor in eastern Norway who were "the best in the area and worthy of a ballad." In the winter they make extra money by spending a fortnight at their forest hut cutting wood to bring down the rivers. The Solung are "the very best woodsmen, they learn to use the ax as children."[4]

Like the people of Solor, many of the Upper Midwest's new immigrants worked in the woods to supplement farm income, and other immigrants sustained Old World woods songs in the new land. The region's Bavarians and Austrians exulted in "The Jolly Lumberjack" (*"Tiroler Holzhackerbuam Marsch"*), a mainstay of contemporary "Dutchman" polka bands that was recorded by John ("Whoopee John") Wilfahrt's Concertina Orchestra in Minneapolis in 1929 and by Milwaukee's Heinie and His Grenadiers in 1935.[5]

In the Upper Midwest, however, far more songs regarding labor were composed or significantly modified than were imported in their entirety. Immigrants who claimed and cleared their own land, like the Walloons who settled Door County, Wisconsin, sought riches in farms and full bellies. They modified *"La Faridondon, La Faridondaine,"* a seventeenth-century Belgian song, to suit their nineteenth-century experience.

Nous-estans quites po l'Amerique	We are setting out for America
I nos faut foute one crole.	We are going to get drunk.
No f'rans peter l'djambon.[6]	We shall treat ourselves to ham.

Not even lake-effect snow and five months of winter daunted their heir, Arthur "Zeke" Renard (see fig. 2), who, more than a century later, snug in his farm house and push-pulling a button accordion, sang a song learned from

Fig. 2 Arthur Renard

his mother about a crop of "canadas" safe in his root cellar: *"Dji m' fou d' ca, dj'a des canadas . . . pour passer mon hivier"* ("I don't care a rap about it. I've got 'canadas' [potatoes] to pass the winter away").[7]

Other rural immigrants' sons and waves of turn-of-the-century peasant newcomers, however, had neither potatoes nor a place to put them. The good land was either taken or beyond their means. Many hired themselves out to milk cows, make hay, harvest hops, and thresh grain. Hired workers on small farms often worked, ate, and slept side by side with the farm family. The awkwardness of boarding an unrelated adult in a farm family's home inspired numerous jokes involving sexual liaisons between farm family members and assorted hired men and women.

Songs circulated on this theme as well. Barney McCarthy, an Irishman living on Beaver Island, Michigan, learned the following ditty in the lumbercamps. It concerns a lusty wife, a gullible farmer, and a willing, well-hung hired man. McCarthy finished his performance with the typically Irish *declamando* or spoken ending.

Titter-ry-an

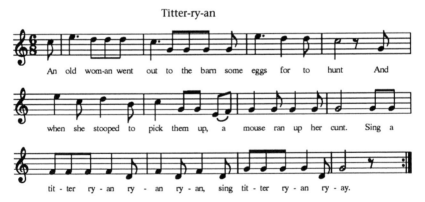

An old woman went out to the barn,
Some eggs for to hunt.
And when she took to pick them up
A mouse ran up her cunt.

Chorus:
Sing titter-ry-an, ry-an, ry-an,
Sing titter-ry-an, ry-ay.

She ran to the barn door,
She hollered loud and shrill.
She hollered to her husband
Who was working at the mill.
(chorus)

Her husband came running
As fast as he could fly.
He said, "Wife, oh dearest wife,
I thought I heard you cry."
(chorus)

"Now I have a mouse
Way up in my cunt,
And if he doesn't get turned around
I fear he'll gnaw his way out."
(chorus)

He put his arms around her waist.
He laid her on the floor.
And every time he missed that mouse
By an inch and a half or more.
(chorus)

He ran to the barn door.
He hollered loud and shrill,
He hollered to the hired man
Who was working at the hill.
(chorus)

The hired man came running
As fast as he could fly.
He said, "Master, dearest master,
I thought I heard you cry."
(chorus)

"My wife has a mouse
Way up in her cunt,
And if she doesn't get turned around,
I fear he'll gnaw his way out."
(chorus)

He put his arms around her waist.
He put her on the ground
And every time he took a jab,
He turned that mouse around.
(chorus)

Now just to show you
Her husband was deceived:
And when she got all the screwing she wanted
The mouse ran out of her sleeve.
(chorus)[8]

Threshing inspired the bulk of the region's agrarian labor songs. While a "ring" of neighbors generally handled grain threshing in Michigan, Wisconsin, and Minnesota prior to the introduction of combines in the 1930s, the prior era required seasonal armies of hired workers. Some were itinerant laborers making another stop on the annual round, some were tradesmen after extra cash, many were Scandinavians—Swedes and Norwegians.

During the Great Depression Axel Mattson, a butcher from Badger, a hamlet near Rouseau in northwestern Minnesota, gathered together a team, a wagon, and a crew of men to travel to North Dakota to thresh. The work was hard and the pay, for that era, was good. On the way home Mattson and his fellows gathered in the back of the wagon to play cards, imbibe, and make up a song in Swedish.

Kom Mina Pojkar
Translation by John Berquist
Swedish transcription by Philip Martin and Jean Johnson

Kom mina pojkar, kom allihopa,	Come all my boys, come all together,
Så resar vi til Nord Dakota	We're on our way to North Dakota
O harvest*en o treskingen,*	For the harvest and the threshing,
O tjäna pengar att vinteren.	To earn a little money for the winter.
Til Nord Dakota, *det har jag varit,*	To North Dakota, that's where I've been,
O mina pengar har illa farit.	But my money didn't do so well.
O drickar cider *o* ginger *ol.*	We drank cider and ginger ale.
Nu huudpinne det blir min lonn.	And now all I have left is a headache.[9]

Axel Mattson's composition, above, is one of a cycle involving Scandinavians, itinerant labor, strong drink, an aching head, and squandered money. "Ole Olson the Hobo from Norway" follows the immigrant from his arrival in New York City to St. Paul, Minnesota. Bruce Bollerud, who performs the song with the Goose Island Ramblers, was raised on a farm in Iowa County, Wisconsin: "We milked fifty cows and we had a lot of hired men. Some of them were 'newcomers' from Norway. They still had thick accents and spoke Norwegian a lot." One of them, Roy Anderson, played a three-row button accordion and sang about "Ole Olson." Another hired man, Bert Vinje, knew the song as well. In Bruce Bollerud's recollection:

The hired man on the farm was something like—you know, you see these documentaries on the cowboy out in the west—and they were like that. They worked real hard. They were usually single guys. They usually didn't have a lot of close relatives nearby. They worked real hard and then, when they got paid, they would go on a big drunk. And they might be out of commission for three, four days, or a week. It's kind of similar to the Ole in the song there—it's really not that different.[10]

The Anderson-Vinje-Bollerud version begins with a chorus stressing that "Ole"—like Irish "Pat" or Polish "Stash"—was a stock name given to all Norwegian males by outsiders.

Ole Olson the Hobo from Norway

Chorus:
Ole Olson, ya they all call me Ole.
I don't know how they found out my name.
I never told none of them fellers,
But they all call me Ole yust the same.

My name is Ole Olson.
I yust come over from Norvay.
I vent to New York and I can't find no vork,
So I tink I head west right away.

Ole Olson in the city of St. Paula,
He yust had one dollar fifty cents.
He bought him a pint of alcohola,
And on a hell of a bender he vent.

Ole Olson met a cop with brass buttons.
He said, "Ole you yust come with me."
He hit me, he slammed me, he banged me,
Locked me up with a big brass key.

"Ole Olson, you hobo from Norway,
You got drunk and you went on a spree.
I fine you ten days and ten dollars,
And I hope you remember the day."[11]

Bjarne Andresen, born in Minneapolis, Minnesota, in 1906 of immigrant parents from southern Norway, likewise grew up with the song that commonly was performed at get-togethers. His version includes three additional verses describing the swindling of a green immigrant by a cunning newsboy who pockets a cash "decoy," then gives short change.

I buy me penny ticket for St. Paul,
Get on in an extra fine car.
The conductor comes round and he tells me:
"Sneak in where those immigrants are."

Oh newsy, he tells me to buy book,
He tell me to take yust one look.
I see where the dollars stick out of a corner,
For a dollar I buy me that book.

But newsy is darn slick with money.
He gives me the change only half.
When I ask for the rest of that money,
Oh newsy gives me the horse laugh.[12]

Nor were the Swedish workers of song much different. The most widespread example of the hardworking, wandering, profligate, tippling Scandinavian-in-verse is "A Swede from North Dakota" who, like Ole Olson, is sentenced to ten days and ten dollars. It dates at least from 1900 and concerns a Swedish hired man's ill-fated trip to the state fair in Minnesota's Twin Cities. Carl Bruce (1887–1980), a native of Gothenburg, Sweden, learned the song in Minneapolis in 1904, two years after immigrating. From 1906 until his death he resided in Rockford, Illinois, where he worked in a factory and entertained in a Swedish theater group as the rural comedian Sven pa Lappen (Sven on the Patch). The song was also recorded by Ragnar Hasselgren and by Ernest ("Slim Jim") Iverson in the 1940s and 1950s, respectively. A second generation Swedish-American, Glenn Ohrlin—born in Minneapolis but best known for his cowboy songs—recorded the song in the 1960s and also included it in his anthology *The Hell Bound Train*. The Swede's versified misadventures were set down by George Milburn in his 1930 *Hobo's Hornbook* and were published two years later as a dialect poem in George Springer's pioneering anthology of Scandinavian humor, *Yumpin' Yiminy*.[13]

The versions are fairly stable in plot. Verses are occasionally combined and the Swede is sometimes Sven, sometimes Swan. Invariably his misadventures lead him from North Dakota to the German and Irish neighborhoods of St. Paul, to Minneapolis where Swedes abound, and back to North Dakota. In the versions offered by Milburn and Ohrlin, the Swede is confronted by a Salvation Army lass in the midst of Minneapolis's heavily Swedish "Seven Corners" district.

> She said, "Vill you vork for Yesus?"
> I said, "How much will Yesus pay?"
> She said, "Yesus don't pay nothing."
> I said, "I won't work today."

"I won't work" was a standard parody of the Industrial Workers of the World's IWW acronym.

Glenn Ohrlin, not surprisingly, first heard the song from his father Bert, who emigrated from Sweden after World War I and worked as a harvest hand in North Dakota and as a lumberjack. Stewart Holbrook's history of American lumberjacks mentions that "loggers had a song about a big Swede who went to Minn-e-a-polis to take in 'the big state fair,'" and E. C. Beck offers a Michigan text (Holbrook 1956:103; Beck 1948:182). The Swede of song figures into at least one woods anecdote:

> A tall Swede left Ellis Island to catch a train west. A Salvation Army lassie stopped him. Shaking her tambourine, she asked: "Sir, will you work for Jesus?" The immigrant deliberated for a minute, then shook his head.
> "Ay tank ay rather work for Louie Sands," he said and kept on walking.

The Scandinavian-born Sands ran camps in the Michigan pineries and was known for hiring Swedes, Norwegians, and Danes (Wells 1978:169–70).

George Springer's text transcription, offered here, emphasizes the characteristic immigrant dialect.

Ay Ban a Svede From Nort' Dakota

> Ay ban Svede from Nort' Dakota
> Vork on farm bout von year,
> Ay ban goin' to Mannasota,
> Yust to luke on da big State Fair.

Gat mey ticket, gat mey bottle,
Dress all op luke aut of sight,
Yump me on a Yim Hill vagon,
Feel so gude ay lak to fight.

Next morning ay ban vake op,
Faller him say ban near Sant Paul,
Ay tal ju ay gat a headache,
Ay ban drenk det alcohol.

Valk roun' street in Sant Paul,
Ant seen Svedemans anyvhere,
Yump on street car go to Minnaplis,
Ju bat planty Svedemans dar.

Valkin' roun' in Sout Minnaplis,
Go bae Stockholm luke for fun,
Har ay find von nice big Svede girl,
She slap mey back say, "Gude dog Swan."

Ay turn roun' en feel so funny,
Naver seen dis girl ay tenk,
Ay ban foxy say, "Hallo, Tillie,
Von't ju come en hor en drenk."

Ve tak drenk en feel so yolly,
En begin to dance en seng,
En ay skol say to all Svede fallers,
Ay skol pay for hull dam teng.

Tillie say ay ban gude faller,
Lukin' mighty gude to her.
She say, "Swan, come on ay show yu
Best time aver did occur."

Riding op in nice blue vagon,
To da city yudge to see,
He say, "Swan, ten days, ten dollars
Cause ju ban on awful spree."

Ay luke in mey pocket gat no money,
Yudge him say can gat no bail,
All ban laft for dis poor Svedeman,
To lay ten days in da yail.

Ay'm goin' back to Nort Dakota,
Gat a yob on a farm somevhere,
A skol say to all Svede fallers,
"Go to hal wit da big State Fair."

Although a staunch teetotaller, the real-life Swedish immigrant Joel Emmanual Hägglund (1882–1915) was jailed nonetheless, and on far more serious charges than his fictive ethnic kinsmen. His labor activities on behalf of the Industrial Workers of the World (the IWW or the "Wobblies") ultimately cost him his life. He was convicted of murder on dubious evidence and executed by a Utah firing squad. Although his activities were in the West, Hägglund, better known as Wobbly bard Joe Hill, exerted a profound influence on labor songs in the Upper Midwest.[14]

Even as Hill awaited execution, the Wobblies were organizing the Agricultural Workers Organization (AWO) which would address conditions in the wheat belt extending from northern Texas through Oklahoma, Kansas, Nebraska, the Dakotas, and into Canada. Hill's "Ta-Ra Ra Boom De-Ay" borrowed the tune and verse structure of the popular turn-of-the-century original to comment on hired labor in the wheat fields. Alvin "Salty" Hougan, a farm boy from Stoughton, Wisconsin, learned the version offered here in the mid-1930s, while playing on the WLS "National Barn Dance," a Chicago radio program that catered to rural and small town audiences throughout the Midwest. Back in Wisconsin, Hougan performed it with the Goose Island Ramblers as a comic song alongside rural standards like "Hey, hey Farmer Gray, haul another load away."

I Worked for a Farmer

I worked for a farmer threshing wheat,
Seventeen hours on hands and feet.
And when the moon was shining bright.
He kept me working day and night.

One day, I am so sad to tell,
I accidentally slipped and fell.
I threw the pitchfork in-between
The cogwheels of the threshing machine.

Well the cogwheels and the bolts and hay
Went a-flying every way.
One of the bolts of the old machine
Hit the farmer on the bean.

One day the farmer, he did say,
"I'm going to town with eggs today,
So grease the wagon up, you mutt,
And don't forget to tighten the nut."

Well I greased the wagon up all right,
But I forgot to put the nut on tight.
When the farmer was on his trip,
The wheel fell off and he broke his hip.

Then the farmer says, "There must be something wrong.
Could it be I work my men too long?
I'll see that something's really done.
I'll change my tactics one-by-one."

So he cut the hours and he raised the pay
And he gave ham and eggs for every day.
Now he works his men from spring to fall
And he has no accidents at all.[15]

Joe Hill was known in the Upper Midwestern forest as well as on the farms. When Aili Kolehmainen Johnson documented Finnish labor songs in the Upper Peninsula of Michigan in the mid-1940s, she found small farmers and loggers still observing the anniversary of Hill's execution every November 19. In their notebooks and on their lips were IWW songs, written in Finnish, among them, *"Lumber Jakk Marssi"* ("March of the Lumberjack"), which begins with a bitter account of dangerous work, filthy dwellings, poor food, and oppressive bosses.

Brothers, men of the timberlands,
We struggle in the forests,
Felling pine and fir.
There is our lovely shack,
The endless beans, salt pork, and margarine.
Our wretched fellows
Bear and wolf,
The louse and the bedbug,
The devilish strawboss,
They thirst for our blood.
(Johnson 1947:336–37)

The song, with its itemization of complaints, resembles the versified "needles" directed at heartless bosses by Anglo-Celtic singers. Bert Taplin (1857–194?) started out in the Wisconsin lumbercamps in 1871 as a swamper, rising to the rank of foreman before leaving the woods in 1907. While he and his fellows were full of praise for open-handed bosses, they reviled "Old Hazeltine." When Helene Stratman-Thomas recorded Taplin in 1941, he told her: "I was in a saloon singing while I was drunk. Along came Hazeltine—God, how I hated him—and I had to sing this song. They stood by the door, the boys, and they wouldn't let him out. He had to stay and listen."

> It's of the Eau Claire River, a stream I'm sure you know.
> It's of a crew of shanty boys who worked through the snow.
> And as to Old Hazeltine, he's a lousy son-of-a-bitch,
> For it is from the poor man that he has grown rich.
> For the cheating, and the robbing, and stabbing of his crew,
> I think he's an old screw.[16]

An unidentified Michigan singer complained with particular venom about the food at a Torch Lake camp.

On the Shores of Torch Lake

Oh our cook she's the daugh-ter of Hon - est John Clark   One taste of her bis - cuits would make an ox fart,   Her pud - ding's as tough and as green as the grass,   and if you would taste 'em you'd hock off your ass.   Der-ry dye oh day, whack fal the dye dee oh did - dle oh day —

Vexed by intolerable conditions, the entire Torch Lake crew reportedly sang the final verse of this needle to the camp boss before walking off the job en masse.

> Oh here's to Tad Minton, the son-of-a-bitch,
> May his ballocks rot off with the seven year itch.
> His pecker will turn like the point of a screw,
> And his arsehole will whistle the red, white, and blue.[17]

Excepting such bawdy examples, the songs of Anglo-Celtic loggers in the Upper Midwest have been well documented, both in print and on record, by such scholars as E. C. Beck, Sidney Robertson Cowell, Alan Lomax, Franz Rickaby, and Helene Stratman-Thomas. The substance of their published works—revealing songs of tragic accidents, unrequited love, skilled and dangerous work, and "catalogues" of lumbercamp life—need not be reiterated here. But the non-English and foreign dialect songs of Midwestern loggers demand attention. "Ole Olson the Hobo from Norway," for example, turns up in the Michigan lumbercamps. After having "yus come down from Minnesota" and visiting a sister who "live in Dakota," Ole continues his misadventures:

> Ay got one fine yob in the river,
> Chasing the trees down the stream
> Vit a big pole in one hand,
> Oh, vasn't it grand?
> Ven the trees make a bend down river
> Ay give a big whoop and a yell;
> My feet go co-plosh in the water,
> And ay tank ay ban gone to Hell.[18]

Scandinavian loggers recited as well as sang such dialect pieces in the camps.

Fig. 3 William F. Kirk as "The Harvest Hand"

Perhaps the most popular recitations were published in 1905 by William F. Kirk (1847–ca. 1926), a Chippewa Falls, Wisconsin, journalist who probably doubled as a dialect comedian in the "opera houses" of the Upper Midwest (see fig. 3). Like the Swede Hjalmer Peterson, who billed himself as Olle i Skratthult (Ole from Laughtersville), Kirk called himself the Norsk Nightengale and dressed as a Scandinavian *bondkomiker* (peasant comedian) in clunky shoes, highwater pants, an illfitting jacket festooned with an oversized flower, and a felt workman's cap pulled over pudding-bowl hair. He also dressed as a hired hand on Dakota grain harvests, and as a Scandinavian logger toting his crosscut saw or "Swedish fiddle." The preface to Kirk's *Norsk Nightengale, Being the Lyrics of a Lumberyack*, associates his verses with "the residents of Northern Wisconsin and Minnesota where the 'lumberyack' lives and thrives." No doubt they were recited there by Scandinavian loggers in the lumbercamps. E. C. Beck recorded the versions "Yim," "Tillie Olson," "A Good Fellow," and "Olaf" in the Michigan woods.[19]

Since Kirk's writings are long out of print and difficult to obtain, it is worth reprinting an example here.

Olaf

> Yust two years ago last venter
> Ay meet Olaf op in camp;
> Ve ban lumberyacks togedder.
> Every morning ve skol tramp
> 'Bout sax miles yust after breakfast
> Till ve come to big pine-trees;
> Den our straw boss he skol make us
> Vork like little busy bees.
>
> Olaf, he ban yolly faller,
> He skol taling yoke all day;
> Sometimes he sing dis har ragtime,
> Yust to passing time avay.
> And at night, ven ve ban smoking
> After supper, he skol make
> All us lumberyacks to laughing
> Till our belts skol nearly break.
>
> Me and Olaf bunked together,
> And sometimes he taling me
> 'Bout his vife and little Torger,
> Who ban living cross big sea.
> "Ay ban saving dough," says Olaf;
> "And next summer, ef ay can,
> Ay skol send for vife and baby;
> Den ay ban a happy man!"
>
> One night Olaf getting letter
> Ven ve coming back to camp;
> He yust tal me, "Little Torger,"
> And his eyes ban gude and damp.
> Dis ban how ay know vy Olaf
> Never taling no more yoke,—
> Vy he yust sit down at night-time,
> Close by me, var he skol smoke.

A sober antidote to Kirk's "The Lumberyack," in which the hardworking Scandinavian typical in song blows his "whole venter's dough" on "drenk and headache," "Olaf" presents an instance that was not unusual among immigrant loggers.

Finnish loggers, especially, versified about the hardships of lumbercamp life, often incorporating IWW ideology. Those laboring in northern Wisconsin sang:

> A wretched home, this cheerless camp!
> And "finer people" sneer, make cracks:
> "You ruffians, bums, bearded lumberjacks!"
>
> Our wages are the rags we wear,
> Our scraps of food no one digests.
> Our beds are bunks, and fleas our only guests.
> (Kolehmainen and Hill 1951:38)

Arthur Kylander is perhaps the most noted songster amongst Finnish Wobblies. Born in Finland, Kylander (1892–1968) early in this century, working as a lumberjack in both Maine and Minnesota before moving to California in the 1940s where he started a tree farm. As Pekka Gronow has observed, Kylander "combined humor with a biting social commentary." He published several volumes of *Humoristisia Lauluja* (Humorous Songs) and recorded twenty sides for Victor between 1927 and 1929.[20]

"Lumber Jäkki," recorded during Kylander's first session in New York, is still performed today. It invokes, then sardonically undercuts, romantic notions of lumbercamp life. The "red card" of the final verse is an IWW membership card.

Lumber Jäkki
Translation by Tellervo Zoller

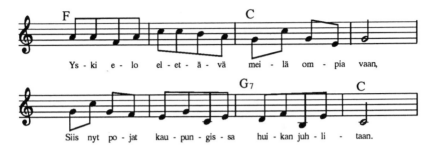

Ys - ki e - lo   el - et - ä - vä   mei - lä om - pia vaan,

Siis nyt po - jat   kau - pun - gis - sa   hui - kan juh - li - taan.

Terveisiä korvesta,
Sydän maalta, salolta,
villin luonnon laitumilta, metsän povesta.
Missä riemut kaupungin
Poissa on ja muutenkin
Pojat siellä elää saa kuin munkit luostarin.
Niinpä kärsivällisyys se yli kuohahti.
Lumber-Jäkki kämpän jätti sekä päätteli:
Yksi elo elettävä meillä ompia vaan,
Siis nyt pojat kaupungissa hiukan juhlitaan.

Tunnelmasta korpien,
Herrat laulaa ihaillen.
Kuinka kaikk' on runollista alla honkien.
Lumber-Jäkki eikös vaan,
Onnen poika tosiaan,
Kuin saa siella honkain alla elää eloaan.

Ruokana,—no tietysti, on tuore liha ain',
Säilytetty Chicago'ssa vuosikymmenen vain.
Siellä marjat makiat on eessä mansikat;
"Binssiksi" tok' kaupungissa niitä haukkuvat.

Siellä ilta myöhällä,
Pojat kuin on petillä,
Silloin tällöin kajahtaapi kumma sävelmä.
Äänen sen jos kuulisi
Herrat, varmaan luulisi,
Etta pojill' kämpässä on iltakonsertti.
Mutta unen helmoissa jo pojat uinahtaa
Ja iltaseksi syödyt "binssit" ne ne soinahtaa.
Hongat säestää huminallaan, paistaa täysi kuu.
Runollista, tottamaar se onkin, eikös juu?

Kyllä on siell' korvessa
Niin runollinen tunnelma,
Että kaupunkiinkin vielä sieltä tultua,
Silmissä on neitonen,

Herran jee, niin suloinen!
Olkoon ijältänsä vaikka kuudenkymmenen.
Oikeimpa se mieli oisi suukko suikata,
Halata ja kiikutella hiukan polvella.
Kuin on täynnä runollista korven tunnelmaa,
Voihan siinä muutenkin viel' hiukan hairahtaa.

Miellä metsän pojilla
Ei oo toki hienoja
Vaatteita ja muitakaan ei herras tapoja.
Myös ei sanahelinää
Käytä metsan pojat nää,
"No perkele" on tervehdys kuin tuttu yllättää.
Kumarrukset, hienot vaatteet, helkse sanojen,
Peittona vain voipi olla häijyn sydämmen.
Ne, ne sopii ruhtinaalle, diplomaatille.
Vaan ei meille, lokareille, korven pojille.

Viime varsyss' laulussa,
Lauletaan nyt ajasta
Kuin Lumber-Jäkit astuvat tass kohti korpea.
Ei Jäkki niinkuin nykyinen
Se ero näät on sellainen
Ett', joka miehen taskussa on kortti punainen.
He silloin työnsä tuloista saa osan suuremman
Ja herroille he antavat sen korven tunnelman.
Kämpän seinät tutisee ja korpi kumajaa,
Kuin kumoukselliset laulut illoin kajahtaa.

Greetings from the wild,
From the wilderness, from the backwoods,
From the pasture of wild nature, from the bosom of the forest,
Where the delights of the city
Are lacking and
The guys live there like monks in a cloister.
Thus patience overflowed.
Lumber Jack left the camp and concluded:
We have only one life to live,
Guys let's go and celebrate in the city.

About the atmosphere of the wilderness,
The bosses sing with admiration,
How everything is poetic under the pines.
For food,—of course, is fresh meat
Stored in Chicago only for a decade.
There are sweet berries in front of him, strawberries,
They are called "bins" [beans] in the city.

Late at night
When the guys are in bed,
Now and then a strange melody sounds.
If the bosses would hear it
They would surely believe
That the guys are having an evening concert at the camp.
But the guys are already sleeping
And the "bins" [beans] they've eaten for supper are ringing.
The pines are accompanying their murmuring, the full moon is shining.
Certainly it's very poetic, isn't it?

Yes, there in the forest
It is so poetic
That when they arrive in the city
They have girls on their minds.
Good God, so sweet!
She may be sixty years old,
One would like to kiss her,
Hug and rock her on the knee.
If one is full of the atmosphere of the wilderness,
It is easy to make all kinds of mistakes.

My guys of the forest
Don't have fancy
Clothes nor other genteel manners.
These forest guys don't use fine language.
"Oh devil," is the greeting when surprised by a friend.
Bowing, fancy clothes, and meaningless words
May cover up a mean heart.
They are becoming of a prince or of a diplomat,
But not of us, loggers, guys of the forest.

In the last verse of the song
We sing from a time
When the Lumber Jacks return to the wild.
He is not a jack of today.
The difference is such that every man carries in his pocket a red card.
They will be getting a bigger piece of the results of their labors,
And they will leave to the bosses the atmosphere of the forest.
The walls of the camp are shaking and the wilderness rings
When the revolutionary songs resound in the evening.[21]

"Jingo" Viitala Vachon's brother Wilho owned most of Arthur Kylander's records, including "Lumber Jäkki," which she learned to sing in the early 1930s. The Viitalas lived in the "big timber area of Toivola, Michigan," where Jingo was born in 1918. Meaning "Vale of Hope," Toivola was chiefly a settlement of Finns who had begun to farm, fish, and log in the wake of successive strikes in the Copper Country of Michigan.[22] Injury and death from mining accidents were excessively common early in this century in the

Copper Country, and in the iron mines of Michigan, Wisconsin, and Minnesota. Many miners doubtless saw themselves in this verse, translated here from the original Finnish, which appeared in the ethnic press in 1915.

> For many a year he had toiled in the mine,
> And for wages he had pocketed
> An ailing body besides his bread,
> A caved-in chest and a crooked spine.
> (Kolehmainen and Hill 1951:36)

Some left the mine for a farm, like the Viitalas, or for factory work, but most simply hoped that their children's fate would be better. Jingo Vachon captured such sentiments in a "Finnglish" dialect song about an immigrant in the mines of Ishpeming:

Finn from Is'peming

I'm a Finn from Ispeming
I vork here in ta mine.
I got a vife who spends her life
Yust keeping me in line.
See's cute an small, a Polak doll,
But, boy, see soor can roar,
"You big dumb Finn from Ispeming,
Go sovel ta iron ore!"

Full of yoy, a country boy
I came across ta sea
To find ta gold tat I vas told
Vas vaiting here for me.

But ven I came I found no fame
Upon tis golden sore;
All I found down in ta ground
Vas yust ta iron ore!

I met a girl, her name was Pearl,
Her last name I von't tell.
I never trite to say it right,
It take too long to spell.
A man tat looked at her vas hooked
For good an' evermore.
I still don't see vy see picked me
To sovel her iron ore.

So by my side my plussing pride
Stood on our vedding day;
A dream in vhite, by candle light,
I heard her sveetly say,
"I luf you, Ike," ten Iris Mike
He yelled in from ta door,
"I'll kill tat Finn from Ispeming
An sovel his iron ore!"

Oh, how I vis to farm an' fis
Ta vaters deep an' blue,
An' own my home an vun two cows
An' ten a boat or two.
But seems to me I'll alvays be
A miner evermore,
Yust a Finn from Ispeming
Who sovels ta iron ore.

So tat's ta vay now day by day
My life is rolling on;
I'm home at night to luf and fight
Ten back to vork at dawn.
An' kids I got a nice big lot,
First vun - two - tree, ten four,
An' now tere's ten, I'll tell you men,
I sovel ta iron ore!

I get a dream tat makes me scream
An' svear an' sveat an' pray;
I dream I die an' vonder vy
St. Peter blocks my vay.
"You got no soul, go soveling coal,"
He tells me at ta door,
"You're yust a Finn from Ispeming
Who soveled ta iron ore!"[23]

Croatian and Slovenian miners in the Upper Midwest sometimes bent songs toward their occupations. The sons of Nikola and Maria Belopavlovich—Mike Bell, Dan Belo, and Paul —grew up in Michigan's Copper Country where Nikola finally settled his family after seven trips back and forth. House parties with singing were frequent at the Belopavlovich home through the 1930s. One standard, *"Oj Maricka Peglaj"* ("Oh Marie Is Ironing"), concerning an immigrant woman's household chores, was expanded with a reference to the Calumet and Hecla Mining Company which employed the men:

> *Oj Maricka peglaj—peglaj, peglaj, peglaj.*
> Calumet and Hecla—Hecla, Hecla, Hecla.[24]

Beyond the western end of Lake Superior, Slovenians have worked on Minnesota's Vermillion and Mesabi iron ranges, and in port cities like Duluth from whence the ore is shipped to distant mills. Their loyalties, understandably, were to the Congress of Industrial Organizations (the CIO), heir to the Wobblies in the 1930s, rather than to the historically exlusive American Federation of Labor (the AFL), which owed its roots to pre-industrial craft guilds. Despite the 1955 merger of the two mega-unions, workers still maintain loyalties to one or the other branch. Accordionist Frankie Smolz of Minnesota's Mesabi Iron Range was still entertaining workers decades later at his union hall with an adaptation of *"Stirje Fantje Spilajo"* (popularly known as "EIO Polka"), a Slovenian folk song in which a barmaid says she would rather work in the fields with a young man than count money with an old grandpa. Smolz's use of *"Ja sam"* (I am) in the second line retains his Slovenian language, albeit ungrammatically, in an American context.[25]

CIO Song

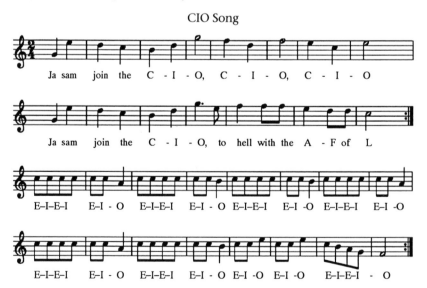

Ja sam   join   the   C - I - O,   C - I - O,   C - I - O

Ja sam   join   the   C - I - O,   to   hell   with the   A - F of   L

E–I–E–I   E–I - O   E–I–E–I   E–I - O E–I–E–I   E–I -O   E–I–E–I   E–I -O

E–I–E–I   E–I - O   E–I–E–I   E–I - O E–I -O E–I -O   E–I–E–I - O

Other Great Lakes cities echoed with the foreign labor songs of factory workers. In post-Civil War Chicago, organizations like the Socialist Labor Party and the International Working People's Association sponsored parades, picnics, and dances. The xenophobic *Chicago Tribune* disparaged an 1885 dance: "Every variety of step might have been witnessed yesterday. The 'Bohemian dip,' the 'German lunge,' the 'Austrian kick,' the 'Polish romp,' and the 'Scandinavian trot.'"[26]

Posters in German and English alike summoned workers to Chicago's Haymarket Square in 1886 in support of the eight-hour day. When a bomb disrupted the otherwise peaceful meeting, killing six policemen and wounding some fifty more, the state proscecuted eight of the rally's leaders. While no one presented evidence linking any of the men to the actual bombing, they were convicted of having said or written things that might have spurred someone else to action. One committed suicide, four were hanged, and the other three served lengthy prison terms. Songs in German and Yiddish marked their passing. The final verse of Charles Diether's "The Eleventh of November, 1887," refers to the interment in Waldheim Cemetery of five men whose German surnames, excepting Albert Parsons, are evident.

> And Waldheim's voice calls out loud and louder,
> Already the slaves are breaking their chains!
> Soon it will thunder and lightning out of the dark grave,
> The structure of tyranny will fall in ruins.
> And laughing friendly the avenging angel welcomes
> And lisps: "Parsons, Spies, Lingg, Fischer, Engel."[27]

While such songs as "The Eleventh of November" clearly addressed a labor issue, the enormous involvement of immigrant laborers in the Midwestern economy sometimes blurred the distinction between songs of labor and songs of immigration. Furthermore, in many instances, the distinction between American and foreign songs was also blurred, particularly for the many immigrants from eastern and southern Europe who came to the industrialized cities of the Midwest between 1890 and World War I. In this period, the stereotypical immigration story in which an entire Old World family bundles up its worldly goods to make a single one-way voyage to America often was not representative. For many Italians, Slavs, Finns, and Hungarians, emigration began as an extended form of migrant labor, primarily by males whose original intention was to earn enough cash to buy land, outfit a business, or build a house in the homeland. Residing in boardinghouses in America and traveling by railroad and steamship, the migrant workers made several round trips to take care of obligations on both sides of the Atlantic. While frequent two-way journeys became difficult during the years of the Depression and

World War II, they have resumed since the 1950s as immigration has increased. Moreover, affordable air fares have made the trip to and from the homeland quicker and less arduous than in steamship days.

For many nationalities, the concepts of immigration and migrant labor are very similar. Macedonian Slavs even use the identical word, *pečalbar*, to denote both harvest-time farm laborers who leave their villages for other regions and emigrants to America, Australia, or Western Europe. Pečalbar songs, which like the Scandinavian dialect poem, "Olaf," focus upon the consequences of separation from loved ones, are sung both in America and the Old Country. Alexandra Buling, who emigrated from Beram, Macedonia to Elgin, Illinois, in the 1970s, sings a well-known Pečalbar song, *"Sudbo Moja"* ("My Destiny"), which queries:

Što si sudbo me odnela	Destiny, why have you carried me away
V zemlja nepoznata?	To the unfamiliar land?[28]

Many of the *pečalbar* songs are from the viewpoint of those left behind. In Lorain, Ohio, steelworker-musician Paul Vangeloff sings *"Amerika Pusta Bila"* ("May America Be Barren"), a village girl's lament cursing the continent that has stolen away her young man. By the 1970s, when Australia, Canada, and Western Europe replaced the United States as the major destination of emigrants, the curse was broadened in a new version, *"Tuginata Pusta Bila"* ("May Foreign Parts Be Barren"), which Gary, Indiana, singer and bouzouki player Linda Pappas, the American-born daughter of Macedonian Slavs from Kostur, Greece, learned from records by Macedonian Gypsy singer Esma Redžepova.[29]

In Chicago, Croatians from the Adriatic island of Lošinj sing Old Country songs based upon their seafaring traditions in which jilted fiancées and abandoned spouses of sailors either curse their faithless lovers, *"Gdi on črni gavran da ga ne pojide?"* (Where is the black raven to eat him?) or curse the prostitutes who tempted them:

Oj proklinja mlade zis Inglenterra	Oh cursed be you young girls in England
Če ste njemu i košuju pojile?	Did you even have to eat up his shirt?

Rather than relying upon a supernatural curse, the female protagonist in a well-known Croatian song from the Dalmatian coast, *"O Da Mi Je Cimentati More,"* wishes to pave the ocean so her lover can ride back to her on a donkey.[30]

That the women left behind in the village had reason to be concerned is made clear in a Polish American song, "Iron Foundry Polka," recorded in Chicago in the 1960s by a band called the Starlights.[31] In typical Polish Amer-ican polka style, the verses are alternately Polish then English. The song concerns the not-uncommon phenomenon of a family's breakup after lengthy separation.

Iron Foundry Polka
Translation by Edmund and Helen Zawacki

Mo - ja żen - ka w kra - ju, a ja w A - mer - y - ce —

Mo - ja żen - ka w kra - ju, a ja w A - mer - y - ce —

Ja cięź - ko pra - cu - ję, ja cięź - ko pra - cu - ję

Ja cięź - ko pra - cu - ję, w że - laz - nej fab - ry - ce. —

Moja żenka w kraju, a ja w Ameryce (2x)
Ja ciężko pracuję (3x) w żelaznej fabryce
Ja ciężko pracuję (3x) w Krengla w fabryce.
Kocajh że innego, ja cię nie zabraniam (2x)
Aja z Ameryki (3x) do ciebie nie zwracam.

My wife is in the homeland and I am in America.
I work hard in the steel mill.
I work hard in Krengel's steel mill.
Go ahead and love another, I don't forbid you
Because from America I am not returning to you.

Another Polish song which shares the line about working hard in a steel mill, but which reveals a less sanguine attitude about life in America, was recorded in 1938 by Alan Lomax from the Romel brothers, Sylvester and Adolph, in Posen, Michigan, a farming community near the shores of Lake Huron, which included a fair share of Poles who had worked for a time in Chicago factories.

W Żelaznej Fabryce
(In a Steel Mill)
Translation by Edmund and Helen Zawacki

Mam ja dav - no mro - laj - i bi - ał - ę knj - i - ki—

A sam się za - bier - am, a sam się za - bier - am do tyj A - mer - y - ki—

Mam ja davno mrolaji białę knjiki,
A sam się zabieram, a sam się zabieram
Do tyj Ameryki.

Przyjachałem, przyja . . . do tyj Ameryki,
Znalazłem robotę, znalazłem robotę
W żelaznej fabryce.

Jak robię, tak robię, roboty pilnuję,
A Anglik nade mnę Anglik nade mną
Mnie się godamuje.

Jak on godamuje, roboty nie rzucę,
Gdy Pan Bog da zdrowie, gdy Pan Bog da zdrowie,
Da kraju powrocę.

Wo tyj Ameryce odbierają wo co oblata
A mlode dziewcząta odbierają wianki,
Bo w tyj Ameryce, bo w tyj Ameryce
To są same niedowiarki.

For a long time I tended white horses.
I am preparing to go to America.

I arrived in that America.
I found work in a steel mill.

How I work, I work, as best I can,
But the English "goddamns" me all the time.

Even though he "goddamns" me, I'm not going throw the job away,
And if Lord God grants me health, I'll return to the homeland.

In America they snatch whatever wealth flies by
The way maidens snatch up wreaths,
 Because in America there's nothing but unbelievers.[32]

The final verse's scorn for materialism—money is seized in the way that Old Country maidens seize bachelors' wreaths tossed in the Vistula as a spring courting ritual—is an oft-repeated immigrant's critique. The sentiment is echoed in *"L'Emigrante Disilluso"* ("The Disillusioned Immigrant"), recorded by Frank Amato of Detroit in 1952. A newcomer resents the lack of respect for his noble lineage in a free-wheeling money-oriented capitalist America. The song is a dialogue, however, and what one newcomer regards as a despicable preoccupation with "money, money, money," another regards as a democratic opportunity to rise up in the world through hard labor:[33]

L'Emigrante Disilluso
(The Disillusioned Immigrant)
Translation by Sabina Magliocco

Un sig - no - re e - mig - ran-te e as - sa - i el - e - gan-te, co' la tes-ta va - gan - te

di-scen-dent di san-gue blù— Dall' A-mer-i-ca è ar-ri-va-to, an-cor-a non è un me-se

E già s'ha im-par-a-to la più bel-la pa-ro-la ing-les-e: Mu- ni, mu-ni, mu-ni! Si

im-par-a-to a dir'; Quest'-or-a vo-le tro- var-e, e pres-to ri-tor- na-re— O, che

so-gno che s'ha so- gna-to, se la pig-lia co' s'o co- gna-to; ca la sen-za stru-zi-o-ne,

fors'- e-ra un me-le- o-ne— Mu- ni, mu-ni, mu- ni! Dov' è quel-la mu- ni

So- gnai un so-gno bar-bar-o tro- var-lo all' al-be-ro. Mu- ni, mu-ni, mu- ni

Me sta-te-vi on-de   sta';   se l'A - me-ri-ca è co- sì me ne vo-glio ri-tor- nar'!

Un signore emigrant, e assai elegante,
Co' la testa vagante, discendent di sangue blù
Dall' America è arrivato, ancora non è un mese,
E già s'ha imparato la più bella parola inglese.

Money, money, money!
Si è imparato a dir';
Quest'ora vole trovare, e presto ritornare.
O, che sogno che s'ha sognato, se la piglia co' s'o cognato;
Ca senza struzione, fors'era un meleone.
Money, money, money!
Dov'è quella money?
Sognai un sogno barbaro; sognai trovarlo all'albero.
Money, money, money!
Me statevi onde sta';
Se l'America è così, me ne voglio ritornar'!

Alle cinque ogni mattino, una sveglia mi fa saltare
Da un piccolo lettino per andare a lavorare.
Quando l'ero dall'Europa, io campavo come un papa;
Avevo le camarere e mi chiamavano "Cavalere."
Ogni giorno era festa, ogni giorno era siesta;
Due ore di lavora, cinquecento lire d'oro;
Qui non vedo neanche il piombo, che per sogno mio svanì;
Ma la colpa è di Colombo, che l'America scoprì!

Money, money, money!
Me quale money? M'immaginavo che si trovava in mezzo alle strada,
nda le casalina; ma qua che c'è casalina? Qua si butta sangue dagli
occhi per la moneta. Se t'arriva 'n mezzo viaggio de parte, e va' di corsa!

Sentitemi, compari: imparatevi a zappare;
Dall'America noe c'è titoli perchè son cose inutili.
Lo scarparo e lo barbiere passan' meglio d'un cavalere;
L'automobile tutti hanno; sono nobili e non lo sanno.
Lo suo nonno era ingengnere, lo suo zio era prete,
E voi eran' cavalere, ma qua contate che cosa siete!
M'hanno detto che siete un dotto ca quattro e quattro fanno otto;
Pigliatevi lo stangotto; che facite ancora qua?

Money, money, money!
Dov'è quella money?
Sognai un sogno barbaro, sognai trovarlo all'albero;
Money, money, money!
Ma statevi onde sta':
Se l'America è così, me no voglio ritornar!

An immigrant gentleman, very elegant,
A bit absent-minded and descended from blue-bloods
Arrived in America not even a month ago,
And already he's learned the most important English word.

Money, money, money!
This is what he learned to say.
This is what he now wants to find, so he can quickly return.
Oh, what a dream he had! He takes it out on his brother-in-law;
For without an education he was a redneck.
Money, money, money! Where is that money?
I dreamed a strange dream; I dreamed of finding it in trees.
Money, money, money! Stay right where you are;
If this is what America's like, I want to go back!

At five o'clock each morning, an alarm clock makes me jump
Out of bed to go to work.
When I was in Europe, I lived like a pope;
I had servants who called me "Sir."
Every day was a holiday, every day was a rest;
Two hours of work, five-hundred golden *lire*.
Here I don't even see lead, which disappeared as in a dream.
It's all Columbus's fault; he discovered America!

Money, money, money! What money? I imagined it could be found
In the streets, in the outbuildings; but here, who has outbuildings. Here you
Bleed from the eyes for money. If you get a free
Trip back, leave immediately.

Listen to me, *compari:* learn to hoe;
In America there are not titles because such things are useless.
The cobbler and the barber are better off than the gentleman;
Everybody has a car: they're noblemen and they don't know it.
His grandfather was an engineer, his uncle was a priest,
And you were a gentleman, but what does that count for here?
They told me you were learned, because four and four make eight;
Up yours! What are you still doing here?

Money, money, money!
Where is that money?
I dreamed a strange dream; I dreamed of finding it in trees.
Money, money, money!
Stay right where you are;
If this is what America's like, I want to go back!

Amato's counterpoint to disillusionment—the notion that America was a wonderful land for those who sought work, money, and the chance to be better off as a New World tradesman than as a noble across the Atlantic—was echoed in the late 1950s by Stan Wolowic and the Polka Chips. The popular

Chicago Polish polka band celebrated the era's relative prosperity for construction workers in a song that, in typical Chicago polka style, alternated English with Polish verses.

The Bricklayer's Song
Translation by Edmund and Helen Zawacki

Mu - la - rze, mu - la - rze — co wy tu ro - bi - cie —

Po jed - nej ce-giel-ce, po jed - nej ce-giel-ce, do -mu u - kła -dzie - cie —

We build the buildings tall, we build the buildings small.
Red brick and mortar for two and a quarter,
On pay day we save it all.

Mularze, mularze, co wy tu robicie?
Po jednej cegielce, po jednej cegielce
Domu układziecie.

[Bricklayers, bricklayers, what are you doing?
One brick at a time we are putting up a house.]

Mularze, mularze, czego wy tu chcecie?
Czy wapna, czy gliny, czy ładny dziewczyny,
Wszystko dostaniecie.

[Bricklayers, bricklayers, what do you want here?
Some lime or clay or a beautiful girl?
You will get everything you want.]

In summer we make our gold, winter will come, it's cold.
Then we won't labor, it's just love thy neighbor,
And sweethearts we have to hold.[34]

Whether satisfied or disillusioned, whether commenting from intimate personal experience or through the heightened rhetoric of mass movements, whether toiling with a wooden scoop in a cranberry bog or with trowel, brick, and mortar atop a scaffold, the Upper Midwest's workers have performed and composed songs in many languages and dialects for more than a century. Our essay has provided a glimpse of their rich traditions, but, more importantly, it offers an invitation to further research.

University of Wisconsin, Madison
Wisconsin Arts Board, Madison

Notes

While some of the songs treated here are drawn from books and articles, most are culled from sound recordings. Some were commercially issued on 78-RPM discs, on 45-RPM "singles," on 33 1/3-RPM long play or LP recordings, and on cassette. None has yet, to our knowledge, appeared on a compact disc. LPs and cassettes often include useful information on their "jackets," in their "J-cards," or in accompanying booklets, and we have relied upon those sources as well. In addition, we have made use of field recordings. Some of these recordings were undertaken for public institutions and have been deposited in an archive, but many are in the personal collections of researchers. We are especially indebted to Bob Andresen, John Berquist, Paul Gifford, and Toni and Oren Tikkanen for allowing us to use materials from their research. We are likewise grateful to Arnold Alanen, Jean Johnson, Sabina Magliocco, Philip Martin, Tellervo Zoller, and Edmund and Helen Zawacki who cheerfully provided translations and insights into the various foreign songs. Archie Green's editorial suggestions led us to new sources.

1. Comments on the "Cranberry Song"'s composition and the first verse given here were recorded from Frances Perry by Helene Stratman-Thomas, Black River Falls, Wisconsin, August 14, 1946. Perry reckoned her version of the song was the "original," composed by Barney Reynolds of Mather about 1895. Perry sings her version on *Folk Music from Wisconsin*, ed. Helene Stratman-Thomas, Library of Congress L55. The second verse presented comes from a completely different version of the song recorded from A. P. Jones of Black River Falls by Helene Stratman-Thomas in 1946. Jones's version is printed in full in James P. Leary's book accompanying a series produced by Judy Woodward for Wisconsin Public Radio. The thirteen radio programs and corresponding publication have been issued as a seven cassette/book package, *The Wisconsin Patchwork: Recordings from the Helene Stratman-Thomas Collection of Wisconsin Folk Music* (Madison: Department of Continuing Education in the Arts, 1987), 50.

2. The seminal work on lumbercamp song in the Upper Midwest is Franz Rickaby's *Ballads and Songs of the Shanty Boy* (Cambridge, Mass.: Harvard University Press, 1926). E. C. Beck's trio of books published by the University of Michigan Press are likewise extremely valuable: *Songs of the Michigan Lumberjacks* (1941), *Lore of the Lumbercamps* (1948), and *They Knew Paul Bunyan* (1956). Lumbercamp songs recorded by Helene Stratman-Thomas appear in *Folksongs Out of Wisconsin*, ed. Harry Peters (Madison: State Historical Society of Wisconsin, 1977). Regional logging songs appear on *Folk Music of Wisconsin*; *Songs of the Michigan Lumberjacks*, ed. E. C. Beck, Library of Congress L56; and *Wolf River Songs*, ed. Sidney Robertson-Cowell, Ethnic Folkways FE 4001.

3. The American Folklife Center's conference on ethnic recording stimulated new work and resulted in an influential publication: *Ethnic Recordings in America: A Neglected Heritage*, ed. Judith McCulloh (Washington, D.C.: American Folklife Center, 1982). Richard Spottswood's seven-volume discography has provided researchers with a valuable tool: *Ethnic Music on Records: A Discography of Ethnic Recordings Produced in the United States, 1893–1942* (Urbana: University of Illinois Press, 1990).

4. Alice Everson was recorded by Helene Stratman-Thomas in 1946. Her two songs and summary translations appear on cassette program 8, "Worksongs and Songs About Work," and are treated in an accompanying chapter of the same name in *The Wisconsin Patchwork* (1987).

5. Heinie and His Grenadiers, "Jolly Lumberjack" *("Tiroler Holzhacker Buab'n")*, 78-RPM recording, Decca De 5146, Chicago 1935. John Wilfahrt's Concertina Orchestra, "Jolly Lumber Jack—March," 78-RPM recording, Vocalion Vo 15780, Minneapolis, 1929. Both cited in Spottswood, *Ethnic Music on Records*, vol. 1, pp. 166, 273.

6. Recorded from Alfred Vandertie, Algoma, Wisconsin, by Francoise Lempereur, 1980, and issued on *Anthologie du folklore Wallon, les Wallons d'Amerique* (Wisconsin), LP recording and insert booklet, Centre d'Action Culturelle de la Communaute d'Expression Francaise, CACEF FM 33010.

7. Recorded by Francoise Lempereur for *Anthologie du folklore Wallon*. Information about the song's source came from a tape-recorded interview with Arthur Renard by James P. Leary, Duval, Wisconsin, May 1988.

8. Recorded from Barney McCarthy, Beaver Island, Michigan, in August, 1938, by Alan Lomax for the Library of Congress, AFS 2302 B2.

9. John Berquist of Eveleth, Minnesota, learned the song from Carl Carlson of Rouseau, who acquired it from its composer. Berquist recorded the song in 1985 on *Ya, Sure, You Bet You*, cassette recording, Half Moon Records HM 1005.

10. Tape-recorded interviews with Bruce Bollerud, Madison, Wisconsin, by James P. Leary and Richard March, August 1987, and by Leary, July 1990.

11. Recorded by the Goose Island Ramblers on the LP *The Sounds of Syttende Mai* Cuca 2010.

12. Tape-recording of Bjarne Andresen by Robert Andresen, Duluth, Minnesota, 1977.

13. "The Swede from North Dakota" is offered by George Milburn, *The Hobo's Hornbook* (New York: Ives Washburn, 1930), 139; it is reprinted in Richard E. Lingenfelter, Richard A. Dwyer, and David Cohen, *Songs of the American West* (Berkeley: University of California Press, 1968), 493. "Ay Ban Svede From Nort' Dakota" appears in George T. Springer's *Yumpin' Yiminy: Scandinavian Dialect Selections* (Long Prairie, Minn.: The Hart Publications, 1932), 116–18. Carl Bruce's version, biography and singing are found in the booklet and on the grooves of a double LP documentary recording, *From Sweden to America: Emigrant and Immigrant Songs,* Caprice CAP 2011. Ragnar Hasselgren's 78 RPM "Swedes in North Dakota" appeared in 1948 on the Harmony Music label issued by the Scandinavian Music Company of Berkeley, California. Slim Jim's "I Ban A Swede From Nort Dakota" was recorded before his death in 1958, but not issued until 1980: *Slim Jim,* an LP on Hep Records HEP 00228. Finally, Glenn Ohrlin's LP version is on *The Hell-Bound Train* (Campus Folksong Club CFC 301); see also, Ohrlin, *The Hell-Bound Train, A Cowboy Songbook* (Urbana: University of Illinois Press, 1973), 20–21.

14. This brief sketch is culled from "Joe Hill: Wobbly Bard," in Joyce L. Kornbluh's *Rebel Voices: An I.W.W. Anthology* (Chicago: Charles H. Kerr, 1988).

15. Joe Hill's original, published in the ninth edition of the IWW songbook, is reprinted by Kornbluh, *Rebel Voices,* pp. 16–17. The condensed version acquired by Salty Hougan is sung by K. Wendell Whitford on the Goose Island Ramblers' 1990 cassette, *Midwest Ramblin',* Wisconsin Folk Museum WFM 9001.

16. Taplin's remarks, his song, and its tune appear in Peters, *Folk Songs out of Wisconsin*, p. 91.

17. Recorded from an unidentified singer on Beaver Island, Michigan, in August, 1938, by Alan Lomax for the Library of Congress, AFS 2303 A3.

18. Recorded as "Ole From Norway" from John Frederickson, Frankfort, Michigan, by E.C. Beck. Beck mentions that the song "has been reported from Nebraska and Wyoming," but offers no sources. Beck, *Songs of the Michigan Lumberjacks*, pp. 30–31.

19. William F. Kirk, *The Norsk Nightengale, Being the Lyrics of a 'Lumberyack'* (Boston: Small, Maynard & Company, 1905). Beck cites recitations of Kirk's verses in *Songs of the Michigan Lumberjacks*, p. 30.

20. Gronow's biographical sketch appears in liner notes for the LP *Siirtolaisen Muistoja* (The Immigrant's Memories) Finnish RCA PL 40115. The copies we have seen of Kylander's *Humoristisia Lauluja* were privately printed for Kylander, perhaps in the

1950s, in Brooklyn, New York. Data on Kylander's recording sessions appear in Spottswood, *Ethnic Music on Records*, vol. 6, pp. 2581–82.

21. "Lumber Jäkki" ("Lumber Jack") was recorded September 29, 1927, in New York City, on a 78-RPM disc, Victor Vi 80185. See Spottswood, *Ethnic Music on Records*, p. 2581.

22. A brief biography of Vachon, by James P. Leary, appears in a booklet accompanying the two-LP set *Accordions in the Cutover: Field Recordings of Ethnic Music from Lake Superior's South Shore*, Wisconsin Folk Museum WFM 8602. Vachon offers anecdotes from her Finnish-American experience in three books: *Tall Timber Tales, Sagas from Sisula*, and *Finnish Fibbles* (L'Anse, Mich.: L'Anse Sentinel, 1973, 1975, 1979).

23. Seven of Jingo Viitala Vachon's songs and poems, including "Finn From Is'peming," appear in *An Anthology of Verse about Michigan's U.P.*, ed. William J. Finlan and Margaret Gilbert (Escanaba, Mich.: Photo Offset Printing, 1965).

24. Tape-recorded interview with Dan Belo and Mike Bell, Tamarack Mills, Michigan, by James P. Leary and Thomas Vennum, September 21, 1986, for the Smithsonian Institution. The brothers' adaptation of "Oj Maricka Peglaj" is quoted elsewhere in James P. Leary, "Folklore of the Upper Peninsula," *1987 Festival of American Folklife Program* (Washington, D.C.: Smithsonian Institution, 1987).

25. Tape-recorded interview with Frankie Smolz on Minnesota's Mesabi Range by John Berquist, ca. 1983.

26. Bruce C. Nelson quotes from the *Chicago Tribune* in "Dancing and Picnicking Anarchists? The Movement below the Martyred Leadership," in *Haymarket Scrapbook*, ed. Dave Roediger and Franklin Rosemont (Chicago: Charles H. Kerr Publishing Company, 1986), pp. 76–79. The *Scrapbook* also includes articles and reproduces documents regarding Czech, Danish, German, Italian, and Polish workers in nineteenth-century Chicago and Milwaukee.

27. A spate of songs, composed in the wake of the Haymarket trials, including English versions of non-English examples, are presented in "The Eight-Hour Day and the Haymarket Affair," a chapter in Philip S. Foner, *American Labor Songs of the Nineteenth Century* (Urbana: University of Illinois Press, 1975), 216–34.

28. Tape-recorded interview with Alexandra Buling, Elgin, Illiois, by Richard March, May, 1977, for the Chicago Urban Ethnic Folklore Project undertaken by the American Folklife Center at the Library of Congress.

29. Tape-recorded interview with Paul Vangeloff, Lorain, Ohio, by Richard March (March 1979), for the Greater Cleveland Ethnographic Museum's Balkan Slavic Music Project; tapes deposited at Cleveland State University. Tape-recorded interview with Linda Pappas, Gary, Indiana, by Richard March (April 1976), for the Gary Project of Indiana University's Folklore Institute. Esma Redžepova recorded "Tuginata Pusta Bila" in Yugoslavia, Jugoton LP Y61142.

30. Richard March learned the Lošinj seafaring songs from family oral tradition in the 1960s. Noted singers were his maternal aunts and uncles: Christina Karlich, Lena Sokolich, Joseph Grbac, and Kreso Grbac. Dalmatian song about cementing over the sea appears in *Selection of Folk Songs and Dances* (Zagreb: Matica Iseljenika, 1977), 38.

31. The Starlights, Vocal by Max Kawa, "Iron Foundry Polka" b/w "Tony's Polka," 45-RPM, Ampol 507.

32. Recorded from the brothers Adolph and Sylvester Romel, Posen, Michigan, in September, 1938, by Alan Lomax for the Library of Congress, AFS 2320 A3. Sylvester Romel was interviewed in Posen in September, 1989, by James P. Leary for the Michigan Traditional Arts Program. He remembered the song vividly and sang along with a recording of his singing from fifty-one years prior.

33. Frank Amato, vocal, with guitar by S. Pelione and mandolin by A. Catania,

"L'Emigrante Disilluso," United 3945–B, 1952. Amato recorded at least two other songs on the United label, all on 78-RPM discs, regarding life in America: "Terra Di Paradisu," 3944–A and "Bella California," 3942–A. We thank Paul Gifford of Flint, Michigan, for making these recordings available.

34. Stan Wolowic and the Polka Chips, "Bricklayer's Song," on the LP *Polka Party,* Tele House CD2034 (originally issued on ABC-Paramount).

References Cited

Beck, E. C. 1941. *Songs of the Michigan Lumberjacks.* Ann Arbor: University of Michigan Press.

———. 1948. *Lore of the Lumbercamps.* Ann Arbor: University of Michigan Press.

Holbrook, Stewart. 1956. *Holy Old Mackinaw: A Natural History of the American Lumberjack.* New York: Macmillan.

Johnson, Aili Kolehmainen. 1947. "Finnish Labor Songs from Northern Michigan." *Michigan History* 31: 336–37.

Kolehmainen, John I., and George W. Hill. 1951. *Haven in the Woods: The Story of the Finns in Wisconsin.* Madison: State Historical Society of Wisconsin.

Kornbluh, Joyce L. 1988. *Rebel Voices: An I.W.W Anthology.* Chicago: Charles H. Kerr.

Leary, James P. 1981. "The Peasant Songs of Jerry Novak." *North Country Folk* 1:5–7, 30.

———. 1987. *The Wisconsin Patchwork: Recordings from the Helen Stratman-Thomas Collection of Wisconsin Folk Music.* Madison: Department of Continuing Education in the Arts.

Peters, Harry. 1977. *Folk Songs out of Wisconsin.* Madison: State Historical Society of Wisconsin.

Wells, Robert W. 1978. *Daylight in the Swamp!: Lumberjacking in the Late Nineteenth Century.* New York: Doubleday.

Jeff Ferrell

The Brotherhood of Timber Workers and the Culture of Conflict

The Song the Capitalist Never Sings

I want to be a working man and with the workers roam,
The cross-roads for my palace car, a bull-pen for my home;
I want to be a member of that free, untrammeled band,
A ball-chain on my ankle and a pick-axe in my hand.

I want to be a working man and hear the bosses sing
The praise of "honest labor" while the big blue whistles ring;
To cheer the starry banner 'till my empty insides bust,
And be a company sucker 'till my ragged form is dust.

—Covington Hall, in *The Rebel*, 1912[1]

In the Deep South of 1910–14, a radical and impoverished union of lumber workers—the Brotherhood of Timber Workers (BTW)—stood up against the powerful southern lumber trust. The BTW did so by building a broad-based, inclusive union which wove racial and ethnic minorities, women, and other outsiders into a united opposition to the trust. Women were active members of the union and helped lead it through its most critical strike. Blacks constituted roughly half the union's membership and a significant portion of its leadership; the involvement of Hispanics was such that one lumber trust report put "Presumably Union (All Mexs. are)" beside the name of a Hispanic lumber worker.[2] Farmers and small merchants likewise participated in the union and actively supported it. In battling the southern lumber trust, the Brotherhood also utilized a stock of innovative strategies and tactics that blended secrecy and deception with confrontation and direct action in the workplace. Many of these orientations evolved in conjunction with the Industrial Workers of the World (IWW, the Wobblies), the daring and progressive national union with which the BTW affiliated in 1912. And, in all its work of organization and confrontation, the Brotherhood developed and drew on a vigorous counter-culture to that of the southern lumber trust and the social order of which it was a part. The BTW thus created for itself and its members a distinctive and defiant style and utilized weapons of ideology and interpretation throughout its battles.

The Brotherhood of Timber Workers and the culture of conflict that it created emerged not only out of a national setting permeated by collective rebellion against capitalism, but also a regional history of organized and unorganized resistance to the abuses of the southern lumber trust. The Brotherhood embodied workers' resistance to long hours and low wages, but perhaps even more so their rebellion against the trust's systematic control of their lives. Southern lumber workers suffered on the job under the efficiencies of scientific management and the inequities of the "scrip" payment system; lived in company housing inside tightly controlled company towns; and attended churches, schools, and YMCAs designed to create an economical and complacent work force.

As the Brotherhood began to succeed in organizing resistance to these systems of social control, the southern lumber trust responded with the blacklisting of BTW members and the shutdown and restructuring of mills in which BTW members worked. Despite this, BTW organization and strike activity increased. A strike against the Galloway Lumber Company at Grabow, Louisiana, climaxed with the 1912 Grabow "riot," which resulted in a number of dead and injured, and in the arrest, indictment, and jailing of BTW president A. L. Emerson and approximately sixty BTW members and support-ers on murder charges. Following the defendants' acquittal, the trust precipi-tated a strike at the American Lumber Company in Merryville, Louisiana, and with the help of local deputy sheriffs and the Good Citizens' League, broke the strike by the summer of 1913. A final BTW strike—the "Sweet Home Front" strike—began late in 1913 and ended in the summer of 1914.[3]

Networks of ideology and interpretation

This brief chronological sketch, of course, masks more than it reveals, reduc-ing the conflict to a sequence of dates and events. What were the social dynamics that linked these events? How was the Brotherhood able to produce and disseminate an active counter-culture and to utilize its cultural and ideological weapons against the might of the southern lumber trust during the Grabow trial, the Merryville strike, and elsewhere?

To begin with, the Brotherhood regularly engaged in what one lumber industry journal labelled "incendiary speeches at nights and on Sundays."[4]

BTW President A. L. Emerson reported to the May, 1912, BTW convention:

> Since January 1, 1911, I have traveled over 11,000 miles. I have made 257 public speeches—85 talks in halls and in the woods to small crowds of union men. I have had 37 speeches broken up by the companies and their pimps. I have missed three or four speeches on account of cold, two on account of sickness, and some two or three on account of missed connections.[5]

More was involved than simple speech-making, however. The speeches were often made at social gatherings such as barbeques and picnics, some directly organized by the Brotherhood. Also, BTW gatherings—especially those held on weekends—often incorporated a march to a nearby mill, with the intention of confronting and/or converting "scab" labor employed in the mill, and arousing public sympathy.[6]

A network of Brotherhood literature supported its speechmaking. At the 1912 convention, the Grand Executive Board recommended

> more educational literature to better educate our fellow workers. We recommend that each Local's membership purchase or subscribe to all such publications and pamphlets as will enlighten them in the knowledge of Unionism.

The convention responded by adopting the recommendation and empowering the Grand Lodge "to print as many copies" of speeches by leaders like Covington Hall and Bill Haywood "as they deem necessary."[7] So effective was this dissemination of literature that the New Orleans *Times-Democrat* reported

> the whole country as far west as the Sabine River has been literally plastered over with Socialistic literature of every description . . . in the shape of newspapers, booklets, leaflets, tracts and magazines, and it is being sent here from all sections of the country.[8]

Prior to the Grabow trial, the BTW placed Covington Hall in charge of publicity; according to Hall, his

> first act was to get out a weekly bulletin with the latest news from our side. . . . Each week, up to the opening of the trial (and throughout) we issued a bulletin, distributing it over West Louisiana and East Texas, and elsewhere, mailing bundles to trusted men to hand out. They did a good job. The bulletins were distributed everywhere . . . and the prosecuting attorney began to ask prospective jurors the question: "Have you read the Defense Bulletin?"[9]

Merryville strikers also distributed leaflets widely. In direct fashion, strikers threw them to "scabs" through the windows of trains, and on the station platform. The importance of these leaflets and circulars to the BTW's efforts was perhaps best captured in an incident during the Grabow trial. Desiring to prejudice prospective jurors, the lumber companies distributed a fake IWW

Table 1: A Sample of BTW Circulars	
Title	*Topic*
An Appeal to Timber and Lumber Workers	Union organization
Wage Scale	BTW wage demands
A Parable (reverse of "Wage Scale")	Union organization
"$20,000 To See Him Hang"	Appeal for aid, Grabow trial
Shall Emerson Die?	Grabow incident, appeal for aid
Barbarous Louisiana	Lake Charles jail conditions
Shall More Murder Be Done?	Lumber trust activities; appeal for aid
To All Negro Workers and Especially to the Negro Forest and Lumber Workers of the South	Appeal for racial solidarity and aid
The Grabow "Conspiracy"	Grabow trial
To the Members and Sympathizers of the B of TW	BTW protest at opening of Grabow trial
Louisiana—A Rival to Despotic Russia	Legal/economic harassment
Labor, the Creator of Wealth, is Entitled to All it Creates	Appeal for aid, Merryville strike[10]

bulletin extremely militant in its tone; not surprisingly, Covington Hall responded with a counter-bulletin ridiculing the companies' attempt.[11]

Unionists utilized newspapers extensively in conjunction with these leaflets and circulars. BTW leaders like Jay Smith emphasized the necessity of the union's having its own newspaper, whereby the union could generate publicity—"our greatest weapon"—and exercise some control over "the sources of information and education." The BTW thus started *The Lumberjack,* a newspaper edited by Covington Hall and described as "a new machine gun of the revolution."[12] Though beset by financial difficulties, harassed in both its production and distribution by the southern lumber trust, and eventually relocated and renamed, *The Lumberjack* was widely and effectively utilized by the Brotherhood. The Merryville, Louisiana *Times*—which a lumber industry journal attacked as "the most anarchistic publication in the English language"—was another BTW organ, reportedly operated by A. L. Emerson.[13] The DeRidder, Louisiana *News,* like other rural newspapers based in the BTW's area of greatest strength, also supported the union.[14] Late in the conflict Covington Hall established *Rebellion,* which provided support for the final efforts of the timber workers.

Beyond these newspapers stretched a formidable network of socialist, labor, and union newspapers. The *Appeal to Reason* (Girard, Kansas) and the *National Rip-Saw* (St. Louis) were widely read. A BTW member arrested after the Grabow "riot" told the arresting officer, "Wait until I get my *Rip-Saw* and *Appeal to Reason*. I cannot go to jail without taking them papers with me," and when asked about his Bible responded, "No, these papers are all I want."[15] The prosecution in the Grabow trial thus questioned prospective jurors as to whether they had read these papers, with "one juror being challenged peremptorily by the State because he had read one copy of 'The Rip-Saw.'"[16] BTW leaders cited the *Rip-Saw*, along with the *Industrial Worker, Solidarity, The Rebel, The International Socialist Review,* and *The Coming Nation,* as six newspapers that played a critical role in the battle to free Emerson and the other Grabow defendants.[17] The *Rip-Saw*, an industry-oriented paper, sent a "star" reporter to the region and supported the Brotherhood's efforts; the *Industrial Worker* and *Solidarity* represented official IWW positions; *The International Socialist Review*, a Chicago-based monthly, publicized the BTW's fight through articles by Covington Hall and others.

The Rebel, published in Hallettsville, Texas, served as the official weekly paper of the Socialist Party of Texas. The paper's remarkable growth during the BTW conflict—from 2,340 subscriptions in July, 1911, to 23,599 in January, 1914—indicated its popularity not only among Texas socialists, but also among the timber workers of East Texas and western Louisiana. *The Rebel's* partisans distributed over 15,000 copies of its special timber workers' edition (Aug. 17, 1912) in the lumber districts.[18]

Even this accounting, however, does not exhaust the newspaper network available to the Brotherhood. *The Rebel, The Lumberjack,* and *The International Socialist Review* formed part of what came to be known as the "rebel press," a group of publications that also included *The Strike-Bulletin* (Clinton, Illinois) and *The Argus-Star* (Huntington, West Virginia). In Louisiana, *The Weekly Record* (New Orleans) and the Leesville *Toiler* also publicized and supported the BTW. Moreover, throughout the conflict *The Rebel* documented the existence of numerous socialist newspapers in the region that constituted, at the minimum, a broad network of potential support for the BTW.

The role of these newspapers and circulars in the conflict was defined, though, not only by the breadth of their distribution, but by the heterogeneity of their content. They certainly served as vehicles for the dissemination of information. Circulars issued by the Brotherhood, for example, incorporated accounts of BTW battles, lists of demands, instructions for BTW members, and appeals for aid; pro-BTW newspapers like *The Rebel* published regular accounts of strikes and legal battles, and innumerable appeals for financial

Table 2: A Sample of Regional Socialist Newspapers

Newspaper	Locality
Clarion	Sugden, Oklahoma
The Eye-Opener	Memphis, Tennessee
Fort Worth Socialist	Fort Worth, Texas
The Habt-Acht (German)	Hallettsville, Texas
The Herald	Mingus, Texas
The Investigator	Berryville, Arkansas
The Laborer	Dallas, Texas
The Militant	Tyler, Texas
New Century	_____, Oklahoma
The New Era	Hallettsville, Texas
New Forum	Winfield, Louisiana
The Oak Valley Socialist	Oak Valley, Texas
The Pitchfork	Dallas, Texas
Pozor (Bohemian)	Hallettsville, Texas
The Questioner	Abbeville, Louisiana
The Sledgehammer	Barton, Florida
Social Democrat	Memphis, Tennessee
Social Democrat	Okla. City, Oklahoma
The Socialist	Abbeville, Louisiana
The Socialist	Comanche, Texas
The Socialist	Texarkana, Texas
The Southern Worker	Huntington, Arkansas
Sword of Truth	_____, Oklahoma
Workin' Stiff	Shawnee, Oklahoma[19]

support. But beyond this, the circulars and newspapers became vehicles for the definition of the Brotherhood as an organization, for the interpretation of the Brotherhood's collective activity, and for the construction of the Brotherhood's style. The circulars and newspapers certainly disseminated straightforward prose reports structured much like those in other media sources of the period, but they also disseminated poems, songs, parables, aphorisms, and cartoons. While they were certainly the conduits for official pronouncements of the BTW and the IWW, and for the writings of union leaders like Covington Hall and Bill Haywood, they also functioned as conduits for the creative outpourings of the membership, and thus were critical to the sort of participatory style which the BTW promoted. These elements of style and interpretation can best be seen in the documents themselves.

The documents

The Brotherhood produced and circulated a remarkable number of documents, only a few of which are included here. Moreover, the BTW drew from a wide spectrum of ideological resources in constructing this literature and utilized it to examine broad-ranging issues. BTW literature drew on the Southern/Confederate heritage; Christianity; Democratic, Republican, and socialist traditions; and the more general ethos of labor versus capital. In a single circular, for example, the BTW's Committee of Defense quoted Andrew Jackson, Thomas Jefferson, Abraham Lincoln, Karl Marx, and Christ.[20] This literature at the same time covered issues ranging from religion to politics and class conflict.

Within this heterogeneous literature perhaps the most striking theme, and the one most critical to the BTW's creation of a distinct style, was *defiance*. Covington Hall's poem "Us the Hoboes and Dreamers" warned

> We shall laugh to scorn your power than now holds the South in awe,
> We shall trample on your customs, we shall spit upon your law;
> We shall outrage all your temples, we shall blaspheme all your gods,
> We shall turn your Slavepen over as the plowman turns the clods!

Hall's "The Fight is On" likewise proclaimed

> To hell with the statutes and with the laws. . . .
> To hell with courts, in crime grown old!
> To hell with justice bought and sold![21]

In E. F. Doree's "A Parable," a lumber mill owner concludes a long debate with a union representative by asking, "Well, what in _____ do you want?" and the representative replies, simply, "The earth and the machinery of production."[22] The Brotherhood was never more insolent, however, than in its attacks on the leadership of the southern lumber trust, and especially John Henry Kirby, its pompous, patronizing head. BTW writers labeled Kirby "Con H. Jirby," "Director General of the Guntoters," and the "Texas Jackass," and BTW poems like "Coming" warned,

> We are coming, "brother" Kirby, we are coming good and strong,
> And the day isn't distant when you'll sing another song.[23]

This defiance surfaced in other forms as well. During the conflict, enemies accused the BTW of sabotage, and at times the union claimed this practice. Whatever the actual extent of the sabotage, BTW literature in regard to it was clearly intended to communicate a defiant—and threatening— message. The BTW and the IWW popularized symbols such as the wooden shoe (from the sabots, or wooden shoes, with which French workers fouled machinery), and the black cat (the "Sabo-Tabby Kitten") and otherwise advocated sabotage through poems and essays. In the midst of the Merryville strike, the *Industrial Worker* ran a carefully constructed warning:

> Scabs!
> Attention
> Brotherhood of Timber Workers
> On Strike at Merryville, La.
> Take Warning!
> American Lumber Co.
> Going crazy.
> Everybody's doin' it!
>   Doin' what? Nawthin'.

A few months later, the paper published the following editorial:

> **S**oap stops water from making steam in boilers.
> **A**safetida keeps patrons from struck theatres.
> **B**y working slow profits are greatly reduced.
> **O**il containing emery makes machinery strike.
> **T**elling trade secrets wins battles for workers.
> **A**ccidents often are an aid in winning strikes.
> **G**uerilla warfare always gets the bosses' goat.
> **E**nds that are revolutionary justify the means.[24]

THE SOUTHERN BOSS IS UP A TREE!

From *Industrial Worker*, 2 November 1911.

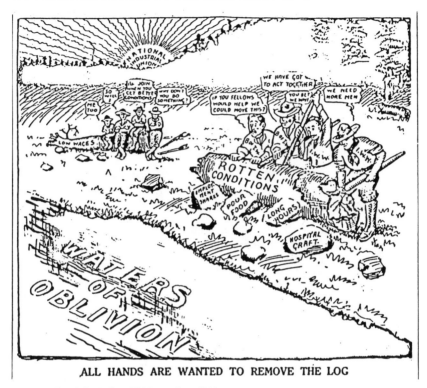

ALL HANDS ARE WANTED TO REMOVE THE LOG

From *Industrial Worker,* 23 November 1911.

The Lumberjack likewise published the poem "Saw Mill 'Accidents,'" by The Wooden Shoe Kid, and the *Industrial Worker* ran "Don't Do It, Boys," a lengthy "warning to wayward lumberjacks," which began

> We are sure that no self-respecting lumber worker would ever resort to that terrible thing called sabotage. We wish to warn all workers against it. You don't know what sabotage is, you say? Well perhaps it is best to tell you so that you may take warning,

and went on to detail all manner of sabotage (not) to be used. The results of sabotage efforts were reported with similar craft.[25]

Conventional notions of religion received as little respect in the BTW's literature as did conventional notions of property and property rights. Brotherhood writers defined the Christ event as a root metaphor for the struggles of labor and denied the legitimacy of the Christian church as organized and utilized under capitalism. Covington Hall poems such as "Might is Right," "Rebellion," "The Ways of Kings, Crowned and Uncrowned," and "Jesus Christ," for example, offered a straightforward message: the church and state powers of Judea martyred Christ in the same way that the powers of capitalism and the state now persecute labor.

Moreover, the literature of the BTW ridiculed and parodied many of the sacred texts and textual forms of western Christianity. The *Industrial Worker* urged its readers to "all join in and sing the famous hymn that starts thusly":

> What a friend we have in Kirby
> All our sins and griefs to bear;
> In dividing labor's product
> Give to John the larger share.

The Rebel also published a hymn—Covington Hall's "The Lumberjack's Thanksgiving Hymn"—which made reference to Kirby and other leaders of the southern lumber trust:

> Thank God for this—John Kirby lives,
> Buchanan still his bounty gives;
> That Downman's star is still on high,
> And corporations never die. . . !

Late in the conflict, *The Rebel* published "The 23rd Psalm (With apologies to R. K. James)," which began

> The Lumber King is my master;
> I know only want.
> He maketh me to go down in deep forests;
> He leadeth me beside tall trees.
> He thinketh not of my soul;
> He leadeth me in paths of danger for his profit's sake.[26]

IWW organizer and BTW leader Phineas Eastman wrote the outrageous "A Workin' Stiff's Prayer." It included the following passages:

> Oh Lord, we approach thy throne this day, in the spirit, and through thy meek (?) servant, our Holy (?) Minister, do thank thee for the blessings that thou hast seen fit to take from us and bestow upon our earthly mentors. . . .
>
> We are becoming rebellious, though, Oh Lord, and have begun to question the right of a few of thy stewards to cop everything that is conducive to happiness, leaving us everything that is productive of wretchedness; and we are beginning to take a delight in being disobedient, and if you in the wisdom you are credited with, but which we doubt, do not see fit to give orders to said stewards to divide fair with us, we are going to put such a Hell of a crimp in their pocketbooks that they will have to come down from their lofty perches and go to work or starve. . . .
>
> And, if it be true that you are the God who has so tenderly provided for our masters' comforts at our expense, then we will set up another God—call it Industrial Freedom—and proceed to worship it devoutly, despite our masters' policemen, sheriffs, militia, gunmen and priests. . . .

> We have called our masters' bluff, Oh Lord, and they are depending upon you to lead them out of a bad situation, and, Oh Lord, all we ask is that you help them as little as you have helped us. Amen.[27]

The Brotherhood also utilized its literature to define the union and its membership. In speeches and writings, for example, the Brotherhood conceptualized itself in terms of the One Big Union (OBU), the IWW's notion of an eventually all-powerful union integrating workers of every industry.[28] E. F. Doree's "A Parable," distributed as part of a BTW "Wage Scale" circular, taught a lesson about the OBU through a parable about a victory won through the cooperation of all workers and unions.[29] As seen above, the BTW also brought about remarkable racial integration and solidarity and used its literature to reinforce this. BTW leader Ed Lehman announced, in the usual defiant style,

> There are white *men,* Negro *men* and Mexican *men* in this Union, but no niggers, greasers or white trash! All are *men* on the side of the Union, and all the greasers, niggers and white trash are on the side of the Lumber Trust. . . .

Covington Hall's "A Miracle in Dixie"—a parody of the Christmas story—recorded the miraculous racial solidarity within the BTW, and began:

> And it came to pass that a miracle happened in the land of Dixie, forasmuch on the morning of a red day three Clans of Toil awakened from a hard superstition and the Anglo-Americans and the Afro-Americans and the Mexic-Americans arose and gathered together around the council fire. . . . [30]

Finally, the BTW utilized its literature to engage the literature of the southern lumber trust in "style warfare."[31] As noted previously, when the lumber companies had the Burns Detective Agency distribute a fake IWW circular in an attempt to prejudice prospective jurors, Covington Hall countered with "All About Bums, the Big Sensation," a bulletin which "parodied the agency's circular throughout. . . . " According to Hall,

> my bulletin was not only a sensation but caused a big laugh at the Burnsite's expense. When I returned to Lake Charles I found everybody laughing except the "Bum's" manager, Kinney, and his "defectives," who all were breathing fire and brimstone, and threatening me with revenge. It taught me to get everybody laughing at the enemy if possible; there is nothing so effective "in getting him!" [32]

The Brotherhood likewise "got" John H. Kirby. Kirby had answered an inquiry as to his role in the conflict with a self-serving letter. The BTW responded with a parody entitled "A Lumber Lord's Letter" and signed "Con. H. Jirby." Published in the *Industrial Worker,* the parody included such passages as

In your letter you say: "It is your brains that is trying to destroy the Timber Workers' Union." This is a mistake. I never had any brains. . . . As I am, all men could be, for any man can be a millionaire if he can hypnotize 5,000 other men into letting him take eighty percent of the products of their toil.[33]

These literary battles were even fought within the realm of poetry. The lumber industry journal *Southwest* published the poem "A Heartfelt 'Lay,'" by W. C. Lay of Noble, Louisiana. An attack on the BTW and its leader "Lord Emerson," the poem began:

> Let us alone and let us work,
> While others around us their
> Duty shirk,

and included the verse,

> And where is R. A. Long, J. H. Kirby and E. A. Frost?
> Against whose interest this fight was waged and lost.
> They are still furnishing the all needful proceeds of toil,
> And a higher class of gentlemen never graced our soil.[34]

The Brotherhood, of course, counterattacked. *The Rebel* reprinted the poem under the heading "The Worm Turns" and later published Covington Hall's response, "A Dirty 'Lay'":

> Once there was a Company sucker
> And he hatched a dirty lay,
> And through a dirty paper
> Had his dirty little say.
>
> In a shameless, harpy ballad,
> In a rotten, dirty song,
> He gloated over murder
> And he licked the boots of Long.
>
> And that thrift might follow fawning,
> Lest his rented job be lost,
> He [grovelled] unto Kirby
> And he toadied unto Frost.
>
> And the currish, cringing coward
> Yelpt, in glee, in ghoulish hymn
> While man stood in the shadow
> Of the gallows, dark and grim.
>
> In a turkey-buzzard paper,
> In a carrion-crowish way,
> In a puke he called a poem,
> Yawpt the Company sucker, Lay.[35]

Conclusions

The literature of the Brotherhood of Timber Workers, and the ideologies and interpretations that it carried, played a critical role in the conflict. Far from an epiphenomenon which simply "documented" the actual conflict, the literature constituted a fundamental and active component. Speeches transmitted the perspectives of the Brotherhood's leaders, functioned as the centerpoints of social gatherings, and instigated collective action. Poems and essays about sabotage held perhaps greater tactical importance than the sabotage itself, as they both cleverly disseminated information to the membership and created an atmosphere of defiance and intimidation. And, when the southern lumber trust attempted to utilize its own literature to undercut the Brotherhood's efforts, and to redefine the conflict and its participants, the BTW employed its literary prowess to counterattack effectively. In studying the BTW or other historical instances of collective rebellion, then, we investigate social documents and the culture they embody not as avenues for getting at workers' lives and actions, but as the very building blocks of social life and social action.

In this light, our understanding of labor history and radical social change also broadens. While successful labor movements certainly mobilize individuals, they at the same time, and as part of the same process, create and mobilize bodies of knowledge and understanding. For members of the Brotherhood or other radical movements, speeches, poems, and parables—and as much so, caricatures, cartoons, and songs—are repositories of style and meaning. They serve to create a collective style and perspective in which members participate as surely as they do in picket lines or protest marches. Similarly, when we investigate the social networks within which a movement is located, and on which it draws, we investigate not only individuals, institutions, and interaction as traditionally thought of, but also networks of shared concepts through which the ideology of the movement is developed and disseminated. The history of workers' rebellion is inevitably the history of workers' culture.[36]

Recent developments in social theory and social action—developments often grouped under the heading "postmodernism"—have caused concern that style has now replaced substance, that the increasing attention paid to stylistic and aesthetic orientations today leaves little room for the "real" substance of social life.[37] As we have seen, though, style was as critical to the southern timber workers who constituted the Brotherhood as it was to the young leftists of the 1960s, the punks and postmoderns of the 1970s and

1980s, and the Chinese students of 1989, and style remains a substantive component of any collective rebellion. The ongoing importance of style as an element of collective action can be glimpsed in a remarkable parallel, between an *Industrial Worker* editorial which appeared during the BTW conflict and the Jefferson Airplane's "We Can Be Together," written some fifty-five years later:

> The moment a movement becomes respectable in the eyes of those who are not wage workers, that moment it loses its revolutionary character. It dies. . . . We are not "undesirable citizens." We are not citizens at all. We are rebellious slaves, scorning the morals, ethics and institutions of the Plunderbund. There-fore we are not respectable. We admit it and we are proud of it.

> We are all outlaws in the eyes of America.
> In order to survive we steal,
> Cheat, lie, forge, fuck, hide and deal.
> We are obscene, lawless, hideous
> Dangerous, dirty, violent, and young. . . .
> We are forces of chaos and anarchy.
> Everything they say we are we are,
> And we are very proud of ourselves.[38]

Regis University
Denver

Notes

I presented a version of this paper at the annual meeting of the Pacific Sociological Association (1988), Las Vegas. An abbreviated version appeared in Labor History, *Summer, 1991.*

1. *The Rebel* (Hallettsville, Texas; December 14, 1912), 4.
2. American Lumber Company list in John H. Kirby Papers, Houston Metropolitan Research Center, Houston Public Library, Houston, Texas.
3. See Jeff Ferrell and Kevin Ryan, "The Brotherhood of Timber Workers and the Southern Lumber Trust: Legal Repression and Worker Response," *Radical America* 19/4:54–74, for additional information on the conflict and its legal and political dimensions. For more on the company towns and social control, see Jeff Ferrell, "East Texas/Western Louisiana Sawmill Towns and the Control of Everyday Life," *Locus* 3/1:1–19.
4. *The St. Louis Lumberman* (St. Louis; August 15, 1912), 60.
5. Brotherhood of Timber Workers, *Minutes of the Second Annual Convention* (Alexandria, Louisiana, 1912), 2.
6. See *The St. Louis Lumberman* (August 15, 1912), 60; Charles R. McCord, "A Brief History of the Brotherhood of Timber Workers" (Master's thesis, University of Texas at Austin, 1959), 54–55; Merl E. Reed, "Lumberjacks and Longshoremen: The I.W.W. in Louisiana," *Labor History* 13/1:49; James R. Green, "The Brotherhood of Timber Workers, 1910–1913: A Radical Response to Industrial Capitalism in the Southern U.S.A.," *Past and Present* 60:180, 188; Covington Hall, *Labor Struggles in the Deep South* (unpublished manuscript, no date), 141–54; operative's report to Kirby Lumber Company (June 16, 1912), Kirby Papers.
7. Brotherhood, *Minutes*, 3, 22.

8. New Orleans *Times-Democrat* (New Orleans, August 5, 1912), 1; see also (August 4, 1912) Section II:1.

9. Hall, *Labor Struggles,* 156, 158.

10. These circulars were generally signed either by BTW leaders like Jay Smith and E. F. Doree, or by the Brotherhood's Defense Committee. Some of the original circulars can be found in the Kirby Papers; others were reproduced in whole or part during the conflict in journals such as the *Industrial Worker, The Rebel, Southwest,* and *The St. Louis Lumberman.* For a more detailed listing, see Jeff Ferrell, "The Brotherhood of Timber Workers and the Southern Lumber Trust, 1910–1914" (Ph.D. diss.,University of Texas at Austin, 1982), 349–51.

11. See Philip S. Foner, *History of the Labor Movement in the United States,* Volume IV: *The Industrial Workers of the World, 1905–1917* (New York, 1965), 252; the *Industrial Worker* (Spokane, March 6, 1913), 4; (February 27, 1913), 4; Hall, *Labor Struggles,* 171– 72; *Southwest: Southern Lumber and Industrial Review* (Houston, October 1912), 26.

12. Smith in *The Rebel* (August 9, 1913), 3; *Industrial Worker* (January 23, 1913), 4; see Hall, *Labor Struggles,* 98; *Industrial Worker* (June 5, 1913), 3.

13. *Southwest* (October 1912), 26.

14. See George T. Morgan, "No Compromise–No Recognition: John Henry Kirby, The Southern Lumber Operators' Association, and Unionism in the Piney Woods, 1906–1916," *Labor History* 10/2:199.

15. New Orleans *Times-Democrat* (August 3, 1912), 4.

16. "The Grabow 'Conspiracy,'" original circular in Kirby Papers.

17. See *The Rebel* (February 8, 1913), 2. Reporters for both *Appeal to Reason* and *National Rip-Saw* circulated in the region—see the New Orleans *Times-Democrat* (August 3, 1912), 1, 4. See also Green, "Radical Response," 179; and Grady McWhiney, "Louisiana Socialists in the Early Twentieth Century: A Study of Rustic Radicalism," *The Journal of Southern History* 20/3:322.

18. See *The Rebel* (August 24, 1912), 4; (August 31, 1912), 3, 4.

19. These socialist newspapers are cited in editions of *The Rebel,* 1911–14.

20. See the *Industrial Worker* (August 22, 1912), 4.

21. Joyce Kornbluh, *Rebel Voices: An I.W.W. Anthology,* new edition (Chicago, 1988), 260; *The Rebel* (November 23, 1912), 3. For more on Covington Hall and his literary works, see David Roediger, ed., *Covington Hall, Dreams and Dynamite: Selected Poems* (Chicago, 1985); and Ferrell, *The Brotherhood,* 406–31.

22. Original circular, Kirby Papers.

23. *The Rebel* (August 17, 1912), 1.

24. *Industrial Worker* (December 26, 1912), 8; (June 12, 1913), 2—emphasis in original.

25. *Industrial Worker* (December 26, 1912), 2. See Kornbluh, *Rebel Voices,* 56–57; *Industrial Worker* (May 30, 1912), 3; (February 27, 1913), 1, 4; Ferrell and Ryan, "Legal Repression," 64–66.

26. *Industrial Worker* (July 17, 1913), 2; *The Rebel* (September 14, 1912), 2; (April 4, 1914), 2.

27. *Industrial Worker* (February 27, 1913), 3.

28. See, for example, Covington Hall, "The Victory of the Lumber Jacks," *The International Socialist Review* 13/6 (December 1912), 470–71; A. L. Emerson speech typescript (July 4, 1912), Kirby Papers.

29. Original circular in Kirby Papers.

30. Quoted in Hall, *Labor Struggles,* 190 (emphasis in the original); *The Rebel* (December 21, 1912), 2.

31. See Stuart Cosgrove, "The Zoot-Suit and Style Warfare," *Radical America* 18:38–51; Peter York, *Style Wars* (London, 1980/1983).

32. Hall, *Labor Struggles,* 171–72.

33. *Industrial Worker* (May 30, 1912), 3; see John H. Kirby to T. H. Dillon (April 13, 1912), Kirby Papers.

34. *Southwest* (August 1912), 77.

35. *The Rebel* (October 30, 1912), 3; (December 14, 1912), 1.

36. See, for example, Robbie Lieberman, "People's Songs: American Communism and the Politics of Culture," *Radical History Review* 36: 63–78.

37. On postmodernism, see, for example, Hal Foster, ed., *Postmodern Culture* (London, 1985); the various essays collected in *ICA Documents* 4: *Postmodernism* (London, 1986); The 2nd January Group, *After Truth: A Post-Modern Manifesto* (London, 1986); Jean-Francois Lyotard, *The Postmodern Condition: A Report on Knowledge* (Minneapolis, 1984); and Norman K. Denzin, "Postmodern Social Theory," *Sociological Theory* 4:194–204. Among the critiques of postmodernism, see, for example Fredric Jameson, "Postmodernism, or The Cultural Logic of Late Capitalism," *New Left Review* 146: 53–92; Jurgen Habermas, "Modernity—An Incomplete Project," in Foster, *Postmodern Culture,* 3–15; and J. G. Merquior, "Spider and Bee: Towards a Critique of the Postmodern Ideology," in *ICA Documents* 4: 16–18.

38. *Industrial Worker* (Oct. 24, 1912), 2; Jefferson Airplane, "We Can Be Together," *Volunteers,* RCA (1969).

Richard Ellington

Fellow Worker Guy Askew: A Reminiscence

The Industrial Workers of the World, founded in Chicago in 1905, carried American labor far beyond the limitations imposed by then-existing craft unionism. The IWW saw craft loyalists pitting one group of workers against another, showing intolerance to all except skilled labor, and effectively excluding women, blacks, and foreign-born workers. In response to narrow craft divisions and a policy of collaboration with employers, the IWW proposed that "The working class and the employing class have nothing in common." From inception, the IWW advocated a broad-based union, taking in all workers, and organized on "industrial" lines: all workers in the same industry in the same union.

The "One Big Union" concept caught on quickly and spread like a smoldering fire, blazing up not only in the accepted form of strike activity, but also in a variety of new tactics innovated by IWW organizers. These rebels shaped a veritable guerrilla warfare of sit-down strikes, rule-book strikes, and sabotage—defined by the IWW as the purposeful withdrawal of efficiency on the job. Restless, footloose organizers mingled freely with the hobo community, priding themselves on their ability to get around the country quickly and easily on freight trains.

From the beginning, the IWW formed a singing organization. When the Salvation Army bands drowned them out on skid roads where the jobless congregated, Wobblies began writing their own texts to be sung to the tunes played by the "Sallies." Soon they circulated the songs, first on little cards, then in the famous *Little Red Songbook*, a living organism that changed with each edition as editors added new material and dropped the old. Currently, in its thirty-fifth edition, the tradition remains, with songs by new scribes resting comfortably next to those by classic writers like Joe Hill and Ralph Chaplin.

The IWW's policy of sticking strictly to economic action and of staying out of electoral politics made the organization attractive to anarchists like

Guy Askew and myself. It also placed the IWW in opposition to the Communist Party. When the IWW refused to affiliate with the Red Trade Unions
organization (circa 1921), the Communist Party tried unsuccessfully to imple-
ment a strategy of "boring from within," hoping to take over the industrial
organization by subterfuge. Askew's response to such left rivalry typified that
of many of his fellow workers, men and women who defined themselves as
old-time Wobblies.

That aside, it would be a mistake to consider Askew, himself, as "typical"
in any way. In an organization so heavily leavened with highly individualistic
men and women from every part of society, all members add to a rich
painting their own hue or tint. Wobblies still identify themselves as workers
who can shape One Big Union by job action and creative imagination—
songs, poems, cartoons, union-hall murals, hall posters, tiny agitational
stickers. Indeed, IWW members like Guy Askew dedicated themselves on and
off the job to "painting" a bright new world.

*   *   *

He signed the letters in a variety of ways: "Skidroad Slim," "Old 110 Cat,"
"Right Guy," and sometimes even formally with his full name, Guy B. Askew
(see fig. 1). The file of his correspondence in front of me covers about ten
years, from 1956 to just before his death in 1966. It's quite an imposing sight,
half a dozen file folders stuffed to overflowing. The letters are written on what
was obviously whatever kind of paper he could scrounge. Most of them are on
various sizes of cheap ruled tablet paper and, while a few of them are written
in ballpoint pen, most are in a blunt number two pencil. Even the few that
start in pen often break off midway and go back to the more familiar pencil.
Depending apparently on his health and personal circumstances, the flow of
the letters had a strange, almost tidal pattern, ebbing off to a sparse one a
month on occasion then, in response to some moon of his own, rising to two
or three a week for a month or so, or even two a day on rare occasions.

I first saw one of his letters in 1956, when I handled the literature sales for
the Libertarian League, a small anarchist group in New York, and also
collected the mail from our post office box. I was going over a couple of days'
worth of mail with Russell Blackwell, an older comrade with an unpredictable
sense of humor. He tossed me a letter with a groan and muttered something
about another damned Askew tirade. In puzzlement, I looked at the strange,
old-fashioned scribble that was to become so familiar in the next few years. It
opened with a complaint that two weeks previously he had sent us some small
sum—I think it was a quarter—requesting a pamphlet, and hadn't yet received the pamphlet. He went on to give us a severe lecture on how this was

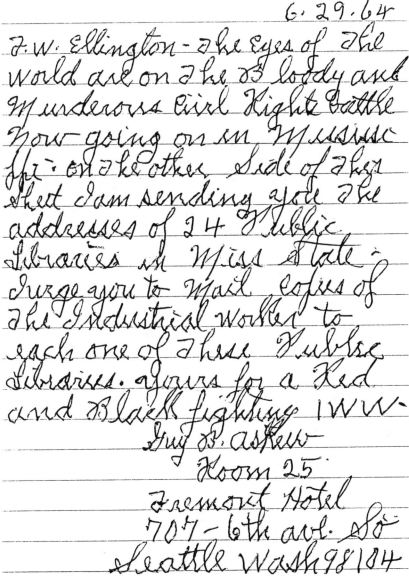

6.29.64

F.W. Ellington - The Eyes of The world are on The FBI loddy and Murderous Civil Right battle now going on in Mussissippi - on The other side of this sheet I am sending you The addresses of 24 Public Libraries in Miss State; I urge you to mail copies of The Industrial Worker to each one of These Public Libraries. Yours for a Red and Black fighting IWW-

Guy B. Askew -

Room 25

Fremont Hotel

707 - 6th ave. So

Seattle Wash 98184

Fig. 1 *Courtesy Archives of Labor and Union Affairs, Walter P. Reuther Library, Wayne State University*

no way to run an organization. Russell was laughing by then but I didn't see anything terribly funny about it. I remember asking him if he had indeed got the quarter and mailed the pamphlet. He admitted that he might well have missed it since he often threw Askew letters away unread. We got into an argument about it; Russ suggested, finally, that I go ahead and write the old man myself and see how long my patience held out. I took the dare and I suppose it was about six months until I found myself getting to the point where I occasionally filed those letters away unread if I happened to be busy when they arrived.

Later, as my circle of acquaintances in the anarchist movement widened, I found that we were far from being an isolated target and that, in some circles, "Askew letter" was almost a standing joke. Slowly a picture emerged of this old man sitting alone in a skid road hotel in Seattle grinding out these letters day after day to anyone he thought might read them. Since I had replied courteously, I became the addressee of choice for all of Guy's missives to the Libertarian League—or just about anything else in New York for that matter. At first, being a fairly conscientious correspondent, I felt compelled to answer each one—a compulsion Russ Blackwell found hysterically funny. It took a while before I got to the point where I would let the pile grow a while, sometimes for several months, before I wrote him back. It was only with a solid stack of them in front of you that you could readily see how much repetition there was and how many of them really required no answer. As a matter of fact, it soon became obvious that Guy didn't really expect answers any more often than that. He did expect us to fill his little literature orders promptly, but a letter in reply every few months was quite enough to keep him happy.

The real flood broke loose when I became active in the IWW, especially after a group of us reopened the General Recruiting Union branch in New York and started some modest agitational and organizing activities. He got tremendously excited by this and began to pour letters at us at a frenetic rate. The IWW was close to being totally dormant at that time. There were very few young members, and the older members had begun to die off or sink back into inactivity. As an anarchist and former IWW member, Askew saw in our little group the possible fulfillment of his hopes for a resurgent IWW with a heavily anarchist orientation—what he called "a red and black IWW." His letters were full of bits of advice, warnings, tirades, diatribes, and screeds against anything and everything, phrased in his own fiery language and filled with revolutionary fervor. Occasionally there would be a break in this outpouring and a sudden spontaneous expression of affection, as in the following from 1959:

> I love you Militant IWWs for the Enemies you have Made in New York City.
> Keep up the good work in fighting the Job Sharks, Educating and Organizing the
> Wage Slaves into the Revolutionary IWW. Yours for a Black and Red fighting
> IWW, Guy B. Askew

Some place along the line I finally realized that, much as his letters might annoy and infuriate some people or just plain bore the life out of a lot more, I *liked* Guy B. Askew. We had never met of course, but I began to develop a strong comradely feeling for him, and also a realization that, even if he seemed a little crazy by the standards of our current society, he was a warm human being, and we shared a lot of basic ideas. I also came to realize that, as an old timer, he must have been around many interesting situations in his time. I began to query him about the past generally and about himself personally. I immediately ran up against a peculiar attitude that I was to encounter time and time again in older radicals, particularly some of the older anarchists. Although they are usually not averse to talking about the past to a sincere and interested audience, most of them tend to clam up totally when asked anything personal about themselves. It has to do, in most cases, with an aversion to what they usually refer to with a sneer as "the cult of the individual," a feeling that no "I" is important, only "we."

Guy was fairly typical of this attitude. He never refused my requests for personal information—he simply ignored them. Occasionally, a tiny snippet of information would drop in, almost by accident. I can thus state that he was probably born about 1896 in New Salem, Illinois; that he was a member of the IWW for twenty-five years or so; was a Class War prisoner for four months in 1923 in the Yakima County jail and probably also in other jails; and that he spent some time in New York in 1925, where he worked for a time at a hospital on Staten Island. His life during the time I knew him was simple enough. He lived a precarious existence in a Seattle skid road hotel at Dearborn and Eighth Avenue South, where he probably existed on social security or welfare. He spent his time reading, writing letters, and occasionally going up to the old IWW hall, though he never stayed there long, since he obviously didn't get along too well with the other old Wobblies who hung out there. He spoke often of taking the unsold copies of the IWW's *Industrial Worker* each month after the new issue had arrived and distributing them in any way that he could, rather than see them go to waste. He spoke of few friends and no one that he saw regularly. One or two of the young anarchists in Seattle visited him occasionally, took him out to dinner, and bought him some stamps and writing paper, but these visits were rare. Obviously, correspondence filled his life. Typical of the way he would occasionally drop in a personal remark is this excerpt:

> I am a firm believer in this circus type of Advertising for both the IWW and LL [Libertarian League]. In my younger days I traveled with Circuses and Carnivals as a Barker (Ballyhoo) Man for Side Shows. I have also Soapboxed for the IWW Many Times in North Dakota, Yakima Valley and Elsewhere and always enjoyed it very much. (July, 1959)

Finally, early in 1960, I got to Seattle and went down to his hotel to meet him. I don't really know what I expected but he was definitely a surprise. Physically, he was short, thin, wiry, almost delicate in build, but it was the voice that startled me. I guess I had built up an image from all his written fire and brimstone of a fierce, snarling voice, and what I found instead was a thin, reedy voice, almost a whisper, not so much conspiratorial as perhaps a little frightened. We spent several hours talking though he was obviously ill at ease having anyone visit him in his little room. I presented him with a box of fluorescent chalk (he was an inveterate graffiti artist, scrawling IWW slogans on walls and fences all over the area). His eyes lit up when I explained how it would glow in the dark.

My family and I were en route from New York to California with a complicated schedule so I didn't get back for a planned second visit. But when we arrived in Berkeley, the flow of letters started up again immediately. I found, over the years, that if I asked specific questions he would respond willingly with whatever he could remember from the early days. Occasionally, I'd forget and mention one of his pet peeves, which would bring forth another flood of fire-and-brimstone denunciations. Religion usually triggered an outburst, as did any mention of the communists—he used the expression "Commie Gimlet" almost as one word, equivalent perhaps to a southerner's "damyankee." Dave Van Ronk and I had put together a collection of satirical folksongs called "The Bosses' Songbook" and out of idle curiosity I sent Guy a copy, warning him carefully that they were satires and not to be taken seriously. He was a strong advocate of the IWW's Little Red Songbook and when I mentioned I was interested in anything he might remember about other early songs of the IWW, he sent back the following:

A Wobbly Good and True
by Paul Walker

I was riding one day on a train far away, wishing there was a Wobbly near, when it did just seem, like someone in a dream, came a Wob with a hearty cheer.

Chorus:
With some one like you, a Wob good and true, we'd like to rule this world and all that it produces. Day and night, for the greedy parasites, just to give each slave his right. And then we'll have peace, the master class will cease to divide us while we're on the job. The boss will be surprised to find us organized and every slave will be a Wob.

Now he said, Look here Son, I don't know where you're from, but I know that you're true blue. Let us hope that some day all wage slaves will say, Hurrah for the O.B.U.!
(chorus)

The tune to this song is "Let the Rest of the World Go By." Fellow worker Paul Walker was a fine looking, highly intelligent young colored boy who composed this song and sang it in the IWW hall in Aberdeen, Washington in 1923. He had a beautiful voice. You know the tune F. W. Walker used—"We'll build a sweet little nest, Way out in the West, and Let the rest of the World Go By." The IWW must not be satisfied with writing about its history; it must be making history. (March 14, 1958)

Later that week he sent me the following verses, probably his own composition:

Tune: "Darktown Strutter's Ball"

Oh, we'll all organize in the IWW. We'll all take out that little red card. We'll all unite to fight our masters, To the wage slave system we'll bring disasters. We'll fight for better working conditions By direct action on the jobs. Fellow Workers do get wise, One Big Union Organize. We're going to win in the good old Wobbly way.

Oh get you ready for a new war sonny! Don't you hear your masters call? A-bombs, H-bombs, not so funny, And the radiation, it's a honey. We'll not fight their wars at all. With a world-wide General Strike We'll put all the masters on the hike And we'll win that fight in the good old Wobbly way.

Oh when the revolution's over A free society we will make. All the industries, all the land, All the wealth we're going to take. Oh red and black they are our colors, Our banners will wave in every land. So come on and join the band, Be a fighting union man, And we'll win this fight In the good old Wobbly way. (March 21, 1958)

Two months later he sent along the following, again without comment. I do not know if it was his own composition or quoted from memory:

Tune: "Little Old New York"

East Side, West Side, All around the town, You'll find us Junior Wobblies Where fun loving workers are found. We all stand together, We joined the grand O.B.U. We're going to fight for freedom And to our cause we'll be true.

Wage slaves, wage slaves, Hear our call today: To organize for a better world Where all are free and gay. No longer shall the master Make a hell of every hearth. We'll spoil their dirty game of grab And drive them from the earth.

Wage slaves, wage slaves, Of all lands unite. We must fight our masters To make conditions right. Don't matter where you came from, Your race or color or creed, If we all stand united, All wage slaves will be freed.

East Side, West Side, All around the town, You'll find us singing our Wobbly songs Wherever we are found. Boys and girls together, Determined to be free, For we are libertarians Wherever we may be. (May 26, 1958)

Another letter shortly after touched on several of his pet peeves as an aside to some more comment on IWW songs:

Back around World War I, a group of IWWs was being tried before a jury here in Seattle under the Criminal Syndicalism Law then on the statute books of Wash. state. The D.A. read from the IWW songbook to the jury a song whose content contained the following:

I got a job once thrashing wheat, Worked 16 hours with hands and feet, And when the moon was shining bright, They kept me working all the nite. I'm very sorry, I hate to tell, I accidentally slipped and fell, My pitchfork went right in between Some cog wheels on that thrash machine. etc.

Attorney George Vanderveer let it go until he made the closing speech for the IWW Members. Then he said to the Jury: "Ladies and Gentlemen of the Jury, the wage slave was an unorganized Scissor Bill and not an IWW member. They are good union men and will not work 16 hours a day for any boss." The Jury was out only a short time and brought in a Not Guilty verdict in favor of the IWW defendants. There was a book on Sabotage put out by the IWW (though not officially) many years ago and I think the author was Elizabeth Gurley Flynn, now an old political hack of the Moscow Communist Party. She is one of Hennacy's pals sorry to say. [Referring to Ammon Hennacy of the Catholic Worker.] (June 3, 1958)

Other letters revealed a particular antipathy to alcohol:

In 1923, the IWW's largest and most active year, it had a membership in good standing of over 83,000 members. Of these, over 75% was young and under 35 years of age. Card playing, drinking and drunks was not allowed in the halls. There was no old dead timber those days, sitting around the halls playing cards all day. A large part of the sincere and active members those years was young anarchists. The black cat was on the walls and the wooden shoe was on the secretary's desk or hall committee's desk. (May 30, 1962)

So many of the unfortunate wage slaves are victims of that foul social disease called "chronic alcoholism." During the 1917–23 time (the IWW lumberjacks' strike here in the Pacific Northwest), the IWW sent strong arm squads and closed up all the boot legging joints. The money the jacks would have spent for rotgut booze went to feed the picket lines and to support the strike. The winos in time became nothing but human wrecks. It is capitalist poison for the wage slaves; as they can't fight the booze and their capitalist masters at the same time. A whiskey glass and a woman's ass make a horse's ass of the wage slave class. (August 10, 1963)

I should note that I never attempted to "humor" Guy; I would often argue hotly with him and he would respond in kind. He appreciated my honesty, and when I called him on the little doggerel verse quoted above as being a slur on women, he backed off a bit and, perhaps anxious to demonstrate that he was not a total misogynist, gave me his own views on sex:

Now comrade Ellington, I think young IWWs and anarchists who are Sincere and True should mate up with the opposite sexes—we have a very much better chance of keeping them with us *and* these movements that way. For most anarchists and IWWs to marry Scissor Bills and Scissorines it works out no good for our idealistic causes as we have learned by hard experiences. Try and keep your young members clean and healthy. Keep them off the booze and dope as much as possible. Teach them sex hygiene—also birth control if they don't want too many kids. But if they have kids bring them up IWWs and anarchists if possible. Find a place too for the old timers. Many years ago a member of the North Dakota Nonpartisan League told me you IWWs should get your love mates and breed your own IWWs. I now know he was right in many respects on that score. Weak-minded IWWs and anarchists can be weaned away from our cause by the Sex Power of stronger minded Scissor Bills and Scissorines. (undated)

His occasional reminiscences about the early days of the IWW were fascinating to me. Though he never actually admitted it, I was quite sure he had been a "110 cat" himself, one of the rank-and-file practitioners of direct action on the job. I found these occasional snippets of information worth saving:

Some old IWW stickers. Read and bring up to date: Join the armed services and get a wooden coffin to match your wooden head. Why does the black cat and the wooden shoe mean hard luck for the boss class? Join the IWW and find out. Slow down. The hours are long, the pay is small, so take your time and buck them all. Speed up slaves, your masters need the money. Whenever you speed up on the job or work long hours, you're scabbing on the unemployed. The road to freedom is strewn with rocks and thorns! Put on the good old wooden shoe; it will not hurt your corns. —Joe Hill From back in the good old days when the black cat was on the wall and the wooden shoe was on the secretary's desk in IWW halls. (May 14, 1958)

At that time [not specified] the IWW had 15,000 members active and militant all the way from Oklahoma to Saskatchewan, a thousand mile picket line through the small grain belt. Strikes, picket lines, free speech fights; with hundreds filling jails and stockades, speakers and mass meetings all up and down. It took a red card to ride the freights and many railroad workers belonged to the IWW then and demanded red cards of all who rode the boxcars to and from the harvest fields. There was no auto tramps in those days and the picket lines functioned part of the time on the freight trains with cooperation of the train crews. There was flying squadrons traveled the harvest fields, sent out by I.U. 110, who checked up on all traveling and job delegates. If found crooked or drunk they lifted their credentials and took proper action on them. The IWW run the hijackers, bootleggers and tin horn gamblers out of the harvest belt. They sure kept the migratory wage slaves sober and clean. News boys and literature all through the drive and IWW songs was heard all over the small grain country of the northwest. (June 3, 1958)

It was the migratory wage slaves, hoboes and tramps that built the IWW in the first place. These Boomers could beg, mooch and rustle. They kept the hobo jungles clean and could cook damned good eats—mulligan stews, good jamaica and had silver mounted tongues. They went on the jobs to organize, agitate and raise hell in every way possible. They put up IWW stickers, passed out leaflets, sold papers and the *Little Red Songbook*. They never was afraid of a good free speech fight or going to jail. (September 4, 1958)

The IWW made and held the best conditions that ever existed before and since in the logging camps of the Pacific Northwest. They had no labor contracts signed with the lumber companies nor did they want any. They was always free to strike any time the bosses did not meet their demands. In Sept., 1923, the IWW struck the logging camps and their chief demand was release of all political class war prisoners from the Masters' bastilles. The double-deck bunks was done away with by cutting the top bunks off and throwing them out of the doors. They used many types of strikes: slow-down strike, intermittent strike and picket line strike. They was rough and tough as hell, but when they got through they had made the northwest logging camps the best in the world. After burning their own bedrolls, they made the companies furnish clean blankets, clean sheets and pillowslips, decent and comfortable beds, lots of good food in the kitchens, new and neatly painted bunkhouses, shower baths and laundry rooms, and in many instances only 4 men slept in each bunk-house. If the company allowed the blankets and sheets to get dirty, the IWW members took them outside, piled them up and set fire to them and burned them up. Industrial direct action all the way through gets good results. First IWW strike started in the short log country of Idaho in June, 1917, spread to the logging camps of Washington, Montana and Oregon. At the time, the IWW paper, *The Industrial Worker*, became a daily paper during these strikes. The 8 hr. day was won by blowing the whistles and going into camps. That meant 8 hrs. from camp to camp. They went to and from work on the company's time, and the wooden shoe and the black cat was used against the companies as well as against the finks and scabs that showed up. (May 5, 1959)

Up until 1928, the local branch of the IWW had the cutest bunch of girl and boy Junior IWWs you could want to meet or hear sing its songs. The IWW branch had a large hall at 512 1/2 Second Ave. above the Florence Theater. They put on a show every Saturday nite at 8 pm. Admittance was free but good collections was taken at these entertainments. A light lunch was sold during a 10 minute intermission and after the show was over F. W. James P. Thompson spoke at an IWW mass meeting—sometimes before the show to large crowds at the corner of Washington and Occidental on Skidroad. He always spoke there twice a week, starting at 7 pm. All these IWW shows was based on the class struggle and the IWW preamble. They had a damned good piano, good musicians, good singers and actors and comedians, and these wonderful little Junior IWWs sang 5 or 6 songs at each show and they was given free lunches and candy bars for their wonderful cooperation. There was little red Junior IWW cards for them. Some of our Juniors was only 7 and 8 years old—smart, pretty and cute as hell. These kids sold IWW papers and literature at these entertainments and the hall was always so crowded with workers of all ages that many had to stand up. An IWW speaker would also make a 5 or 10 minute talk at these shows. Sometimes we put on a play such as *The Kangaroo Court*. The little IWW songbird, Katie Phar, brought much free talent to these IWW entertainments and directed them. She died in 1943 and now sleeps in Lakeview Cemetery just below the greenhouse in Volunteer Park. A red tombstone marks the graves of her father, an IWW, and herself. (May 9, 1959)

Many years ago some anarchists and IWWs published in Los Angeles a fiery little magazine called *The Wooden Shoe*. It advocated sabotage, which means the conscientious withdrawal of efficiency by the wage slaves on the job. It told of the best method of using direct action strike methods by the slaves on the jobs. The effects of emery dust in the oiling systems of machinery, sugar in the gasoline tanks of autos, etc. It told threshing crews to slow down, don't wear out the farmers' and threshers' machinery. As I remember, it was sponsored by no organization. Slaves wrote in their experiences in turning the Sab Cat loose on the jobs against their industrial masters, also the scabs and finks. The boss class fears the strikes on the job more than any other kind because they are the most effective and they have to pay the slaves for waging these job strikes against them. The black cat and the wooden shoe means hard luck for the boss. Hucksters even sold *The Wooden Shoe* on street corners here in the West, and *The Wooden Shoe* and Emma Goldman's *Mother Earth* could be found in IWW halls all over the country. (May 3, 1959)

Occasionally simply mentioning a name would trigger some information. The following two letter excerpts pretty well cover the extremes of his opinions:

Many old timers in the IWW and outside of it will remember Sam Cohen, a very forceful and excellent soapboxer, who spoke on the skidroads of many cities from New York City to Seattle and Frisco and L.A. in California. Sam often traveled with IWW members and was often in its halls throughout the country. Sam was an anarchist and was always very friendly to the IWW in all his soapbox speeches. He drew big crowds when he exposed the Soviet despotism and the phoney and false commies. Sam was said to have been born in Russia of Jewish parents. He carried papers and documents which exposed the commies. On many occasions they tried to get them away from him. On one occasion in Spokane, Wash., a girl threw acid in Sam's face, trying to blind him but failed to do so. I have heard Sam Cohen died some years ago in California: Many of us old timers who gave him support at his soapbox mass meetings miss him very much. (December 31, 1963)

This old battle-ax haybag may try to line up again in the IWW, but keep her out as she is an expelled member of the organization. She is a natural born pie-card. I think she was in the IWW at the most two or three years. She was a good looking young cunt who came into the harvest fields of the Northwest and fell in love with a young IWW member who induced her to take out a card. She was on pie and led a good life most of the time she carried a card. Besides being on pay, members came in from the jobs and gave her five and ten dollar bills. Sex Appeal—ha! ha! (June 3, 1958)

There was quite a bit of discussion in the IWW at the time about the annoying problems created by being listed on the U.S. attorney general's "subversive list." Again, Guy said straight out what a lot of us felt—that maybe the attorney general was right, we were subversive and proud of it:

> Since its formation in 1905, the IWW has always been on the shit list of the Master Class—and when it was persecuted the most was when it grew the fastest. So being on the subversive list is not keeping it back, only the inactivity of its dues paying members is doing that. (April 30, 1958)

> Some old Wobs are cry babies. "Please get us off your subversive list oh Masters." Ha! ha! IWW always had the slogan years ago—"Make your laws in union halls. The rest can go to hell." (June 3, 1958)

The Libertarian League and the New York IWW branch occasionally took part in small "united front" actions with the Catholic Worker group and later, in California, I would lend them a helping hand on occasion with an old truck I had. This, and our long friendship with Ammon Hennacy, nettled Askew often. He was particularly infuriated when Ammon opened a Catholic Worker house in Salt Lake City and called it "Joe Hill House." He responded bitterly to the writeup on the opening of the house: "Well, F. W. Joe Hill, Kropotkin, etc. in the murals are right next to Jesus Christ, Virgin Mary and the Holy Family in A. H.'s Joe Hill House in Salt Lake City, Utah. ha! ha! ha!" (January 4, 1962).

Later that year, I got the following. I reproduce it in full because I think it's a typical—one might even say "classic"—example of an Askew letter.

> F. W. Ellington - We are still Safe and Sound and our hotel is OK after the Big Storm last nite. Hurricane Freda was a rough old gal. I sure hope the magazine *Wobbly* hits the field soon and regular. In my opinion the Catholic Worker movement is strictly Phoney and several of its top notchers such as Ammon Hennacy and Dorothy Day are soft toward the commies and the old political hack Gurley Flynn. I am surprised that Robert Nichols hangs around the phoney outfit in Salt Lake City so long. It's OK to cover the slaves in their bread lines with IWW and LL literature, but to hang around them all the time! Oh hell, I couldn't stand it. The sun is shining beautiful outside at this writing— quite a change from the hell the old gal Freda gave Seattle and the Northwest last nite. The Kremlin Commie Bastards have sure taken over Cuba and shafted the Revolution with the help of Dictator Fidel Castro, the Murderous Son of a Bitch. Yours for a Red & Black IWW, the LL and the Free Society. Guy B. Askew PS. F. W. Ralph Chaplin wanted to have the *Industrial Worker* take the lead in exposing the Kremlin Commie Rats to the wage slaves, and he was right. But some of the God Damned Marxian Centralist Bastards in the IWW made it Hell for him so that's why he stopped paying dues in the IWW before he died. F. W. Chaplin was a good editor and a good man. (October 13, 1962)

By 1966 the letters weren't coming as often and the handwriting was getting noticeably shakier. He had been trying, in his own way, to help out a small IWW organizing campaign in Washington state and the postscript to his last letter proudly told me: "I am putting out lots of IWW leaflets and stickers and *Industrial Workers* for F. W. Underwood here in Seattle" (April 22, 1966).

But of all the letters he wrote, this one from 1963 touched me the most. I knew he had known Wesley Everest and asked him what he could tell me about the man. He replied:

> F. W. Wesley Everest, who defended the IWW hall in Centralia, Wash., with a German Luger gun against an American Legion mob Nov. 11, 1919 and died a horrible death at the hands of this lumber trust mob, was perhaps the world's greatest labor martyr, though largely unheralded and unsung across the USA. Though quiet, he was strictly a direct actionist for the IWW, though never in the limelight. F. W. Everest was a very active job delegate in the logging camps. Sold IWW papers, literature, song books and put out leaflets to the lumberjacks and worked in logging camps from the time he was a kid in Washington state. A good, generous, kind-hearted Wob with his fellow workers, he had a hot temper and was a good fighter against the enemies of the IWW. He was a sharp shooter with a gun or rifle and was damned good in a fist fight also. You and F. W. Wesley Everest would have been good pals. (August 10, 1963)

Berkeley, California

Editor's Note. Richard Ellington died on May 26, 1991, in Berkeley, California. During visits and with phone talks, I had kept him posted on the progress of this collection of essays on work songs. Sadly, he could not read his contribution in its final form. Thus, I use this editorial note to say goodbye to Dick: typographer, anarchist, Wobbly. We first met in 1959 in Greenwich Village. In one of the strange eddies of the "folksong revival," an unlikely crew of amateur performers, neophyte scholars, science-fiction buffs, left libertarians, and Village habitués had contributed to *Caravan,* a folksong "fanzine." For a few short years, we looked critically at emergent "revival" dogmas. Within our caravansary, Dick and I shared a special interest in IWW treasures.

Early in 1987, Ellington designed and printed a catalog, "Wobbly"—80 Years of Rebel Art for an exhibit at the Labor Archives and Research Center, San Francisco State University. Dick generously contributed the booklet to LARC's growth. Renewing friendship at the exhibit's opening, I told him of my commitment to a memorial volume for folklorist Richard Reuss. Ellington described his massive correspondence with Guy Askew and, subsequently, offered this reminiscence—essentially a portrait of a rank-and-file rebel, a creator and carrier of workers' traditions. The article now stands in remembrance of Reuss, Askew, and Ellington.

Sam Richards

The Joe Hill Legend in Britain

Conceivably the best known industrial or political song in the British trade union and labor movement is the American composition "Joe Hill" by Alfred Hayes and Earl Robinson. Hardly a union activist has not heard it, many can sing along with it, and all who in any way concern themselves with singing informally at weekend schools and conferences seem to know it.

The transcription below is from the singing of George Strattan, a Scot, who has lived in various parts of England for much of his working life. When the recording was made, 30 April 1981, he had fairly recently retired from work, having been active in his union, AUEW–TASS (Amalgamated Union of Engineering Workers—Technical, Administrative and Supervisory Section). He now lives in Liverpool and is active in the peace movement.

Joe Hill

1. I dreamed I saw Joe Hill last night
   Alive as you and me.
   Says I, "But Joe you're ten years dead."
   "I never died," said he,
   "I never died," said he.

2. "In Salt Lake City, Joe," says I
   Him standing by my bed,
   "They framed you on a murder charge."
   Says Joe, "But I ain't dead,"
   Says Joe, "But I ain't dead."

3. "The copper bosses killed you, Joe,
   They shot you, Joe," says I.
   "Takes more than guns to kill a man,"
   Says Joe, "I didn't die,"
   Says Joe, "I didn't die."

4. And standing there as big as life
   And smiling in his eyes
   Says Joe, "What they could never kill
   Went on to organize,
   Went on to organize."

5. From San Diego up to Maine
   In every mine and mill,
   Where working men defend their rights
   That's where you'll find Joe Hill,
   That's where you'll find Joe Hill.

6. I dreamed I saw Joe Hill last night
   Alive, as you and me.
   Says I, "But Joe you're ten years dead."
   "I never died," says he,
   "I never died," says he.

(Original key: G ♩ 120 freely)

I dreamed I saw Joe Hill last night

A - live   as   you   and   me

Says   I 'But Joe   you're   ten years dead'

'I   nev - er   died'   said   he

'I   nev - er   died'   said   he.

Some idea of the popularity of the song can be gained from a trade union colleague of George Strattan's, Ian Parr, who does most of his singing in the Merseyside area. He claims that when his colleagues realize that he is prepared to sing to them there is an automatic assumption: "You must know 'Joe Hill.' Sing us 'Joe Hill.'" Apparently, until a few years ago Ian, who is in his thirties, did not know the song and felt obliged to learn it, such was the pressure on him to sing it.

The usual context for singing at conferences or weekend schools is a common room or bar, often after hours. Sometimes it is loosely organized by one singer who acts as an MC. More often it is an informal affair, probably dominated by a handful of singers whose repertoires can extend to an hour or so. Some singers deliberately hold "Joe Hill" back since it is a difficult song to follow because of the depth of meaning it holds for many of those present.

The song has made Joe Hill himself into a legend. In its original usage the word 'legend' was exclusively applied to the orally circulating accounts of the lives of saints. If Joe Hill can be seen as a secular saint, or labor martyr, he is certainly a legend even in this narrow sense. His life story is usually clothed in sometimes contradictory and mythological detail. Like many other legendary figures from Hereward the Wake to Che Guevara, Joe Hill is said to be at his people's side in time of need, a notion entirely created by the song and the lore surrounding it.

Legends may be true or false. Often they are both. More important than matters of literal truth are the questions: What do they mean to those who know them, and how did they become generally current? Even so, it is instructive to look at the facts as closely as possible if only to see how much or little the legend deviates from them.

Entire books have been written about Joe Hill; I give the bare bones. The song commemorates an actual event and a well-known American agitator, Joe Hill. He was born in Sweden as Joel Emmanuel Hägglund and became Joseph Hillstrom some time after he moved to the USA. Subsequently, he became better known as Joe Hill of the Industrial Workers of the World (IWW), nicknamed "The Wobblies." This was a revolutionary syndicalist organization formed out of a combination of smaller groupings which preached the gospel of "One Big Union." Its recruitment methods included street-corner speaking and frequently brought its members into conflict with the Salvation Army, which used similar tactics. In fact, the Salvation Army and the Wobblies competed for the same members, often unorganized migrant workers.

The Wobblies, from the outset, recognized the power of song and music in their campaigns and, fortunately for them, numbered talented songsters in their ranks. These included Mac McClintock who had already written "Halle-lujah, I'm a Bum" and "The Big Rock Candy Mountain," both destined to become part of the folklore of the British, Canadian, and Australian labor movements as well as the American. Richard Brazier, who was on the General Executive Board of the IWW, remembered many years later:

> What first attracted me to the IWW was its songs and the gusto with which its members sang them. Such singing, I thought, was good propaganda since it had originally attracted me and many others as well; and also useful since it held the crowd for Wobbly speakers who followed. (Brazier 1968:91)

The IWW local in Spokane eventually produced its own songbook, The Little Red Songbook, to replace the five-cent song card previously sold on the streets. The book was initially 28 pages long, and 10,000 copies were printed, all of which were sold in a month. None of Joe Hill's own songs were in the first edition, although, says Brazier: "He was largely responsible for its success and expansion in size" (1968:103). After the circulation of several booklets locally produced in Spokane, the national IWW office in Chicago undertook to keep the popular songbook in print.

Joe Hill's immortalization in song stems from his arrest, conviction, and execution for allegedly murdering a grocer and his son in Salt Lake City, Utah, in 1914. He was convicted on very slender circumstantial evidence and his execution will always rank among the United States' judicial scandals.

A detailed biography of Joe Hill did not appear until Gibbs Smith's meticulous study (1969). Previous writers on Hill had leaned heavily on colorful or sensational accounts. John Greenway quotes IWW leader Ralph Chaplin's account of Hill's life as told to him by a "wino" in a Cleveland saloon who claimed to be Hill's cousin. Said Chaplin: "Word by word, drink by drink, I got the story out of him and wrote it down in my notebook" (1953:190).

According to the Cleveland wino, Joe had been a porter and odd job man in New York, travelled the states widely, and worked as a longshoreman on freight steamers out of San Pedro on the Honolulu run. He joined the IWW at this time. He was musical, harmless, not too interested in women, and fond of Chinese food. He never understood why his songs became so popular. As Greenway points out, this has to be taken with a grain of salt, especially as a later researcher, Wallace Stegner, came to a very different conclusion based on interviews and documentary evidence. To quote Greenway:

> Stegner re-examined the court records and other documents pertaining to Hill's trial, searched through contemporary newspapers, and interviewed old Wobblies who remembered Hill. His conclusions, briefly, are that Hill's activities during his four years as a Wobbly are vague, that he was not a misogynist . . . but on the contrary was continually in trouble because of women; that, far from being an expert instrumentalist, he could not learn to play the guitar; that the record of Hill's strike activities is questionable if not erroneous; that although Hill was always well dressed, he had no visible means of support; that it was the general impression among old time Wobblies that Hill was a crook; that Hill was probably guilty of the murder for which he was convicted. (191)

This may be a little harsh, although it does serve to blow some of the romance away. A more recent account of Hill's trial, by Philip Foner, shows what has generally been assumed all along: that Hill was framed by pig-headed authorities and never given a fair trial. This does not exclude the possibility of Hill being the seedy, shadowy character that Stegner suggests.

Foner's book is extremely detailed. He shows how the so-called evidence submitted against Hill was inconclusive. The Utah police and judiciary, heavily influenced by the Mormon church, fanatically hated the IWW. During the murder investigations, Hill was arrested along with other suspects. This was probably pure chance. When it was found out later that he was in the IWW, his chance of a fair trial disappeared. Moreover, Joe Hill was a stubborn man; apparently, he could have submitted to the court an alibi which may have freed him, but he refused to do so on the grounds that it was legally irrelevant; that is, he should not have had to prove his innocence; it was up to the court to prove his guilt. Also, he insisted that his alibi would have involved other people, in particular a woman whose honor he did not want to damage. He composed a moving "Last Will" in rhyme and sent a telegram to IWW leader Bill Haywood in Chicago: "Goodbye Bill: I die like a true rebel. Don't waste any time mourning, organize." Hill faced the firing squad next day with the words: "Fire—go on and fire."

Hill immediately became a labor martyr in the United States. Thirty thousand people went to his funeral, which was held in Chicago because he had indicated in prison that he did not want to be found dead in Utah. Hill had been the subject of a massive campaign which included workers all over the United States, not to mention the Swedish government, and President Wilson, who was apparently unable to influence the Utah judiciary. About 1932, Alfred Hayes wrote a simple Joe Hill poem; in 1936, Earl Robinson set it to music. Ironically, this Hayes-Robinson piece became better known than all Hill's own efforts with the possible exception of "The Preacher and the Slave."

How and when did the Hayes-Robinson song of 1936, which deals with a specifically American occurrence, pass into British folklore? Although the trial and execution of 1915 were big news across the Atlantic, they were less so in Britain which, in any case, was preoccupied with the First World War. A few persons on the British Left may have known "Joe Hill" as a poem before the Second World War. However, I have not come across any. Those people in Britain who know the song generally agree that it was the black actor and singer, Paul Robeson, who really popularized it.

Gibbs Smith, Lori Taylor, and others indicate that the Hayes-Robinson song reached Spain during the Civil War as Lincoln Brigade members carried it across the Atlantic from New York. Paul Robeson reported learning it at the London Workers' Theatre in 1938. Despite such notes of early "travel," most Robeson fans in England fall back on biographer Marie Seton to account for the song's popularity in Britain. Seton tells how Robeson premiered the song during 1947 in Salt Lake City. Robeson was booked to give a concert at the University of Utah, in the very city in which Joe Hill had been tried and shot. "Some of the people had noticed the song 'Joe Hill' on the program. It had never been sung on any local stage. What was it?" (1958:176). Then Robeson began the song: "I dreamed I saw Joe Hill last night." Marie Seton's description of what happened next is written with due sense of irony:

> Robeson's voice tapered into the silence. The audience were stunned. Who would have thought that a towering black man would arise to fling the charge of murder to the "copper bosses" who had snuffed out the life of white Joe Hill? Suddenly the applause broke loose. Most people clapped with all their might; but the hands of some clenched in their laps. The concert continued calmly to its close.

At the end of the Salt Lake City concert, Robeson addressed the audience, telling them that he was retiring for a few years from concert work and was going to sing from then on "for my trade union and college friends; in other words, only at gatherings where I can sing what I please"(Seton 1958:177). Paul Robeson did exactly as he said, in doing so encountering racism and political censorship. Eventually, in February 1949, however, he took on a professional concert tour of England. He sang for political meetings during this tour, and it was then that many British people heard "Joe Hill" for the first time. Its impact was immediate.

Listeners paid the £1 ticket for his Royal Albert Hall performance, but even more heard him in Lincoln's Inn, London, where he sang at an open air meeting for the international peace organization, the Stockholm Peace Petition. My own parents were among those who attended, and their account tallies in every way with others I have heard and recorded. All who were present remember the towering Robeson's opening sentence: "I stand here the son of a slave." Thousands of people packed together to hear the speeches and the slave's son sing, among other songs, "Joe Hill." Rarely can a song have started on its road into folklore in so spectacular a fashion. The Lincoln's Inn meeting was the only time my mother heard the song, and yet she remembered enough of it to use as a nursery song after I was born a couple of months later.

All who attended the meeting recall its atmosphere of drama, which one informant described as "magical." Its political background must at least partially explain this. Those who attended were left sympathizers. The timing was in the latter part of the 1945–50 Labor government. With a majority in parliament of 154, the Attlee government was widely expected to follow socialist policies. However, by the time of the Lincoln's Inn meeting there was a feeling of disappointment. It was leftist opinion that nationalization had been botched by over-compensation to the previous owners of unprofitable industries, the profitable sectors being left alone. Legislation for the Health Service had been blocked by the resistance of the doctors and had not produced the fully socialist-style service expected. Squatters exposed the poor housing situation. Sir Stafford Cripps instituted an economic squeeze at home, and abroad the Cold War had started in earnest. Labor support was visibly dwindling, as was to be decisively seen in the result of the 1950 general election. My father described the relationship between these facts and the Lincoln's Inn meeting:

> From having an overwhelming majority in the House of Commons we slipped. We thought the Tories were all finished, but they began to creep back. It seemed whatever government you got in you had the same policies. Then one evening, feeling disillusioned and isolated, we went along there (Lincoln's Inn) and the Square was completely packed with people, and all you could see was arc lights. We were right at the back. And there was this big black guy singing this song and everything seemed possible again. It was a very uplifting occasion.

George Strattan, whose version of the song has been given, was also there. He remembers the meeting as significant politically, as well as in a personal sense: "I suppose it was in my days when I was becoming politically involved, and you remember some of the demonstrations." In these circumstances we begin to comprehend the power of Joe Hill as a symbol.

The song was helped by print. Of the numerous appearances it had in left-wing inspired songbooks, a few in my possession are no doubt typical. An undated *Topic Songbook* prints four verses with music.[1] By 1960 Eric Winter, editor of the songbook, *And Since We're in Good Company,* found it unnecessary to print the tune even though all the other items in the book had tunes (1960:8). "Joe Hill" appeared in the Labor Party songbook and on its song sheet.[2] Furthermore, there were numerous sound recordings by Paul Robeson and, also, in 1954, by Joe Glazer for Folkways Records. Although the Folkways catalogue was hardly the standard fare of the High Street record shop, even in the diverse 1950s, it was influential, certainly in the London area among left-wing people. The Communist Party owned Collets record shop in New Oxford Street, thus helping popularize Folkways discs in England. A Pete Seeger recording was also available at the time.

When the British folksong revival of the late 1950s and 1960s gathered momentum, enthusiasts expended considerable argument on the question of whether English, Scots, or Irish revival singers should sing their own country's folksongs in preference to then-current American songs. Much of this discussion centered on the London Singers' Club and the powerful personalities and ideas of Ewan MacColl and Peggy Seeger. Their position gained considerable support. It was a simple but logical argument: there are native folksongs in any country or region and, on the whole, revival singers are more convincing when they stick to their own culture.

As a corrective against the pseudo-American skiffle prevalent at the time, this rigid line was justified. Even so, it side-stepped a salient fact of British labor folklore: that many songs of American origin had circulated orally and in print long before the idea of folk revival was widely accepted. It is not possible to label songs like "Hallelujah I'm a Bum," "The Preacher and the Slave," "Scissor Bill," "Morphine Bill and Cocaine Sue," "The Great Historical Bum," "Poor Man's Heaven," "The Big Rock Candy Mountain,"[3] or "Joe Hill" as American songs, or even as composed-therefore-not-folksongs. A cursory knowledge of the labor repertoire shows that they are sung from Blackpool to Brighton every year, more so than thousands of other items conventionally regarded as folksongs. To this extent, then, these Wobbly and "hobo" songs of American origin have become part of the heritage in Britain just as a high percentage of classic ballads, in past centuries, passed from culture to culture. Had American folklorists limited their view of the nature of American folksong to songs of American origin, they would have had to jettison most of the Appalachian ballads and many nonsense songs, broadsides, and numerous other pieces. In the case of the labor songs, indeed, internationalism is an important component of the philosophy and worldview promoted by the labor movement, even to the point of singing songs in foreign languages, such as "Bandiera Rossa."

After all, a culture or subgroup does not automatically take to itself all songs from elsewhere. A selection is made. An instructive comparison could be drawn between country singer Merle Travis's two famous American mining songs, "Sixteen Tons" and "Dark as a Dungeon." "Sixteen Tons," despite Tennessee Ernie Ford's successful commercial recording, has not yet turned up in all our researches into songs popular in the labor movement. "Dark as a Dungeon" has on many occasions, notably as roared out at Ruskin College one weekend by a group of Kentish miners. (Their other favorites, "Miner's Lifeguard" and "Down in a Coalmine,"[4] are both shaped into present versions by journeyings to and from the United States.) "Sixteen Tons" contains many references which make it specific to aspects of American culture, such as the company store, the straw boss, "raised in the bottom by a mama hound," "mean as a dog," and so on. This tends to make it difficult for a British singer to adapt it to his own culture without parody, or cultural imitation. "Dark as a Dungeon" has no such limitations, and it is sung, and has even spawned versions which show considerable oral change.

Likewise, to sing "Joe Hill" requires no such imitation, despite the localized references to Salt Lake City, San Diego, and Maine. Ian Parr, who sings it with great conviction, answered my comment about this:

I don't think that matters. One of the things is the universality of the labor movement, and everybody accepts that. And the other thing is that it's about somebody who's a trade unionist, an organizer, and I think everybody understands that as well. The line says: "Where workers strike and organize." To be honest you're talking a language that people understand already. Most of the people who attend the weekend schools have heard of Joe Hill or that type of person. Everybody identifies that sort of person.

"Joe Hill" is pressed into service for virtually any left-wing cause. Sung on May Day (International Labor Day) or during a strike, it obviously takes on extra shades of meaning. George Strattan identifies the song strongly with a particular victim of the fight against apartheid in South Africa. Older-style folk singers carry in their minds certain ideas and images which act as emotional memory,[5] helping them to feel the song. George Strattan says:

One reason why I like to sing "Joe Hill" when we have an evening is just to remind people of a very good friend, Dave Kitson, who's now spending his seventeenth year in a South African prison because of his activity against the apartheid regime. Now Dave Kitson lived in London. We worked together in the same area, and I can remember that we used to have socials, and Dave used to be there, and one of his favorite songs was "Joe Hill," so I always associate that with Dave.

"Joe Hill," then, has continued its life in the folklore of the labor movement as a powerful symbolic song, without the aid of the British folk revival to any marked degree. In all probability the song was sufficiently established before 1960 to assure its position as a popular labor song. However, it did get extra help from various American recordings during the 1960s and 1970s, the most significant being those of Pete Seeger and Joan Baez. Few British revivalists have included it in their repertoires. A notable exception is the Scottish group, The Laggan, who recorded it in the late 1970s under the auspices of the Scottish TUC. This was on an LP of best-known and highly regarded labor songs. In this situation "Joe Hill" was as obligatory as "Rule Britannia" on the last night of the Proms. By this time "Joe Hill" had picked up slight oral variations and textual changes that are not without meaning.

For instance, while verse one is identical in all versions, verse two has been subject to editorial change at least once. Most copies are identical to the form given at the beginning of this article. The printed version in *And Since We're in Good Company* changes the rhyming quite radically and alters the phrase "standing by my bed":

"In Salt Lake City, Joe" says I,
Him standing by my side,
"They framed you on a murder charge,"
Says Joe, " I never died."

Verse three about the copper bosses may have caused confusion in some singers' minds. It is not a reference to high ranking police chiefs corrupted by industrial bosses. It is a direct reference to the Utah Copper Company which continually resisted the organization of its workers, hated the IWW, and clearly had some influence over the local judiciary at the time of Hill's trial. The *Topic Songbook* omits this verse entirely, and *And Since We're in Good Company* once again gives a rogue version. Was this Eric Winter's work?

> "The copper bosses shot you, Joe,
> They filled you full of lead."
> "Takes more than guns to kill a man,"
> Says Joe, "And I ain't dead."

Verse four is usually the same, and verse five, in Hayes's original poem, is rarely sung. It does not occur, for instance, in George Strattan's version, nor in Ian Parr's. Many versions, however, have retained one line from it, the third, transposed into the next verse, substituting for the original third line in this verse.

> "Joe Hill ain't dead," he says to me,
> "Joe Hill ain't never died.
> Where working men are out on strike
> Joe Hill is at their side."

Verse six is the focus of the most significant variation, that just referred to. There is general disagreement about line three. Joe Glazer's old Folkways recording has:

> "From San Diego up to Maine
> In every mine and mill,
> Where workers strike and organize,"
> Says he, "You'll find Joe Hill."

"Strike and organize" is a highly charged expression. This line caused some comment from Ian Parr:

> I can do a lot with that penultimate verse, which is really the powerful verse. "Where workers strike and organize." Now you don't have to sing "strike." You can sing "fight." Or you can actually not put a lot of effort into singing those particular words.

It appears that another writer or singer has possibly seen this line as the political point of the song and altered it too. Who it was is difficult to tell. The alternative, and equally current version, and that, incidentally, sung by Paul Robeson, is as George Strattan sings it:

> Where working men defend their rights
> It's there you'll find Joe Hill.

The difference between "strike and organize" and "defend their rights" hardly needs comment. It turns the song from a militant attacking piece to a human rights issue. This may well have suited Robeson who was heavily involved in the basic issues of human rights for black people in America. Most singers end with a repeat of verse one.

"Joe Hill," as previously stated, is possibly the best known labor song in Britain. This popularity extends to other parts of the English-speaking world. This fact alone recommends it to the folklorist as a subject for inquiry. Where a collective repertoire exists over a wide area it may well be the most widely known songs that encapsulate general values in the relevant communities. In English farming communities, for example, "The Farmer's Boy" is a key song. Over a very large area in Britain "McCafferty" and "The Young Sailor Cut Down in his Prime" are commonly found.[6] With southern English Gypsy communities, it is "The Farmer in Chester" (or Leicester). In relation to Irish politics, "Kevin Barry," and amongst English schoolgirls of primary school age "When Suzy Was a Baby" is found everywhere.

Now that some scholars have balanced their interest in the exotic, the rare, the atypical with an equal concern for more usual, commonplace, or typical material, we may expect further studies in this direction. Should this happen, researchers will inevitably encounter the question: Why is this particular song popular as opposed to others which seem to have equal merit or qualification? In the case of "Joe Hill," what is its appeal beyond its memorability and simple repeat chorus line?

Accounting for popularity is a hazardous pursuit. It is insufficient to suggest that the aesthetic merit of the words and melody constitute any more than a highly contentious reason for a song's appeal. The most perfect artistic expressions are no doubt those that most successfully express generally held attitudes and values, a common aesthetic which, of course, begs a most important question. No single factor makes a song popular. Popularity results usually from a concatenation of many factors which, unpredictably, cluster around a particular item.

A structuralist approach to "Joe Hill" would perhaps consist of canvassing the whole genre of labor songs, producing analyses of each item, and discovering recurrent deep structures which would be seen to be most fully expressed in this one item. Here we speculate, since no such analysis has been carried out. Indeed, it would be difficult to accomplish any form of analysis which involved surveying the whole field of British labor songs when so much basic fieldwork remains to be done.

I will, however, suggest three factors about "Joe Hill" that seem notable, and can be examined purely in the light of the song itself and performers' views of it. First, it is tempting for a folklorist to see created in this song a modern version of the death and resurrection theme. Notwithstanding the unlearned romanticism which this theme used to attract from dilettante folklorists, it hardly needs restating that it is archetypal. Its immediacy and tenacity can be seen in modern society by the number of reports of well-known people who have supposedly been sighted after death—James Dean, Jimi Hendrix, Charlie Parker, Che Guevara, John Lennon, Adolf Hitler, and many more.

None of these cases give great cause for thought for present purposes. With Joe Hill, though, the notion of the resurrected hero, even if only created by Alfred Hayes's poem, does present one special problem. Vast numbers of those who know or respond to the song —trade unionists, people on the political left—are motivated by agnostic or atheistic philosophies. The spirit that pervades gatherings of organizers, activists, or delegates at conferences and schools is one of conscious, material negotiation for collective rights. Joe Hill himself, in real life, dismissed religion and the religious as "pie in the sky," as one of his best known songs puts it (Fowke and Glazer 1973:155). In this he certainly expressed a common attitude found amongst left-wing sympathizers.

Writing about the notion of death and resurrection and rebirth as an archetype, Joseph L. Henderson has claimed that "modern man continues to respond to profound psychic influences of a kind that, consciously, he dismisses as little more than the folk tales of superstition and [of] uneducated peoples" (1964:100). This perhaps states the case adequately enough for present purposes. Despite its apparent lack of relevance to twentieth-century scientific ideas, the symbolic impact of the resurrection of the God-king figure is sufficiently strong to recur in modern guises. It may not be fanciful to see the resurrection and rebirth theme in the central theoretical moment of revolutionary socialism. Capitalism would be seen as bringing about the temporary death of the human spirit. This is a partial death, and the human spirit is to be reborn in nobler form in the rising of the proletariat. The period of death is usually conceived as a sleep, as explicitly stated in many a socialist song, "The Internationale" among them:

> Arise ye starvelings from your slumbers
> Arise ye criminals of want
> For Reason in revolt now thunders
> And at last ends the age of cant.[7]

The device in "Joe Hill" that rationalizes, or makes credible, the entire poem is that of the dream. This puts the idea on acceptable ground and involves no quasi-religious ideas, even for the duration of a short song. At the same time, though, it permits the use of a powerful symbol that elicits a response which may not have been acceptable if it had been presented in any other way. Indeed, the usual interpretation of this song involves a climax on the penultimate verse and then a relaxation of tension for the last verse which is a repetition of the first and restates the dream idea. This can be seen as a passionate climax, a flight of fancy in which the resurrection of Joe Hill, combined with the things he says in the song, almost becomes believable. If this is plausible, the quieter restatement of the first verse beginning "I dreamed . . . " is more than a musical or poetic coda put in for purely aesthetic effect. Dreams, in fact, occur frequently in labor songs. Visions, utopian or class-vengeful, may be in an immediate practical sense considered naive or hopelessly idealistic, but many a flight of egalitarian fancy is prefaced by such a verse as:

> Kind friends gather near I want you to hear
> A dream that I had last night.[8]

A second factor which, I would contend, has had some influence on the popularity of "Joe Hill" is the considerable amount of additional material (such as anecdotes about Hill himself) that has clustered around the song. In this "Joe Hill" is similar to other key songs such as "McCafferty" or "The Young Sailor Cut Down in His Prime," both of which are the focus of folk beliefs. (It may, of course, be said that the songs have attracted the beliefs.) In the case of "Joe Hill" there is a widely printed "Last Will" written as a poem. Also, Hill's final words have been altered in oral tradition. This "last testament," in its variant forms, has appealed to those involved in left-wing politics. Leftists have seen Hill's cause as greater than any individual, a view perhaps challenged by more recent approaches. Hill's last words were not precisely those maintained by folk belief, but the folk version has a greater sense of drama. I can certainly remember having such anecdotes presented to me as true.

A final point concerning the popularity of the song: it is widely believed to be both factually and ethically true. Herbert Halpert's observations on truth in folksongs are useful here (1964:xii–xx). In his inquiry into the folksinger's belief in the factual basis of his songs, Halpert lists eight phenomena that account for the way singers may be said to "believe in" the truth of what they are singing. Four of these, rationalization of textual corruptions, localization of place names, respect afforded to aged singers who have passed songs on, and verification by ex-participants in events sung about, do not seem relevant to "Joe Hill." The other points require comment.

The emotional participation of the singer is intense. George Strattan and Ian Parr, singers with differing approaches, both sing it passionately with the carefully managed climax already referred to. Halpert mentions the way some singers verify the content of their songs by reference to actual phenomena. This may be more relevant in a culture less reliant on printed sources. With "Joe Hill" we have books and other printed sources, orally circulating anecdotes, and, more recently, Bo Widerberg's film, *The Ballad of Joe Hill* (1971), all of which figure in some way in conversations about the song.

The final and in this case most important factor Halpert mentions concerns the ethical truth of a song. A song is believed to be true because "such things could be so" (1964:xix). Trade union audiences consciously see Joe Hill as a symbol of the fighting spirit of the labor movement. Ian Parr says: "They know bloody well that he was a union organizer who died for being an organizer." Although actual death for trade union activities is rare in Britain, if not unknown,[9] it is widely believed in the labor movement, at least among activists, that justice is not objectively pursued in a society of exploiters and exploited. On the contrary, it is said to be stacked against the working class, and a well-known string of references from the Tolpuddle Martyrs through labor history to the present can be marshalled together to prove the point. Those in power, those with most to lose, it is believed, will stop at nothing in their fight against organized labor, not even at framing a man and executing him. With the singers that Halpert studied, "they feel that human nature can be relied upon to be consistent." With "Joe Hill" it is not human nature that is commented upon, but class nature.

Yet it must not be assumed that "Joe Hill" is an ultra-leftist's anthem. When I asked Ian Parr, who requested the song on his weekends and conferences, whether it was solely agitators and politicos, he replied: "No. Anybody really. Anybody."

Notes

This article originally appeared in Folk Music Journal *(1983), titled "Joe Hill: A Labour Legend in Song." We reprint it with permission of editor Ian Russell. Since its publication, new material has appeared in album notes by Lori Elaine Taylor for* Don't Mourn—Organize *(Smithsonian/Folkways Records 40026, 1990), and in a chapter by Archie Green, "Singing Joe Hill," in* Wobblies, Pile Butts, and Other Heroes: Laborlore Explorations *(Urbana: University of Illinois Press, 1993). Some factual and stylistic details in the 1983 piece have been altered to conform to current knowledge about Joe Hill.*

The interviews with Ian Parr (Clywd) and George Strattan (Liverpool) were recorded in April 1981 and those with my parents (Devon) in May 1981.

1. *Topic Songbook: Words and Melodies of Old and New Favorites* (London: Workers' Music Association, n.d.), 47. John Miller, archivist, gives the date as 1952-53.

2. *The Labor Party Song Sheet* (London: Labour Publications Department, n.d.), Song no. 51. The inclusion of songs composed in the early 1960s gives a rough clue to the date.

3. "Hallelujah I'm a Bum" and "The Preacher and the Slave," Fowke and Glazer (1973:126, 155); "Scissor Bill," *IWW Songs to Fan the Fames of Discontent* (1973:22–23); "Morhpine Bill and Cocaine Sue," Best and Best (1955); "The Great Historical Bum," *Sing* 3:51; "Poor Man's Heaven," Palmer (1974:324–26); and "Big Rock Candy Mountain," Lomax (1960:422–23).

4. The Tennessee Ernie Ford recording issued by Capitol on a 78-RPM disc CL14500 in 1955. See also Travis (n.d.). For a version of "Miner's Lifeguard" current in Britain, see A. L. Lloyd, *Come All Ye Bold Miners* (London: Lawrence and Wishart, 1978), 290–91. For two distinct versions of "Down in a Coalmine" current in Britain, see Lloyd (1978), 35–37.

5. Emotional memory is a concept used by Constantin Stanislavsky in the training of actors. See *An Actor Prepares* (London: Geoffrey Bles, 1942), 163–92.

6. For "McCaffery," see also A. E. Green, "McCaffery: A Study in the Variation and Function of a Ballad," in three parts, *Lore and Language* 1 (August 1970):4–9, (January 1971):3–12, and (July 1971):5–11.

7. English version. Eugene Pottier wrote words in French in 1871; music by Deygeyter, 1888. "The Internationale" arranged by Alan Bush for soprano, alto, tenor, and bass, and performed by the Glasgow Socialist Singers, can be heard on Workers Music Association disc WMA 101, n.d.

8. "Poor Man's Heaven," from Palmer (1974:324–26).

9. For example, Freddie Matthews, a miner on picket duty, was run over by a lorry during the 1972 miners' strike. A number of songs were written concerning this incident. Most accessible is "Freddie Matthews" by Ron Elliott, a miner's son, originally published in *Garland,* vol. 3 (London, privately published, October 1974) and reprinted in Sam Richards and Tish Stubbs, *The English Folksinger* (London and Glasgow: Collins, 1979), 112.

References Cited

Baez, Joan. 1970. *Woodstock.* 12-inch LP, SD 3-500, Cotillion.
Best, Vic, and Beth Best, eds. 1955. *Songfest.* New York: Crown.
Brazier, Richard. 1968. "The Story of the IWW's Little Red Songbook." *Labor History* 9:91.
Dunstan, Ralph. 1929. *The Cornish Song Book.* London: Reed Brothers.
Foner, Philip S. 1970. *The Case of Joe Hill.* New York: International Publishers.
Fowke, Edith, and Joe Glazer. 1973. *Songs of Work and Protest.* New York: Dover
Glazer, Joe. 1954 *Songs of Joe Hill.* 10-inch LP, FA 2039, Folkways.
Greenway, John. 1953. *American Folksongs of Protest.* Philadelphia: University of Pennsylvania Press.
Halpert, Herbert. 1964. "Truth in Folk-Songs: Some Observations on the Folk-Singer's Attitude." In John Harrington Cox, *Traditional Ballads and Folk-Songs Mainly from West Virginia,* edited by George Herzog, Herbert Halpert, and George W. Boswell, xii–xx. Philadelphia: American Folklore Society.
Henderson, Joseph L. 1964. *Man and His Symbols.* London: Aldus Books.
Hubbard, Jane A. 1982. "Children's Traditional Games from Birdsedge? Clapping Songs and Their Notation." *Folk Music Journal* 4:253–54.

IWW Songs to Fan the Flame of Discontent. 1973. 34th ed. Chicago: Industrial Workers of the World.

Laggan, The. n.d. *I Am the Common Man.* 12-inch LP, KLUB03LP, Scottish Trades Union Congress.

Lomax, Alan. 1960. *The Folk Songs of North America in the English Language.* New York: Doubleday; London: Cassell.

MacColl, Ewan, and Peggy Seeger. 1977. *Travellers' Songs from England and Scotland.* London: Routledge and Kegan Paul.

Palmer, Roy, ed. 1974. *A Touch on the Times: Songs of Social Change 1770–1914.* Harmondsworth, England: Penguin.

———. 1977. *The Rambling Soldier.* Harmondsworth, England: Penguin.

Purslow, Frank, ed. 1965. *Marrow Bones: English Folk Songs from the Hammond and Gardiner MSS.* London: E.F.D.S.

Robeson, Paul. n.d. *Joe Hill.* 10-inch 78-RPM LP, TRC 95–78, Topic.

Seeger, Pete, and Arlo Guthrie. 1975. *Together in Concert.* Two 12-inch LPs, K64023, Reprise

Seton, Marie. 1958. *Paul Robeson.* London: Dobson Books.

Smith, Gibbs. 1969. *Joe Hill.* Salt Lake City: University of Utah Press.

Strattan, George. 1981. "Joe Hill." On *An English Folk Music Anthology.* Two 12-inch LPs, FE 38553, Folkways.

Travis, Merle. n.d. [but after 1964]. *The Best of Merle Travis: 21 Years A Country Singer.* 12-inch LP, ST21010, Capitol.

Winter, Eric. 1960. *And Since We're in Good Company.* London: Sing.

Norm Cohen

Worksongs: A Demonstration Collection of Examples

Dick Reuss's continuing interest in labor and occupational folksong culminated in his compilation, *Songs of American Labor, Industrialization and the Urban Work Experience: A Discography* (1983). In it, he defined his scope of interest as "musical descriptions of the labor and industrial experience and urban work life of the United States and Canada." In an afterword to Reuss's survey, Archie Green briefly discussed the problem of defining "labor song," and its relation to "occupational song" and other terms.

Generally, we use the broad term, "occupational song" to denote a piece in which descriptions of work or work conditions, or attitudes towards work form a significant textual element. "Labor song" serves as a subcategory of "occupational song," generally geared to trade unionism, often hortatory or polemical in tone, but its precise boundaries are difficult to fix. We use "work song" to identify an item that is actually sung during the work process. This implies that we can always ascertain whether a particular song was sung to accompany work.

In *Long Steel Rail: The Railroad in American Folksong* (1981), I faced a similar problem of categorization while posing the question, "What is a railroad song?" I used examples to show that definition based on what railroaders actually sang often proved unrewarding: in fact, railroaders frequently sang whatever was popular at the time, without reference to work.

Our choice, then, is either (a) a contextual definition—we can't identify a given song as a "worksong" unless we are given its context; or (b) a prescriptive definition—for example, requiring a worksong to be an occupational piece (as defined above) that is sung during the work experience. If we choose the former, we will find some relatively stable worksong traditions—with the same texts occurring over and over, but also "nonce" worksongs sung to accompany work only by an individual singer or an isolated group. If we choose the latter, we will arbitrarily discard the nonce worksongs to give our chosen material some textual consanguinity and thus be able to identify a text as a worksong without knowing about its circumstances of performance. While the latter may simplify the analyst's task, it seems to deny the reality of the work/song event itself.

Consequently, I prefer alternative (a), but favor those occupational songs that have some reference to work, job circumstance, or attitudes concerning work. In this brief survey, I discuss the most common types of worksongs (by my definition) found in various American traditions and offer textual examples of each. A bibliography and discography follow my opening discussion and examples. This listing provides a typological framework for the ethnographic/case-study methods employed by our monograph's other contributors. Bibliography and discography have long served as twin pillars supporting the structure of folksong scholarship. While individual students continue to delve into the histories of particular songs, performers, and events, thereby linking artists and their creative works with social history, discography and bibliography, together, remind us that one *sine qua non* of folksong is continuity: the recycling of themes, phrases, tunes, and entire songs from one place and time to another.

I now turn to work, the subject of worksong itself. Worksongs are sung as an integral part of work activity. Singers believe that such songs contribute positively to the execution of their tasks. Specifically, singing paces the activity of a single worker, coordinates the motions of a group of workers, diverts the mind from the oppressive tedium of a monotonous task, or cheers flagging spirits. Some of the examples in this survey were once meant to affect the actions not of humans, but of animals, inanimate objects, or divine agents. These songs could equally well be regarded as either worksongs or ceremonial songs, performed under circumstances of labor but directed towards nonhuman agents believed to play a role in the satisfactory completion of the task.

In preindustrial or primitive societies, worksongs have been recorded accompanying a variety of tasks—agricultural, pastoral, domestic. In different societies, at varying times, these have included rope making, grape treading, house building, corn grinding, tree felling, bale toting, weaving, and fishing. In the United States, worksongs have been satisfactorily documented for only a few occupations. The preeminent example in the Anglo-American folk tradition is sea shantying. Soldiers for uncounted generations have sung marching songs to help synchronize their steps and rouse their spirits, but there has been no scholarly treatment of such songs beyond mere collection and publication (generally greatly expurgated). The collection of pastoral and agricultural worksongs has been far more successful in outlying parts of the British Isles than in the United States, though the bulk of material was collected early in the twentieth century.

The documented Afro-American folk tradition in this country is much richer in work songs than the Anglo-American: numerous examples of axe songs, riverboat roustabout songs, tie-tamping chants, steel-laying hollers, and shoeshine patters have been preserved in sound recordings—some in artificially recreated circumstances, but others, more importantly, in actual unperturbed work situations.

Another category of worksongs consists of those in which the individuals who are supposed to be influenced are not the workers themselves. These include the chants of tobacco auctioneers; the street cries of peddlers, vendors, tinkers, grinders, ragmen, and junk collectors; the sing-song of railroad conductors; and, by extension to contemporary media, the singing commercials of radio and television and the voiceless mechanical jingles of outdoor ice cream vendors' trucks.

The examples in this collection are drawn from the British Isles and North America—in the latter case, from both Anglo-American and Afro-American traditions. The texts are all given in English, although in some cases the original language of the song was Gaelic. The examples are divided into six categories, most of which can be characterized as containing songs intended primarily for coordination, direction, supplication, or solicitation. All the songs, as well, perform the function of diversion, a function which often grew in importance as other elements atrophied.

(a) Domestic worksongs. This category includes spinning, weaving, and waulking songs, most of which were originally sung in Gaelic. ("Waulking" is a dialectal form of "walking," a near obsolete term for "fulling," or beating and pressing, wool fibers to cause them to shrink and thicken.) The waulking songs are group coordinative; the others are solo songs, sometimes with traces of supplication still apparent. Most songs in this category were collected a half-century ago or more, and it seems to be the case that the use of such songs is on the wane.

(b) Agricultural and pastoral worksongs. Mostly originally supplicatory, they seem to have become primarily diversional. In this broad category are butter-churning, grain-grinding, milking, and sheep-shearing songs, from both Celtic British and Anglo-American traditions. Related corn-shucking and rice-thrashing songs appear in category (d) below. As in the case of the previous category, there is little evidence that these songs are still being used in real work situations.

(c) Sea chanties. Although scattered earlier references exist, as well as some printed examples of sea shanties believed to date from the fifteenth century, the English language shanty flourished between ca. 1815 and the end of the nineteenth century. Shanties, all of which are labor coordinative, can be classified according to the type of work they accompanied: (1) *hauling songs,* for intermittent operations (e. g., raising and lowering sails), including halyard, short haul, bowline, bunt, hand-over-hand, and walkaway shanties; and (2) *heaving songs,* for continuous work (e. g., raising anchor), including capstan, windlass, and pump shanties. Notwithstanding this taxonomy, in many instances the same song has been placed in different categories by diverse writers. Clearly, many songs served alternate functions for different crews.

(d) Afro-American (gang) worksongs. In the Afro-American tradition (and the African one whence it came), the worksong served both coordination and diversion functions. White taskmasters found an additional function for the worksong: antebellum slave owners considered slave songs as conducive to greater work output and demanded fast, lively music. In the case of prison camp worksongs, a further function was to serve as an outlet for frustrations and aggressions. Prison worksongs divide into solo and group songs, the former sung by individual workers in cotton and cane fields. Group songs can be divided into axe (or crosscutting, or double-cutting) songs, used for felling trees; flatweeding songs, used for any kind of hoe work; and cotton picking or canecutting songs, which, like the individual songs used for this activity, tend toward greater lyrical and melodic complexity than the preceding three types.

(e) Songs and chants of direction. In this category, which is not altogether distinct from the preceding one, I put musical pieces in which a primary function of the singer is to direct or organize the actions of other workers. With the passage of time, any particular type of chant may acquire filler lyrics that do not serve this primary purpose; indeed, one can collect (and some of the examples given below demonstrate this) texts in which the lyrical element dominates, and the directions or instructions are very intermittent. Sometimes, the fact that a particular piece is a direction chant is apparent only when many related texts are available for comparison.

(f) Street cries. A handful of examples from city streets of both Britain and the United States represent what used to be commonly heard a half-century ago or more, but is now almost entirely replaced by mechanical or electronic music. Whenever used, the function of these songs was purely solicitational. In the first four of these categories, workers have often shown no particular preference for song texts that describe or relate to the work experience itself.

In other words, it is often impossible to tell, from the text of a song alone, whether it is, or can be, used as a waulking song or as a capstan shanty or as a cotton-picking song. Often, the same text can, with only slight modification in tempo, serve several different work functions. In choosing these examples, I have favored texts that do relate to the work itself, and in this regard my selections may not be entirely representative.

Domestic worksongs

A.1. ["Spinning Song."] [Unidentified informant, collected by Mrs. Richard C. Thompson in Arkansas. From Scarborough, *On the Trail of Negro Folk-Songs*, p. 215].

> Spin, ladies, spin all day (2),
> Sheep shell corn,
> Rain rattles up a horn,
> Spin, ladies, spin all day (3).

A.2. "Spin, Wheel, Spin." [Sung by Mrs. Callow, Cardle Veg, Maughold, Isle of Man. Collected by Mona Douglas, 1918–20. From Kennedy, *Folksongs of Britain and Ireland*, p. 192. Translated from the Manx Gaelic.] Versions of this song have been collected as part of a folktale very similar to "Rumpelstiltskin."

> Spin, wheel, spin (2),
> Every branch upon the tree,
> Spin above for me.
> With the King the wool-man,
> With myself the spool-man,
> So old Trit-Trot,
> He'll ne'er have her always.
> Spin, wheel, spin,
> Sing, wheel, sing,
> Every slate upon the house
> Spin above for me.
> With the King the white wool,
> With myself the spool-man
> So old Trit-Trot,
> He'll ne'er have her always.
> Spin, wheel, spin,
> Run, wheel, run,
> Every wave upon the shore,
> Spin alone for me.
> With the King the grey wool,
> With myself the spool-man,
> So that when the weaver comes,
> He'll ne'er have her always.

A.3. ["Weaving Song."] [Sung by Annie Johnston, Castlebay, Barra, Scotland, September 1951. Issued on Columbia AKL 4946: *Folk Songs from Scotland.* Translated from the Gaelic.]

> Wait today until tomorrow,
> Until I spin you a shirt;
> The loom is in Patrick's wood,
> The flax has been sown and has not grown.
> The milkmaid is unborn to mother,
> The Queen has the bobbin;
> And the wool is on the sheep in the wilderness,
> And the King of France has the shuttle-pin.

A.4. ["Waulking Song."] [From Miss Peigi MacRae, North Glendale, and Miss Annie MacDonald, Lochboisdale, South Uist. Collected by Margaret Fay Shaw. From Shaw, *Folksongs and Folklore of South Uist*, p. 207. Translated from the original Gaelic.] This is one of the few waulking song texts that refers to the waulking process itself.

> *Refrain:* Waulk, o ho, the cloth of the lads (3).

> From hand to hand, the cloth of the lads.
> Let me waulk quickly, the cloth of the lads.
> Let me waulk with joy, the cloth of the lads.
> Sing with love, the cloth of the lads.
> Put into a roll, the cloth of the lads.

Agricultural and pastoral worksongs

B.1. "Come, Butter, Come." [Sung by Miss Annie Johnston while churning. Recorded in Barra, Scotland, June 1951. Issued on Columbia AKL 4946: *Folk Songs from Scotland.* Translated from the original Gaelic.]

> Buttermilk to the wrist and butter to the elbow,
> Come, churn, come.
> There's a gulp here, there's a clatter there,
> There's a better thing than the right here,
> There's a better thing than wine,
> Come, churn, come.
> Buttermilk to the wrist and butter to the elbow,
> Come, churn, come.
> The blackbird will come, the thrush will come,
> The music will come from the fairy knoll.
> The cuckoo will come and the jackdaw will come,
> The skylark will come;
> Come, churn, come.
> Buttermilk to the wrist and butter to the elbow,
> Come, churn, come.

B.2. "Come, Butter, Come." [Sung by Irene Williams, Rome, Mississippi. Collected by John A. and Ruby T. Lomax, 1940, Library of Congress recording AFS 4011 A3.] A very similar text was published in seventeenth-century England. Perdue has found other related versions throughout Georgia.

> Come, butter, come.
> Mistus standin' at the gate,
> A-waitin' for the butter cake to come, butter, come.
> Come, butter, come, mistus a-waitin' (2)
> De mis' is a waitin' for the butter cake
> To come, butter, come.

B.3. ["The Grinding Song."] [Sung by Margaret Quayle, Glen Aldyn, Lezayre, Isle of Man. Collected by Mona Douglas, 1925. From Kennedy, *Folksongs of Britain and Ireland*, p. 183. Translated from the original Manx Gaelic.]

> O the oats are great for human and cattle,
> It keeps them warm and gives them mettle,
> And in the straw for the bedding is the best place to cuddle,
>
> *Refrain:* O a-millin', millin'-o,
> An' the corn, the corn is new,
> An' the little oat grain is a-goin' to the mill-o.
>
> O the wheat is good for bread and cake baking,
> It's good with cheese and salt and butter,
> It's good at home and it's good in the chapel,
> *(refrain, with changing last line)*
>
> An' the little wheat grain is a-goin' to the mill-o.
> O the grain of the barley is the best of any,
> And it's only from barley I'll take my tally,
> It cheers and it banishes melancholy,
> An' the little barley grains are a-goin' to the mill-o.

B.4. ["The Milking Song."] [Sung by Mrs. Faragher, Kerro Glass, Kirk Michael, Isle of Man. Collected by Mona Douglas, 1929. From Kennedy, *Folksongs of Britain and Ireland*, p. 187. Translated from the original Manx Gaelic.] An excellent example of the supplicatory function of a folksong.

> Give your milk, cow, give your milk,
> While I sing my song to you;
> Let the milk-churn fill and spill
> With your milk, my dear old cow.
>
> *Refrain:* Blessings of God I'll put upon you,
> Father, Son and Holy Ghost,
> And also Blessed Mary,
> Give more milk, my cow.

Yours is good milk, fine and healthy,
From the butter there'll be cream.
Do your best to give me plenty,
Then your barley share you'll gain.
(refrain)

B.5. "Shear Um." [Text from Mr. T. C. Fertic, Kissimmee, Florida. From Alton C. Morris, *Folksongs of Florida* (Gainesville: University of Florida, 1950. Reprint, New York and Philadelphia: Folklorica, 1981), p. 184.]

Makes no difference how you shear um,
Makes no difference how or when;
Makes no difference how you shear um,
Just so you shear um clean.

Shanties

C.1. "Haul the Bowline." [Sung by Richard Maitland at Sailors' Snug Harbor, Staten Island, New York. Recorded by Alan Lomax, 1939. Library of Congress recording AFS 2531 B2, issued on LP album L 26.] There is an unconvincing argument that this short-haul shanty dates back to the reign of Henry VIII. At any rate, it is a good 150 years old. The pull comes on the last word *haul* of each refrain.

Haul the bowline, the long-tailed bowline,

Refrain: Haul the bowline, the bowline haul.
Haul the bowline, Kitty, oh, my darling, *(refrain)*
Haul the bowline, we'll haul and haul together, *(refrain)*
Haul the bowline, we'll haul for better weather, *(refrain)*
Haul the bowline, we'll bust, we'll break our banner, *(refrain)*

C.2. "Away Rio." [Sung by Capt. Leighton Robinson, as shantyman, with Alex Barr, Arthur Brodeur, and Leighton McKenzie as chorus (joining in on *italicized* words), at Belvedere, California. Recorded by Sidney Robertson Cowell, 1939. Library of Congress recording AFS 4232A, issued on LP album L 27, where it is titled "Rio Grande."] An outward bound capstan shanty used for heaving up anchor, this song refers to the port of Rio Grande in Brazil.

Oh, Rio Grande lies far away,
'Way Rio!
Oh, Rio Grande lies far away,
And we're bound for the Rio Grande.

Refrain: And away, Rio, it's away, Rio!
Singing, fare you well, my bonnie young girl
And we're bound for the Rio Grande.

I thought I heard our old man say,
'Way, Rio!
I thought I heard our old man say,
"We're *bound for the Rio Grande*." (refrain)
Two dollars a day is a sailor's pay . . . *(refrain)*
So it's pack up your donkey, and get underway . . . *(refrain)*
Oh, I left my old woman a month's half pay . . . (refrain)
So heave up our anchor, away we must go . . . *(refrain)*

Kenneth Shoesmith's drawing "The Monkey's Orphan," frontispiece, in the public domain, in Frank C. Bowen's *Sea Slang* (London: Sampson Low, Marston, 1929)

C.3. "Reuben Ranzo." [Sung by Noble B. Brown at Millsville, Wisconsin. Recorded by Helene Stratman-Thomas and Aubrey Snyder, November 1946. Library of Congress recording AFS 8394 B3, issued on LP album L 26.] One of the most rousing of the halyard shanties, numerous hypotheses for the identity of Ranzo have been offered.

Poor old Reuben Ranzo,
Refrain: Ranzo, boy, Ranzo
Poor old Reuben Ranzo,
Refrain: Ranzo, boy, Ranzo

He shipped aboard a whaler, *(refrain)*
But Ranzo was no sailor. *(refrain)*

He could not do his duty, *(refrain)*
For neither love nor beauty. *(refrain)*

He could not find his sea legs, *(refrain)*
Used clumsy, awkward land pegs. *(refrain)*

He could not coil a line right, *(refrain)*
Did not know end from rope's bight. *(refrain)*

Could not splice the main brace, *(refrain)*
He was a seasick soft case. *(refrain)*

He could not box the compass, *(refrain)*
The skipper raised a rumpus. *(refrain)*

The old man was a bully, *(refrain)*
At sea was wild and woolly. *(refrain)*

Abused poor Reuben plenty, *(refrain)*
He scourged him five and twenty. *(refrain)*

He lashed him to the mainmast, *(refrain)*
The poor seafaring outcast. *(refrain)*

Poor Ranzo cried and pleaded, *(refrain)*
But he was left unheeded. *(refrain)*

Some vessels are hard cases, *(refrain)*
Keep sailors in strict places. *(refrain)*

Do not show any mercy, *(refrain)*
For Reuben, James, or Percy. *(refrain)*

The ocean is exacting, *(refrain)*
Is often cruel acting. *(refrain)*

A sailor never whimpers, *(refrain)*
Though shanghaied by shore crimpers. *(refrain)*

C.4. "What Shall We Do With the Drunken Sailor?" [Sung by Richard Maitland; same source as C.1 above. Library of Congress recording AFS 2521 B, issued on LP album L 26.] A walkaway shanty— used when the men were walking away with the slack of the rope, for example when an iron ship was having its hull scrubbed.

Now what shall we do with the drunken sailor,
What shall we do with the drunken sailor, (2)
Early in the morning?

Oh, chuck him in the long boat till he gets sober,
Chuck him in the long boat till he gets sober, (2)
Early in the morning.

Refrain: Ay, hey, and up she rises, (3)
Early in the morning.

Oh, what shall we do with the drunken soldier . . .

Oh, put him in the guardhouse and make him [?bail] sober,
Put him in the guardhouse till he gets sober . . . *(refrain)*

Oh, here we are nice and sober . . . *(refrain)*

Afro-American gang worksongs

D.1. "Grizzly Bear." [Sung by Benny Richardson and group, crosscutting, at Texas State Prison at Ellis. Recorded by Bruce Jackson, 24 March 1966. From Jackson, *Wake Up Dead Man*, pp. 188–89. Recording issued on Rounder 2013: *Wake Up Dead Man*.] In all the songs in this section, *italicized* words indicate group chorus. The group joins in on the *italicized* words. In this ballad text, "grizzly" is always pronounced as three syllables. Jackson discusses the referent of the song, noting that many prison oldtimers he interviewed felt either that "grizzly bear" was a nickname of Joe Oliver, an inmate nicknamed "Jack the Bear," or referred to Carl Luther McAdams, one of the toughest wardens in the Texas prison system.

I'm gonna tell you a story about a *grizzly bear* (2).
He was a great black a-grizzly, *grizzly bear* (2).

Refrain: Well a grizzly, grizzly, *grizzly bear,*
Lord have mercy, *grizzly bear.*

He went a-trackin' through the bottom like a *grizzly bear* (2).
He had a long white tushes like a *grizzly bear* (2). *(refrain)*

You know my mama was afraid of the *grizzly bear* (2)
You know my papa went a-huntin' for *grizzly bear,*
He went a-huntin' in the mornin' for *grizzly bear.*

Well he went a track through the fields like a *grizzly bear,*
He was a-makin' big tracks-a like a *grizzly bear.*

He had a long black hair like a *grizzly bear,*
And every mornin' he will be there, *grizzly bear. (refrain)*

You know my papa went a huntin' for *grizzly bear,*
He died a-huntin' on the Brazos for *grizzly bear.*

It was early one mornin', *grizzly bear,*
I heard a shootin' and a callin' and *grizzly bear.*

He find the bear on old Brazos, *grizzly bear,*
He found him down on old Brazos, *grizzly bear*

You know I ain't scared o' no *grizzly bear,*
Because the workin' squad they killed him there, *grizzly bear.*

Well-a grizzly, grizzly, *grizzly bear,*
Well Lord have mercy, *grizzly bear.*

D.2. "Take This Hammer." [Sung by Joseph "Chinaman" Johnson and group, logging, at Texas State Prison at Ellis. Recorded by Bruce Jackson, 21 August 1965. From Jackson, *Wake Up Dead Man*, pp. 238–39.] Though used here as an axe song, "Take This Hammer" has also been used as a hammering (or spike-driving) song by railroad construction workers.

This old hammer killed John Henry,
This old hammer *killed John Henry,*
This old hammer *killed John Henry,*
But it *won't kill me, oh boys, won't kill me.*

Take this *hammer, take it to the sergeant,* (3)
Tell him I'm *gone, oh boys, tell him I'm gone.*

If he asks you *what got the matter* (3)
Had too long, *oh boys, had too long.*

If he asks you, was I laughin' (3)
Tell him I was *cryin', oh lord, tell him I was cryin'.*

If he ask you, was I runnin' (3)
Tell him *I was flyin', oh lord, tell him I was flyin'.*

If he ask you any more questions, (3)
You don't *know, oh boy, you don't know.*

D.3. "Pick a Bale o' Cotton." [Sung by Louis "Bacon and Porkchop" Houston and group, Texas State Prison at Ramsey. Recorded by Bruce Jackson, 17 August 1965. From Jackson, *Wake Up Dead Man*, pp. 99–101.]

Well it's never will I *pick a bale o' cotton,*
But it's never will I *pick a bale a day.*

Well I'm goin' to the new ground, *pick a bale o' cotton,*
Well I'm goin' to the new ground, *pick a bale a day.*

Refrain: How in the world can *I pick a bale o' cotton,*
How in the world can *I pick a bale a day.*

Well you big enough and black enough to *pick a bale o' cotton . . . (refrain)*

I got a little baby brother can *pick a bale o' cotton . . . (refrain)*

You got to jump-a down and turn around to *pick a bale o' cotton . . .*

Well, old Eli Hawkins can *pick a bale o' cotton . . . (refrain)*

Well, I'm goin' to the new ground to *pick a bale o' cotton . . .*

Well you big enough and black enough to *pick a bale o' cotton . . . (refrain)*

I got a little baby sister can *pick a bale o' cotton . . . (refrain)*

D.4. ["Timber Lay Down."] [Taken down by hand by Walter Jekyll, ca. 1905, Port Royal Mountains, Jamaica; recording data and informants' identities not given. From Jekyll, *Jamaican Song and Story*, pp. 185-86.] This Jamaican timber-cutting song was also used for digging and other kinds of field labor.

> Timber lay down 'pon pit, Timber;
> Cut 'im make we go 'way, Timber;
> Me want go 'way ya soon, Timber;
> Timber lay down 'pon pit, Timber;
> Timber, timber oh Timber;
> Me wanty go 'way ya soon, Timber;
> Me want go home back-a yard, Timber;
> A cedar timber oh, Timber;
> Lash the saw make we go home, Timber;
> Timber lay down 'pon pit, Timber.

D.5 "Peas an' the Rice." [Sung by Julia Walker, Georgia Sea Islands. Collected by Lydia Parrish. From Parrish, *Slave Songs of the Georgia Sea Islands*, p. 232.] Walker remembered singing this song in her youth while hulling rice.

> Peas an' the rice, peas an' the rice,
> Peas an' the rice done done done done,
> Peas an' the rice, peas an' the rice done done done done.
> New rice an' okra, eat some an' lef' some,
> Peas an' the rice, peas an' the rice done done done done.

D.6 ["Corn-husking Song."] [Quoted by Thomas C. Thornton, *An Inquiry Into the History of Slavery* (Washington, D.C.: W. M. Morrison, 1841), pp. 120–22. Reprinted by Epstein, *Sinful Tunes and Spirituals*, pp. 173–74. Only part of the text is given here.] Thornton claimed to recall this song from having heard it sung by plantation slaves twenty-five years earlier, i.e., 1816.

> Leader: I loves old Virginny.
>
> *Chorus: So ho! boys! so ho!*
>
> I love to shuck corn. *So ho! . . .*
> Now's picking cotton time. *So ho! . . .*
> We'll make the money, boys. *So ho! . . .*
> My master is a gentleman. *So ho! . .*
> He came from the Old Dominion. *So ho! . . .*
> And mistress is a lady. *So ho! . . .*
> Right from the land of Washington. *So ho! . . .*
> We all live in Mississippi. *So ho! . . .*

The land for making cotton. *So ho!* . . .
They used to tell of cotton seed. *So ho!* . . .
As dinner for the negro man. *So ho!* . . .
But boys and gals it's all a lie. *So ho!* . . .

Direction songs and chants

E.1. ["Tie Tamping Chant."] [Called by Henry Truvillion at Wiergate, Texas. Recorded by John A. and Ruby T. Lomax, 1940. Library of Congress recording AFS 3973 A2, issued on LP album AFS L 8, where it is titled "Tamping Ties."] For nearly twenty years Truvillion had been head track layer for the Wiergate Lumber Co., which built railroads to haul big logs out of the woods to the sawmills. This rendition was "staged."

Tamp 'em up solid,
All the livelong day.
Tamp 'em up solid,
Then they'll hold that midnight mail.
The captain don't like me.
Won't allow me no show.
Well, work don't hurt me,
Don't care where in the world I go.
Work don't hurt me,
Like the early rise.
Well, work don't hurt me,
But that's the thing that hurts my pride,
That hurts my pride, (3).

E.2. ["Steel Laying Holler."] [Chanted by Rochelle Harris, Tennessee State Penitentiary at Nashville. Recorded by John A. Lomax and Alan Lomax, 1933. Library of Congress recording AFS 181 A1.]

Aw right, aw right, ev'rybody get ready.
Come on down here, come on, boys.
Bow down, boys, bow down.
Aw right, up high.
Aw right throw 'way.

Aw right, le's move on down 'n' git another one.
Aw right, bow down.
Aw right, head high.
Throw 'way.

Aw right, boy, da's aw right now.
Move on down ag'in.
Bow down, up high.
Throw 'way.

That's aw right, boy, now let's move on down again.
Aw right, up high.
Aw right, throw 'way.

Come on down here, boys, come on down now, come on now.
Now, boys, now, stop.
An' I want you to listen at me, now.
I'm gonna tell you a sad warnin' now.
Now bow down ea—sy, boys, bow down.
Now I got ta raise her now, head high, boys.
Throw [it] away.

Aw right now, boys, that's not made aw right,
Let's go on down and get another one.
Aw right, now.
Stop everybody now and listen to me, boy, don' get hurt;
You want to go home lookin' aw right.
Aw right, bow down; up high,
Throw away.

That's made aw right,
But let's go on down and get another one.
Aw right now, down everybody.
Aw right, up high,
Aw right, throw away now.

E.3. ["Heaving the Lead Line."] [Called by Sam Hazel at Greenville, Mississippi. Recorded by Herbert Halpert, 1939. Library of Congress recording AFS 3097 A, B1 & 4. Issued on LP album AFS L 8.] Hazel, eighty-six years old when recorded, chants the sounding calls as he heard them while roustabouting on the Ohio and Mississippi rivers. "Mark twain" means two fathoms (twelve feet) deep; "quarter less twain" means two fathoms less a quarter (= 10.5 feet).

Now we're stuck there . . . [?] . . . to a bar,
For the lead line drapped off right now.
Well, old deck hand, when you git on top,
I'm gonna hear that line, I wanta . . . [?]
Let the old boat draw.
Lord, I'm throwin' lead line on the la'board side.
Quarter less twain,
Don't you change your mind.
Heave it in the water just-a one more time.
Eight feet and a half, Mr. Pilot, will you change your mind.
Run him on a slow bell, (2)
Quarter less twain on the sta'board side.
Mr. Pilot, will you change your mind.
Drap it on over on the left-hand side.
Tell me there's a buoy, a buoy right on the bar.

The light is twisted, and you can see just how.
Pull a little over to the la'board side.
Lawd, lawd.
Quarter less twain, (4),
Lawd, lawd, now send me quarter less twain.
Throw the lead line a little higher out.
I've gone low down, so mark twain.
Mark twain.

Come ahead, Mr. Pilot, a little bit strong.
I've done got over, and I believe we're gonna
Done throw the lead line over—
No bottom here.

Street cries

F.1. ["Watermelons."] [Denton, Texas, recording data not given. From Hurley, "Come Buy, Come Buy," p. 122.]

Oh, good old red ripe watermelons!
Oh, they're red ripe and sweet as honey.
You can save money.
You can cut 'em and plug 'em
They are red ripe.
Oh, lady, lady, you can eat the meat
And pickle the rind
And save the seed 'til plantin' time.

F.2. ["Young Lambs."] [Sung by Mr. Such at Cheltenham, Gloucestershire, England, 13 August 1921. Collected by Cecil Sharp. From Karpeles, *Cecil Sharp's Collection of English Folk Songs*, vol. 2, p. 586.]

Young lambs to sell, young lambs to sell,
They're four for a penny, sixteen for a groat,
But finest young lambs that ever was bought!
If I'd as much money as I could tell
I'd never cry out: young lambs to sell.

F.3. ["Tamales."] [From Dallas, Texas; recording data not given. From Hurley, "Come Buy, Come Buy," p. 118.]

The world goes around,
And the sun comes down,
And I got the best
Hot tomales in town.

F.4. ["Charcoal."] [From Travis County, Texas; recording data not given. From Hurley, "Come Buy, Come Buy," p. 134.]

My hands is black, my face is black,
And I sell my coal two bits a sack;
Chah-coal!

F.5. ["Baskets and Chairs."] [Sung by Agnes Collins, in Adelaide Road, Hampstead, London, 16 May 1908. Collected by Cecil Sharp. From Karpeles, *Cecil Sharp's Collection of English Folk Songs*, vol. 2, p. 583.]

All kinds of fancy chairs, easy arm-chairs.
Will you buy a pretty basket,
Clothes basket, cheap basket, flo'r basket?
We've all kinds of chair.
For I say, ladies don't delay.
Come and buy your chairs and baskets today;
Buy 'em of the maker,
For we are sons of the jolly basket-makers.
We mean to sell 'em all and make no more.
Come and buy your parlor rugs today.
Buy 'em of the maker.

F.6. ["Lavender Song."] [Sung by lavender man in Juliet Williams's studio, London, 16 July 1912. From Williams, "London Street Cries," in Broadwood et al., p. 61.] The earliest printed reference to a lavender seller's song is a London publication of 1804. The tune used then was the revival hymn "Happy Day." This cry was the basis for the song "Who Will Buy?," in the musical, *Oliver!*, written by Lionel Bart (1960).

Buy my sweet scented lavender,
Sixteen branches for a penny;
You'll buy it once, you'll buy it twice,
Sixteen branches for a penny.
This thyme will scent your clothes
And pocket handkerchiefs,
There's sixteen blue branches a penny;
Now dear ladies don't delay,
Buy my lavender sweet from Mitcham today,
Buy my blue lavender,
Sixteen branches a penny.

F.7. ["Chimney Sweep."] [New Orleans; recording data not given. From *American Street Cries*, chorus for mixed voices, a cappella, arranged by Elie Siegmeister, pp. 1–5. The "American Ballad Singers" series of Native American Folk-Songs. Copyright 1940 by Carl Fischer, New York. Reprinted by B. A. Botkin, ed., *Sidewalks of America* (Indianapolis and New York: Bobbs-Merrill, 1954), p. 576.]

Romanay, romanay, romanay, lady,
I know why yo' chimley won' draw;
Stove won' bake, an' yuh can' make no cake,
An' I know why yo' chimley won' draw.
Romanay, romanay, romanay, lady (2).

Venice, California

Annotated Bibiography

Abrahams, Roger D. 1974. *Deep the Water, Shallow the Shore. Three Essays on Shantying in the West Indies.* Austin and London: University of Texas Press for the American Folklore Society, Vol. 60 in Memoir Series. The first essay reviews earlier scholarship and reports; the others explore the ways shanties are used in three different communities: Newcastle, Nevis; Plymouth, Tobago; and Barouallie, St. Vincent. Texts of forty-five shanties, many with tune transcriptions, collected by the author in 1963–67, are presented.

Allen, William F., C. P. Ware, and L. M. Garrison. 1867. *Slave Songs of the United States.* New York: A. Simpson. [Reprint, New York: Oak, 1965.] Among the 136 text/tunes given, which the editors collected from slaves in the early 1860s, are 12 "rowing songs" (nos. 5, 14, 17, 27–33, 36, and 46), including the first collected version of "Michael Row the Boat Ashore," the only song the editors noted was used only for rowing. From islands off the coast of Georgia and South Carolina.

Barrow, David C., Jr. 1882. "A Georgia Corn-Shucking." *Century Magazine* 24, 873-78. [Reprinted in *The Negro and His Folklore in Nineteenth-Century Periodicals*, edited by Bruce Jackson. Austin and London: University of Texas Press for the American Folklore Society, 1967. Vol. 18 in Bibliographical and Special Series.] An important early description of a corn-shucking ceremony, with transcriptions of texts and tunes.

Botkin, B. A., ed. 1954. *Sidewalks of America.* Indianapolis and New York: Bobbs-Merrill. [Reprint of "Street Cries Set to Music—Sounds Henceforth Forbidden in New York—Passing of the Noises That for More than a Century Have Individualized the Trades of the Street Vendors—Each with a Character of Its Own." The New York *Sun* (September 20, 1908).] A brief discussion with transcription of eleven examples, including "umbrellas to mend," "kettles to mend," "scissors to grind," "bananas," "ole clo's," etc. The Botkin volume includes two more articles on American street cries.

Brakeley, Theresa C. 1950. "Work Song." In *Funk & Wagnalls Standard Dictionary of Folklore, Mythology, and Legend,* edited by Maria Leach, 1181–84. New York: Funk & Wagnalls. An excellent general survey of worksongs, with references to many types throughout the world (but no examples).

Broadwood, Lucy, et al. 1919. ["Street Cries."] *Journal of the Folk Song Society* [London] 6:43–79. Several articles on street cries, mostly collected by Juliet Williams in London; includes historical discussions by Broadwood, Frank Kidson, and others.

Colcord, Joanna C. 1924. *Roll and Go, Songs of American Sailormen.* Indianapolis: Bobbs-Merrill. [Reprinted as *Songs of American Sailormen* (New York: Bramhall House, 1938).] Early collection of American sea shanties, collected by the author in the field in 1890–99; some of the texts have been doctored based on other sources.

Courlander, Harold. 1963. *Negro Folk Music U.S.A.* New York and London: Columbia University Press. The chapter on worksongs contains a useful discussion of the structure and style of Afro-American worksongs in the U.S. and the West Indies, with commentary also on their African antecedents. Many of the illustrative examples are taken from the published books and sound recordings of other collectors and include prison camp gang worksongs, rice threshing and pounding songs, rowing and roustabout songs, and one shoeshine patter.

Dargan, Amanda. 1983. "Street Cries, Auction Chants, and Carnival Pitches and Routines" in the Recorded Collections of the Archive of Folk Culture. A Library of Congress Folk Archive Finding Aid. Washington, D.C.: Archive of Folk Culture, Library of Congress (xerox). This fifteen-page discography describes all the pertinent material found in the Archive, identifying each item briefly (with first line of text), and giving performer, place and date, and collector, if known. Most of this material is available for public listening. The Archive has also compiled a "Selected Bibliography of Street Cries," printed together with a "Selected Discography of Street Cries."

Doerflinger, William M. 1951. *Shantymen and Shantyboys: Songs of the Sailor and Lumberman.* New York: Macmillan. Doerflinger's collection, audio-recorded in northeastern United States and eastern Canada in the 1930s and 1940s, illustrated the close musical cultures of the whaling and lumbering industries. Forty-five shanties are presented in the first three chapters with words and music and, in some cases, alternate texts. The fourth chapter, "The Rise of Shantying," presents a historical overview.

Epstein, Dena J. 1977. *Sinful Tunes and Spirituals: Black Folk Music to the Civil War.* Urbana: University of Illinois Press. Primarily a critically analyzed bibliography of the various kinds of written sources pertaining to antebellum music, Epstein's study is an essential tool for anyone with a serious interest in the subject. One chapter devoted to worksongs includes several very early texts and descriptions and references to many others.

Gordon, Robert W. 1938. *Folk-Songs of America.* New York: National Service Bureau. Chapter 3 of this series, originally published in the *New York Times Magazine* (January 16, 1927), was subtitled "Negro Work Songs from Georgia" and presented three "pulling song" coast or dock shanties, two hammering songs, and three rowing songs, with commentary (text only, no tunes).

Hugill, Stan. 1966. *Shanties from the Seven Seas: Shipboard Work-Songs and Songs Used as Work-Songs from the Great Days of Sail.* London: Routledge & Kegan Paul. Possibly the most comprehensive collection of sea shanties, including not only British and American but also Norwegian, Swedish, German and French shanties, Hugill's material was collected early in this century during his own maritime voyages. The songs are grouped into families (based on text), rather than by class of shanty (i.e., capstan, halyard etc.). Other collections are consulted for background material and related texts.

———. 1969. *Shanties and Sailors' Songs.* London: Herbert Jenkins. A valuable complement to the author's earlier collection, this work is devoted half to texts and half to general discussions on the historical background of shanties, how they were used, and how and when collected.

Hurley, Elizabeth. 1953. "Come Buy, Come Buy." In *Folk Travelers: Ballads, Tales, and Talk,* edited by Mody C. Boatright, Wilson M. Hudson, and Allen Maxwell, 115–38. Austin: Publication of the Texas Folklore Society, vol. 25. A discussion, with examples of Texas street cries, including doughnuts, watermelons, tamales, hominy, charcoal, kindling wood, etc., but with very scanty documentation.

Jackson, Bruce. 1972. *Wake Up Dead Man: Afro-American Worksongs from Texas Prisons.*

Cambridge, Mass.: Harvard University Press. The best available treatment of the subject, Jackson's study includes sixty-five different worksongs collected during his own fieldwork in 1964–66, some with several alternate texts. Careful documentation, meticulous transcriptions, and extensive background on the songs, the singing tradition, and the social context contribute to this book's value.

Jekyll, Walter. 1907. *Jamaican Song and Story: Annancy Stories, Digging Sings, Ring Tunes and Dancing Tunes*. London: David Nutt. [Reprint, New York: Dover, 1966.] Jekyll's important early collection, first published under the auspices of the British Folk-Lore Society, was reprinted with three supplementary new essays. Among the 145 songs that Jekyll collected and notated are 37 "digging songs," songs used for various kinds of field labor, including tree-felling, field-clearing, and crop-planting.

Karpeles, Maud, ed. 1974. *Cecil Sharp's Collection of English Folk Songs*. London: Oxford University Press. Volume two of this substantial collection by one of the great fieldworkers in both England and the United States includes three text/tunes collected by Sharp in 1908 and 1921 of street cries: "Baskets and Chairs," "Young Lambs," and "Lavender."

Kennedy, Peter. 1975. *Folksongs of Britain and Ireland*. London: Cassell. This ponderous collection of 360 songs from field recordings includes several Manx Gaelic domestic worksongs (with English translations), including grinding, washing, milking, baby-washing, and spinning songs.

Lomax, John A., and Alan Lomax. 1934, 1964. *American Ballads and Folk Songs*. New York: MacMillan. The first volume of collectanea from the fieldwork of two of America's most distinguished folksong collectors contains several chapters devoted to Afro-American worksongs and one including a few sea shanties. In the former category are five railroad construction songs (tie-tamping, tie-shuffling, tracklining, etc.) and eleven prison-gang construction songs. Unfortunately, subsequent research in several instances has revealed that the song texts presented were often conflated from different sources. For serious textual analysis it is best to rely on the original recordings themselves, most of which are available in the Archive of Folk Culture in the Library of Congress.

———. 1941. *Our Singing Country: A Second Volume of American Ballads and Folk Songs*. New York: Macmillan. Unlike its predecessor, this volume gives recording dates and locations and Archive of Folk Song index numbers for the field recordings transcribed herein. One chapter includes fifteen Negro gang songs, mostly transcribed directly from the recording of black prisoners, but a few taken from the singing of the Lomaxes, who learned them from prisoners.

Odum, Howard W., and Guy B. Johnson. 1926. *Negro Workaday Songs*. Chapel Hill: University of North Carolina Press. Collected in 1925–26 from blacks of Tennessee, Georgia, and the Carolinas by two sociologists, these texts provide a good sampling of what was sung in day-to-day work situations. Documentation is generally vague, as is the contextual background, but numerous examples of gang and individual songs are included.

Parrish, Lydia. 1942. *Slave Songs of the Georgia Sea Islands*. New York: Creative Age Press. [Reprint, Hatboro: Folklore Associates, 1965.] Text/tunes to songs collected by the author in the years following 1912. Among them are fourteen worksongs: ten shanties (plus ten more without tunes), four rice planting or thrashing songs (plus several fragments), a rowing song, and some chain gang cutting songs (without tunes).

Perdue, Chuck. 1969. "Come Butter Come." *Foxfire* 3:20–24, 65–72. A collection of thirty-four butter-churning chants obtained by the author (mostly by mail correspondence) from Georgia, with some historical background and references to other related published material.

Scarborough, Dorothy. 1925. *On the Trail of Negro Folk-Songs.* Cambridge, Mass.: Harvard University Press. [Reprint, Hatboro: Folklore Associates, 1965.] Material collected throughout the South, either hand annotated or with aid of phonograph. The chapter on worksongs includes corn shucking songs, rubbing (i. e., washboard) songs, shine (i. e., shoe shine) reels, a spinning song, a woodchopper's song, a butter-churning song, pick and hammer, road work, and muleskinner songs. A few tune transcriptions are included.

Shaw, Margaret Fay. 1955. *Folksongs and Folklore of South Uist.* London: Routledge and Kegan Paul. Among the material, collected by the author on one of the islands of the Scottish Hebrides in 1929–35, are six milking songs, three spinning songs, and thirty-two waulking songs (used for waulking, or fulling, newly woven cloth). Texts, tunes, and English translations as well as documentation are given.

Walser, Robert J. 1981." Sea Shanties and Sailors' Songs: A Preliminary Guide to Recordings in the Archive of Folk Culture." Washington, D.C.: Archive of Folk Culture, Library of Congress (xerox). This five-page discography lists and describes the various collections of shanties and other sailors' songs that have been collected for, or deposited in, the Archive of Folk Culture, from both the British Isles and North America.

Wheeler, Mary. 1944. *Steamboatin' Days: Folk Songs of the River Packet Era.* Baton Rouge: Louisiana State University Press. One of the few booklength studies dealing with folksongs of the river packet boats of the Ohio River, collected by the author from black roustabouts. The text reads well, but the documentation is often scanty. One chapter deals with worksongs.

White, Newman I. 1928. *American Negro Folk Songs.* Cambridge, Mass.: Harvard University Press. [Reprint, Hatboro: Folklore Associates, 1965.] Material collected mostly by White's students in Alabama and North Carolina in 1915–25. One chapter is devoted to gang worksongs, mostly very fragmentary, few with tunes. Another chapter deals with farm and plantation labor songs, mostly very brief, with no tunes.

Discography

Blow Boys Blow: Sea Songs and Shanties (Tradition TLP 1026). Sung by A. L. Lloyd and Ewan MacColl, accompanied by Alf Edwards (concertina), Ralph Rinzler (guitar, banjo, mandolin) and Steve Benbow (guitar).

Haul on the Bowlin'and Other Chanties and Foc'sle Songs (Stinson SLP 80). Sung by A. L. Lloyd and Ewan MacColl, accompanied by Alf Edwards (concertina).

Thar She Blows!—Whaling Ballads and Songs (Riverside RLP 12–635). Sung by A. L. Lloyd and Ewan MacColl, accompanied by Peggy Seeger (banjo and guitar) and J. Cole (harmonica).

A Sailor's Garland (Prestige International 13043). Sung by Ewan MacColl and A. L. Lloyd, accompanied by Alf Edwards (concertina) and Dave Swarbrick (fiddle).

Off To Sea Once More (Stinson SLP 81). Sung by A. L. Lloyd and Ewan MacColl, accompanied by Alf Edwards (concertina). These five albums, recorded in the 1950s, are among the most listenable recreations of maritime ballads and shanties available. The performers, Lloyd and MacColl, are Britishers with extensive experience in the field of folk music as performers as well as collectors, writers, and editors. The selections on these albums can be taken to be accurate renditions of what very good shantymen would have sounded like if recorded in their heyday. The Riverside, Tradition, and Prestige albums are out of print, but are worth hunting for in used record bins. All have brief but informative back jacket notes by the performers. The Tradition and Prestige albums contain the largest number of shanties.

Sea Shanties (Topic 12TS234). Sung by Roy Harris, A. L. Lloyd, Ian Manuel, Bernard Wrigley, and Martyn Wyndham-Read. An excellent collection of nineteen shanties, arranged, produced, and documented by Lloyd. The seven-page booklet includes text/tune transcriptions, good notes, and general background material. The recordings, all a capella, were made in 1974.

American Sea Songs and Shanties: Folk Music of the United States from the Archive of Folk Culture, edited by Duncan Emrich (Library of Congress L 26/27). This double album includes twenty-one selections, all but two of which are shanties, recorded by five one-time shantymen between 1939 and 1946. All are sung a capella; most are solo performances. The renditions are often at a slow but traditional tempo, by singers well past their prime. While aesthetically perhaps not so exciting as performances on other albums listed here, these are nevertheless probably closer to the sounds of the typical shantyman.

Stan Hugill Reminisces: Shanties and Stories of Life under Sail (Greenwich Village Recordings GVR 217). On this disc, recorded at a live concert in England in 1979, shanty expert Hugill sings eleven not-so-common shanties (with audience as chorus) from black and white shantymen, interspersed with some of his own recollections from his maritime experiences.

'Tis Our Sailing Time (Folk Legacy FSI-97). Sung by The Boarding Party (Jonathan Eberhart, Bob Hitchcock, Tom McHenry, K. C. King, and David Diamond). Because of the decline in the practice of shanty-singing on ships, recordings made in recent years increasingly will necessarily feature singers with little or no actual shipboard experience of shantying. This 1983 album features five American and English singers some of whom at least have experience in the navy if not on shanty-singing vessels. Renditions are tasteful and lively, mostly a capella with solo lead and chorus. Some ten of the sixteen selections have been used as shanties—including one shanty learned from black crewmen of a menhaden fishing vessel out of Mayport, Florida. A fifteen-page booklet by Eberhart with texts and background material is enclosed.

Afro-American Spirituals, Work Songs, and Ballads (Library of Congress AFS L 3). Various performers; edited by Alan Lomax.

Negro Work Songs and Calls (Library of Congress AFS L 8). Various performers; edited by B. A. Botkin. These two LPs, first issued as 78 RPM sets in 1942 and 1943, respectively, offered the first opportunity for nonfolklorists to hear genuine worksongs recorded in the field. Mostly from the fieldwork of John A. Lomax and Alan Lomax in 1933–1940, these selections were recorded with rather primitive equipment, but their musical value is still evident. AFS L 3 includes eight worksongs from prison groups in Texas, Arkansas, Mississippi, Tennessee, and South Carolina. AFS L 8 includes two railroad construction chants from Texas and Tennessee, three Mississippi riverboat worksongs, a Bahamian launching song, and four prison gang songs from Texas and Arkansas. Enclosed booklets contain text transcriptions, recording data, and background information.

Negro Prison Songs (Tradition TLP 1020), various performers; recorded and edited by Alan Lomax. In 1947, Lomax returned to the South with the first portable tape machine on the market to rerecord the traditions that he and his father had earlier documented for the Library of Congress. This LP contains what are possibly the most musically exciting examples of prison worksongs available. An enclosed fourteen-page booklet includes text transcriptions and commentary by Lomax.

Negro Prison Camp Work Songs (Folkways FE 4475), various performers; recorded by Toshi and Peter Seeger, John Lomax, Jr., Chester Bower, and Fred Hellerman at Ramsey and Retrieve State Farms, Texas, in 1951. These recordings were made indoors, simulating the actual working environment, which may account for the tendency of the singers to increase their tempo during the performance of a song.

Prison Worksongs (Folk Lyric A–5; reissued as Arhoolie 2012), various performers; recorded and edited by Harry Oster. This album includes a broader variety of prison worksongs than most similar LPs. In addition to hammer, axe, and hoeing songs, there are plowing, track-lining, and gravel-shoveling songs, a spiritual used to accompany work on an electric sewing machine, and another sung by two license plate stamping press operators. Recorded in the Louisiana State Penitentiary at Angola in 1959; back jacket liner notes by Oster.

Wake Up Dead Man: Black Convict Work Songs from Texas Prisons (Rounder 2013), various artists; recorded and edited by Bruce Jackson to accompany his book of the same name (see Bibliography). These selections were recorded in 1965–66; taken together with Jackson's book, they offer the best-documented recordings of the black prison camp worksong tradition.

Virginia Traditions: Virginia Work Songs (Blue Ridge Institute BRI 007). Various performers; edited by Glenn Hinson. This 1984 publication includes five prison songs collected at the State Penitentiary in Richmond in 1936 by John A. and Alan Lomax; and four menhaden fishing shanties from Weems, Virginia, and from off the New Jersey coast, collected between 1950 and 1980. Of particular interest are several recordings from work situations rarely heard on commercial discs: crab-cracking, ship-caulking, and oyster shucking, all recorded in 1979–80 near the Virginia coast by Hinson. An illustrated thirty-six page booklet by Hinson includes complete recording data, text transcriptions, notes on the singers and songs, and background information on Afro-American work songs in general. The sound quality of the Lomax field recordings is rather poor.

John Crow Say . . . Jamaican Music of Faith, Work & Play (Folkways FE 4228). Various performers; recorded in Jamaica by John Storm Roberts. Issued in 1981, this album includes three digging songs: "Kissander," "Rosibella," and "Half a Whole" [sic], recorded in Maryland, St. Andrews Parish, "in field conditions to the rhythm of picks." Includes a four-page brochure with very sketchy documentation.

The Ballad Hunter: Lectures on American Folk Music (Library of Congress AFS L 49–53), by John A. Lomax. This five-LP set, recorded in 1941, includes ten half-hour radio broadcast lectures written and narrated by Lomax. Each lecture includes brief selections from Lomax's field-recordings. Part IV: *Rock Island Line*, includes four prison camp songs from Gould, Arkansas, recorded in 1934 and 1939. Part V: *Two Sailors*, includes two shanties by J. M. Hunt and one canal song by Capt. P. Nye. Part VIII: *Railroad Songs*, includes several excerpts from rail tamping and track laying songs. Documentation for these examples is often sketchy.

Waulking Songs from Barra (Tangent TNGM 111: vol. 3 of the series, Scottish Tradition), various singers. Though waulking songs, according to the jacket notes, have not been sung on the Hebridean island of Barra since World War II, there were still singers, most of them in their seventies and eighties at the time, who remembered using the songs when these recordings were made in 1965–67. The seven songs are all sung in Scottish Gaelic; also included is one set of pipe reels that were played at the dances that took place when the waulking itself was completed. An eight-page brochure includes Gaelic texts and translations, notes on the songs, and general background on the waulking song in its context. Recorded and documented by the School of Scottish Studies, University of Edinburgh.

Folk Songs from Scotland: Lowland and Highland (Columbia AKL 4946: vol. 6 of the series, *World Library of Folk and Primitive Music*, edited by Alan Lomax), various singers. The forty-three abbreviated selections on this LP are intended to provide a broad overview of Scottish folk music. Among the selections are several seldom-recorded examples of domestic worksongs: a milking song, a weaving song, a spinning song, and three waulking songs, as well as a rowing song, all in Scottish Gaelic. Sewn-in notes include song texts and translations, as well as some documentation and commentary.

The Music of New Orleans: The Music of the Streets (Folkways FA 2461), various singers; edited by Samuel Charters. Among the selections, recorded by Charters or Harry Oster in 1957–58, are some very short street cries by vendors (e.g., watermelon, coal, etc.), and shoeshine patters.

Street Cries and Creole Songs of New Orleans (Folkways FA 2202), sung by Adelaide van Way. One section of this album, recorded ca. 1956 by a North Carolina-born folk song collector and performer/interpreter, is a set of nine a capella street cries from various American cities, including a hominy man, sand seller, pepper pot, ragman, horseradish seller, flower vendor, cantaloupe vendor, praline seller, and scissors grinder.

Contributors

Norm Cohen, author of *Long Steel Rail: The Railroad in American Folksong* (1981) and editor of Vance Randolph's *Ozark Folksongs* (1982), has recently completed an annotated discography of traditional recorded Anglo-American music (Garland, 1994). Since 1969 he has been Executive Secretary of the John Edwards Memorial Foundation/Forum. He has written extensively on American folk music for thirty years and has edited or annotated numerous sound recordings, most recent of which is *Folksong America: The Folk Revival* (1991).

John Cowley has published many articles on blues and black music. As a mature student, he has just completed his doctoral dissertation on aspects of black music in the English-speaking Caribbean, for the University of Warwick, England. He produced the Flyright-Matchbox series of LPs and is a contributor to the *Blackwell Guide to Blues Records* and *Black Music in Britain.* More recently, he collaborated in the compilation and production of two LPs devoted to early recordings of Trinidad carnival music, issued by Matchbox records.

Doug DeNatale is the director of the Center for Folklife and Oral History at the University of South Carolina. In 1987, he served as the project coordinator for the American Folklife Center's Lowell Folklife Project in Massachusetts. His recent publications include "The Dissembling Line: Industrial Pranks in a North Carolina Textile Mill," in *Arts in Earnest, North Carolina Folklife* (1990) and "Oral History" in the *Encyclopedia of American Social History* (1992).

David King Dunaway is Associate Professor at the University of New Mexico and Visiting Fellow at City University (London). A past consultant to UNESCO, he currently produces a radio series on the folklore and literary history of the Southwestern U.S. for the National Endowment for the Humanities.

Richard Ellington was an early-1960s participant in the Greenwich Village folksong revival scene, a contributor to *Caravan,* a folksong "fanzine," and held from those early times an interest in IWW labor songs. In 1987, he designed and printed a catalogue, *"Wobbly"—80 Years of Rebel Art,* for an exhibit at the Labor Archives and Research Center, San Francisco State University. He died on May 26, 1991, in Berkeley, California.

Jeff Ferrell is Associate Professor of Sociology at Regis University, Denver, Colorado. His work has appeared in journals ranging from *Social Justice, Labor History,* and *Radical America* to *Contemporary Sociology, Youth and Society,* and the *Journal of Popular Culture.* His book, *Crimes of Style: Urban Graffiti and the Politics of Criminality,* is forthcoming from Garland.

Archie Green, now retired, was Professor of Folklore and English at the University of Texas, Austin. He is author of *Only a Miner,* numerous studies of laborlore, and, most recently, *Wobblies, Pile Butts, and Other Heroes* (1993). In the decade from 1965 to 1975, he lobbied for the American Folklife Preservation Act in Washington, D.C., and has been active, since its inception, in the John Edwards Memorial Forum (formerly Foundation), an archival association in the area of folklore and vernacular music.

Michael Heisley is a native Texan whose research interests include Mexican and Chicano folklore, folksong, and the folklore of the United States. He produced *Las voces de los campesinos* (a record album of songs from the farm workers' movement) and compiled *An Annotated Bibliography of Chicano Folklore from the Southwestern United States.* Formerly Curator of Folklore at the Southwest Museum in Los Angeles, he currently teaches in the Folklore and Mythology Program at the University of California, Los Angeles.

Glen Hinson is Assistant Professor of Folklore and Anthropology at the University of North Carolina, Chapel Hill. His research interests include African American vernacular poetry, tourism and commoditization in the American South, and African American gospel performance. His is currently preparing a manuscript on trajectories of transcendence in African American gospel.

Joyce Kornbluh, editor of *Rebel Voices: An IWW Anthology* and author of numerous books and articles on labor history and labor education, recently retired as director of the Program on Women and Work at the Labor Studies Center at the University of Michigan. A workers' educator for over four decades, she also has been active in workers' culture and popular culture movements. She is on the National Executive Board of the Labor Heritage Foundation, and received its annual Joe Hill Award in 1992.

Donald Lance is Professor of English Linguistics at the University of Missouri-Columbia. He has been Secretary of the Missouri Folklore Society since 1981 and was General Editor of the *Missouri Folklore Society Journal* from 1980 to 1990. He has published in the fields of Spanish-English bilingualism, dialectology, folklore, and linguistics.

James Leary divides his time between an associate professorship in the Folklore Program at the University of Wisconsin, Madison, and the Wisconsin Folk Museum, Mt. Horeb. His research interests and publications concern the occupational folklife and traditional music of the Upper Midwest. He has produced *The Wisconsin Patchwork: Recordings from the Helen Stratman-Thomas Collection of Wisconsin Folk Music.*

Robbie Lieberman is Assistant Professor of History at Southern Illinois University, Carbondale; from 1984–1991 she directed the Peace Studies Program at the University of Missouri-Columbia. She is author of *My Song Is My Weapon* (1989), and a book on communism and the American peace movement in the 1950s is forthcoming from Syracuse University Press.

Richard March is Traditional and Ethnic Arts Coordinator for the Wisconsin Arts Board. He manages folk arts grant programs, coproduces the "Downhome Dairyland" radio series for Wisconsin Public Radio, and has coordinated ethnic projects with the Smithsonian Institution. He is also an active polka musician, playing button accordion in the Madison area.

Brenda McCallum headed the Popular Culture Archives at Bowling Green State University prior to her death on August 25, 1992. She established the Archive of American Minority Cultures at the University of Alabama, contributing to its holdings materials and audio recordings from her own extensive fieldwork in Alabama. Many of the materials in the Archive were used in the acclaimed NEH-funded radio series *Working Lives*, and the NEA-funded radio program *In the Spirit*, a profile of Alabama's black religious music.

Judith McCulloh is Executive Editor at the University of Illinois Press. She has served as President of the American Folklore Society and been on the editorial boards of several publications, including the *Journal of American Folklore* and *American Music*. She has coedited *Folklore/Folklife* (1984) and *Stars of Country Music: Uncle Dave Macon to Johnny Rodriguez* (1975), and edited *Ethnic Recordings in America: A Neglected Heritage.*

John Minton is Assistant Professor of Folklore at Indiana University–Purdue University, Fort Wayne. His research interests include Anglo- and Afro-

American folklore of the southern United States, North American folksong and folk narrative, and folklore, media, and popular culture.

Sam Richards has performed as a folk revival singer in Britain, and his folklore research interests include many aspects of Westcountry life: farming communities, children, gypsies, and travellers. In 1986, with the support of the local arts council, he established The Westcountry Folklore Center.

Neil V. Rosenberg is Professor of Folklore at Memorial University of Newfoundland, where he was the first Archivist of, and later the Director of, the MUN Folklore and Language Archive. He has also served as President of the Folklore Studies Association of Canada and the Atlantic Canada Institute. He is author of *Bluegrass: A History,* and is presently sound recordings review editor for the *Journal of American Folklore.* He is editor of *Transforming Tradition: Folk Music Revivals Examined* (1993).

Rebecca Schroeder is the former Reference Librarian and Director of Publications at the Missouri State Library in Jefferson City. She is active in the Missouri Folklore Society and currently serves as the Society's archivist. She was co-editor of the 1986–1987 and the 1989–1990 issues of the *Missouri Folklore Society Journal.* Her primary research interest is in the history of folksong collection in Europe, Great Britain, and North America.

Lori Taylor is a Utahn who, unlike Joe Hill, does wish to die in Utah. Meanwhile, she works as Assistant Archivist in the Folkways and Folklife Archives of the Smithsonian Institution in Washington, D.C., where she explores the mysteries of labor, punk, and folk revival music communities. She is active in the Occupational Folklife and Popular Music sections of the American Folklore Society. She edits *Ethnopop.*